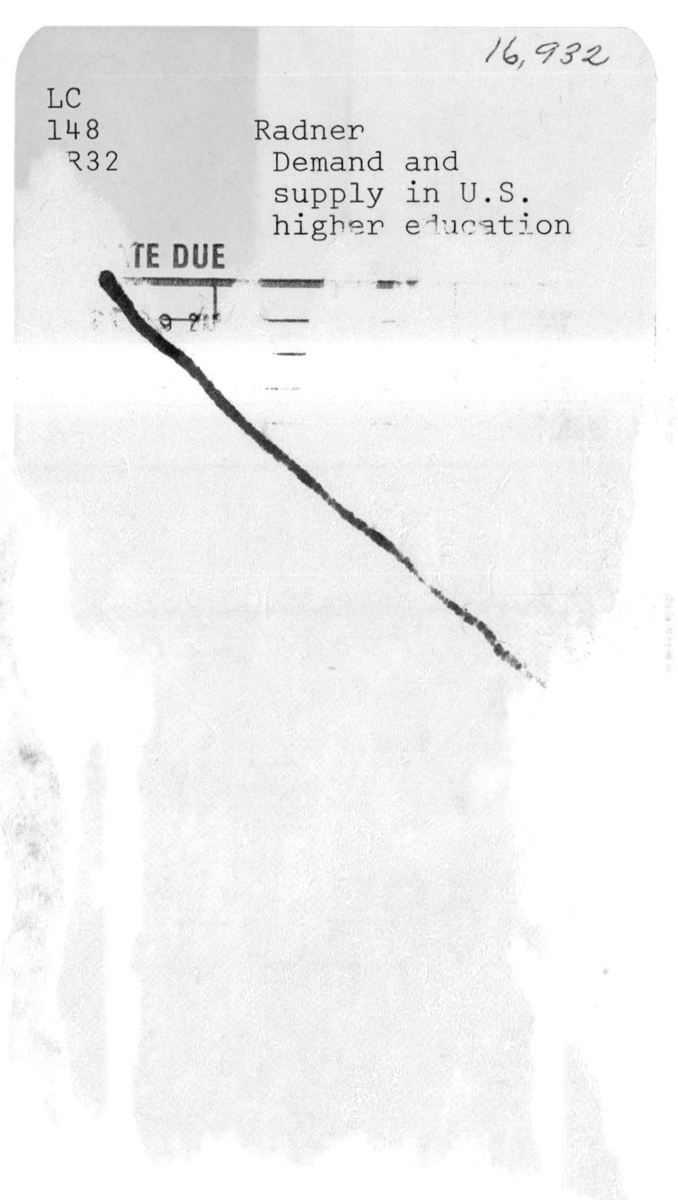
16,932
LC
148
R32
Radner
Demand and
supply in U.S.
higher education
TE DUE

Carnegie Commission on Higher Education
Sponsored Research Studies

DEMAND AND SUPPLY
IN U.S. HIGHER EDUCATION
Roy Radner and
Leonard S. Miller

FACULTY BARGAINING:
CHANGE AND CONFLICT
Joseph W. Garbarino and
Bill Aussieker

COMPUTERS AND THE
LEARNING PROCESS IN
HIGHER EDUCATION
John Fralick Rockart and
Michael S. Scott Morton

WOMEN AND THE POWER TO CHANGE
Florence Howe (ed.)

THE USEFUL ARTS AND
THE LIBERAL TRADITION
Earl F. Cheit

TEACHERS AND STUDENTS:
ASPECTS OF AMERICAN
HIGHER EDUCATION
Martin Trow (ed.)

THE DIVIDED ACADEMY
PROFESSORS AND
POLITICS
Everett Carll Ladd, Jr.
and Seymour Martin Lipset

EDUCATION AND POLITICS
AT HARVARD
Seymour Martin Lipset
and David Riesman

HIGHER EDUCATION AND EARNINGS:
COLLEGE AS AN INVESTMENT AND A
SCREENING DEVICE
Paul Taubman and Terence Wales

EDUCATION, INCOME, AND HUMAN
BEHAVIOR
F. Thomas Juster (ed.)

AMERICAN LEARNED SOCIETIES
IN TRANSITION:
THE IMPACT OF DISSENT
AND RECESSION
Harland G. Bloland and
Sue M. Bloland

ANTIBIAS REGULATION
OF UNIVERSITIES
Richard A. Lester

CHANGES IN UNIVERSITY
ORGANIZATION, 1964–1971
Edward Gross and Paul V. Grambsch

ESCAPE FROM THE DOLL'S HOUSE:
WOMEN IN GRADUATE AND PROFESSIONAL
SCHOOL EDUCATION
Saul D. Feldman

HIGHER EDUCATION AND
THE LABOR MARKET
Margaret S. Gordon (ed.)

THE ACADEMIC MELTING POT:
CATHOLICS AND JEWS IN
AMERICAN HIGHER EDUCATION
Stephen Steinberg

LEADERSHIP AND AMBIGUITY:
THE AMERICAN COLLEGE
PRESIDENT
Michael D. Cohen and
James G. March

THE ACADEMIC SYSTEM IN
AMERICAN SOCIETY
Alain Touraine

EDUCATION FOR THE PROFESSIONS OF
MEDICINE, LAW, THEOLOGY, AND SOCIAL
WELFARE
Everett C. Hughes, Barrie Thorne,
Agostino DeBaggis, Arnold Gurin,
and David Williams

THE FUTURE OF HIGHER
EDUCATION:
SOME SPECULATIONS AND
SUGGESTIONS
Alexander M. Mood

CONTENT AND CONTEXT:
ESSAYS ON COLLEGE EDUCATION
Carl Kaysen (ed.)

THE RISE OF THE ARTS ON THE AMERICAN
CAMPUS
Jack Morrison

THE UNIVERSITY AND THE CITY:
EIGHT CASES OF INVOLVEMENT
George Nash, Dan Waldorf, and Robert E. Price

THE BEGINNING OF THE FUTURE:
A HISTORICAL APPROACH TO GRADUATE
EDUCATION IN THE ARTS AND SCIENCES
Richard J. Storr

ACADEMIC TRANSFORMATION:
SEVENTEEN INSTITUTIONS UNDER PRESSURE
David Riesman and Verne A. Stadtman (eds.)

WHERE COLLEGES ARE AND WHO ATTENDS:
EFFECTS OF ACCESSIBILITY ON COLLEGE
ATTENDANCE
C. Arnold Anderson, Mary Jean Bowman, and
Vincent Tinto

NEW DIRECTIONS IN LEGAL EDUCATION
Herbert L. Packer and Thomas Ehrlich
abridged and unabridged editions

THE UNIVERSITY AS AN ORGANIZATION
James A. Perkins (ed.)

THE EMERGING TECHNOLOGY:
INSTRUCTIONAL USES OF THE COMPUTER IN
HIGHER EDUCATION
Roger E. Levien

A STATISTICAL PORTRAIT OF HIGHER
EDUCATION
Seymour E. Harris

THE HOME OF SCIENCE:
THE ROLE OF THE UNIVERSITY
Dael Wolfle

EDUCATION AND EVANGELISM:
A PROFILE OF PROTESTANT COLLEGES
C. Robert Pace

PROFESSIONAL EDUCATION:
SOME NEW DIRECTIONS
Edgar H. Schein

THE NONPROFIT RESEARCH INSTITUTE:
ITS ORIGIN, OPERATION, PROBLEMS, AND
PROSPECTS
Harold Orlans

THE INVISIBLE COLLEGES:
A PROFILE OF SMALL, PRIVATE COLLEGES
WITH LIMITED RESOURCES
Alexander W. Astin and Calvin B. T. Lee

AMERICAN HIGHER EDUCATION:
DIRECTIONS OLD AND NEW
Joseph Ben-David

A DEGREE AND WHAT ELSE?
CORRELATES AND CONSEQUENCES OF A COLLEGE EDUCATION
Stephen B. Withey, Jo Anne Coble, Gerald Gurin, John P. Robinson, Burkhard Strumpel, Elizabeth Keogh Taylor, and Arthur C. Wolfe

THE MULTICAMPUS UNIVERSITY:
A STUDY OF ACADEMIC GOVERNANCE
Eugene C. Lee and Frank M. Bowen

INSTITUTIONS IN TRANSITION:
A PROFILE OF CHANGE IN HIGHER EDUCATION
(INCORPORATING THE 1970 STATISTICAL REPORT)
Harold L. Hodgkinson

EFFICIENCY IN LIBERAL EDUCATION:
A STUDY OF COMPARATIVE INSTRUCTIONAL COSTS FOR DIFFERENT WAYS OF ORGANIZING, TEACHING-LEARNING IN A LIBERAL ARTS COLLEGE
Howard R. Bowen and Gordon K. Douglass

CREDIT FOR COLLEGE:
PUBLIC POLICY FOR STUDENT LOANS
Robert W. Hartman

MODELS AND MAVERICKS:
A PROFILE OF PRIVATE LIBERAL ARTS COLLEGES
Morris T. Keeton

BETWEEN TWO WORLDS:
A PROFILE OF NEGRO HIGHER EDUCATION
Frank Bowles and Frank A. DeCosta

BREAKING THE ACCESS BARRIERS:
A PROFILE OF TWO-YEAR COLLEGES
Leland L. Medsker and Dale Tillery

ANY PERSON, ANY STUDY:
AN ESSAY ON HIGHER EDUCATION IN THE UNITED STATES
Eric Ashby

THE NEW DEPRESSION IN HIGHER EDUCATION:
A STUDY OF FINANCIAL CONDITIONS AT 41 COLLEGES AND UNIVERSITIES
Earl F. Cheit

FINANCING MEDICAL EDUCATION:
AN ANALYSIS OF ALTERNATIVE POLICIES AND MECHANISMS
Rashi Fein and Gerald I. Weber

HIGHER EDUCATION IN NINE COUNTRIES:
A COMPARATIVE STUDY OF COLLEGES AND UNIVERSITIES ABROAD
Barbara B. Burn, Philip G. Altbach, Clark Kerr, and James A. Perkins

BRIDGES TO UNDERSTANDING:
INTERNATIONAL PROGRAMS OF AMERICAN COLLEGES AND UNIVERSITIES
Irwin T. Sanders and Jennifer C. Ward

GRADUATE AND PROFESSIONAL EDUCATION, 1980:
A SURVEY OF INSTITUTIONAL PLANS
Lewis B. Mayhew
(Out of print, but available from University Microfilms.)

THE AMERICAN COLLEGE AND AMERICAN CULTURE:
SOCIALIZATION AS A FUNCTION OF HIGHER EDUCATION
Oscar Handlin and Mary F. Handlin

RECENT ALUMNI AND HIGHER EDUCATION:
A SURVEY OF COLLEGE GRADUATES
Joe L. Spaeth and Andrew M. Greeley
(Out of print, but available from University Microfilms.)

CHANGE IN EDUCATIONAL POLICY:
SELF-STUDIES IN SELECTED COLLEGES AND UNIVERSITIES
Dwight R. Ladd

STATE OFFICIALS AND HIGHER EDUCATION:
A SURVEY OF THE OPINIONS AND EXPECTATIONS OF POLICY MAKERS IN NINE STATES
Heinz Eulau and Harold Quinley
(Out of print, but available from University Microfilms.)

ACADEMIC DEGREE STRUCTURES, INNOVATIVE APPROACHES:
PRINCIPLES OF REFORM IN DEGREE STRUCTURES IN THE UNITED STATES
Stephen H. Spurr

COLLEGES OF THE FORGOTTEN AMERICANS:
A PROFILE OF STATE COLLEGES AND REGIONAL UNIVERSITIES
E. Alden Dunham

FROM BACKWATER TO MAINSTREAM:
A PROFILE OF CATHOLIC HIGHER EDUCATION
Andrew M. Greeley

THE ECONOMICS OF THE MAJOR PRIVATE UNIVERSITIES
William G. Bowen
(Out of print, but available from University Microfilms.)

THE FINANCE OF HIGHER EDUCATION
Howard R. Bowen
(Out of print, but available from University Microfilms.)

ALTERNATIVE METHODS OF FEDERAL FUNDING FOR HIGHER EDUCATION
Ron Wolk
(Out of print, but available from University Microfilms.)

INVENTORY OF CURRENT RESEARCH ON HIGHER EDUCATION 1968
Dale M. Heckman and Warren Bryan Martin
(Out of print, but available from University Microfilms.)

The following technical reports are available from the Carnegie Commission on Higher Education, 2150 Shattuck Ave., Berkeley, California 94704.

RESOURCE USE IN HIGHER EDUCATION:
TRENDS IN OUTPUT AND INPUTS, 1930–1967
June O'Neill

MAY 1970:
THE CAMPUS AFTERMATH OF CAMBODIA AND KENT STATE
Richard E. Peterson and John A. Bilorusky

MENTAL ABILITY AND HIGHER EDUCATIONAL ATTAINMENT IN THE 20TH CENTURY
Paul Taubman and Terence Wales

AMERICAN COLLEGE AND UNIVERSITY ENROLLMENT TRENDS IN 1971
Richard E. Peterson

PAPERS ON EFFICIENCY IN THE MANAGEMENT OF HIGHER EDUCATION
Alexander M. Mood, Colin Bell, Lawrence Bogard, Helen Brownlee, and Joseph McCloskey

AN INVENTORY OF ACADEMIC INNOVATION AND REFORM
Ann Heiss

ESTIMATING THE RETURNS TO EDUCATION:
A DISAGGREGATED APPROACH
Richard S. Eckaus

SOURCES OF FUNDS TO COLLEGES AND UNIVERSITIES
June O'Neill

TRENDS AND PROJECTIONS OF PHYSICIANS IN THE UNITED STATES 1967–2002
Mark S. Blumberg

NEW DEPRESSION IN HIGHER EDUCATION—TWO YEARS LATER
Earl F. Cheit

PROFESSORS, UNIONS, AND AMERICAN HIGHER EDUCATION
Everett Carll Ladd, Jr. and Seymour Martin Lipset

A CLASSIFICATION OF INSTITUTIONS OF HIGHER EDUCATION

POLITICAL IDEOLOGIES OF GRADUATE STUDENTS: CRYSTALLIZATION, CONSISTENCY, AND CONTEXTUAL EFFECT
Margaret Fay and Jeff Weintraub

FLYING A LEARNING CENTER: DESIGN AND COSTS OF AN OFF-CAMPUS SPACE FOR LEARNING
Thomas J. Karwin

THE DEMISE OF DIVERSITY?: A COMPARATIVE PROFILE OF EIGHT TYPES OF INSTITUTIONS
C. Robert Pace

TUITION: A SUPPLEMENTAL STATEMENT TO THE REPORT OF THE CARNEGIE COMMISSION ON HIGHER EDUCATION ON "WHO PAYS? WHO BENEFITS? WHO SHOULD PAY?"

THE GREAT AMERICAN DEGREE MACHINE
Douglas L. Adkins

The following reprints are available from the Carnegie Commission on Higher Education, 2150 Shattuck Ave., Berkeley, California 94704.

ACCELERATED PROGRAMS OF MEDICAL EDUCATION, *by Mark S. Blumberg, reprinted from* JOURNAL OF MEDICAL EDUCATION, *vol. 46, no. 8, August 1971.**

SCIENTIFIC MANPOWER FOR 1970–1985, *by Allan M. Cartter, reprinted from* SCIENCE, *vol. 172, no. 3979, pp. 132–140, April 9, 1971.**

A NEW METHOD OF MEASURING STATES' HIGHER EDUCATION BURDEN, *by Neil Timm, reprinted from* THE JOURNAL OF HIGHER EDUCATION, *vol. 42, no. 1, pp. 27–33, January 1971.**

REGENT WATCHING, *by Earl F. Cheit, reprinted from* AGB REPORTS, *vol. 13, no. 6, pp. 4–13, March 1971.**

COLLEGE GENERATIONS—FROM THE 1930s TO THE 1960s, *by Seymour M. Lipset and Everett C. Ladd, Jr., reprinted from* THE PUBLIC INTEREST, *no. 25, Summer 1971.**

WHAT'S BUGGING THE STUDENTS?, *by Kenneth Keniston, reprinted from* EDUCATIONAL RECORD, *American Council on Education, Washington, D.C., Spring 1970.**

THE POLITICS OF ACADEMIA, *by Seymour Martin Lipset, reprinted from David C. Nichols (ed.),* PERSPECTIVES ON CAMPUS TENSIONS: PAPERS PREPARED FOR THE SPECIAL COMMITTEE ON CAMPUS TENSIONS, *American Council on Education, Washington, D.C., September 1970.**

*The Commission's stock of this reprint has been exhausted.

INTERNATIONAL PROGRAMS OF U.S. COLLEGES AND UNIVERSITIES: PRIORITIES FOR THE SEVENTIES, *by James A. Perkins, reprinted by permission of the International Council for Educational Development, Occasional Paper no. 1, July 1971.**

FACULTY UNIONISM: FROM THEORY TO PRACTICE, *by Joseph W. Garbarino, reprinted from* INDUSTRIAL RELATIONS, *vol. 11, no. 1, pp. 1–17, February 1972.**

MORE FOR LESS: HIGHER EDUCATION'S NEW PRIORITY, *by Virginia B. Smith, reprinted from* UNIVERSAL HIGHER EDUCATION: COSTS AND BENEFITS, *American Council on Education, Washington, D.C., 1971.**

ACADEMIA AND POLITICS IN AMERICA, *by Seymour M. Lipset, reprinted from Thomas J. Nossiter (ed.),* IMAGINATION AND PRECISION IN THE SOCIAL SCIENCES, *pp. 211–289, Faber and Faber, London, 1972.**

POLITICS OF ACADEMIC NATURAL SCIENTISTS AND ENGINEERS, *by Everett C. Ladd, Jr., and Seymour M. Lipset, reprinted from* SCIENCE, *vol. 176, no. 4039, pp. 1091–1100, June 9, 1972.*

THE INTELLECTUAL AS CRITIC AND REBEL, WITH SPECIAL REFERENCE TO THE UNITED STATES AND THE SOVIET UNION, *by Seymour M. Lipset and Richard B. Dobson, reprinted from* DAEDALUS, *vol. 101, no. 3, pp. 137–198, Summer 1972.*

THE POLITICS OF AMERICAN SOCIOLOGISTS, *by Seymour M. Lipset and Everett C. Ladd, Jr., reprinted from* THE AMERICAN JOURNAL OF SOCIOLOGY, *vol. 78, no. 1, July 1972.*

THE DISTRIBUTION OF ACADEMIC TENURE IN AMERICAN HIGHER EDUCATION, *by Martin Trow, reprinted from* THE TENURE DEBATE, *Bardwell Smith (ed.), Jossey-Bass, San Francisco, 1972.*

THE NATURE AND ORIGINS OF THE CARNEGIE COMMISSION ON HIGHER EDUCATION, *by Alan Pifer, based on a speech delivered to the Pennsylvania Association of Colleges and Universities, Oct. 16, 1972, reprinted by permission of the Carnegie Foundation for the Advancement of Teaching.*

AMERICAN SOCIAL SCIENTISTS AND THE GROWTH OF CAMPUS POLITICAL ACTIVISM IN THE 1960s, *by Everett C. Ladd, Jr., and Seymour M. Lipset, reprinted from* SOCIAL SCIENCES INFORMATION, *vol. 10, no. 2, April 1971.**

THE POLITICS OF AMERICAN POLITICAL SCIENTISTS, *by Everett C. Ladd, Jr., and Seymour M. Lipset, reprinted from* PS, *vol. 4, no. 2, Spring 1971.**

THE DIVIDED PROFESSORIATE, *by Seymour M. Lipset and Everett C. Ladd, Jr., reprinted from* CHANGE, *vol. 3, no. 3, pp. 54–60, May 1971.**

JEWISH ACADEMICS IN THE UNITED STATES: THEIR ACHIEVEMENTS, CULTURE AND POLITICS, *by Seymour M. Lipset and Everett C. Ladd, Jr., reprinted from* AMERICAN JEWISH YEAR BOOK, *1971.**

**The Commission's stock of this reprint has been exhausted.*

THE UNHOLY ALLIANCE AGAINST THE CAMPUS, *by Kenneth Keniston and Michael Lerner, reprinted from* NEW YORK TIMES MAGAZINE, *November 8, 1970.**

PRECARIOUS PROFESSORS: NEW PATTERNS OF REPRESENTATION, *by Joseph W. Garbarino, reprinted from* INDUSTRIAL RELATIONS, *vol. 10, no. 1, February 1971.**

. . . AND WHAT PROFESSORS THINK: ABOUT STUDENT PROTEST AND MANNERS, MORALS, POLITICS, AND CHAOS ON THE CAMPUS, *by Seymour Martin Lipset and Everett C. Ladd, Jr., reprinted from* PSYCHOLOGY TODAY, *November 1970.**

DEMAND AND SUPPLY IN U.S. HIGHER EDUCATION: A PROGRESS REPORT, *by Roy Radner and Leonard S. Miller, reprinted from* AMERICAN ECONOMIC REVIEW, *May 1970.**

RESOURCES FOR HIGHER EDUCATION: AN ECONOMIST'S VIEW, *by Theodore W. Schultz, reprinted from* JOURNAL OF POLITICAL ECONOMY, *vol. 76, no. 3, University of Chicago, May/June 1968.**

INDUSTRIAL RELATIONS AND UNIVERSITY RELATIONS, *by Clark Kerr, reprinted from* PROCEEDINGS OF THE 21ST ANNUAL WINTER MEETING OF THE INDUSTRIAL RELATIONS RESEARCH ASSOCIATION, *pp. 15–25.**

NEW CHALLENGES TO THE COLLEGE AND UNIVERSITY, *by Clark Kerr, reprinted from Kermit Gordon (ed.),* AGENDA FOR THE NATION, *The Brookings Institution, Washington, D.C., 1968.**

PRESIDENTIAL DISCONTENT, *by Clark Kerr, reprinted from David C. Nichols (ed.),* PERSPECTIVES ON CAMPUS TENSIONS: PAPERS PREPARED FOR THE SPECIAL COMMITTEE ON CAMPUS TENSIONS, *American Council on Education, Washington, D.C., September 1970.**

STUDENT PROTEST—AN INSTITUTIONAL AND NATIONAL PROFILE, *by Harold Hodgkinson, reprinted from* THE RECORD, *vol. 71, no. 4, May 1970.**

COMING OF MIDDLE AGE IN HIGHER EDUCATION, *by Earl F. Cheit, address delivered to American Association of State Colleges and Universities and National Association of State Universities and Land-Grant Colleges, Nov. 13, 1972.*

MEASURING FACULTY UNIONISM: QUANTITY AND QUALITY, *by Bill Aussieker and J. W. Garbarino, reprinted from* INDUSTRIAL RELATIONS, *vol. 12, no. 2, May 1973.*

PROBLEMS IN THE TRANSITION FROM ELITE TO MASS HIGHER EDUCATION, *by Martin Trow, paper prepared for a conference on mass higher education sponsored by the Organization for Economic Co-operation and Development, June 1973.**

**The Commission's stock of this reprint has been exhausted.*

Demand and Supply in U.S. Higher Education

Demand and Supply in U.S. Higher Education

by **Roy Radner**
Professor of Economics and Statistics
University of California, Berkeley

and **Leonard S. Miller**
Assistant Professor of Social Welfare
University of California, Berkeley

with the collaboration of **Douglas L. Adkins**
Assistant Professor of Economics
Graduate School of Business Administration
New York University

and **Frederick E. Balderston**
Professor of Business Administration
and Chairman, Center for Research in Management Science
University of California, Berkeley

A Report Prepared for
The Carnegie Commission on Higher Education

McGRAW-HILL BOOK COMPANY
New York St. Louis San Francisco
Düsseldorf Johannesburg Kuala Lumpur London Mexico
Montreal New Delhi Panama Paris São Paulo
Singapore Sydney Tokyo Toronto

The Carnegie Commission on Higher Education, 2150 Shattuck Avenue, Berkeley, California 94704 has sponsored preparation of this volume as part of a continuing effort to obtain and present significant information for public discussion. The views expressed are those of the authors.

DEMAND AND SUPPLY IN U.S. HIGHER EDUCATION

This book was set in Palatino by University Graphics, Inc. It was printed and bound by The Maple Press Company. The designer was Elliot Epstein. The editors were Nancy Frank, Janine Parson, and Michael Hennelly for McGraw-Hill Book Company and Verne A. Stadtman and Karen Seriguchi for the Carnegie Commission on Higher Education. Andre Hanneman edited the index. Milton J. Heiberg supervised the production.

Library of Congress Cataloging in Publication Data

Radner, Roy, date
Demand and supply in U.S. higher education.

Bibliography: p.
Includes index.
1. College attendance—United States. 2. Education, Higher—United States. I. Miller, Leonard S., joint author. II. Carnegie Commission on Higher Education. III. Title.

LC148.R32 331.1'26 74-23180
ISBN 0-07-010113-2

123456789MAMM798765

Contents

List of Figures

List of Tables

Foreword

It has become a familiar fact in the last few years that higher education in the United States is facing a dramatically different outlook, in terms of its rate of growth, from the situation that prevailed in the 1960s. In the mid-1960s, exceptionally rapid growth, with all of its consequences, was taken for granted. As we move into the mid-1970s, much of the time and attention of those involved in the planning and study of the future of higher education is concerned with the implications of a rate of growth that is already greatly reduced and can be expected to continue to decline, and perhaps become negative, as we move into the 1980s.

The present volume—the work of sophisticated econometricians—is based on studies that were initiated during the rapid growth period. Yet it includes a surprising number of investigations that shed light on the implications of slower growth and on the ways in which the future rate of growth could be affected by policy changes.

Research on the economics of education has become an important branch of economics only in the last 10 to 15 years, despite recognition by Adam Smith and other early economists of the importance of education in relation to economic development. A significant aspect of recent research efforts is the study of the demand of students for enrollment in higher education, with increasing emphasis on (1) how student demand varies among types of institutions and (2) on the relation between student demand and the supply of student places in these institutions. In the present volume, the authors present an extremely useful review of the development of this research and then go on to present the results of their own efforts, which represent advances in methodology over much of the earlier research. Their findings and those of earlier investigators, with particular reference to the impact of changes in "price" (tuition) on student demand, played an important role in the development of the economic model of higher education used by the National Commission on the Financing of Postsecondary Education—a model that, incidentally, needs to be refined and modified before it can be seriously used for actual forecasting.

An important methodological innovation was the use of the *ratio of cost of attendance to family income* in the investigation of the impact of changes in cost on student demand, and the analysis of how the influence of changes in this ratio was related to the influence of student ability. It was found that the cost-to-income ratio played a considerably more important role in affecting the demand of low-ability than of high-ability students. High-ability students "appeared to be willing to sustain substantially higher financial burdens in order to attend" an institution of higher education than low-ability students and were also strongly attracted to highly selective institutions. Interestingly, also, among the students of comparatively low ability, the more able were especially likely to elect not to go to college at all. Two aspects of these findings that warrant further investigation are (1) the role of student aid in supporting the demand of highly able students, especially for admission to selective institutions, and (2) the role of comparative employment opportunities in explaining the choices of the more able among the relatively low-ability students. The authors, quite rightly in my opinion, emphasize the importance of continued development of open-door and comprehensive community colleges, as did the Carnegie Commission, in providing more attractive, occupationally oriented educational opportunities for students for whom a strictly academic program has little appeal.

The authors then go on to analyze faculty-student ratios, developing an innovative method of estimating *marginal* faculty-student ratios—critical for educational planning—by investigating the way in which average ratios vary with enrollment at both the graduate and undergraduate levels. They find that there are economies of scale in the use of faculty in undergraduate institutions up to an FTE enrollment of 3,000 to 4,000, but not beyond that. No such clearcut result was obtained for universities. These findings are essentially similar to those presented in the Carnegie Commission's report *The More Effective Use of Resources* (1972).

To what extent do high faculty-student ratios tend to be found in institutions that are otherwise characterized by relatively high quality, as measured by comparative faculty salaries and proportions of Ph.D.'s on the faculty? Although a positive relationship prevailed in universities, public four-year colleges, and private M.A.-granting institutions, two-year colleges and private four-year colleges with high faculty salaries displayed a tendency to substitute quantity of faculty for one of the faculty quality variables, while in private four-year colleges with relatively low salaries no significant relation was found between the quality variables and faculty-student ratios. In universities, another quality variable—American Council on Education ratings of graduate programs—was investigated and was found to be associated particularly with faculty-student ratios at the graduate level rather than with the other quality measures. The findings are important because they indicate that these relationships are complex and that differing approaches to improvement of quality need to be considered in different types of institutions.

On the critical issue of the future job market for Ph.D.'s, the authors explore the implications of deliberately raising faculty-student ratios and increasing the percentage of Ph.D.'s on faculties. This is an attempt to determine how much Allan Cartter's path-breaking and pessimistic findings could be modified by policy adaptations designed to improve or "smooth" out the job market for Ph.D.'s. They find that such policy changes—which would be dependent, of course, on allocating adequate financial resources to higher education—would improve the demand for faculty significantly over Cartter's estimate but would not vitally alter the outlook for a poor job market for Ph.D.'s in the late 1970s and in the 1980s. Again, the authors explore certain policy implications and urge greater emphasis on development of Doctor of Arts programs *or* changes in Ph.D. programs to provide greater emphasis on breadth of training and on preparation for teaching. Such changes, they argue, would produce holders of doctorates who would be better qualified to teach in public community colleges, where the increased demand for faculty will be relatively high.

An aspect of these results that requires further exploration is the question of how much both the Cartter and the Radner-Balderston findings require modification on the basis of the recent decline in enrollment rates, chiefly among young white males, that has been occurring since enrollment projections that they used were developed. Prospects for future enrollment growth among college-age young people may be even less favorable than these projections indicate. On the other hand, some critics are arguing that it is erroneous to assume we are approaching a "steady state," because rapidly increasing enrollment of adults will offset the impact of the decline in the college-age *population* that is bound to occur in the 1980s—reflecting the diminishing size of cohorts born from about 1964 on. The new Carnegie Council is now developing revised enrollment projections designed to measure the possible impact of these changes.

Probably the most methodologically innovative part of the book begins with the development of a very sophisticated dynamic input-output model of the education system in Chapter 10. The model is then used to investigate resource requirements for a universal two-year college program. This is of special significance because of the growing interest in "two years of free access" or "two years of higher education in the bank," which the Carnegie Council is also studying. Although there are numerous ways in which "two years of free access" might be implemented, of which the particular universal two-year college program explored by Radner and Miller is only one, the analysis and data will be useful in exploring other possible approaches as well. They have developed, for example, detailed state-by-state estimates of the possible impact on enrollment. They also show, in an analysis of implementation in a five-year, ten-year, or fifteen-year period, that the most gradual of these three alternatives would involve the least strain on the existing system and the most economical use of resources.

Another extremely interesting application of aspects of the model relates to the impact of a drastic increase in the faculty-student ratio in the teaching of disadvantaged students in elementary and secondary schools. Thoroughly familiar with the controversy over the findings of the Coleman Report to the effect that variations in resource inputs do not greatly effect outcomes, in terms of student performance in the public schools, the authors nevertheless argue that it is at least plausible to assume that an increase in the faculty-student ratio (for disadvantaged students only) from the present 1 to 25 to something on the order of 1 to 6 would appreciably improve the performance of such students. Here again, they find that gradual implementation would have advantages. The estimated overall cost of about

$12 billion, of which only about $1 billion would be at the higher education level, is high, but appropriate social accounting would weigh this against the social costs of high unemployment and crime rates among those emerging from ghetto schools. On the other hand, remembering Conant's *Slums and Suburbs* (1961), we must recognize that the educational system alone cannot solve the problems of slum youngsters in the absence of other measures, such as adequate low-cost housing, aimed at improving the environment in which they grow up. Despite this qualification, the results are of special interest, not only in connection with the critical need for improvement in ghetto schools, but also in relation to the exceedingly poor current and future job market prospects for teachers. Among teachers' associations, there is a strong tendency to argue that a surplus of teachers is not inevitable if adequate resources are allocated to the schools.

Finally, the volume includes valuable estimates of annual changes in the stock (or total number) of educated persons by field of training. These estimates are based on a painstaking and elaborate analysis of the annual number of degrees awarded at three levels, involving numerous adjustments of U.S. Office of Education data and application of survival rates based on mortality data to determine changes in the stock. They should prove particularly useful to analysts who are concerned with changing patterns of demand and supply by field of study.

Perhaps the most important contribution of this innovative volume is in its demonstration that researchers should be wary of uncritical acceptance of the results of studies based on a single set of assumptions. By making use of sets of alternative assumptions in much of their analysis, the authors demonstrate not only that rather widely differing results can be obtained, but also that a number of different assumptions are quite plausible in attacking problems of estimating future developments in higher education. Their work will be intensively studied by those engaged in similar analyses, and the policy implications of many of their findings will be of interest to a wide audience.

Clark Kerr
Chairman
Carnegie Commission
on Higher Education

June 1975

Demand and Supply in U.S. Higher Education

gramming assistance of Charles Yarborough and Ernie Haberkern. In particular, Sunny Yoder did most of the data collection and statistical analysis for Chapter 7, and Sharon Bush did the same for Chapter 9.

Grace Katagiri supervised the initial stages of manuscript preparation; Emily Thomas and Carol de Ruiter typed the manuscript; Terry Jue did the preliminary drawings for the many figures; Alice Kwong and Virginia Thompson contributed their expertise at various stages of the process. Finally, Emily Thomas valiantly earned her spurs by supervising the final preparation of a long and difficult manuscript.

The authors also gratefully acknowledge the comments provided by Joseph Froomkin, Gus Haggstrom, Stephen Hoenack, Kenneth Roose, and Finis Welch, who read parts of various drafts, and those of Margaret S. Gordon, who read the entire penultimate draft. Gus Haggstrom provided essential enrollment projections, and Daniel McFadden made available computer programs and advice essential to the use of his conditional logit method. The demand study would not have been possible without the cooperation of Denis Donovan and the Center for Research in Higher Education at the University of California, Berkeley, who made available the data from the SCOPE project.

Finally, we owe the greatest debt of all to Clark Kerr, who first inspired our faith in public higher education, then inspired and encouraged this project on the econometric study of higher education, and finally waited patiently (or impatiently) for the outcome. The modest results of our research could not match his grand vision of an econometric model of United States higher education, but we hope they contribute something to the realization of his much grander vision of higher education in the United States and in the world.

Roy Radner
Leonard S. Miller
Berkeley, California

Authors' Preface

The research for this volume was initiated at the end of 1967 under the auspices of the Carnegie Commission on Higher Education. The major financial support for the project was provided by the Carnegie Commission, with substantial support also coming from the National Science Foundation. The research reported in Chapters 8 and 9 was also supported in part by the Ford Foundation through its Program for Research in University Administration at the University of California. The project made substantial use of the research and computing facilities of the University of California, Berkeley; the State University of New York, Stony Brook; and New York University.

Financial support is not everything. Just as important was the support we received from Irene Miller and Virginia Radner during a long and sometimes demanding project.

The undersigned were jointly and directly responsible for the conduct of the research reported in all but Chapters 8 and 9 and for the preparation of the volume. D. Adkins did the research for and writing of Chapter 8. F. E. Balderston and R. Radner collaborated on Chapter 9.

Space limitations did not permit the inclusion in the present volume of all the background tables and explanations of methodology that were included in an original, and considerably longer, draft of this volume. This additional material will be available in two technical reports sponsored by the Carnegie Commission, one by D. Adkins (1975) relating to Chapter 8, and one by L. S. Miller and R. Radner (1975) relating primarily to Chapters 3, 4, 5, 11, and 12.

The authors gratefully acknowledge the research contributions of Sharon Bush, Everett Ehrlich, Deborah Gordon, Alice Kwong, Brian Morris, and Sunny Yoder, and the computer pro-

1. *Introduction*

Higher education in the United States may be thought of as a giant industry in which (1) the "inputs" are students with various characteristics and qualifications, the services of faculty and other professionals, and all the other usual kinds of material and service inputs and (2) the "outputs" are graduates (and dropouts) with various characteristics and qualifications, research, public service, and occasionally even entertainment and other consumer goods and services. Even the category "goods in process" has its analogy in the case of students who are partway through a particular education program.

If this picture is at all appropriate, then we shall be led naturally to study the demand for outputs, the supply of factors, the technological relationships within the industry, and the like. Note, however, that the "supply of student inputs" from the point of view of the education industry corresponds to what is usually regarded as the "demand for places" by potential students. Colleges and universities do not sell in any direct way their output of graduates in the market for educated labor, nor are they usually thought of as selling their places to students. Furthermore, the hypothesis of profit maximization is no doubt even less appropriate to the education industry than to most conventional industries.

Lest some readers be put off by what might appear to them as an excessively cold or quantitative approach, we should emphasize at the outset that our view of United States higher education as an industry is in no way inconsistent with the view that the most important output of this industry is education in one or more of its loftiest senses. At the heart of every industry are processes of transformation—in this case the transformation of students, teachers, and knowledge. As economists, we shall be most concerned with the resource allocation aspects of these processes, especially the allocation of human resources.

In the present volume we report on the results of a project designed to estimate statistically several aspects of demand and supply in United States higher education and to illustrate the possible uses of the resulting econometric models for policy research. Although we had an overall view of the education industry in mind, we did not produce a single, unified econometric model, nor did we seriously consider such an ambitious goal. We have instead focused on three aspects: (1) estimation of the demand for freshman places by potential students as a function of cost of attendance, student family income, student academic ability and other traits, and school selectivity; (2) estimation of the relationship between student-faculty ratios and institutional characteristics; and (3) estimation and projection of the stocks of educated persons, by age, sex, highest degree, and field of specialization, together with the dynamic relationships between stocks and flows.

Our aim in this project has been not only to add to the scientific description and understanding of the education industry but also to provide a set of related models that can contribute to the debate on policy issues. Effective policy analysis requires, of course, not just good projections based on the assumption of unchanging trends but also estimates of how policy instruments affect target variables.[1] To illustrate the use of quantitative models for policy purposes, we present three exercises in policy analysis, centering on models of input-output relationships: (1) a set of alternative forecasts of academic demand for new Ph.D.'s, showing the effects of alternative faculty personnel policies; (2) estimates of human and financial resource requirements of alternative universal two-year college programs; and (3) estimates of the impact on higher

[1]For the classic discussion of this question, see Jacob Marschak's paper, "Economic Measurements for Policy and Prediction" (Marschak, 1953). The econometric reader will recognize at several points in our own work our struggles with the problems of *identification of structural parameters* and *specification of policy instruments.* We shall not, however, provide any systematic explanation of these issues. See, for example, the famous Cowles Commission Monograph 14 (Hood & Koopmans, 1953), of which the paper by Marschak is the first chapter.

education of significant compensatory education programs in the primary and secondary schools.

Thus the topics of our project, and the present volume, are divided between basic and applied research. There are a number of important topics with which we have not dealt, either because they are being intensively studied by others (e.g., the benefits of higher education, the supply of finance in different sectors) or because we could not deal with them given the available data and/or time. In particular, we had hoped to make more progress on studies of the supply and pricing of places by private institutions and of the factors influencing the demand for educated persons by the United States economy. The latter study appeared to require good estimates of the stocks of educated persons, which did not exist previous to the research reported in this volume. Furthermore, it is doubtful whether one can get a good explanation of the dynamics of the industrial demand for educated persons from the study of aggregate statistics alone. As longitudinal studies of individuals and firms become more available, economists and sociologists will be in a better position to deal effectively with these questions.

Since each chapter of the volume contains a summary, we felt it would be superfluous to include a chapter-by-chapter summary here. On the other hand, some readers may find it useful at this point to have a brief indication of those of our results that have some relevance to current policy issues. Accordingly, the remainder of this chapter is devoted to such observations, organized around three interrelated topics: influencing the demand for higher education, increasing equality of opportunity, and effective use of educational resources. We shall also incorporate into the discussion some remarks on needed directions of new research.

Our study of the demand for freshman places in institutions of higher education was based on the SCOPE sample survey and focused on both the economic and noneconomic factors that influence individual choices of high school seniors among available alternative postsecondary options (Chapters 3 through 5). Three variables were revealed as most important in explaining these choices: (1) a measure of ability-to-pay, (2) a measure of academic ability or aptitude, and (3) a measure of the academic selectivity of alternative postsecondary institutions available to the particular individual. In terms of explanatory power, ability-to-pay seemed best measured from the available data by the simple ratio of out-of-pocket cost to family income. As one would expect, demand varied inversely with ability-to-pay. However, the influences of ability-to-pay and academic selectivity varied substantially among potential students of different measured academic ability. First, ability-to-pay had the weakest influence among high school seniors with high academic ability and the strongest influence among those with low academic ability. Second, among seniors with high academic ability, there was a positive attraction between higher-ability seniors and more selective colleges and universities, whereas among seniors with academic-ability test scores below the median for the United States population, the higher the academic ability of the senior, the more likely he or she was to elect to go to work rather than go to college. (For seniors in the lower half of the academic-ability distribution, open-access junior colleges were usually the only available college option.)

These differences in demand behavior among students of different academic ability would appear to have subtle, but important, implications for financial aid policy, for policies designed to increase access to higher education, and for substantive changes in curricular programs. Financial aid programs based solely on family-income criteria may have disappointing results as far as increasing higher education enrollment among potential students with lower academic ability is concerned, and also among potential students with low family incomes (because of the statistical correlation between income and measured academic ability). Increasing the supply of freshman and sophomore places in colleges and universities, and lowering admission standards, may also have disappointing effects on enrollment if corresponding curricular changes are not made to make programs more useful and attractive to those in the middle and lower ranges of academic ability.

A notable feature of our demand study is the attempt to distinguish the influence of factors affecting demand from the causal influences on supply. The use of our model to project the effects on demand of changes in cost, income, ability, and selectivity is illustrated in Chapter 4, together with measures of how sensitive these projections are to errors in the estimated parameters of the demand model. We have not attempted to integrate these calculations into a national model of demand. However, an important step in this direction has been made by the National Commission on the Financing of Postsecondary Education (1973), using the results of our study.

Improving access to higher education requires increasing the supply of places and of faculty, as well as manipulating demand. In some respects, these two aspects are interdependent. For example, since the cost of living away from home can be a significant fraction of the total out-of-pocket cost of going to college, the availability of lower-cost institutions within commuting distance has an important influence on the demand for higher education in a given geographic area.

Student-faculty ratios represent an important aspect of the "technology" of the higher education industry and influence the supply of the "output" of the industry. In Chapters 6 and 7 we report how student-faculty ratios have varied through time and across institutions. In particular, we relate student-faculty ratios to various institutional variables, such as level of degree granted, control, size, average faculty salary, fraction of the faculty who hold the Ph.D. degree, and, where applicable, fraction of students at the graduate level and quality of the graduate program.

We have used this information, together with enrollment projections, to estimate the academic demand for Ph.D.'s between now and 1990 (Chapter 9). The conclusions of this exercise confirm in general terms those of Cartter (1971); namely, the holders of doctoral degrees will probably confront a declining *academic* demand during at least the next decade, throwing an increasing proportion of new doctorates into competition for nonacademic employment. Our study goes beyond Cartter's in that (1) we disaggregate our projections by institutional type (level and control), and (2) we calculate our projections under each of a series of different policy assumptions and under different projections of enrollment. These different policy assumptions imply, in turn, different projections for the evolution of student-faculty ratios, percentages of faculty with the Ph.D., and distributions of Ph.D.'s among the various sectors of higher education. The implications of these projections for decision makers at various levels (government, institutions of higher education, students) are spelled out in the last section of Chapter 9.

The cross-sectional study of student-faculty ratios provides interesting evidence on the nature of returns to scale to faculty inputs. There is strong evidence of increasing returns to scale in undergraduate (four-year) colleges with fewer than 3,000 students. Thus, holding the other variables constant, there is increasing inefficiency in the use of faculty as student enrollment declines below 3,000 in any one-institution. This conclusion is roughly consistent with the Carnegie Commission's analysis of cost data (*The More Effective Use of Resources*, 1972, p. 41). (To this one might add that small faculties find it difficult to provide the breadth and richness of programs that one can usually find in larger institutions.) Of course, such judgments should not be applied in blanket fashion to all institutions regardless of their goals, but the results of the statistical analysis do suggest that many very small colleges with "normal" aspirations and goals could operate more efficiently at a larger scale.

Analysis of the data for 93 (Ph.D.-granting) universities in our sample revealed no evidence of either increasing or decreasing returns to scale. Our sample of universities included only those with substantial graduate enrollments, and the average size in both public and private categories was about 11,000 full-time-equivalent students.

It is often assumed that lower student-faculty ratios are correlated with higher quality of instruction; indeed, "quality" is sometimes defined in terms of student-faculty ratios (and other variables). Our study does not reveal any clear pattern in this connection, except in the case of the universities, where there is a definite inverse correlation between the student-faculty ratios in graduate education and the quality of graduate instruction. (In order to measure this relationship it was, of course, necessary to estimate separate "faculty input coefficients" for undergraduate and graduate education within the same institution; the method for doing this is described in Chapter 7.) This relationship between the input of faculty per graduate student and the quality of graduate instruction assumes increasing policy importance as both public and private universities face increasing financial difficulties. There is a danger that, in a period in which there seems to be an excess supply of Ph.D.'s, support of graduate education will be scaled down in such a way that the *quality* of graduate education in the major universities of the country will suffer. Furthermore, if (as we predict) the federal government plays an increasingly explicit role in the support of graduate education, especially at the doctoral level, it will be particularly important to recognize this relationship in the standard support formulas that will inevitably be established. Finally, the time series show a gradual but unmistakable increase in student-faculty ratios during the 1950s and 1960s (provided one adjusts for the changing percentage of graduate students in the universities). The relative deficiency in the academic demand for Ph.D.'s that would be developing in the 1970s and 1980s if student-faculty ratios remained unchanged will provide higher education with the opportunity to reverse that historical trend and restore the ratios to their 1950 values.

The changing market for teachers will also provide the opportunity for increasing equality of access to higher education during the next two decades, in at least two different ways. First, the growth of the junior college system could have an important role in increasing equality of educational opportunity, since it would not only make a modest amount of postsecondary education available to almost all high school graduates but also provide an additional chance for talented students with poor backgrounds to overcome their initial educational handicaps and go on to qualify for entrance to four-year colleges and to universities. In Chapter 11 we explore the consequences —in terms of enrollments, teacher requirements, and costs—of bringing the nationwide enrollment in the first two years of college up to a level of 90 percent of all high school graduates. Such an exercise requires a more sophisticated model of the higher educational system than that used in Chapter 9; we use a dynamic input-output model, which is developed in Chapter 10.

The resource requirements for such a "universal two-year college plan" depend upon the speed with which the plan is put into effect. We calculate these requirements for three alternative start-up periods: 5, 10, and 15 years. With regard to possible bottlenecks in the training of higher education faculty, none of the plans appears to pose any feasibility problems, although the faster start-up periods are somewhat more wasteful in their resource use. However, in view of the results of our demand studies, there might be serious problems in generating the required student demand. When the plans reached full operation, they would imply a 13.5 percent expansion in undergraduate enrollment and an 18.5 percent expansion in higher education costs. It must be kept in mind, however, that the percentage of high school graduates *currently* going on to some type of postsecondary education varies considerably from state to state, so that the impact of such a plan would vary correspondingly.

Further progress in increasing equality of educational opportunity at the level of higher education probably requires an increase in academic achievement at the primary and secondary levels. Low achievement at these levels is highly correlated with certain disadvantages in the student's background, especially poverty and racial discrimination. One class of methods that has been proposed for eliminating this obstacle is "compensatory education." Generally speaking, compensatory education involves allocating more than average resources to the education of students from disadvantaged backgrounds. These additional resources may take the form of specialized programs, of an increase in the general quality of teachers, of an increased number of counselors, of improved facilities, etc. A particularly simple form of compensatory education is a decrease in the student-teacher ratio. Such a form of compensatory education in the primary and secondary schools can affect higher education in at least two ways. First, it can increase the output of high school graduates who are qualified to enter institutions of higher education. Second, it can increase the demand for teachers, some or all of which will be met by increasing the output of institutions of higher education.

In Chapter 12 we present estimates of the resource requirements of compensatory education plans in which the student-teacher ratio for disadvantaged students in United States primary and secondary education would be reduced from its present level to a target level of 6 to 1. This target level has been chosen to illustrate the quantitative impacts on *higher education* of a *dramatic* change in the student-teacher ratio for disadvantaged students in primary and secondary education. Little is known about the relative efficacy of different student-teacher ratios, although it would appear that small changes cannot be expected to produce significant results in achievement. Nevertheless, it seems to us plausible that such a low ratio, coupled with appropriate teaching techniques, could produce substantial gains in achievement among students.

The techniques used to obtain the projections in Chapter 12 are similar to those used in the case of the universal two-year college plans. Again, start-up periods of 5, 10, and 15 years are considered.

By 1987, when all the plans would have reached full-scale operation, an increment of approximately 1 million primary and secondary school teachers would be needed. This is equal to half of the 1969 stock of practicing elementary and secondary school teachers. Although this need not place a great strain on the system in the long run, all the plans would appear to face bottlenecks in teacher training if all the additional teachers were new college and university graduates. However, various sources of relief of such bottlenecks suggest themselves and are discussed in Chapter 12.

On the cost side, by 1987 the annual cost increments for all plans would be about $12 billion (1966–67 prices), not counting capital costs for primary and secondary schools. This is probably a low estimate, since we have used moderate estimates of teacher salaries and have not accounted for any increase in costs per teacher that might be needed to tap the present reserve. Of this $12 billion, only about $1 billion represents costs induced in the higher education sector. Although the different start-up times of the plans do not affect the long-run annual costs, they do affect the initial costs. Longer start-up times result in smoother time series of higher education faculty and student requirements, which are more efficient from the point of view of resource utilization. Thus the initial induced higher education cost of the 5-year plan is $1.6 billion, whereas the corresponding initial cost of the 15-year plan is only $600 million.

A third major component of the empirical effort of our project has been the estimation of the number of persons in the United States labor force (active or potential) who hold degrees from American colleges and universities, classified by 44 educational specialties, by degree of highest attainment, by sex, and by age (Chapter 8). In a sense, these estimates give a detailed picture of the existing stock of "human capital," as that term has been used recently by economists, that is, a picture of the surviving cumulated output of the education industry. Up to now, there have been available data on the occupational composition of the labor force, but economists and statisticians have not been able to discover any stable relationships between occupational classifications and educational requirements. With respect to human capital, attention has been focused almost exclusively on the level of educational attainment (and not in much detail above the fourth year of college), with the result that there has been a striking gap in our information about the composition of the stock of degreed manpower and womanpower by educational specialty. The estimates presented in Chapter 8 represent an attempt to fill that gap, at least partially.

Because of the apparent absence of close and stable links between occupational requirements and educational requirements, it is difficult to draw immediate inferences from these new estimates with respect to general questions of labor-force policy. Individual disciplines and specialties will no doubt find the historical trends of considerable interest, however, especially in conjunction with more detailed forecasts of academic and nonacademic demand.

Nevertheless, one striking set of conclusions with regard to the sex distributions in these stocks calls for comment. If one looks only at gross aggregates, then one might get the impression that modest but not insignificant progress has been made toward sexual equality in the population of collee-degree-holders since 1930. In 1971, 42 percent of that population was made up of women, as compared with 36 percent in 1930. However, if one disaggregates by highest degree attained, one sees that the bachelor's and doctorate stocks have maintained a remarkably stable sex ratio from 1930 to 1970; in both cases the percent female was somewhat higher in 1930 than in 1970. The percent female in the second-level stock has risen gradually over the same period. But a disaggregation of the second-level stocks by educational specialty shows that this trend is associated primarily with changes in specialty proportions, away from male-dominated specialties and toward female-dominated specialties. In fact, at the 44 category level of disaggregation, the sex ratios have stayed remarkably constant for most of the specialties, at all three levels. Thus if we look at the sex ratios within specialties at each level, there is little evidence of a lessening of inequality between the sexes.

One of the most important female-dominated specialties is,

of course, primary and secondary school teaching. If the academic market in higher education continues to worsen, more and more men may be driven to compete with women for places in primary and secondary education. Thus women may be threatened with losing some of the numerical gains that appear in the aggregate statistics. On the other hand, this pressure, in the atmosphere of an awakening spirit of women's liberation, may finally result in the opening up of many specialties to women and may promote a more fundamental movement toward equality of the sexes in the stock of human capital than we have seen during the past 40 years.

We complete this chapter with some brief reflections on desirable directions of future research. On the demand side, we have used new methods of estimating demand relationships from individual longitudinal response data. (These methods were based largely on a statistical technique developed by D. McFadden.) The elaboration of these methods was initially quite time-consuming, and this prevented us from utilizing all but a small fraction of the data available in the SCOPE sample. In addition, data available from Project TALENT now include sufficient geographic detail to allow the application of our methods. Thus an obvious follow-up of the research reported in Chapters 3 through 5 would be to extend the analysis to more of the SCOPE data and to the Project TALENT data.

However, further mining of available sample surveys will have definite limitations. New surveys, with questions that are more sharply relevant to policy issues, would shed more light on questions of financial aid policy (such as the differential effects of grants, loans, and work-study), on questions of curricular appeal, and on various locational problems.

Questions of demand are intimately related with questions about institutional "pricing" and admissions policy. Little is known, at least quantitatively, about the dynamics of application, admission, and acceptance and about the dynamics of institutional tuition and financial aid policy.

More effective use of resources could be promoted by new research into measuring inputs and outputs in higher education, or new measures of "value added." In any case, in an era of increasing demand for accountability, a good defense against the misuse of oversimplified "productivity measures" by the philistines around (and among) us is a thorough understanding of the quantitative as well as the qualitative relationships in the various processes of education and research.

The threatened crisis of excess capacity in the higher education industry can be transformed into an opportunity to increase quality and equality at all levels of education. Although there are many gaps in our basic information, in this arena a great deal can be accomplished by policy research that draws together known facts and relationships to spell out the costs and requirements of various proposals. Here the urgent need is to demonstrate the economic feasibility of a number of attractive ideas that are too easily dismissed as infeasible in the absence of careful analysis. The debunking of such myths of economic infeasibility may be the first step toward developing political feasibility of proposals hitherto regarded as utopian.

In sum, the higher education industry, primarily in the hands of nonprofit and government institutions, has not engaged in enough market research (vis-à-vis potential students), has too long avoided understanding the quantitative aspects of its internal resource use, and has been too timid in developing and evaluating bold proposals for the social use of its own powerful resources. We hope that econometric research will provide the tools, data, and analyses to help remedy this situation.

2. Demand for Higher Education: Review and Critique of the Literature

Econometric estimates of the demand for higher education in the United States have a comparatively recent history. As far as we are aware, the literature on the subject begins in 1967, the year we started our own research on the subject. The first studies were pioneering in many ways, but as we shall see, they did not satisfy both of the criteria that we felt were important for a model that could be used for policy purposes: (1) The model should describe the joint demand for different types of institutions of higher education, and (2) there should be a satisfactory solution of the "identification problem"; i.e., the effects of varying demand behavior by potential students should be separated from the effects of varying supply behavior by institutions of higher education. (See the fuller discussion of these problems in the Introduction.)

In this chapter we shall review six demand studies that appeared between 1967 and 1972. A seventh study, which is very similar in method to our own, will be discussed in Chapter 3.

We begin our review with the paper by Campbell and Siegel (1967), who estimated from aggregate time-series data the relationship between numbers of students in four-year colleges, average college tuition, and average family income for the period 1927 to 1963. To describe their results more precisely, for each of the nine years for which data were available during that period, we define:

R_t = the proportion of people in the United States between the ages of 18 and 24 who are enrolled as resident degree undergraduates in four-year institutions in year t

Y_t = an estimate of real disposable income per United States household in year t

P_t = an index of tuition costs (deflated by consumer prices) in year t

A linear regression of the logarithm of R_t on the logarithms of Y_t and P_t, based on nine annual observations during the period 1927 to 1963, yielded an estimate of the income elasticity[1] of 1.20 and an estimate of the tuition elasticity of $-.44$. Both elasticities were significantly different from zero at the .025 level, and 93 percent of the variance of R_t was explained by the estimated regression.

The Campbell-Siegel regression presents us with an example of the "classical" identification problem of demand analysis. Variations in disposable income and tuition ("price") over time could cause changes in the demand for places in institutions of higher education. However, variation in these variables could also be associated with variations in the *supply* of places. The observed variable R_t reflects the result of interactions between demand and supply behavior, and therefore the parameters of the two behavioral relationships could well be confounded in the estimates of the regression coefficients. In this case, the regression coefficients would be biased estimates of the corresponding parameters of the true demand equation. A detailed analysis of such possible biases would require the specification of a complete model of demand and supply behavior, and the nature of the interactions between supply and demand, which we are not prepared to do here. In any case, such analyses are typically inconclusive without more detailed data that permit the identification of individual parameters. Nevertheless, some speculation on the structure of the "market" for college and university places may help us interpret the Campbell-Siegel results.

First, we may consider the temporal structure of supply and demand decisions. Institutions fix their tuition fees in advance

[1]If a variable X depends on a variable Z, the *elasticity of* X *with respect to* Z is defined as the derivative of the logarithm of X with respect to the logarithm of Z. If this elasticity is denoted by η, then, for small changes, a p percentage change in Z is associated with an ηp percentage change in X. We shall follow convention in speaking of the "Z elasticity of X"; sometimes, however, the variable X is understood; e.g., "income elasticity" means the "elasticity of proportion enrolled R_t with respect to income Y_t."

of the period of application and admissions, so that in any one year the tuition fees can be taken as predetermined. Enrollment targets, or nominal "capacities," are also typically determined in advance; to the extent that these targets are feasible, then, enrollments are also predetermined! In this case, the interpretation of the coefficients in the Campbell-Siegel regression would be difficult indeed, since enrollment and tuition in any one year would be responses to variables in previous years, which are not included in the regression.

Just how "predetermined" enrollments and tuition fees are no doubt depends on many circumstances. In years in which demand threatens to fall short of enrollment targets, individual institutions may make some adjustments in admissions standards, but aggregate enrollment is more likely to be determined primarily by demand. In years in which demand exceeds enrollment targets, some institutions, especially in the private sector, will maintain their enrollment limits, whereas others, especially public institutions that are new or at the community college level, will be able and willing to allow enrollments to exceed targets. Recall, however, that R_t refers only to enrollment in four-year institutions.

What would one expect the "supply function" for higher education to look like? Since one does not think of institutions of higher education as profit maximizers, the classical theory of the firm should not be uncritically applied to higher education. Suppose that institutions of higher education (1) have limited financial resources; (2) face downward-sloping demand curves (in terms of tuition fees) but retain some "monopolistic power" because of location, special programs or status, price discrimination based on residence requirements, alumni loyalties, etc.; (3) have preferences with regard to total size and mix of student types; and (4) attempt to obtain a preferred student body, subject to the above constraints and possibly others imposed by legislatures, alumni, etc. Considerable differences in preferences and (especially) in constraints can be expected among the different sectors of higher education.

Most institutions can influence tuition fees and financial aid "packages," but for most public institutions changes in tuition fees must be approved by legislatures, coordinating councils, or other public agencies. Even private institutions are reluctant to charge as much as the traffic will bear, either for social reasons

FIGURE 1
The supply of places as a function of tuition

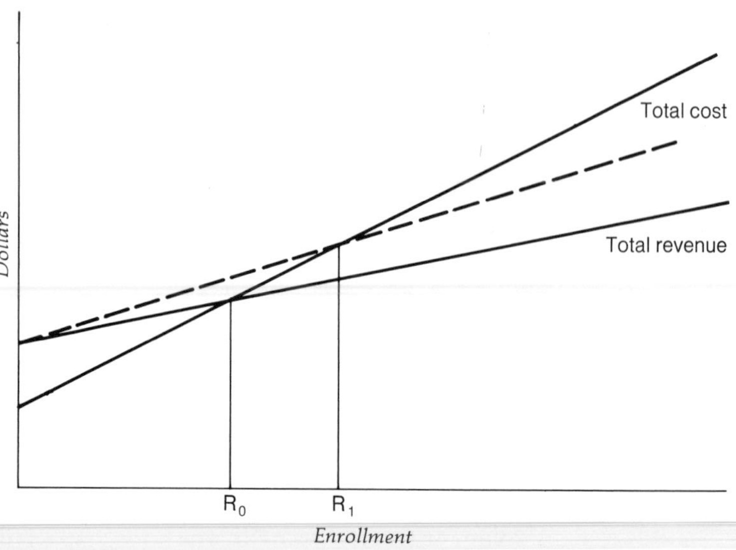

or because such a policy would reduce income from gifts and bequests. It is probably rare that tuition fees cover marginal costs per student, even at private institutions, so that an increase in tuition permits an increase in the level of enrollment at which the institution can break even. This is illustrated in the accompanying graph (Figure 1). The slope of the (solid) total revenue line is the average tuition fee per student, and the intercept of the total revenue line on the vertical (dollar) axis is the sum of money available from sources other than tuition fees. The enrollment R_0 is determined by the condition that total revenue equal total cost. If tuition fees are increased, the new total revenue line is the dotted line, and the new break-even enrollment is R_1. Thus, other things remaining unchanged, an increase in tuition fees will permit an institution to increase its supply of places.

Through the use of financial aid, institutions are able to engage in "price discrimination" among different types of students. There is little doubt that institutions have used financial aid to compete for desirable students, although the official policy of the College Scholarship Service (C.S.S.) is that financial aid should be used only to compensate for inequalities of income and wealth, and the activities of the C.S.S. have gone far toward promoting that policy among its member institutions. In any case, nominal tuition need not be a good measure of the average "price" charged by an institution, and, in particular, an increase in tuition can be offset in the aggregate by increases in financial aid.[2]

In the classical theory of the firm, the average income of consumers would not normally be a variable in the supply function of an industry. In the case of higher education, however, average national family income probably does influence supply with a lag as short as one year. In the case of public institutions, the availability of public funds is closely related to tax receipts, whereas gifts to private institutions are closely related to personal and corporate incomes, and returns from endowments also depend on the state of the economy.

To summarize the results of this rough analysis, there is reason to suspect that an aggregate time-series regression of enrollment on family income and tuition would reflect parameters of supply behavior as well as those of demand behavior. In the supply response, one might expect increases in the supply of places to be associated with increases in disposable income, and also with increases in tuition fees, ceteris paribus. In particular, although the elasticities estimated by Campbell and Siegel have the signs that one would expect from a demand function, it is difficult to draw any conclusions from the actual numerical magnitudes of the coefficients.

The Campbell-Siegel paper investigated how aggregate enrollment in four-year institutions varied over time with variations in average family income and tuition. In the same year, Hoenack (1967) reported on a cross-sectional analysis of demand for freshmen places at the University of California, based on data for the year 1965. The Project TALENT survey (Flanagan et al., 1964) was used to obtain data, with follow-up information, on high school seniors in California. The demand study was actually in two parts. The first part concerned the enrollment at the Los Angeles campus of the University of California by eligible students from high schools in the Los Angeles area. The second part concerned the enrollment of

[2]The Carnegie Commission on Higher Education has in fact recommended that public institutions gradually increase tuition fees relative to the private institutions, with an offsetting increase in financial aid, so that the average price paid by students would remain the same, but there would be a redistribution of price discrimination in favor of the poorer students. See the Carnegie Commission report, *Higher Education: Who Pays? Who Benefits? Who Should Pay?* (1973, pp. 114–118).

eligible students at campuses outside their residence communities; here separate equations were estimated for the University of California campuses at Berkeley (UCB), Davis (UCD), and Santa Barbara (UCSB), and an aggregate function was estimated for UCLA, Riverside (UCR), and Irvine (UCI), all of which are in, or close to, Los Angeles.

The two parts of the study were used to estimate demand functions for each campus or campus group. The commuter demand equation for UCLA was assumed to be applicable at all campuses. The total demand for freshmen places at each campus was estimated to be a weighted sum of the commuter and noncommuter demands. The weights for each campus were determined by the percentage of freshmen on that campus who lived with their parents. The separate campus demand functions were aggregated to obtain a total demand function for freshmen places in the University of California system, but this aggregate function was not reported.

In Hoenack's study, the dependent variables for each high school—say, h—were:

A_{hc} = the number of seniors who attend UC campus c

E_h = the number of seniors *eligible* to attend the UC system (i.e., satisfying the admissions requirements)

The independent variables for each high school h were:

P_{hc} = a measure of the cost of attending UC campus c for a resident of the high school district h (actually, several alternative measures were tried)

P_h^S = the cost of attending the nearest state college

P_h^J = the cost of attending the nearest public junior college

Y_h = an estimate of the median income of families in the census area of high school h

G_h = the number of seniors graduating from high school h

U_h = a measure of the unemployment rate in the region of high school h

W = a measure of the average wage rate for the region

The commuter equations included as well an estimate of the daily cost of commuting. Students' time was valued at $2.40 per hour.

Alternative regression specifications were tried; they were usually linear-logarithmic, although sometimes some of the independent variables were not transformed. Ordinary least-squares regressions were estimated for combined income brackets and for various combinations of income-quartile disaggregations.

To give a flavor of Hoenack's results, we include one of his estimated equations as an example:

$$\begin{aligned}\log \frac{(A_{\text{UCR}+\text{UCI}+\text{UCLA}})}{E} = {} & \underset{(9.21)}{19.11} + \underset{(1.86)}{.002G} + \underset{(3.48)}{1.992} \log P_{\text{UCB}} \\ & - \underset{(-3.44)}{5.740} \log P_{\text{UCLA}} + \underset{(3.20)}{1.9866} \log P_{\text{UCSB}} \\ & + \underset{(2.32)}{1.5473} \log P^S + \underset{(1.70)}{0.98} \log P^J + \underset{(1.81)}{0.69} \log Y \\ & + \underset{(.20)}{0.50} \log U - \underset{(-3.07)}{2.45} \log W \\ & - \underset{(-3.28)}{0.000126} (P_{\text{UCB}} + P_{\text{UCSB}}) \log Y \\ & + \underset{(3.43)}{0.000346} P_{\text{UCLA}} \log Y - \underset{(-2.27)}{0.00067} P^S \log Y \\ & - \underset{(-1.77)}{0.00007} P^J \log Y;\end{aligned}$$

R^2; = .99; DW = 2.10; all income brackets; 90 observations; t values in parentheses (Hoenack, 1967).

Hoenack found an average price (cost) elasticity of demand of −.85. This value varied from −1.12 for the lowest income bracket to −.71 for the highest. He reported that state colleges appear to be close substitutes for UC campuses. If state college prices were to rise simultaneously with UC price increases, but by only two-thirds as much, the students' price elasticity for UC would diminish substantially (in absolute value). Average UC price elasticity values fall from −.85 to −.51; the lowest income group's values decrease from -1.12 to $-.68$, and the highest income group's values decrease from $-.71$ to $-.48$.

The decision to commute or to live away from home was apparently significantly affected by the wage rates prevailing in the hometown area. It was not affected by the unemployment rate.[3]

Income elasticities are not reported. However, the elasticity implied by the sample equation above is approximately .7.

Hoenack made a limited attempt at extending his demand formulation to the state and junior colleges in California. No estimates are actually presented, but Hoenack claims to have been unsuccessful at explaining attendance at the state college geographically nearest each high school and successful at explaining the proportion of high school seniors attending their nearest junior college. According to his report, a $100 increase in junior college tuition would diminish enrollment by approximately 7 percent.

Hoenack's study made substantial progress in two directions. First, he was able to address the identification problem by using as dependent variables the ratios of the number of high school seniors attending various UC campuses to the number of seniors in the high school *eligible* to attend the UC system. It is a reasonable assumption that, within the range of variation to be covered by the demand equations, every formally eligible senior who wanted a place in the UC system could in fact have been supplied one. Second, Hoenack made progress in describing the joint dependence of demand for places at different institutions—in this case, different campuses of the UC system. The possibilities of substitution among alternative choices were also reflected in the use as explanatory variables of the nearest state college and junior college "prices" and of the unemployment and wage rates in the region. Nevertheless, Hoenack did not attempt to estimate a complete model of choice by high school seniors from among the full range of alternatives that they faced. His statistical analysis was hampered by not having measures of family income for individual students, not to men-

[3]The wage rate effect was stronger in southern than in northern California. A 1 percent increase in wages in the hometown area decreased the proportion of eligibles enrolling away from home by 3 to 5 percent in the south and decreased enrollment in the north by approximately 1.75 percent.

tion other measures of family background or measures of academic ability other than eligibility for the UC system. Finally, his study was confined to California, whose system of public higher education was better developed than that of any other state. Further progress in these various directions constituted an important goal of our own research, which we shall describe in Chapter 3.

Three econometric studies of the demand for higher education appeared in 1969. The expansion of our military involvement in Vietnam led Galper and Dunn (1969) to study the effect of the growth of the armed services on higher education demand. A team of consultants in Massachusetts worked on a study to help in the comprehensive planning of higher education in the state (Massachusetts Metropolitan Area Planning Council, 1969).[4] At the national level, Feldman and Hoenack (1969) submitted a report to the Joint Economic Committee of Congress on the demand for higher education and its relation to public policy.[5]

Galper and Dunn (1969) followed the lines opened up by Campbell and Siegel. Using a distributed lag specification, they estimated the short-run effect of the growth of the armed services on the demand for four-year college enrollment. Their estimate of the elasticity of enrollment with respect to the annual rate of growth of the armed services was −.26 and with respect to discharges was .13. The estimated income elasticity was .69, a value close to that found by Hoenack in his California study.

The Massachusetts Metropolitan Area Planning Council (1969) took as its task the development of a coordinated and comprehensive public policy for higher education in the state. In the study for this council to which we have referred, the principal problem was the explanation of the proportion of high school graduates who went on to higher education. The unit of observation was the state. The dependent variable measured, for each state, the percentage of 1960 tenth-grade students who attended college in 1963. The independent variables included

[4]Results of this study were also reported in Corazzini, Dugan, and Grabowski (1972).

[5]See also Hoenack (1971) for further discussion of public policy aspects of the nature of, and demand for, higher education.

data on the students in each state and data on the "environment" within the state. The data on the students (including the enrollment percentages) came from the Project TALENT sample survey; the variables were:

- Father's education, regarded by the authors as a proxy for socioeconomic status (SES) or for family income
- Academic ability, as measured by performance on standardized tests

The state environment variables were indices of:

- Junior college tuition
- Public four-year university tuition
- Teachers college tuition
- Private four-year university tuition
- Average income of production workers, a proxy for the opportunity cost of attending college rather than being employed
- The rate of unemployment

The enrollment percentages also came from Project TALENT data. For each state, the data on students were available as statewide averages, as well as averages for each sex and for each SES (father's education) quartile.

For each of the six subgroups, the Massachusetts study presented a linear regression (across states) of the enrollment percentage on the independent variables listed above. A corresponding regression was also estimated using the statewide averages (i.e., after polling the group averages for each state). The results of these seven regressions are reproduced in Table 1.

Consider first the regression based on the statewide averages (see the first line of Table 1). In this regression, the coefficient of teachers college tuition (P_c) is not significantly different from zero. In order to facilitate a comparison with the other studies we have discussed, we computed the elasticities of percentage enrolled with respect to the several independent variables.[6] The

[6]These elasticities were calculated at the sample means.

TABLE 1 ***Regression results of enrollment rates (in percentage terms) of 1960 tenth graders in higher education: aggregated and disaggregated data***

		Independent variable								
Percentage enrolled	*Constant*	P_j	P_u	P_c	P_p	E	Y	A	U	R^2
E_T	14.431	−.0111 (−3.14)	−.0265 (−2.32)	.0081 (1.26)	−.0087 (−2.06)	2.839 (4.21)	−3.622 (−1.03)	.176 (5.72)	.834 (2.04)	.769
E_{TM}	13.993	−.0132 (−3.42)	−.0438 (−2.39)	.0009 (1.04)	−.0116 (2.17)	3.265 (4.87)	−2.066 (−1.81)	.208 (5.22)	1.553 (2.16)	.806
E_{TF}	5.094	−.0093 (−2.96)	−.0153 (−3.60)	−.0231 (−1.37)	.0106 (0.87)	2.576 (2.87)	−1.041 (−1.19)	.131 (3.67)	.427 (1.41)	.721
E_{LSES}	1.573	−.0072 (−2.06)	−.0125 (−1.71)	−.0059 (−1.04)	.0018 (0.57)	1.762 (2.52)	−1.347 (2.29)	.041 (1.56)	.776 (1.34)	.537
E_{2SES}	4.156	−.0093 (−1.49)	−.0137 (−1.81)	−.0122 (.96)	−.0014 (−1.09)	.853 (2.17)	−1.590 (1.08)	.053 (2.02)	.316 (1.22)	.412
E_{3SES}	5.912	−.0051 (−1.19)	−.0097 (−1.91)	−.0017 (−1.36)	−.0045 (−1.74)	.907 (2.08)	−1.003 (.96)	.069 (2.12)	−.315 (−.58)	.450
E_{HSES}	5.590	.0006 (.57)	−.0126 (1.68)	0055 (.86)	−.0041 (2.09)	.267 (1.21)	0.688 (0.54)	.045 (2.23)	−.065 (−1.89)	.491

NOTATION:

R^2 = coefficient of determination
( ) = t statistic
E_T = total enrollment rate in college of 1960 tenth graders (in percent) in state
E_{TM} = total male enrollment rate (in percent)
E_{TF} = total female enrollment (in percent)
E_{LSES} = enrollment rate of low socioeconomic quartile
E_{2SES} = enrollment rate of second quartile
E_{3SES} = enrollment rate of third quartile
E_{HSES} = enrollment rate of high socioeconomic quartile
P_j = tuition at junior colleges in state
P_u = tuition at four-year public universities in state
P_c = tuition at teachers colleges in state
P_p = tuition at four-year private universities in state
E = paternal education, ranked by educational attainment groups, of zero to seven years, eight years, one to three years of high school, high school degree, one to three years of college, college degree, more than five years of college
Y = average hourly earnings of production workers
A = ability
U = unemployment rate

SOURCE: Massachusetts Metropolitan Area Planning Council (1969, Table 6, pp. 38–39).

tuition (price) elasticities (excluding teachers college tuition) are:

Junior college	*Four-year public university*	*Four-year private university*
−.09	−.18	−.19

Thus, the tuition elasticities for four-year institutions are about twice as large (in absolute value) as the tuition elasticity for junior college.

The coefficient of the unemployment rate (U) was statistically significant in this equation, but the coefficient of the wage rate (Y) was not. This result is just the opposite of what Hoenack found.

The authors of the Massachusetts study rightly caution their readers against interpreting the effect of father's education as purely a family-income effect. Nevertheless, since the authors did present a table showing a national relationship between income and educational attainment (from census data), we could not resist the temptation to compute an implied income elasticity, which we estimated to be .23. This estimate should, of course, be taken with an appropriate grain of salt.

When the data were grouped by sex of student (see regressions 2 and 3 of Table 1), percentage enrollment of males appeared to be more closely related to the tuition and ability variables than the percentage enrollment of females was. Here are the tuition elasticities that we computed, corresponding to these two regressions:

	Junior college	*Public university*	*Private university*
Males	−.096	−.27	−.23
Females	−.081	−.10	Not significant

Regarding ability, the regression coefficient for males is almost 1½ times that for females.

These estimates are consistent with the findings elsewhere that males appear to have higher rates of return on education than females. The price elasticities suggest that men attend college for economic reasons more than women do, and the coefficients on the ability variable suggest that differences in women's ability are not perceived to be as valuable as equal differences in men's ability.

When the data were grouped by quartile of father's education, the proxy for socioeconomic status (SES), the coefficients of many of the tuition variables ceased to be significant (see regressions 4 through 7 in Table 1). The pattern of these coefficients is plausible if one considers that actual demand in different SES groups is concentrated in different types of institutions. For example, using one-tailed tests and a .05 level of significance, junior college tuition and public university tuition are significant for the second lowest SES group, while for the two higher SES groups only the public and private university tuitions are significant.

The disaggregation by SES also affected estimates of the importance of the other explanatory variables. For example, father's education is significant for the lower three quartiles, the wage rate is (negatively) significant for the lowest SES group, unemployment is never significant, and ability rather uniformly affects the upper three groups.

Feldman and Hoenack (1969) also examined the variation of enrollment percentages among states, using a formulation and data similar in many respects to those of the Massachusetts council's study. However, Feldman and Hoenack included more independent variables in their regression analysis, and the functional form of the regression equation was somewhat different. Using Project TALENT data on the proportion in each state of 1960 tenth-grade high school students who in 1963 attended any college offering degree-credit courses, they estimated a regression of a logistic transformation[7] of these proportions on (1) average tuition fees for different types of institutions; (2) average proximity of the state's population to each type of institution; (3) labor-market variables (earnings and unemployment duration rates); (4) average state performance on aptitude tests; (5) urban-rural population composition; (6) a transformation of education of parents, as a proxy for family

[7]If P denotes the proportion enrolled, then the logistic transformation of P is $\ln[P/(1-P)]$, where ln denotes the natural logarithm (to the base e).

income; (7) regional dummy variables; and (8) interaction terms among the above variables.

The results of this regression analysis are illustrated in Figures 2 through 5. Figures 2 through 4 show the estimated effects

FIGURE 2 ***The estimated effects of a $100 increase in tuition at four-year public institutions on enrollment proportions***

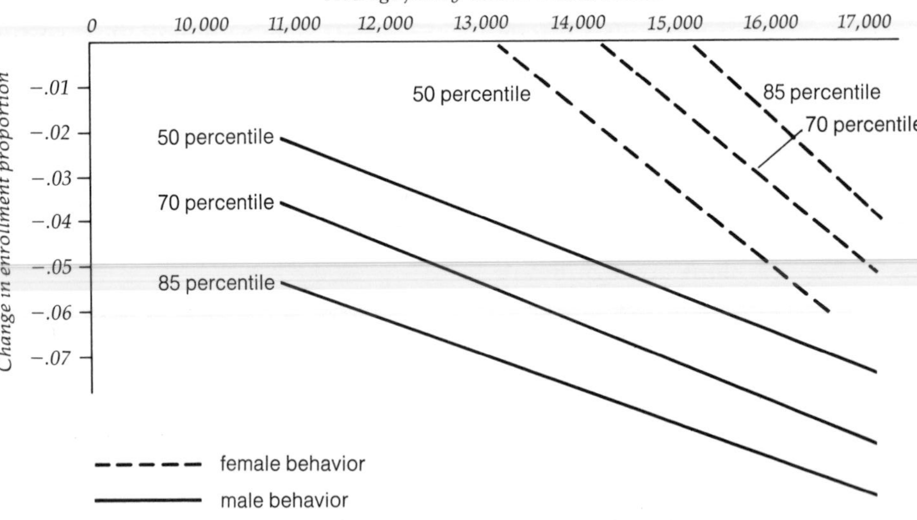

FIGURE 3 ***The estimated effects of a $100 increase in tuition at four-year private institutions on enrollment proportions***

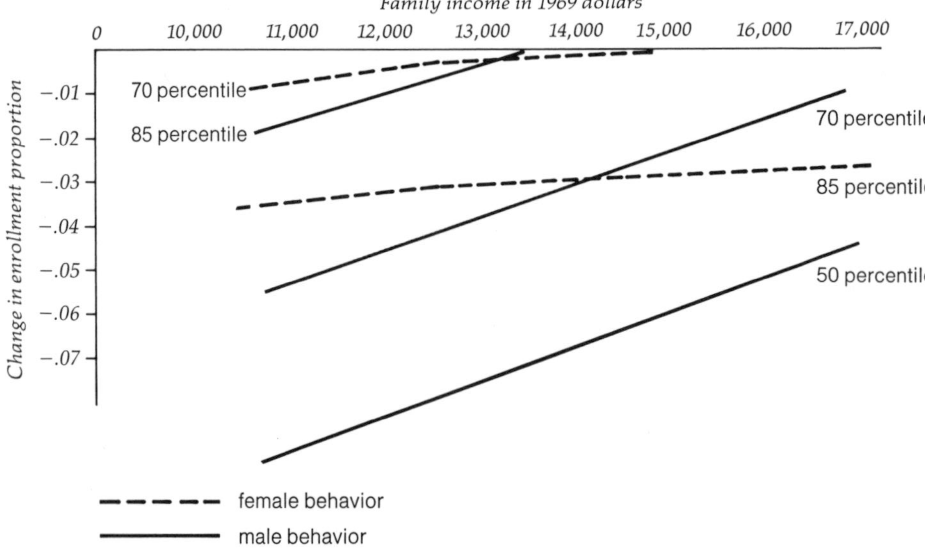

FIGURE 4 ***The estimated effects of a $100 increase in tuition at two-year institutions on enrollment proportions***

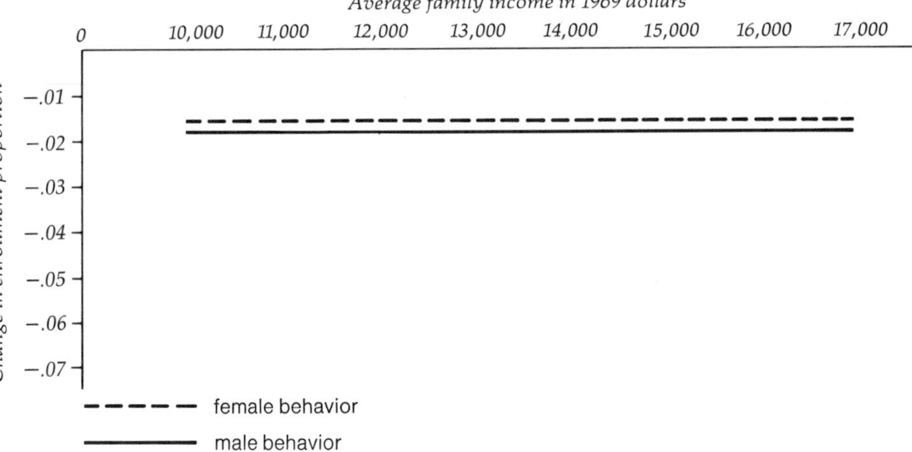

on enrollment proportions of a $100 increase in tuition at three different types of institutions. Figure 5 shows the corresponding effects of a $1 increase in the average hourly wage rate. Each of the figures show how the indicated effect depends on some of the other independent variables (sex, ability, test-score percentile, family income).

In some respects, the Feldman-Hoenack regression confirmed the results of the Massachusetts council's study. Male enrollment proportions were more responsive to changes in four-year college tuition than female enrollment proportions, but the coefficients of two-year college tuition were roughly the same for the two sexes. Also, a comparison of Figures 2 and 3 with Figure 4 shows that, in general, the effects of changes in two-year college tuition were less than the effects of equal changes in four-year college tuition.

However, the results implied by Figure 2 are rather puzzling. Why should the effect on male enrollment proportions of a $100 change in tuition at four-year public institutions increase as average family income increases and also as average ability increases? These results are the opposite of what one would expect a priori, and indeed they are the opposite of what is implied by Figure 3 for the four-year private institutions. As Feldman and Hoenack themselves comment, "The suggestion that the responsiveness of enrollment proportions to changes in tuition can be higher in higher family income and test score groups . . . certainly is not intuitively obvious."

FIGURE 5 ***The estimated effects of a $1.00 increase in the hourly wage rate on enrollment proportions***

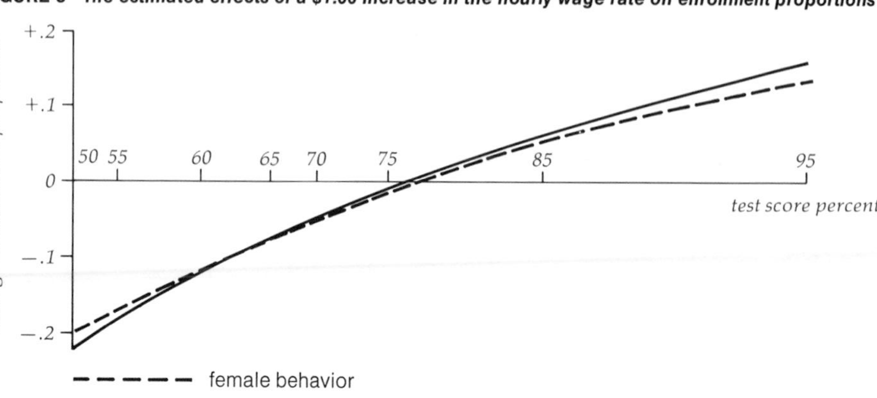

Figure 5 shows what, in our opinion, is the most interesting of the Feldman-Hoenack findings: the change in enrollment proportions associated with a $1-per-hour increase in wages by average ability of students. The suggested interpretation is that higher-ability students tend to take on more part-time jobs and attend college instead of working full time when economic conditions improve, whereas lower-ability students, reevaluating the gains from college against the increased opportunity cost of attending, tend to drop out of college when economic conditions improve.

In all the aforementioned studies, demand estimates were derived from the use of ordinary least squares. Our own demand estimates, which are reported in the following three chapters and in Miller and Radner (1975), are based on another estimation procedure. A recent paper by Kohn, Manski, and Mundel (1972) is similar in methodology to our own research and is reviewed in detail in Section 3.7 of the next chapter. To end on a dynamic note, since the completion of the writing of this review we have received a paper by Ghali, Miklius, and Wada (1974). They estimate the price elasticity and cross-price elasticities of demand for enrollment at the University of Hawaii also using a methodology similar to our own. We do not comment further on their study in this book.

tative explanatory variables, did not, of course, generate a perfect fit between predicted and observed choice frequencies. An examination of the response residuals shows that one can get improved predictions of choices by taking into account the stated academic aspirations and expectations of the high school seniors, their high school curricula, and the educational aspirations that parents have for their children. The timing of the choice of a career is also important, early choices being associated with greater demand for high-cost/high-selectivity institutions than would be predicted by the four primary quantitative variables alone.

However, whether or not students perceive their parents to be concerned about their *current* education does not seem to provide additional explanatory power, nor are students' expectations regarding their own careers associated in any clear way with the pattern of response residuals. Indices of "fate control," self-motivation in problem solving, broad academic interest, and time preference were not significantly associated with the response residuals. Taking account of sex did not improve predictions of the demand for all IHEs together, but did slightly improve the predictions of the distribution of demand among the IHEs.

In order to quantitatively describe the changes in choice probabilities that are associated with changes in the four major explanatory variables, we examined the elasticities of demand with respect to these variables. Formulas for these elasticities and numerical estimates for a variety of student types are presented in Section 3.6.

We conclude this chapter with some comments on recently reported work in progress by Kohn, Manski, and Mundel, who have further experimented with a model and approach similar to ours.

3.2. A CONDITIONAL LOGIT MODEL

We imagine that each high school senior—hereafter called a "student"—faces a set of alternative postsecondary *options.* This set includes attendance at various types of institutions of higher education, as well as the alternative of not going to any such institution. Our statistical model is designed to relate the relative frequencies of choices to the characteristics of the individual student and his options. The availability of data and the results of experiments with different formulations led us to concentrate on the following variables (whose precise definitions are given below):

A_i = an academic-ability score for student i

Y_i = a measure of family income for student i

S_j = a measure of the selectivity or quality of option j

C_{ij} = the out-of-pocket dollar cost to i of option j (set equal to zero for the option "no school")

We assume that the probability that student i chooses option j is a function of these variables and the *set* of options available to i, which we shall denote by J_i. We assume further that this functional relationship can be expressed in terms of two intermediary variables, to which (for the convenience of discussion) we have given the names *cost-income ratio* and *academic interaction*, defined respectively by

$$R_{ij} = \frac{C_{ij}}{I_i}, \quad Z_{ij} = \frac{A_i S_j}{1{,}000}.$$

The particular functional relationship is a generalized form of logit analysis. For each i and j, define f_{ij} and F_{ij} by

$$\begin{aligned} f_{ij} &= \gamma R_{ij} + \alpha Z_{ij}, \\ F_{ij} &= e^{f_{ij}}, \end{aligned} \tag{1}$$

where γ and α are parameters to be estimated. The conditional probability P_{ik} that student i chooses option k from the set J_i of alternative options available to him, given the values of the variables R_{ij} and Z_{ij}, is assumed to be determined by the equation

$$P_{ik} = \frac{F_{ik}}{\sum_{j \in J_i} F_{ij}}. \tag{2}$$

Note that this implies that the odds for any pair of alternatives j and k are equal to the ratio F_{ij}/F_{ik} and that the logarithm (to the base e) of these odds is equal to $f_{ij} - f_{ik}$, or

$$\gamma(R_{ij} - R_{ik}) + \alpha(Z_{ij} - Z_{ik}). \tag{3}$$

The parameters γ and α of this model can be estimated from observations on a sample of students. For each student i we need to know:

1. The set of J_i options available to i
2. The values of the cost-income ratio R_{ij} and the academic interaction Z_{ij} for each option j in the set J_i.
3. The option—say, O_i—actually chosen by i; we shall call this i's *choice*

We shall not describe the details of the estimating procedure that we have used, except to note that the student's choices have a generalized multinomial distribution, in which the probabilities of these choices, which are given by equation (2), vary from observation to observation. The parameters can be estimated by the method of maximum likelihood. Both the computational algorithm and the large-sample properties of the resulting estimators that we have used are due to D. McFadden.[1]

The model that we have just described is an example of what McFadden has called a *conditional logit model.* Such models have been extensively studied in connection with the theory of stochastic choice (see, for example, Luce and Suppes, 1965). In this theory, the term f_{ij} in equation (1) may be interpreted as the utility to student i of option j. From the point of view of the observer, the stochastic nature of i's choice may be due to the fact that the observer has not been able to observe all the variables relevant to i's choice (i.e., the "true" utility is really different from f_{ij}) or to the fact that i's choice behavior is to some extent inherently random.

The usefulness of the conditional logit model does not depend, however, on the validity of its interpretation in terms of stochastic choice and utility theory. Its distinctive feature is that it provides a natural way to describe and estimate, from statistical data, the relationship between observed choices from discrete sets of options and a number of explanatory or

[1]Our own application of McFadden's work was based on McFadden (1968). A more recent reference is McFadden (1973).

independent variables, in terms of a small number of parameters. In this sense it serves as a natural analog, for the case of discrete, qualitative dependent variables, of the method of least-squares regression for continuous random variables.

In particular, the conditional logit model incorporates in a very natural way a feature of demand that we consider to be quite important, namely, the *joint dependence* of the demand for different options. This is clear from equations (1) and (2), which imply that if the utility of a particular option increases, then the probability of that option will increase at the expense of the probabilities of the other options. In other words, an increase in the *relative* demand for one option must decrease the total relative demand for the other options.

One possible drawback of the conditional logit model, as we have applied it, is a feature that has been called *independence of irrelevant alternatives*. From expression (3) we see that the odds for any pair of alternative options do not depend on the characteristics of the other options. In particular, if a certain option j is removed from the set J_i of options available to student i, the model predicts that the corresponding probability P_{ij} will be reallocated to all the other options in J_i *in the same proportions as the original probabilities*. For example, consider a group of students who all have the same set of options—say, "university," "state college," and "job"—and who are identical with respect to the explanatory variables R_{ij} and Z_{ij} for each of the three options j. Assume that such students would choose among these three options with relative frequencies .5, .3, and .2, respectively. Suppose now that the first option, "university," were removed from their set, for example, because of an increase in admissions standards at the university. The conditional logit model would predict that these students would now choose between the two remaining options with relative frequencies .6, and .4, respectively. However, it is quite plausible that most of the students who would have chosen the university had they been eligible would now choose to go to the state college rather than go immediately into the labor market, which would result in relative frequencies of, say, .75 and .25.

Extensions of the conditional logit model have been considered that do not have the property of independence of irrelevant alternatives. In one such extension, the student is assumed to make a *sequence* of choices, narrowing down the set of alternatives at each step. For example, the student might first decide whether to go on to higher education and then, if the first decision were affirmative, decide which available type of institution to attend. Each step in the sequence of choices could be represented by a conditional logit model. We have not attempted to apply any such extensions of the model in our own statistical analysis, but in Section 3.7 we shall describe one such attempt by Kohn, Manski, and Mundel (1972).

In our application of the conditional logit model to the estimation of demand, we attempted to meet the identification problem through the specification of the sets J_i, which reflected the student's eligibility to attend different institutions and the location of the student's family residence in relation to these institutions. This is discussed in more detail in Section 3.3 and in Miller and Radner (1975).

3.3. THE DATA AND THE MEASUREMENT OF THE VARIABLES

The measurement of the variables in the conditional logit model was based primarily on data from the SCOPE sample survey (School to College: Opportunities for Postsecondary Education), which is part of a continuing longitudinal study conducted at the Center for Research and Development in Higher Education, University of California, Berkeley. We had available to us observations on a sample of 4,434 high school students who were seniors in 1966 from California, Illinois, Massachusetts, and North Carolina. The data from the SCOPE survey that we used included, for each student:[2]

1 The score on an aptitude test similar to the College Board Scholastic Aptitude Test (SAT); this score was transformed into an expected SAT score, hereafter called *ability*.

2 The student's estimate of parents' income.

3 The student's answers to various questions concerning attitudes, aspirations, and socioeconomic background.

4 The location of the student's home.

5 The option chosen by the student the following year, which was either attending a particular institution of higher education or not attending any such institution.

6 The results of a follow-up questionnaire sent to *parents*, in 1967,

[2]A detailed description of the data is given in Miller and Radner (1975).

including the responses to a request for an estimate of 1966 family income. Not all the parents responded to this questionnaire, and among those who did, not all provided an estimate of income.

The data on family income presented us with a dilemma. On the one hand, the subsample of students whose parents reported their incomes did not appear to be representative. On the other hand, the income estimates reported by the students appeared to be quite unreliable, as shown by a comparison of estimates reported by students and parents in those cases in which the parents did report an estimate of income. These points are illustrated in Tables 2 and 3, respectively, which provide information on the 4,434 students in our sample. Table 2 gives numbers of students classified by ability group, student-reported income, and type of response to the parent questionnaire. As one might expect, the children of responding parents had higher-than-average ability scores and reported higher-than-average family incomes. Table 3 indicates the nature of the relationship between parent-reported income, student-reported income, and student ability, in that group of students whose parents did report income (group 2). This table gives the means and standard deviations of parent-reported incomes in groups of students classified by ability and by student-reported income. The relationship between student-reported and parent-reported incomes is quite feeble, and there is a clear regression effect; i.e., the mean parent-reported income in each group is higher than the corresponding student-reported income for the group, except in the highest income groups.

Because of the possible differences in demand behavior between the students with responding and nonresponding parents, we estimated the conditional logit model separately for the two groups as follows. First, we selected a subsample of students whose parents reported income. This sample was stratified by ability, parent-reported income, and state, with four ability groups and six income groups. We shall refer to this as sample II ("parent reporters").

Using all the SCOPE data for the parent-reporting students, we estimated the relationship between parent-reported income and many of the other student responses concerning socioeconomic status, etc., including the student-reported income. This

TABLE 2 ***Number of students in SCOPE sample A: ability versus student-reported family income***

Ability group	Parent group*	Income: Less than 2,000	2,000 to 3,999	4,000 to 4,999	5,000 to 7,499	7,500 to 9,999	10,000 to 14,999	15,000 to 19,999	20,000 or more	Confidential	Do not know
Upper 25%	1	3	19	31	132	85	107	34	37	57	67
	2	35	9	26	102	127	130	36	50	68	75
	3	0	2	3	7	4	10	7	7	8	10
Middle upper 25%	1	51	18	44	109	87	74	19	22	84	136
	2	34	8	10	75	51	61	17	15	30	67
	3	6	0	2	5	8	3	2	3	6	11
Middle lower 25%	1	86	38	47	160	99	75	18	11	87	197
	2	26	7	14	34	30	31	11	8	25	58
	3	3	0	4	7	4	6	2	2	8	7
Lower 25%	1	175	53	50	93	49	49	11	10	86	213
	2	23	2	14	13	14	17	2	2	14	31
	3	4	1	1	3	1	4	0	0	5	12

*Group 1, nonresponding parents; group 2, responding parents who reported income; group 3, responding parents who did not report income.

TABLE 3 ***Group 2, parent-reported income, mean parent-reported income (in dollars) by ability versus student-reported family income***

	Student-reported income									
Ability group	*Less than 2,000*	*2,000 to 3,999*	*4,000 to 4,999*	*5,000 to 7,499*	*7,500 to 9,999*	*10,000 to 14,999*	*15,000 to 19,999*	*20,000 or more*	*Confidential*	*Do not know*
Upper 25%	14,865	9,985	8,287	10,726	11,336	15,363	19,411	38,981	18,452	16,017
Middle upper 25%	12,712	6,982	10,189	10,856	12,253	14,608	16,138	23,600	15,860	14,432
Middle lower 25%	9,975	6,298	6,064	11,031	15,222	17,788	17,031	19,944	23,799	12,501
Lower 25%	12,390	8,904	9,728	7,314	10,952	17,776	15,765	66,900	11,568	11,614
Mean by student-reported family income	12,685	7,985	8,413	10,618	11,806	15,656	18,061	35,620	18,159	14,083

	Standard deviations									
Ability group	*Less than 2,000*	*2,000 to 3,999*	*4,000 to 4,999*	*5,000 to 7,499*	*7,500 to 9,999*	*10,000 to 14,999*	*15,000 to 19,999*	*20,000 or more*	*Confidential*	*Do not know*
Upper 25%	9,385	10,242	10,285	13,337	7,348	8,976	8,678	24,524	12,765	11,025
Middle upper 25%	11,589	4,687	8,459	10,631	7,477	16,063	5,244	15,701	12,523	14,040
Middle lower 25%	9,849	3,822	2,426	12,153	8,629	15,853	6,689	8,871	31,800	8,203
Lower 25%	18,500	4,096	5,117	2,169	4,067	18,829	1,765	53,100	10,307	11,650
Standard deviation by student-reported family income	19,523	7,260	8,016	11,952	7,453	10,617	7,674	24,732	18,011	11,621

relationship provided an equation that one could use to "predict" parent-reported income from the student responses alone. The estimation of this relationship has some independent interest; it is described in detail in Miller and Radner (1975) and is summarized in Chapter 5. Using this income-predictor equation, we selected a subsample of students whose parents did not report income, stratified by ability, *predicted* income, and state. Again, there were four ability groups and six (predicted) income groups. We shall refer to this as sample I ("parent nonreporters").

After considerable experimentation with separate estimates by state (reported in Miller and Radner, 1975), we concluded that the parameters of demand behavior differed significantly by ability and that a single demand equation for high school graduates who vary considerably in ability would be inadequate. Accordingly, students from the four states were combined, but samples I and II were each divided into four ability groups. The SAT scores that divided the four groups were 400, 475, and 550. Table 4 gives statistics on ability and income, within each ability group, in sample II (parent reporters). Notice that the correlation between ability and income in each

TABLE 4 ***Distribution of ability and income within ability groups, sample II***

Ability group	*(1) Ability: mean (standard deviation)*	*(2) Income: mean (standard deviation)*	*(3) Correlation between ability and income, within ability groups*
High	611.6 (37.7)	16,912.8 (17,711.9)	.116
Medium-high	509.8 (22.1)	13,379.3 (14,170.4)	−.059
Medium-low	440.9 (22.0)	12,656.0 (11,606.8)	.066
Low	317.4 (55.8)	14,030.0 (16,675.9)	.060

group is quite low, which is a result of the stratification design in the selection of the subsample.

The cost and selectivity variables were estimated from separate sources.[3] The location of the student's home was an important piece of information in the estimation of the costs of alternative options, since it could be used to determine which types of institution of higher education were available within commuting distance of the student's home. In California, we also checked with local high schools to determine each student's eligibility at available public institutions. As one can imagine, these procedures were quite time comsuming, so that we were forced to restrict the numbers of students in the stratified subsamples to (approximately) 96 in each sample, in each state. Fortunately, we were still able to get statistically significant results, and we feel that the economic significance of the results was considerably improved by the effort expended on obtaining better measures of cost and eligibility.

The conditional logit model requires the specification, for each student, of the set of alternative options. Obviously, it would have been impractical to treat every institution of higher education (IHE) in the four states as a separate option. For the purposes of estimation, institutions were grouped into nine categories, or "types," defined by average cost and selectivity. The tenth option was that of not attending any IHE. By representing the collection of IHEs in this manner, we were able (1) to preserve individual institution identification for the low-cost options, those within commuting distance of a student's home, and (2) to incorporate the feature of the conditional logit model known as the *independence of irrelevant alternatives* for the closest institutional substitutes. In our representation, if a particular institution in the medium- or high-cost categories denied a student admission, that student would allocate all the probability of attending the rejecting school to another institution of similar cost and selectivity.

Table 5 describes the 10 groups of options, with their corresponding costs and selectivities. In each group, "average selectivity" is a specification of the average ability (SAT score) of students who eventually choose that option. Notice that the nine types of IHE are arranged in ascending order of cost and

[3]See Miller and Radner (1975).

TABLE 5 ***Alternative options, aggregated into 10 types***

			Selectivity
Type	*Description*	*Average cost*	*Average (SAT)*
1	No higher education	.0	374.4
2	Low-cost /low-selectivity	402.5	426.5
3	Low-cost/medium-selectivity	487.4	499.8
4	Low-cost/high-selectivity	542.3	561.9
5	Medium-cost/low-selectivity	1,607.6	445.0
6	Medium-cost/medium-selectivity	1,700.4	496.5
7	Medium-cost/high-selectivity	1,462.6	562.0
8	High-cost/low-selectivity	2,574.6	426.2
9	High-cost/medium-selectivity	2,914.3	517.6
10	High-cost/high-selectivity	3,369.6	573.4

selectivity and could be laid out in a three-by-three table as follows:

Selectivity→			
	4	7	10
	3	6	9
	2	5	8
		Cost→	

The lower-cost schools, types 2, 3, and 4, represent public choices: the community college, the state college, and the university, respectively, within commuting distance of the student's high school. The medium-cost schools are type 5, trade schools and private junior colleges; type 6, public state colleges not within commuting distance of the student's high school and lower-tuition private colleges (primarily within commuting distance); and type 7, state universities away from home. The high-cost schools, types 8, 9, and 10, represent the three selectivity levels of private colleges and universities. They are supposed to correspond roughly to the three achievement levels created by state master plans for the public colleges and universities.

For each high school senior in the sample, we used his SAT score and the location of his home to estimate the set of options (more precisely, the set of option types) available to him. This corresponds to the set denoted by J_i in Section 3.2. The location of the home determined the costs of available options. For example, if his SAT score was too low, then types 4, 7, and 10 would not be available. Since information on eligibility in public institutions differed by state and since institutions typically do not have fixed admissions standards in terms of SAT scores, the procedure for determining eligibility was somewhat complicated. More details are provided in Miller and Radner (1975).

3.4. PARAMETER ESTIMATES FOR SAMPLE II (PARENT REPORTERS)

In this section we shall present and discuss estimates of the parameters γ and α of the conditional logit model, based on sample II (parent reporters). Recall that γ is the coefficient of the cost-income ratio C_{ij}/Y_i and that α is the coefficient of the academic-interaction variable $A_iS_j/1{,}000$ (see equations [1] and [2] in Section 3.2). While estimating the full model, we also estimated two simpler versions in which only one of the variables appeared in the equations. The three resulting specifications are:

Specification	*Explanatory variables included*
1	Cost-income ratio
2	Academic interaction
3	Both

Tables 6 and 7 show the estimates of the parameters in the three specifications, based on the data from sample II, the parent reporters.[4]

As one would expect, estimates of the coefficient γ of the cost-income variable are negative in every specification. Furthermore, they are statistically significant in every case, save the specification including only the cost-income ratio, for the highest ability group. There is a trend in γ from negative magnitudes toward zero as student ability increases.

[4]Only estimates based on sample II will be discussed in this chapter. The estimates for sample I are discussed in Chap. 5, while estimates for other classifications of students (e.g., by state) are discussed in Miller and Radner (1975).

TABLE 6
Parameter estimates for sample II

Academic-ability group	*Specification number*	*Coefficients of* C_{ij}/Y_i	*Coefficients of* $A_iS_j/1,000$
$SAT < 400$, *162 observations*	1	−7.138* (.962)‡	†
	2	†	$-.279 \cdot 10^{-1}$* ($.491 \cdot 10^{-2}$)‡
$400 \leqslant SAT < 475$, *84 observations*	1	−2.700* (.735)‡	†
	2	†	$-.138 \cdot 10^{-1}$* ($.424 \cdot 10^{-2}$)‡
$475 \leqslant SAT < 550$, *72 observations*	1	−2.803* (.865)‡	†
	2	†	$-.113 \cdot 10^{-1}$* ($.377 \cdot 10^{-2}$)‡
$550 \leqslant SAT$, *57 observations*	1	−.116 (.373)‡	†
	2	†	$.182 \cdot 10^{-1}$* ($.395 \cdot 10^{-2}$)‡

*Significant at the .01 level.
†Variable not included in the specification.
‡Standard errors are shown in parentheses.

TABLE 7
Parameter estimates for sample II

Academic-ability group	*Specification number*	*Coefficients of* C_{ij}/Y_i	*Coefficients of* $A_iS_j/1,000$
$SAT < 400$, *162 observations*	3	−3.592* (1.116)†	$-.328 \cdot 10^{-1}$* ($.774 \cdot 10^{-2}$)†
$400 \leqslant SAT < 475$, *84 observations*	3	−2.450* (.907)†	$-.244 \cdot 10^{-2}$ ($.557 \cdot 10^{-2}$)†
$475 < SAT < 550$, *72 observations*	3	−2.364‡ (1.037)†	$-.325 \cdot 10^{-2}$ ($.478 \cdot 10^{-2}$)†
$550 \leqslant SAT$, *57 observations*	3	−1.031‡ (.589)†	$.211 \cdot 10^{-1}$* ($.423 \cdot 10^{-2}$)†

*Significant at the .01 level.
†Standard errors are shown in parentheses.
‡Significant at the .05 level.

The estimates of the coefficient α of the academic interaction variable are negative and statistically significant for the low ability group and positive and statistically significant for the high ability group. For the two intermediate ability groups, the estimates of α are slightly negative, but not significantly different from zero. Thus there is a trend in α from negative to positive values as student ability increases.

The simultaneous variation in α and γ as one moves from the lowest to the highest ability groups is brought out quite clearly in Figure 6, in which the estimates of α in the four ability

FIGURE 6 ***Display of parameter estimates for sample II***

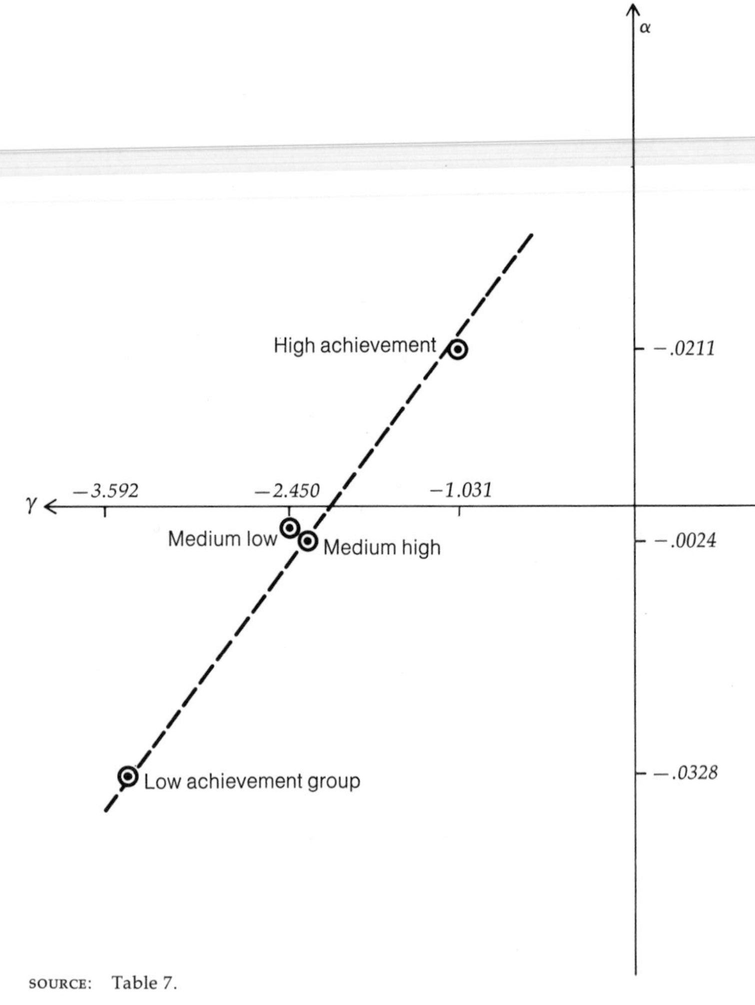

SOURCE: Table 7.

groups are plotted against the corresponding estimates of γ (the estimates are from specification 3, Table 7). Our interpretation of this relationship is twofold. First, students with higher ability can expect to benefit more from higher education, and they or their parents are therefore willing to bear a greater financial burden for a college education, where the severity of the burden is measured by the ratio of cost to family income. Second, high-ability students are attracted to highly selective institutions, and the higher the ability, the higher the attraction. On the other hand, very low ability students are typically restricted to a choice between attending a junior college or an unselective private institution and not attending any IHE; among these students, the more able evidently find it more attractive to work rather than attend these IHEs. The students of medium ability appear not to be much influenced by academic selectivity in their choices among the options available to them.

For each student i in sample II, and each alternative option j in his presumed set of alternatives J_i, one can calculate the probability P_{ij} that he or she would choose option j out of the set J_i. We have done this, using the estimates of the parameters in specification 3. If for each option j ($= 1, \ldots, 10$) we add the probabilities P_{ij} corresponding to all the sample II high school seniors in a given ability group, then we obtain a "prediction" of the number of students in the ability group who would actually choose option j. Dividing this predicted number by the number of students in the ability group, we get a predicted *relative frequency* for each option. In Table 8 these predicted relative frequencies have been compared with the corresponding observed relative frequencies. Small differences between predicted and observed relative frequencies would indicate a good "fit" for the model. On the whole, the fit is relatively good; this question will be examined further in Section 3.5 and in Chapter 5.

To illustrate the use of the model to predict choice probabilities, we shall consider 12 hypothetical high school seniors, differing in family income and ability. All 12 students are assumed to live in a location that offers the same set of local options (within commuting distance) as the Los Angeles metropolitan area. The 12 seniors represent combinations of three income levels and four ability levels. For the purposes of this

TABLE 8 ***Predicted and observed relative frequencies***

Observations	162		84		72		57	
Academic ability	Low		Medium-low		Medium-high		High	
	SAT < 400		400 ≤ SAT < 475		475 ≤ SAT < 550		550 ≤ SAT	
Choice type	Observed relative frequency	Predicted relative frequency	Observed relative frequency	Predicted relative frequency	Observed relative frequency	Predicted relative frequency	Observed relative frequency	Predicted relative frequency
1	.5617	.5134	.2024	.2641	.1806	.2398	.0877	.0294
2	.1728	.2304	.3542	.1831	.2500	.1692	.0877	.0559
3	.10370	.0160	.0595	.0872	.0556	.0700	.0877	.0715
4	.0000	.0002	.0119	.0028	.0556	.0201	.0000	.0435
5	.1420	.1549	.1786	.1501	.1806	.1676	.0351	.0584
6	.0309	.0384	.1310	.1455	.1667	.1288	.1579	.1336
7	.0000	.0001	.0119	.0084	.0417	.0519	.1404	.2035
8	.0247	.0028	.0119	.0027	.0278	.0021	.0175	.0006
9	.0247	.0433	.0238	.1499	.0139	.1314	.0526	.1751
10	.0062	.0005	.0238	.0063	.0278	.0191	.3333	.2285

illustration, the costs and selectivities of the 10 options were assumed to be slightly different from those in Table 5 and are shown in the following chart:

	Option									
	1	*2*	*3*	*4*	*5*	*6*	*7*	*8*	*9*	*10*
Cost	0	290	400	540	2,200	1,300	1,440	3,200	3,200	3,200
Selectivity	374	430	519	564	430	519	564	500	540	625

Table 9 shows the predicted probabilities for each of the 12 hypothetical students among the 10 options, again based on specification 3. Blank cells in the table indicate that the corresponding option was assumed not available to that hypothetical student.

The following comparisons illustrate the information provided in Table 9. A comparison of columns (1) and (5) illustrates the effect of a $6,000 increase in family income (from $6,000 to $12,000) for a 375 SAT student. The student has three options: no school, a local junior college, and a medium-cost/low-selectivity private college (like a technical or trade school). The increase in family income causes a rise of some 6.2 percentage points in the probability of attending an IHE; the probability of not going on to higher education drops from .642 for the $6,000-family-income student to .581 for the $12,000-family-income student. The chances of attending junior college are virtually the same for both students: .271 for the poorer of the two and .268 for the richer of the two. The income-induced increase in freshman enrollment occurs in the medium-cost/low-selectivity schools. The change in the probability of enrollment is from .086 to .151.

Comparison of columns (5) and (6) illustrates the effect of a 100-point rise in SAT score, from 375 to 475, for a student whose family income is $12,000. Notice the drastic reduction in the probability of not attending from .581 to .212. The principal cause of this reduction is the rise in the value of α, the coefficient of the academic interaction variable. The estimate of the coefficient for the 375 student was more than an order of magni-

TABLE 9 ***Predicted probabilities for Los Angeles, California, students:*** ϕ_{ij}

Column		(1)	(2)	(3)	(4)	(5)	(6)	(7)	(8)	(9)	(10)	(11)	(12)
Income Y			*$6,000*				*$12,000*				*$18,000*		
A(SAT)		*375*	*475*	*575*	*650*	*375*	*475*	*575*	*650*	*375*	*475*	*575*	*650*
Parameter	γ	*−3.592*	*−2.407*	*−1.031*	*−1.031*	*−3.592*	*−2.407*	*−1.031*	*−1.031*	*−3.592*	*−2.407*	*−1.031*	*−1.031*
estimates	α	*−.0328*	*−.002845*	*.0211*	*.0211*	*−.0328*	*−.002845*	*.0211*	*.0211*	*−.0328*	*−.002845*	*.0211*	*.0211*
Option													
1		.642	.260	.026	.015	.581	.212	.023	.013	.556	.195	.022	.012
2		.271	.214	.049	.031	.268	.185	.045	.027	.264	.174	.043	.025
3			.182	.142	.102		.160	.131	.090		.152	.127	.086
4				.239	.184			.223	.164			.217	.157
5		.086	.100	.035	.022	.151	.126	.038	.023	.180	.135	.039	.023
6			.127	.121	.087		.134	.121	.083		.135	.120	.081
7				.205	.158			.206	.152			.206	.150
8			.061	.070	.048		.094	.081	.054		.107	.086	.056
9			.057	.113	.084		.089	.132	.094		.102	.139	.097
10					.269				.301				.312

tude more negative than the estimate of the corresponding coefficient for the 475 student.

The probability of attending a junior college diminished from .268 for the 375 student to .185 for the 475 SAT student. That drop arises largely out of the fact that the 475 student chooses higher-quality options. For example, the 475 student's chances of choosing a state college are .294 (the sum of type 3 and type 6).

A comparison of columns (6) and (7) is analogous to the comparison of columns (5) and (6), in the sense that SAT rises by 100 points from column (5) to column (6). We see a continued drastic reduction, down to .023, in the probability of not attending an institution of higher education. The probability of attending junior college has also diminished to under 5 percent. These two results are due largely to the value of α, which is positive for 575 SAT students. This attraction to quality results in a .429 probability of state university attendance. Even with the new university options and the new private option, the probability of state college attendance remains almost as high as it was for a 475 SAT chooser.

The comparison of columns (7) and (8) illustrates the result of adding a more selective option to the feasible set. The 650 student has a .301 probability of attending this more selective institution.

A comparison between columns (8) and (12) is analogous to the comparison between columns (1) and (5). Here we see the effect on the 650 SAT student of increasing family income from $12,000 to $18,000. The income effect seems to be minuscule, but the probabilities of lower-cost options decline, and those of higher-cost options rise.

The effects of changes in the various variables on the choice probabilities are explored further in Section 3.6.

3.5. OTHER EXPLANATORY FACTORS

Thus far we have used only four variables to explain the demand for higher education: cost, family income, student academic ability, and institutional selectivity. The responses to the SCOPE questionnaire included much additional information on aspirations, attitudes, and background, mostly of a qualitative nature. In this section we shall discuss the explanatory value of this information.

Our basic technique is similar to what is sometimes called an "analysis of residuals" in least-squares regression. For example, we wished to examine whether knowledge of the sex of the responding high school senior would enable us to improve our prediction of the senior's choice among available options, beyond what we could do with the conditional logit model alone (using cost, income, ability, and selectivity). To this end, we divided sample II into two parts, by sex; for each sex group we compared the observed choice frequencies with those predicted by the conditional logit model (i.e., by averaging the probabilities predicted for each individual in the group).[5] Large differences between predicted and observed frequencies would indicate that the predictions from the conditional logit model of Section 3.4 could be significantly improved by including sex as an explanatory variable. (The actual results for this variable will be discussed shortly.)

The SCOPE questionnaire included a large number of items, many more than we could examine individually with the above method. We therefore aggregated the items into 21 indices, which are listed in Table 10. The possible values of each index were grouped into two or more categories; thus there were two response categories for index 1, three for index 11, eight for index 13, etc. (For ease of coding, the categories were numbered consecutively, as shown in Table 10.)[6] A number of items figured in more than one index, and a few of the indices represent combinations of other indices. (A description of the individual items and the construction of the indices appears in Miller and Radner, 1975.)

Before doing the actual analysis of residuals, we made two adjustments in our prediction procedure. First, we aggregated the options into 8 types rather than 10. With the original 10 types, we often had too few observations in individual cells when considering an index with several categories. The 8 types we used were obtained by combining the original low- and medium-cost/high-selectivity types and the original high-cost/low- and medium-selectivity types. The new typology, with the revised numbering, is shown in Table 11. In terms of a three-

[5]See the explanation of the construction of Table 8.

[6]Unfortunately, the SCOPE study did not provide any recommendations for the construction of indices from the large set of items. We apologize to the professionals in the field for this exercise in amateur sociology.

TABLE 10 ***Indices of qualitative responses***

Index	*Categories*	*Interpretation*
1	1–2	Conservative
2	3–4	Subindex of conservatism
3	5–6	Fate control
4	7–8	Self-motivation for problem solving
5	9–10	Broad academic interests
6	11–12	Parents' concern with education
7	13–14	Student response to parents' concern
8	15–16	Student academic desires
9	17–18	Index 7 + index 8
10	19–20	Peer-group response at the cost of studying
11	21–23	Actual high school program
12	24–26	Will you ever go to college?
13	27–34	Most satisfaction in life
14	35–40	When was postsecondary school choice made?
15	41–42	Education requirements of preferred jobs
16	43–44	Education requirements of jobs to which the student is indifferent or about which he or she is uncertain
17	45–46	Student attachment to parents
18	47–48	Desire to sacrifice for future payoffs
19	49–50	Parents' desires for student's higher education
20	51–52	Index 6 + ½ (index 19)
21	53–54	Sex of student

NOTE: For ordinal indices, categories are in increasing order.

by-three classification of cost versus selectivity, types 2 through 8 would appear as follows:

<table>
<tr><th></th><th></th><th colspan="3">Cost</th></tr>
<tr><th></th><th></th><th>Low</th><th>Medium</th><th>High</th></tr>
<tr><td rowspan="3">Selectivity</td><td>High</td><td colspan="2">4</td><td>8</td></tr>
<tr><td>Medium</td><td>3</td><td>6</td><td rowspan="2">7</td></tr>
<tr><td>Low</td><td>2</td><td>5</td></tr>
</table>

The second adjustment in our prediction procedure involved making an overall correction in predicted choice frequencies.

Table 11 shows, for each of the eight option types, (1) observed numbers, (2) predicted numbers, (3) observed relative frequencies, (4) predicted relative frequencies, and (5) the differences between (3) and (4), which will be called the *correction constants* and denoted by k_j (for option type j). The predictions are those calculated from specification 3 of Section 3.4. In the calculation of predicted choice frequencies for separate index categories, the predicted frequency from the conditional logit model was adjusted by adding the corresponding correction constant.[7] In other words, for each option type j, we added k_j to the prediction calculated from the conditional logit model alone. The resulting prediction of the probability that student i chooses option j from his set of available option will be called the *corrected choice probability* and denoted by P^*_{ij}.

To illustrate our analysis of residuals, let us consider the classification of high school seniors according to sex, which is coded in index 21, categories 53 and 54; these two categories correspond to males and females, respectively. For each male, we calculated the corrected predicted probabilities of choosing the various options (1 to 8); these probabilities were then averaged over all the males to yield a corrected predicted relative frequency for each option, within the set of males. These *predicted* frequencies were subtracted from the corresponding *observed* relative choice frequencies to yield a *response residual* a_j^{53} of individuals in category 53 (males) to each option j. In a similar fashion, we calculated a response residual a_j^{54} of females to each option j. These response residuals are shown in the accompanying table. Positive response residuals occur in the cases in which the observed relative frequencies are higher than the predicted frequencies.

In order to assess the significance of these residuals, we (1) calculated approximate levels of statistical significance and (2) calculated the ratio of each residual to the corresponding observed frequency. Only the residuals corresponding to option 5 were statistically significant at the 5 percent level. For this option, the two residuals were 40 and 31 percent of the

[7]Similar predictions would have been obtained if the conditional logit equations had included a constant term for each option type. However, in the estimation of the logit equations we were interested in seeing *how much could be explained by the four initial variables alone,* without allowing the intervention of separate constants for each option.

TABLE 11 ***Differences between observed and predicted frequencies, by option type***

	(1)	(2)	(3)	(4)	(5)
Type (j)	*Observed numbers*	*Predicted numbers*	*Observed relative frequencies*	*Average predicted relative frequencies*	*Correction constants k_j [(3)–(4)]*
1	131	127.2003	.3493	.3392	.0101
2	80	66.4680	.2133	.1772	.0361
3	20	19.0140	.0533	.0570	.0026
4	17	20.2639	.0453	.0570	−.0087
5	48	51.7918	.1280	.1381	−.0101
6	37	35.3294	.0987	.0942	.0045
7	18	39.9006	.0480	.1064	−.0584
8	24	15.0197	.0640	.0401	.0239
TOTAL	375	374.9817	1.0000	1.0000	.0000

NOTE:

Option type	*Description*
1	No higher education
2	Low-cost/low-selectivity
3	Low-cost/medium-selectivity
4	Low- and medium-cost/high-selectivity
5	Medium-cost/low-selectivity
6	Medium-cost/medium-selectivity
7	High-cost/low- and medium-selectivity
8	High-cost/high-selectivity

corresponding observed frequencies, respectively. For option 7, the residuals were not statistically significant, but were 63 and 40 percent of the corresponding observed frequencies, respectively. The residuals for option 2 were statistically significant at approximately the 7 percent level. The residuals for option 1 were not close to being statistically significant, nor were they substantial fractions of the corresponding observed frequencies.

These results suggest that taking account of sex would not improve the predictions of the demand for all IHEs together, *beyond what can be predicted from the explanatory variables in the conditional logit model* (cost, income, ability, and selectivity). However, taking account of sex would somewhat improve the predictions of the distribution of demand among IHEs. In

TABLE 12 ***Response residuals, chi-squared, and percentage of observed relative frequency***

	1	2	3	4	5	6	7	8	9
	.0034	−.0026	−.0423*	.0709*	.0117	−.0146	.0509	−.0222	.0162
1	.0188	.0188	5.8174	5.8170	.3543	.3544	2.1772	2.1774	.7993
	.0108	−.0069	−.1577	.1461	.0321	−.0443	.1095	−.0744	.0412
	−.0162	.0122	.0156	−.0263	−.0176	.0220	−.0265	.0116	.0168
2	.5454	.5452	1.0785	1.0789	1.0642	1.0639	.8073	.8070	1.1318
	−.0869	.0522	.0721	−.1268	−.0874	.0966	−.1312	.0529	.0703
	.0048	−.0036	.0018	−.0030	.0114	−.0142	.0154	−.0067	−.0118
3	.1459	.1459	.0543	.0544	1.4058	1.4059	.9801	.9803	1.6672
	.0705	−.0861	.0284	−.0852	.1827	−.3394	.2505	−.1349	−.3268
	−.0024	.0018	.0073	−.0122	−.0079	.0099	.0129	−.0056	−.0078
4	.0336	.0335	.9484	.9487	.6738	.6735	.9306	.9308	.7057
	−.0383	.0546	.1068	−1.7086	−.2061	.1831	.4909	−.1052	−.2898
	−.0418*	.0314*	−.0136	.0228	−.0026	.0032	−.0421	.0184	−.0008
5	4.3039	4.3024	.9229	.9223	.0265	.0264	2.3402	2.3393	.0034
	−.6730	.1771	−.1332	.1331	−.0200	.0257	−.4359	.1296	−.0063
	.0160	−.0120	.0146	−.0245	.0066	−.0083	−.0242	.0106	−.0049
6	.8375	.8383	1.7811	1.7818	.2408	.2412	1.2511	1.2505	.1529
	.1285	−.1513	.1142	−.4897	.0692	−.0814	−.3946	.0920	−.0578
	.0378*	−.0285*	.0053	−.0088	.0074	−.0093	.0174	−.0076	−.0040
7	4.1326	4.1349	.1936	.1940	.2638	.2644	.5544	.5550	.0863
	.4059	−2.0302	.0825	−.4127	.1547	−.1936	.3310	−.1656	−.1102
	−.0017	.0013	.0113	−.0189	−.0091	.0113	−.0039	.0017	−.0036
8	.0222	.0222	3.3781	3.3781	1.2723	1.2723	.1233	.1233	.2006
	−.0191	.0268	.1263	−.8843	−.1573	.1573	−.1110	.0222	−.0719

particular, it would appear that IHEs with low selectivity and high and medium costs are relatively less attractive to males than the model would predict and relatively more attractive to females. These options include mainly private institutions with low selectivity (see Section 3.3). It would also appear that the public junior colleges (option 2) are relatively more attractive to males (and less attractive to females) than the model would predict.

We were somewhat surprised to find that sex does not appear

10	11	12	13	14	15	16	17	18
−.0234	.0296	−.0298	.0331	−.0386	.1455**	−.1095**	.0972**	−.0731**
.7994	1.8211	1.8213	2.6377	2.6380	31.4333	31.4341	14.3660	14.3665
−.0815	.0705	−.1071	.0825	−.1336	.2415	−.6889	.1908	−.3193
−.0243	.0067	−.0068	−.0273	.0319	−.0448*	.0337*	−.0253	.0190
1.1322	.1234	.1235	2.3848	2.3842	4.0143	4.0137	1.2861	1.2857
−.1379	.0287	−.0351	−.1415	.1345	−.2329	.1473	−.1233	.0866
.0171	.0018	−.0018	.0232*	−.0271*	−.0276*	.0208*	.0165	−.0124
1.6670	.0281	.0281	5.4442	5.4446	5.3445	5.3442	1.8667	1.8669
.2179	.0374	−.0306	.3121	−.9362	−2.2209	.2468	.2660	−.2660
.0114	−.0009	.0009	−.0054	.0064	−.0049	.0037	−.0049	.0037
.7055	.0063	.0063	.2923	.2922	.1872	.1871	.1740	.1739
.1580	−.0230	.0161	−.1570	.1099	.0000	.0460	−.2638	.0565
.0012	−.0297	.0299	−.0160	.0187	−.0012	.0009	−.0419*	.0315*
.0033	2.7848	2.7837	.9331	.9324	.0033	.0032	4.1839	4.1825
.0104	−.3492	.1746	−.1543	.1199	−.0090	.0070	−.5184	.1925
.0072	.0026	−.0027	−.0101	.0118	−.0669**	.0503**	−.0449**	.0337**
.1526	.0314	.0316	.5291	.5285	15.8874	15.8847	7.0849	7.0829
.0610	.0276	−.0262	−.1201	.1020	−5.3876	.3078	−1.2039	.2330
.0057	.0047	−.0047	.0014	−.0017	.0117	−.0088	.0049	−.0037
.0859	.0861	.0864	.0091	.0092	.4268	.4274	.0737	.0740
.0880	.1102	−.0883	.0319	−.0320	.3757	−.1446	.1321	−.0662
.0052	−.0149	.0150	.0012	−.0014	−.0118	.0089	−.0017	.0013
.2006	2.7215	2.7215	.0211	.0211	1.6045	1.6045	.0289	.0289
.0609	−.4000	.1647	.0189	−.0224	−.6323	.0903	−.0342	.0171

to be a powerful additional explanatory factor. The particular pattern of significant or nearly significant residuals that does appear might be interpreted as suggesting that males in this sample were somewhat more sensitive to the economic costs and benefits of higher education than females. However, the overall lack of significance of the residuals leads us not to press any particular interpretation of the pattern.

Table 12 gives the response residuals for all 21 indices and all the options. Most indices have only two corresponding cate-

TABLE 12 (continued)

	19	20	21	22	23	24	25	26	27
	−.0070	.0115	.1419**	−.1209**	.1773**	−.0554**	.2156**	.1947**	−.0221
1	.1648	.1647	10.1793	37.4128	14.3806	19.7618	7.8939	8.9772	.0315
	−.0212	.0302	.2249	−.9197	.2766	−.2177	.2875	.2954	−.0608
	.0001	−.0002	−.0545	.0478**	−.0717	.0475**	−.1874**	−.1654**	.0381
2	.0001	.0001	2.0350	7.8659	3.4058	20.2618	9.1808	8.4261	.1076
	.0005	−.0009	−.2695	.2035	−.4302	.1895	−3.3738	−1.8190	.1396
	−.0089	.0146	−.0047	.0068	−.0135	−.0052	.0256	.0142	.0315
3	1.1142	1.1140	.0845	.5812	.5213	1.3046	1.0172	.3749	.2376
	−.2078	.2078	−.1963	.0902	−.5253	−.0967	.4610	.3129	.3468
	.0014	−.0023	.0073	−.0020	−.0026	−.0033	.0346**	−.0061	−.0087
4	.0313	.0314	.2803	.0528	.0356	.8703	7.6775	.1138	.0519
	.0252	−.0821	.6153	−.0260	.0000	−.0610	1.2456	.0000	.0000
	−.0087	.0142	−.0501	.0259	−.0167	.0132	−.0674	−.0333	−.0254
5	.3750	.3746	2.2290	2.7438	.2269	2.2310	1.5756	.5643	.0663
	−.0778	.0918	−.6010	.1721	−.1445	.0905	−1.2133	−.4891	−.2797
	.0136	−.0222	−.0303	.0316*	−.0537*	.0027	−.0245	.0020	.0925
6	1.3840	1.3849	1.7746	6.3972	3.9918	.1483	.4998	.0027	1.2872
	.1170	−.3159	−1.2721	.2040	−2.0937	.0247	−.8818	.0224	.5085
	.0023	−.0038	.0158	−.0090	.0075	−.0078	.0310	.0271	−.0509
7	.0355	.0357	.3777	.4465	.0716	1.1947	.6859	.4976	.2978
	.0416	−.1084	.6629	−.1365	.2920	−.1540	1.1163	.5969	.0000
	.0072	−.0118	−.0255**	.0198**	−.0268**	.0083**	−.0275*	−.0333*	−.0550
8	1.0814	1.0814	7.0962	8.1452	7.0412	7.7016	4.7912	5.2247	1.4123
	.0988	−.2398	.0000	.1761	.0000	.1023	.0000	.0000	.0000

gories, but some have more; in total, there are 54 categories. Table 12 gives the two measures of significance corresponding to each residual. To each column of Table 12 corresponds a category, and the corresponding indices can be determined from Table 10. The rows of Table 12 correspond to different options and are organized as follows: With each option are associated three rows, i.e., three entries in a column; the first entry is the response residual, the second is the corresponding

28	*29*	*30*	*31*	*32*	*33*	*34*	*35*	*36*
.0436	−.0173	.0283	−.1254	−.1219	.0099	−.1456	.1779**	.0666
1.0592	.0310	1.2905	3.5570	1.1286	.0227	2.2551	8.8559	3.7256
.1034	−.0494	.0752	−.7105	−.5283	.0306	−.7278	.3216	.1492
−.0511	.0000	.0091	.1494*	−.1120	−.0216	−.0373	−.0068	−.0191
1.9653	.0000	.1769	5.5296	1.4242	.1352	.2017	.0176	.4065
−.3032	.0001	.0416	.3908	−1.4558	−.1227	−.2798	−.0320	−.0928
.0081	.0465	−.0192	−.0003	.0409	.0215	−.0023	.0449	−.0206
.1690	1.0457	2.5065	.0002	.7467	.3403	.0014	3.1880	1.5206
.1349	.4650	−.5284	−.0111	.5318	.2440	−.0339	.5279	−.5770
.0024	−.0168	−.0036	−.0325	.0407	.0225	.0426	−.0140	.0219
.0163	.2714	.0894	.7361	.2343	.3345	.3555	.2833	2.2883
.0661	.0000	−.0991	−1.1049	.2645	.2551	.3196	−.6560	.4895
−.0067	.0340	.0076	−.0588	−.0204	.0211	.0298	−.0859	−.0104
.0375	.2276	.1409	.9599	.0594	.1731	.1400	3.3008	.1311
−.0503	.2265	.0544	−.6664	−.2655	.1795	.2238	−2.0182	−.0728
−.0261	.0081	−.0097	.0419	.1497*	−.0443	.0479	−.0931**	−.0333
.9526	.0175	.3257	1.0257	4.2624	.6605	.4890	5.9325	2.2733
−.4328	.0806	−.1002	.3566	.6487	−.5015	.3596	.0000	−.6211
.0347	−.0472	−.0067	.0171	.0208	−.0200	−.0291	−.0355	.0061
1.4220	.4957	.1390	.0971	.0569	.1534	.1647	.6596	.0647
.4796	.0000	−.1590	.1939	.2708	−.6800	.0000	−1.6699	.1364
−.0049	−.0073	−.0057	.0085	.0022	.0108	.0938	.0124	−.0112
.1001	.0502	.3114	.0789	.0016	.1015	2.3481	.3832	1.0293
−.1022	−.1460	−.1036	.0964	.0285	.1223	.4692	.1942	−.4191

chi-square statistic (1 degree of freedom), and the third entry is the ratio of the response residual to the corresponding observed frequency. (Thus the response residuals corresponding to the two sexes-–as listed above—have been taken from columns [53] and [54] of Table 12.) Those chi-square statistics which are significant at least at the 5 percent level are marked with one asterisk, and those which are significant at the 1 percent level are marked with two asterisks.

TABLE 12 (continued)

	37	38	39	40	41	42	43	44	45
	−.0767*	−.0390	−.1543*	−.0589	.0539*	−.0461*	−.0673*	.0439*	−.0137
1	4.0463	.6497	5.1214	.7674	5.0180	5.0184	6.1921	6.1917	.3939
	−.2540	−.1561	−2.0835	−.2161	.1123	−.1941	−.2553	.1082	−.0463
	.0336	−.0023	−.0295	.0048	−.0189	.0161	.0554*	−.0361*	.0109
2	1.0524	.0029	.2239	.0062	.8186	.8183	5.5131	5.5139	.3309
	.1345	−.0115	−.1989	.0225	−.0881	.0758	.2103	−.2001	.0531
	.0016	.0037	−.0235	.0138	−.0088	.0076	−.0116	.0075	.0079
3	.0083	.0248	.3558	.1122	.6007	.6006	.7330	.7329	.5629
	.0312	.0732	−.6357	.1520	−.2549	.1092	−.2446	.1317	.1155
	−.0198	.0050	−.0237	.0135	−.0065	.0056	.0204	−.0133	−.0093
4	1.2669	.0272	.1945	.1427	.3388	.3386	2.1469	2.1473	.7710
	−.9490	.0601	−.3203	.2229	−.5658	.0754	.2522	−.6053	−.1769
	.0502	.0277	−.0132	−.0280	.0076	−.0065	−.0006	.0004	−.0083
5	2.8685	.4776	.0573	.2482	.1550	.1552	.0007	.0007	.2239
	.3010	.1846	−.1780	−.3077	.0548	−.0548	−.0053	.0026	−.0793
	.0364	.0019	.0937	.0593	−.0031	.0026	.0071	−.0046	.0138
6	2.0378	.0027	2.3612	1.6004	.0373	.0372	.1432	.1435	.8747
	.2691	.0164	.4218	.3911	−.0381	.0232	.0620	−.0528	.1090
	−.0143	.0182	.0375	.0077	.0056	−.0048	.0031	−0020	−.0079
7	.2791	.2451	.3543	.0214	.1079	.1082	.0239	.0241	.2486
	−.4583	.2733	.3376	.1272	.1619	−.0811	.0512	−.0514	−.1495
	−.0111	−.0152	.1130*	−.0122	−.0298**	.0255**	−.0067	.0044	.0066
8	.6233	.3018	4.6417	.1446	10.2959	10.2959	.3445	.3445	.5554
	−.2653	−.1824	.4358	−.2015	−5.1510	.2240	−.1104	.0662	.0697

Unlike the sex variable, a number of the indices did provide considerable additional explanatory power. The most important of these concerned the students' academic aspirations (index 8), their high school curricula (index 11), and their academic expectations (index 12). It is not surprising that these should be significantly related to the demand for higher educa-

46	*47*	*48*	*49*	*50*	*51*	*52*	*53*	*54*
.0140	−.0270	.0231	.1462**	−.0996**	.1297**	−.0855**	.0157	−.0145
.3939	1.2922	1.2920	28.7357	28.7364	21.7866	21.7873	.4750	.4751
.0346	−.0915	.0583	.2497	−.5291	.2300	−.4111	.0457	−.0411
−.0112	.0258	−.0221	−.0612*	.0417*	−.0429	.0283	.0371	−.0342
.3311	1.5553	1.5558	6.8404	6.8395	3.1802	3.1796	3.4574	3.4581
−.0505	.1114	−.1114	−.3722	.1692	−.2205	.1254	.1483	−.1907
−.0081	.0045	−.0039	−.0045	.0031	.0024	−.0016	.0022	−.0020
.5630	.1503	.1503	.1281	.1280	.0366	.0366	.0374	.0374
−.2146	.0710	−.0868	−.1138	.0487	.0519	−.0280	.0387	−.0387
.0096	.0171	−.0147	−.0016	.0011	.0027	−.0018	−.0102	.0095
.7708	2.0887	2.0891	.0191	.0191	.0519	.0520	.8283	.8280
.2526	.2279	−.7406	−.1243	.0166	.1362	−.0292	−.2633	.1843
.0086	−.0288	.0247	−.0101	.0069	−.0295	.0194	−.0460*	.0424*
.2236	2.2171	2.2161	.2210	.2207	1.8197	1.8188	5.9976	5.9962
.0566	−.2769	.1661	−.0902	.0494	−.3136	.1291	−.3939	.3063
−.0141	.0263	−.0225	−.0464*	.0316*	−.0423*	.0279*	.0174	−.0160
.8755	2.6448	2.6462	6.6906	6.6887	5.5925	5.5909	1.2816	1.2823
−.2013	.2070	−.3036	−1.0066	.2348	−1.0504	.2033	.2085	−.1422
.0081	−.0103	.0088	−.0011	.0007	.0103	−.0068	−.0245	.0226
.2480	.3494	.3488	.0034	.0034	.2954	.2959	2.1349	2.1333
.1867	−.2225	.1778	−.0553	.0110	.3071	−.1182	−.6297	.4006
−.0068	−.0077	.0066	−.0213*	.0145*	−.0305**	.0201**	.0083	−.0077
.5554	.6102	.6102	4.5642	4.5642	9.5548	9.5548	.7872	.7872
−.2090	−.1327	.0948	−1.0806	.1544	−4.5465	.1977	.1153	−.1362

NOTE: Response residuals that are significant at least at the 5 percent level are marked with one asterisk, and those which are significant at the 1 percent level are marked with two asterisks.

tion. The importance of high school curriculum is especially pronounced for options 1 (no HE), 2 (low-cost/low-selectivity), 6 (medium-cost/medium-selectivity), and 8 (high-cost/high-selectivity). This finding serves as a reminder that there are significant lead times in the decisions that affect the demand for higher education and that the use of easily measurable variables such as the proportions of students in different high school programs can significantly improve short-run forecasts of demand for higher education.

Parents' educational objectives are also important. Seniors who perceive their parents to have low educational aspirations for them tend to have significantly higher residuals for no HE and lower residuals for low-cost/low-selectivity, medium-cost/medium-selectivity, and high-cost/high-selectivity institutions. On the other hand, whether or not students perceive their parents to be concerned about their current education does not seem to provide additional explanatory power!

Economists often view the demand for education as related to expectations regarding careers and future labor-market conditions. A few of the indices reflect such a relationship, but not always clearly. Indices 15 and 16 concern the educational implications of career preferences. A definite preference for jobs with high educational requirements (index 15) is associated with positive residuals for high-cost/high-selectivity institutions and with negative residuals for no HE, but the residuals for the intermediate options are not significant. Indifference and uncertainty about jobs with high educational requirements (index 16) is associated with positive residuals for no HE and negative residuals for junior college, but the other residuals are not significant in this case.

The timing of a career choice (index 14) is somewhat important. An early choice is associated with positive residuals for the high-cost/high-selectivity option and with a negative residual for no HE. Students who had not made a career choice by their senior year in high school were associated with significantly positive residuals for no HE.

Index 13 provided eight categories of response to the question: "What do you think will give you the most satisfaction in life?" Among these categories, two had significant associations. Those who chose "leisure time and recreational activities" (category 31) were associated with a significant positive residual for the low-cost/low-selectivity option (public junior college) and an almost significant negative residual for no HE (presumably a job). Those who chose "religious beliefs or activities" (category 32) had a significant positive residual for medium-cost/medium-selectivity institutions.

Many indices that we thought would have additional explanatory power were not, in fact, associated with significant residuals. Fate control (3), self-motivation in problem solving (4), broad academic interest (5), and time preference or ability to sacrifice (18) are examples of such disappointing indices. One explanation is that these indices were too crude as instruments for measuring the underlying variables; another is that the ability (SAT) score already reflected much of the influence of these variables.

A full description of the items that made up the indices, and our code for scoring these items, is provided in Miller and Radner (1975). The formula for calculating the chi-square statistics is also described there.

3.6. ELASTICITIES OF DEMAND

In order to explore the changes in choice probabilities that are associated with changes in the explanatory variables in the conditional logit model, it is convenient to examine the *elasticities of demand* with respect to these variables. Roughly speaking, the elasticity of the probability that individual i chooses option j, with respect to some explanatory variable, measures the percentage change in the probability that is associated with a 1 percent change in the explanatory variable. (A precise definition will be given below.)

To avoid excessive repetition, we shall refer to an elasticity of a probability with respect to an explanatory variable by the name of that variable. For example, the elasticity of the probability that an individual i chooses an option j, with respect to the ability of individual i, will be called an *ability elasticity;* the corresponding elasticity with respect to the cost of option j to individual i will be called a *cost elasticity;* etc.

Tables 13 through 16 present ability, income, cost, and selectivity elasticities for the 12 hypothetical students illustrated in Table 9. The formulas for these elasticities are given in equations (5) through (10) below. It is not necessary to examine the formulas in detail in order to understand the discussion that follows, but both the tables and the formulas bring out the important point that any one elasticity is not a *constant,* but *is itself a function of the explanatory variables.* The elasticities reported in Tables 13 through 16 have been computed using the estimates of the coefficients given in Table 7 (specification 3).[8]

[8]However, for the two middle ability groups, the coefficient of the academic-interaction term was taken to be the average of the two estimated coefficients. Recall that these two estimated coefficients were not statistically significant and that the effect of the corresponding term is not important in magnitude.

TABLE 13 ***Elasticity of the probability of enrolling in type j with respect to individual ability***

Y_i	$6,000				$12,000				$18,000			
A_i	375	475	575	650	375	475	575	650	375	475	575	650
Estimates for α	−.0328	−.002845	.0211	.0211	−.0328	−.002845	.0211	.0211	−.0328	−.002845	.0211	.0211
Column	(1)	(2)	(3)	(4)	(5)	(6)	(7)	(8)	(9)	(10)	(11)	(12)
1	.241	.108	−1.878	−2.508	.289	.117	−1.872	−2.555	.306	.121	−1.872	−2.556
2	−.447	.032	−1.198	−1.740	−.400	.041	−1.192	−1.786	−.383	.045	−1.193	−1.787
3		−.088	−.119	−.519		−.079	−.113	−.566		−.075	−.113	−.567
4			.427	.098			.433	.051			.433	.050
5	−.447	.108	−1.198	−1.740	−.400	.041	−1.193	−1.786	−.383	.045	−1.193	−1.787
6		−.088	−.119	−.519		−.079	−.113	−.566		−.075	−.113	−.567
7			.427	.098			.433	.051			.433	.050
8		−.602	−.349	−.780		−.053	−.343	−.826		−.050	.344	−.827
9		−.116	.136	−.231		−.107	.142	−.278		−.104	.142	−.279
10				.934				.888				.887

Let us consider first the ability elasticities in Table 13. Column (1), for example, refers to a high school senior with a family income of $6,000 per year, an SAT score of 375, and a set of three alternative options: no higher education, a local public junior college, and some medium-cost/low-selectivity institution. According to Table 9, the probabilities that such a student will choose these options are, respectively, .642, .271, and .086. Column (1) of Table 13 shows that a 1 percent increase in ability would increase the probability of choosing no higher education by .241 percent. The effects of larger changes would be approximately proportional, in percentage terms, as long as the changes were not too large. For example, for a 5 percent increase in ability, from 375 to 394, the probability of no HE would increase by about 1.2 percent to .650, the probability of a local junior college would decrease by 2.2 percent to .265, and the probability of a medium-cost/low-selectivity institution would decrease by 2.2 percent to .084.

The magnitude of these changes seems small. In other words, although the coefficient of ability in this group is statistically significant, the effect of the ability variable is nevertheless weak. The ability elasticities in column (4) (income = $6,000, ability = 650) are somewhat larger, but these apply to probabilities that are already rather small. The exception is the high-cost/high-selectivity option, whose probability would increase by 9.34 percent for a 10 percent increase in ability. Thus the difference between a 650 SAT senior and a 715 SAT senior, both with family incomes of $6,000, would be a probability of .249 versus a probability of .269 of choosing option 10.

Table 14 indicates the income elasticities. In column (1), for example, we see the effect on a $6,000, 375 SAT high school graduate. A 10 percent increase in family income, from $6,000 to $6,600, decreases the probability of not going to school by 2.25 percent, .642 to .628; decreases the probability of choosing a public junior college almost imperceptibly, .271 to .270; and increases the probability of choosing the medium-cost/low-quality choice from .086 to .095 (round-off errors are responsible for the fact that the sum of the changes is not exactly zero).

The negative signs in Table 15 indicate the normal price-quantity relationship; price (cost) rises are associated with decreased probabilities of enrollment. The Massachusetts study found that the population had a more inelastic cost elasticity for

TABLE 14 ***Elasticity of the probability of enrolling in type j with respect to family income***

Y_i	$6,000				$12,000				$18,000			
A_j	375	475	575	650	375	475	575	650	375	475	575	650
Estimates for γ	−3.592	−2.407	−1.031	−1.031	−3.592	−2.407	−1.031	−1.301	−3.592	−2.407	−1.031	−1.031
Column	(1)	(2)	(3)	(4)	(5)	(6)	(7)	(8)	(9)	(10)	(11)	(12)
1	.160	−.360	−.226	−.313	−.123	−.233	−.120	−.167	−.094	−.167	−.082	−.114
2	−.013	−.245	−.176	−.263	−.036	−.173	−.096	−.142	−.036	−.129	−.066	−.097
3		−.200	−.157	−.244		−.151	−.086	−.133		−.114	−.060	−.091
4			−.133	−.220			−.074	−.121			−.051	−.083
5	−1.160	.522	.152	.065	.536	.210	.068	.022	.345	.127	.044	.012
6		.161	−.003	−.090		.029	−.009	−.056		.006	−.007	−.039
7			.021	−.066			.003	−.043			.000	−.031
8		.924	.324	.237		.410	.154	.108		.260	.101	.070
9		.924	.324	.237		.410	.154	.108		.260	.101	.070
10				.237				.108				.070

TABLE 15 ***Elasticity of the probability of enrolling in type j with respect to the cost of type j***

Y_i	$6,000				$12,000				$18,000			
A_i	375	475	575	650	375	475	575	650	375	475	575	650
Estimates for γ	−3.592	−2.407	−1.031	−1.031	−3.592	−2.407	−1.031	−1.031	−3.592	−2.407	−1.031	−1.031
Column	(1)	(2)	(3)	(4)	(5)	(6)	(7)	(8)	(9)	(10)	(11)	(12)
1	0	0	0	0	0	0	0	0	0	0	0	0
2	−.127	−.091	−.0474	−.048	−.064	−.047	−.024	−.024	−.043	−.032	−.016	−.016
3		−.131	−.059	−.062		−.067	−.030	−.031		−.045	−.020	−.021
4			−.071	−.076			−.036	−.039			−.024	−.026
5	−1.204	−.794	−.365	−.370	−.559	−.386	−.182	−.185	−.360	−.254	−.121	−.123
6		−.455	−.196	−.204		−.226	−.098	−.103		−.1504	−.065	−.068
7			−.197	−.208			−.098	−.105			−.065	−.070
8		−1.206	−.511	−.523		−.582	−.253	−.260		−.382	−.168	−.173
9		−1.211	−.487	−.504		−.585	−.239	−.249		−.384	−.158	−.166
10				−.402				−.192				−.126

junior colleges than for four-year public colleges and four-year private colleges. Table 15 confirms this finding and, for the students depicted, suggests the relative magnitudes of cost elasticities among the various options. At all levels of income, and at all ability levels, larger percentage changes in demand accompany higher-cost institutions; demand is more elastic as cost rises. This can be seen by comparing the relative size of the elasticities for options 2, 3, and 4 against options 5, 6, and 7 or against options 8, 9, and 10.

Table 15 confirms Hoenack's finding that the cost elasticity for the University of California was greater in magnitude for low income groups than for high income groups (see Chapter 2). One actually sees in Table 15 the extended implication of equation (7) below, that cost elasticities for all higher education options fall as incomes rise.

As the demand for some options increases, the demand for other options decreases. A cost increase in any type leads to a decrease in that type's enrollment probability and an increase in the other institution's enrollment probability. The relationship between a 1 percent rise in the cost of type j and the percentage change in probability of choosing type k ($\neq j$) is called a *cross-cost elasticity* (as distinct from an *own-cost elasticity* if $k = j$). The 10 appropriate tables are not included here, but equation (9) below can be used to compute these responses.

Table 16 gives the selectivity elasticities. In column (1), for example, we see the effect on the $6,000, 375 SAT high school graduate again. If the measure of community college selectivity rises by 10 percent, from 375 to 411 SAT, the probability that a 375 SAT, $6,000-family-income student would enroll in the community college diminishes by 38.6 percent, from .271 to .166. This reduction in community college enrollment probability is accompanied by a rise in the probabilities of the student's two other choices. The alternative options experience a uniform percentage rise of 14.34 percent. Again, the appropriate 10 cross-elasticity tables are not included here. For the record, the probability of no HE increases from .642 to .734, and the probability of the medium-cost/low-selectivity option increases from .086 to .098.

The following equations give the formulas for calculating the various elasticities. First, the elasticity of the probability P_{ij}

TABLE 16 ***Elasticity of the probability of enrolling in type j with respect to a change in the selectivity of j***

Y_i		$6,000				$12,000				$18,000		
A_i	375	475	575	650	375	475	575	650	375	475	575	650
Estimates for α	−.0328	−.002845	.0211	.0211	−.0328	−.002845	.0211	.0211	−.0328	−.002845	.0211	.0211
Column	(1)	(2)	(3)	(4)	(5)	(6)	(7)	(8)	(9)	(10)	(11)	(12)
1	−1.65	−.37	4.42	5.05	−1.93	−.40	4.43	5.06	−2.04	−.41	4.44	5.07
2	−3.86	−.46	4.96	5.71	−3.87	−.47	4.98	5.74	−3.89	−.48	4.99	5.75
3		−.57	5.40	6.39		−.59	5.47	6.48		−.59	5.50	6.51
4			5.21	6.31			5.32	6.47			5.36	6.52
5	−4.83	−.52	5.03	5.77	−4.49	−.51	5.02	5.76	−4.34	−.50	5.01	5.76
6		−.61	5.53	6.50		−.61	5.53	6.53		−.61	5.54	6.54
7			5.44	6.51			5.43	6.56			5.43	6.57
8		−.63	5.64	6.53		−.61	5.54	6.49		−.60	5.54	6.47
9		−.69	5.81	6.78		−.66	5.69	6.83		−.66	5.64	6.69
10				6.27				5.99				5.90

(that individual i chooses option j from the set J_i) with respect to any explanatory variable—say, W—is defined by

$$\eta_{ij,W} = \frac{\partial P_{ij}}{\partial W} \cdot \frac{W}{P_{ij}} \tag{4}$$

provided neither W nor P_{ij} is zero. Using this definition and equations (1) and (2) of Section 3.2, which define the conditional logit model, one can verify the following formulas in a straightforward manner:

$$\eta_{ij,A_i} = \alpha \frac{A_i}{1{,}000} \left(S_j - \sum_{k \varepsilon J_i} S_k P_{ik} \right) \tag{5}$$

$$\eta_{ij,Y_i} = -\frac{\gamma}{Y_i} \left(C_{ij} - \sum_{k \varepsilon J_i} C_{ik} P_{ik} \right) \tag{6}$$

$$\eta_{ij,C_{ij}} = \gamma \frac{C_{ij}}{Y_i} (1 - P_{ij}) \tag{7}$$

$$\eta_{ij,S_j} = \alpha \frac{A_i S_j}{1{,}000} (1 - P_{ij}) \tag{8}$$

$$\eta_{ik,C_{ij}} = -\alpha \frac{C_{ij}}{Y_i} P_{ik} \qquad k \neq j \tag{9}$$

$$\eta_{ik,S_j} = -\alpha \frac{A_i S_j}{1{,}000} P_{ij} \qquad k \neq j \tag{10}$$

Notice that equations (7) and (8) refer to own-cost and own-selectivity elasticities, whereas equations (9) and (10) refer to the corresponding cross elasticities. Notice, too, that for any given j, the cross elasticities corresponding to options $k \neq j$ are the same for all k. This last point is a consequence of the feature of the conditional logit model that was discussed in Section 3.2, whereby the odds between any pair of alternative options do not depend on the characteristics of the other alternatives.

3.7. A COMPARISON OF THE KOHN, MANSKI, AND MUNDEL STUDY WITH OUR OWN

At the conclusion of Chapter 2, in the Introduction, and again in Section 3.1, we have alluded to another ongoing conditional logit higher education demand study, one currently being performed by Kohn, Manski, and Mundel. To conclude this summary of results, we would like to compare their work with our own, bearing in mind, of course, that their work is yet to be completed.

In the large picture both studies have the same basic design, one that enables conditional logit estimation. There are, however, basically four differences between the two studies. The first difference centers about the number of separate decisions a student must make in the process of selecting his or her best postsecondary school option. The difference here is between two choices (using a two-stage decision process) and one choice (using a one-stage decision process). Kohn, Manski, and Mundel employ the two-stage process, and we employ the one-stage process. In a one-stage model the option of not going to an IHE is simply one of the options open to a student. The student chooses either a particular IHE or the not-going option in a single comparison of his or her feasible alternatives. In the two-stage model the best option is determined through a sequence of decisions. First, the student decides whether to go to an IHE. Then, if the student has decided to go, he or she decides which of the IHEs is best.[9]

The reader will recall that the conditional logit model has the feature that has been called "independence of irrelevant alternatives." This feature, previously discussed in Sections 3.2 and 3.3, implies that if an IHE option is removed from the set of options available to a student, the probability corresponding to the removed option is reallocated to all the remaining options in the student's feasible set in proportion to their originally estimated probabilities.

In the two-stage version, removing an institution from a student's feasible set results in an increase in the probability of choosing the other IHEs. The probability of not going remains unchanged. In the one-stage model, the probability of all the

[9]Actually, the Kohn, Manski, and Mundel estimation process follows the reverse order; estimation of the second stage precedes estimation of the first stage. The estimation process begins making conditional logit estimates for the college-attending sample. The estimated model is then used to compute the predicted utility for the attenders' best options and the utilities for the nonattenders' options. The nonattenders' best IHE option is defined as the feasible IHE with the maximum predicted utility. Then the first-stage "go/no-go" model is estimated with a maximum IHE utility variable. This variable takes on the predicted utility for the attenders' revealed preferred option and the predicted utility for the nonattenders' predicted best IHE option. The go/no-go model uses other socioeconomic-demographic and IHE measures as well.

remaining options, including the not-going option, increases. We believe it is more likely that a student would allocate the probability associated with a removed option to a close substitute for that option rather than distribute it among all the remaining options in the feasible set in proportion to their original probabilities. But it is difficult to know which of the two models would actually describe reality more accurately.

On the one hand, if one is concerned with students whose demand for higher education is great, it seems most likely that these students would allocate their probabilities associated with removed options to close substitutes for that option. Thus the two-stage model would appear to be a priori superior to the one-stage model because the probability of attending the removed option is only dissipated over the other higher education institutional choices. Bear in mind, however, that with this type of student the probability of not going computed in the one-stage model is very low. So, in fact, very little of the removed option's probability is actually allocated to the not-going option.

On the other hand, there may very well be an environmental interaction between supply and demand. The existence of particular types of learning centers may actually cause the general demand for all college attendance to be higher. If such an environmental relationship exists, the absence of these centers would cause the demand for higher education attendance to be lower, and the probability of not going should properly rise. This condition is reflected in the one-stage model.

Without calculating the predicted probabilities for different types of students and comparing the two models, it is difficult to judge which model more accurately describes the reality for different types of students. If pushed for a position, however, we like the idea of increased discrimination in regard to the substitutability question, and so on a priori grounds we favor their two-stage model over our own single-stage model.

The second difference between our studies centers around the differences in the way each study handled the academic interaction variable. Kohn, Manski, and Mundel specified two variables, SAT and the square of the difference between the institution's mean SAT and the individual's SAT. But they did not break up their sample into ability groups. We, on the other hand, used only one ability variable, the product of the institution's mean SAT and the individual's SAT, but we broke our sample up into separate ability groups. This difference in treatment led to results which contradicted one another for the low-ability students. The Kohn, Manski, and Mundel results imply that the better of the low-ability students will try to go to better schools. Our results imply that they will be the first to decide that college is not for them. This difference should be investigated further.

We believe that breaking the sample up allows one to estimate separate demand functions by ability groups. This form better captures the interactions between student ability and the perceived relative economic burden of paying for college. Since their study is still in progress, Kohn, Manski, and Mundel may already have broken their sample up in this manner or may have plans to do so. Dividing their sample into more homogeneous ability groups might be the way to further study the difference in predicted behavior of the low-ability students that exists between the two studies.

A third and somewhat related difference between the studies occurs because Kohn et al. used a larger sample and more explanatory variables in their demand specification. To simulate their Illinois students' feasible sets, they first determined all the IHEs within 200 miles of each student's hometown. On the basis of their estimated relationship between the likelihood of admission and student ability, they excluded from that enumeration institutions to which students were not likely to be admitted, and they then portrayed a chooser's choice set with the chosen option and 10 randomly selected options from those which remained. The American Council on Education's (ACE) IHE file provided measures describing the resulting IHE options. With the ACE file, they were able to program the choice-set determination process and consequently were able to simulate choice sets for almost all the Illinois SCOPE sample.

Our own simulation is discussed in detail in Miller and Radner (1975). It resembles, in principle, the method discussed above, but three factors influenced the major differences in our procedures: the unavailability of institutional information and the variation in eligibility to public IHEs by state, which influenced our sample size, and the principle of aggregation consistent with the independence of irrelevant alternatives assumption of the strict utility model, which influenced our description of the feasible set.

First, our study began about two years before that of Kohn et al. When we began, the ACE file did not exist, so consequently we had no central source of institutional description.[10] For example, many of the public IHEs did not require SATs for entry. Naturally, then, institutional SAT measures were unknown. We often estimated our own measures of average institutional ability from the larger SCOPE sample. In addition, we were dealing with students' choice options that are not presently in the ACE file—beauty colleges, schools of cooking, etc. Through correspondence we have learned that these postsecondary choices were classified by Kohn, Manski, and Mundel as "no-goes," that is, not attending an IHE. We classified them as substitutable with two-year colleges. We also learned that a student who chose an IHE outside the 200-mile radius had his or her school choice included in the final choice set.

Second, admission to the public institutions varied by state. We were easily able to simulate student admission to public institutions in Illinois, but in California, for example, where university admission was based entirely on high school performance, we needed additional data.

Third, if one is interested in representing the feasible sets of choosers with a small number of choices, as both of us apparently were, the independence of irrelevant alternatives assumption implies that institutions that appear to choosers as substitutes for one another should be aggregated and represented as a single choice. With such a representation, if a particular institution within a cost and quality classification denies an individual admission, the individual reallocates all the probability of attending that kind of institution to another of its type.

It was in this spirit that we defined substitutability in terms of cost and quality, or selectivity, and aggregated institutions accordingly.

These first two factors forced us to limit our sample size and concentrate our efforts on describing the feasible sets for a smaller sample than that used by Kohn, Manski, and Mundel, but a sample that covered the four surveyed states. The third

[10]See Creager and Sell (1969).

factor suggests that our method of reducing the size of the feasible set resulted in a more accurate description of the options available to a chooser than would result from reducing the size of a feasible set by random selection, given the requirements of a strict utility model.

Many of the additional variables they used were significant. Again, it is difficult to evaluate the gains in explanatory power of these variables. Is the significance due to the importance of these new variables, or is it due to the larger sample size? Further calculations would be required to answer these questions. But a priori, their results should be an improvement over our own.

The final major difference between our studies concerns the questions of stratified versus unstratified samples. We used a stratified sample; they did not. If a single specification does not fit all ability and income levels equally, then the estimates of the parameters will be affected by the distribution of the explanatory variables in the sample. We found that with a stratified sample, a single specification was inappropriate for describing demand. Consequently, on the basis of the distribution of income and ability presented in Table 2, we strongly suspect that their single specification is not applicable to the low-income/lower-ability student population. This in turn suggests that their objective of building policy models falls short of the mark. The importance of this conjecture can be tested by breaking up their sample into groups and making separate estimates for each group, as we have already suggested.[11]

[11]Since this was written, a more recent report has appeared by the same authors, M. G. Kohn, C. F. Manski, and D. S. Mundell, "An Empirical Investigation of Factors Which Influence Gollege-Going Behavior," Report NSF-R-1470, The RAND Corporation, Santa Monica, Calif., 1974.

4. Demand Projections and a Sensitivity Analysis

In this chapter we have two objectives. Our first is to predict demand for the coming decade or two. We shall of course use our estimated model to accomplish this objective. But, since the model is static, based entirely on information about a single year's high school graduates, it should be placed into a dynamic context. We shall argue that historically observed enrollment trends can be made consistent with the model. These historical trends suggest trends in the estimated coefficients. We shall speculate on the new directions in higher education demand entailed by these suggested trends and by further social and economic factors. Finally, these speculations will be made concrete; we shall change the estimated model's coefficients in the speculated directions, use the changed model to forecast new probability distributions of demand, and predict the freshman demand for higher education in the United States to the year 2000.

Our second objective is to explore the sensitivity of the probability distribution of demand to the specific values of the coefficients estimated in the conditional logit model. The technical requirement to meet this objective is to alter the coefficients of the model and then to compare the estimated and predicted probability distributions implied by the estimated and predicted coefficients, respectively. This comparison directly indicates the sensitivity of the demand probability distribution to the coefficients. Since the demand-projection exercise will provide altered coefficients, the second objective will be met concomitantly with the first.

Our results show that, over the broad range of the variables considered, ability affects the joint distribution of demand more strongly than do the economic variables. The fact that ability operates in opposite directions, depending on which end of the ability distribution a student happens to lie in, implies that this variable differs fundamentally from the economic variable, which is significant, but appears to more uniformly affect behavior throughout the ranges of cost and income. The results suggest that primary consideration should be given to the academic-interaction effect and that secondary consideration should be given to the economic effect. We shall proceed accordingly.

Taubman and Wales (1972) compared studies of the fraction of high school graduates continuing on to college, by ability groups, and showed that the historic trend in that fraction is directly related to ability. For example, between 1925 and 1962, the proportion of students attending college averaging in the seventy-fifth and ninetieth ability percentiles has increased from about 54 and 60 percent of high school graduates to about 73 and 88 percent, respectively. Over this same period, the fiftieth-percentile group has moved from about 45 to 50 percent, and the twenty-fifth-percentile group ends the period on about the same percentage it began.

FIGURE 7
Fraction of high school graduates continuing to college at selected percentiles, adjusted

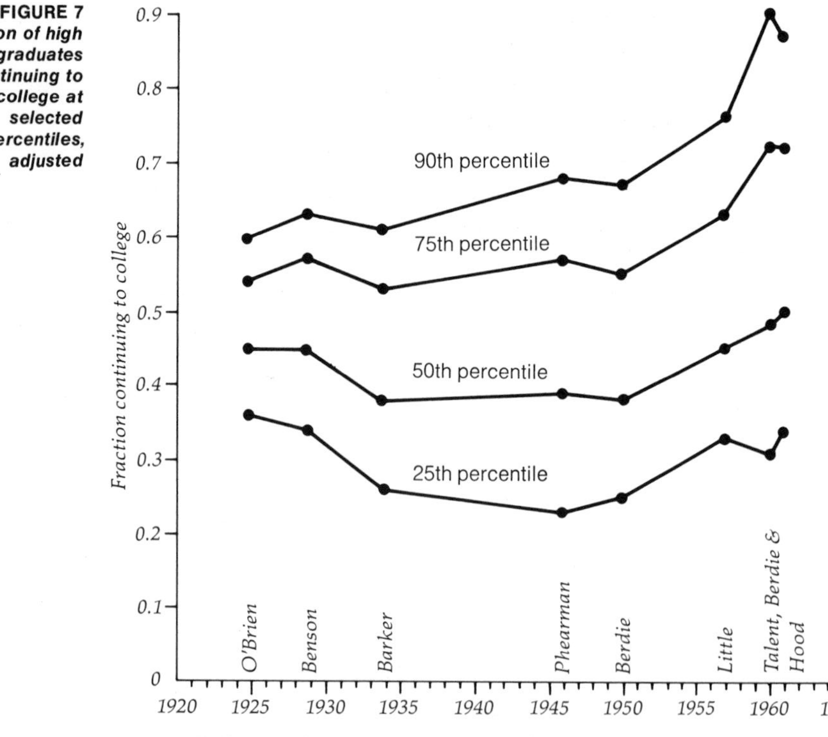

SOURCE: Taubman and Wales (1972, Figure 2, p. 20).

The ninetieth-percentile group moves moderately upward until 1950; thereafter, larger gains are made. The seventy-fifth-percentile group is rather constant until the 1950s and then also moves upward. The fiftieth-percentile group declines somewhat during the Depression, but rises again in the post-1950s, and the twenty-fifth-percentile group declines until after World War II, when they, too, move upward again.

The reported conditional logit estimates are cross-sectionally determined. Taubman and Wales report historically observed results. Can a consistency argument be made between the two?

Let us first consider the effect of supply on enrollment. One of the properties of the conditional logit estimation model is that as the number of options in the feasible sets increases, the probability of attending the previously considered options diminishes. Since not going to college is one of the model's previously considered options, the expansion of the publicly controlled sector, especially the junior and state college institutional growth, would have increased the likelihood that individuals in all ability groups attended IHEs. This result is a consequence of the conditional logit estimation model; the probability of attending school would have increased if the model's coefficients had been stable over the entire period.

We turn now to the aspect of trends in the demand coefficients on enrollment. The effect of changing coefficients in the model is straightforward; negative trends would have decreased going to college, and positive trends would have increased going to college. Just which way demand trends may have been moving for the different ability groups is a little uncertain.

Jencks and Riesman (1968), in their study of the relationship between social stratification and mass higher education, provide some insights. They argue:

> There has clearly been a trend toward popular awareness of the connection between education and adult success. Both rich and poor parents today assume that the social escalator begins in the first-grade classroom and progresses through other classrooms for many years before emerging into the "real" world. Almost all parents today want their children to get an extensive education (p. 98).

Increased popular awareness of the need for a scarce resource, with a high personal payoff, results in greater competition for the use of that resource. The competition leads to winners and losers. For the highest ability group, i.e., the winners, awareness probably results in a positive movement in the academic-interaction coefficient. The increase in demand coupled with the supply-initiated enrollment increase leads to a result consistent with Taubman and Wales's findings for the high ability group. It seems, then, that both supply and demand forces have been acting historically to raise the academic-interaction coefficient of the highest ability group. We see no reason why this trend will stop.

Awareness tends to drive up the trend in the academic-interaction coefficient for the lowest ability group as well, but the competitive failure of this group, relative to that of higher achievers, tends to continuously drive the trend down. Further considerations are needed before any judgment can be reached about the probable future movement of the low achievers' academic-interaction coefficient.

The negative coefficient estimate on the academic-interaction variable reflects, we believe, the alienation of potential students of the lowest ability group from the higher education system. This attitude inhibits enrollment and limits the opportunities of those potential students in question. Changes in the functioning of community colleges toward a program which does not follow the traditional "quality" emphasis of the four-year school would be, in our opinion, the initial step in developing a course of study relevant to the potential student's life-style. This new orientation in higher education is summarized by the program format recommended by the Carnegie Commission (1970, p. 17) for the development of meaningful community college options:

> . . . a variety of educational programs, including transfer education, general education, remedial courses, occupational programs, continuing education for adults . . . cultural programs designed to enrich the community environment . . . within [a] general framework [for] opportunities [of] varying patterns of development and . . . provision of particularly strong specialties in selected colleges. . . .

To retain its effect, however, the program must be coupled with the development of counseling services able to reach potential students while still in high school. These services must be coordinated with placement services and public employment offices and constructed to "encourage students to make wise choices between curricula that are specifically designed to prepare them for an occupation and those that are designed to lead to ultimate career choices" (Carnegie Commission on Higher Education, 1970, p. 17). In our opinion these innovations would mitigate, at least in part, the negative attitudes and effects discussed previously.

The supply of college graduates applying for traditional white-collar jobs has begun to exceed the present demand and, under present projections, will continue to do so at an increasing rate. However, demand for occupational skills, traditionally labeled "blue-collar," is likely to rise. Higher education, especially in the community college sector, could expand in this direction. Because of the relative supply and demand forces, the resulting changes in remuneration rates, and the disintegration of traditional status distinctions, student demand for such action is likley to increase. We believe that the Commission's recommendation ". . . to stimulate the expansion of occupational education in community colleges and to make it responsive to changing manpower requirements" (Carnegie Commission on Higher Education, 1970, p. 21) will increasingly reflect the needs of persons presently opting not to continue in school, as well as those of many who do. We note with interest that the changes in institutional forms necessitated by the considerations of social justice and by the phenomena of supply and demand are similar. Both social and economic trends seem to coincide in demanding radical reorientation of the higher education system.

The following passage from Fryer, contained in Medsker and Tillery (1971, pp. 85–86), probably describes an ideal model (for an urban area):

> . . . a campus totally committed to serving the needs of *individuals* and collectivities in its community. . . . [I]t must find ways to adapt itself to the uniqueness of each of its students, rather than making itself . . . an impersonal obstacle course through which students must compete . . . against each other. . . . [T]he new campus must be intent upon the human condition . . . choosing to respond to the validity of each person's need *as* it exists, *where* it exists.
>
> . . . a campus which takes pains to communicate to all people. . . . [I]t is for them. . . . [S]tructures must invite the city and its people to come in . . . rather than walling them out.

> . . . a campus which in many ways is indistinguishable from the [central] city it serves . . . but an identifiable home base and a source of support for those who need it. . . .
>
> The new campus should set out to intervene in the process of urban deterioration [and contribute to] the city's efforts at self-renewal . . . a center of educational, intellectual, and cultural enrichment. . . .
>
> . . . an experimental campus . . . a laboratory using research evidence, introspection, and response from its community . . . in a constant process of change and self-renewal.
>
> The campus model of governance must be democratic, based on participation in decision-making by all those affected by the outcomes of decisions.
>
> . . . a campus which attempts to recruit and retain sensitive faculty and staff who are concerned people of high energy, commitment, and learning. . . . [It will need] its staff as *ends* as well as means.
>
> . . . a public agency . . . which seeks efficient and effective ways of investing funds so that the public receives maximum return . . . careful coordination within the college . . . and with relevant community organizations and agencies.

To recapitulate, we have been arguing that the typology of cost and quality (as measured by average SAT scores of students) will, under suitable institutional change, become less appropriate to the demand considerations of the low achievers. The net result of this change will be to destroy the present specified demand model or, alternatively, to destroy the implied content expressed by the academic-interaction variable. Adopting this latter perspective, we will adjust the future trend in the lowest ability group's academic-interaction variable coefficient away from its negative value, in a positive direction, toward zero.

Although we have argued for the primacy of the academic-interaction variable, it nevertheless behooves us to consider how the cost-income coefficient might vary. We have alluded to the strong possibility of a correlation in the parameters estimated. If the correct underlying model of demand has these correlations, then forces acting to change the academic-interaction coefficient would also act to change the cost-income coefficient. For example, if the perception of a low achiever changes so that the perceived subjective benefits from a "quality environment" become less costly, then for a given family income, each dollar spent should appear less onerous to the chooser. His or her cost-income coefficient would, accordingly, be less negative. This argument suggests that we adjust the cost-income coefficient away from its negative value, in a positive direction, toward zero.

What if our specifications are biased and the cost-income coefficient is already underestimated? The implication of this possibility on the sensitivity analysis objective of this exercise is that we should see just what the results would be like if this were the case.

Accordingly, we have decided to follow the dictates of both possibilities. In the tables below we have included the series of alternative possibilities discussed in this section. In the first table, Table 17, we present the possibilities for the low achievement group. The presentation of the alternatives is as follows:

1. For comparative purposes the original probability distribution of the lowest ability group is presented for incomes of \$6,000, \$12,000, and \$18,000.
2. An estimate containing only the projected positive movement in the low group's academic-interaction coefficient is then presented. We have moved the coefficient a magnitude of 1.96 times the standard error of the estimates. Unless otherwise commented upon, this magnitude is repeated throughout the exercise.
3. We follow with an estimate containing the positive movement in the academic-interaction coefficient and its possible correlated positive movement in the cost-income coefficient.
4. The final distribution contains the positive movement in the academic-interaction coefficient and the possible negative shift (due to estimate bias) in the cost-income coefficient.

The second and third tables, Tables 18 and 19, present the possibilities of the highest ability group; Table 18 displays the probability distribution for a 575 SAT student, and Table 19 displays the probability distribution of a 650 SAT student. The presentation of the alternatives follows the order of the low achievement group. One slight modification exists. In the third, seventh, and eleventh columns, indicating the possible correlated positive academic-interaction coefficient shift and the positive cost-income coefficient shift, a shift of magnitude 1.96 times the standard error of the cost-income coefficient would

TABLE 17 ***Freshman demand distributions for a 375 SAT student under alternative coefficient estimates***

Y_i	$6,000				$12,000				$18,000			
A_i	375				375				375			
Estimates for γ	−3.592	−3.592	−1.405	−5.779	−3.592	−3.592	−1.405	−5.779	−3.592	−3.592	−1.405	−5.779
Estimates for α	−.0328	−.01762	−.01762	−.01762	−.0328	−.01762	−.01762	−.01762	−.0328	−.01762	−.01762	−.01762
Column	(1)	(2)	(3)	(4)	(5)	(6)	(7)	(8)	(9)	(10)	(11)	(12)
1	.642	.566	.486	.623	.581	.502	.454	.543	.556	.477	.443	.508
2	.271	.329	.314	.325	.268	.318	.303	.326	.264	.311	.299	.319
3												
4												
5	.086	.105	.200	.052	.151	.180	.242	.131	.180	.212	.258	.173
6												
7												
8												
9												
10												

TABLE 18 ***Freshman demand distributions for a 575 SAT student under alternative coefficient estimates***

Y_i	$6,000				$12,000				$18,000			
A_i	575				575				575			
Estimates for γ	−1.031	−1.031	.0000	−2.185	−1.031	−1.031	.0000	−2.185	−1.031	−1.031	.0000	−2.185
Estimates for α	.0211	.0294	.0294	.0294	.0211	.0294	.0294	.0294	.0211	.0294	.0294	.0294
Column	(1)	(2)	(3)	(4)	(5)	(6)	(7)	(8)	(9)	(10)	(11)	(12)
1	.026	.012	.010	.015	.023	.011	.010	.012	.022	.010	.009	.011
2	.049	.030	.025	.036	.045	.027	.025	.030	.043	.027	.024	.028
3	.142	.133	.112	.155	.131	.122	.112	.134	.127	.119	.112	.126
4	.239	.277	.239	.316	.223	.258	.239	.279	.217	.252	.239	.266
5	.035	.022	.025	.018	.038	.023	.025	.021	.039	.024	.025	.023
6	.121	.114	.112	.112	.121	.113	.112	.114	.120	.113	.112	.113
7	.205	.237	.239	.227	.206	.239	.239	.237	.206	.239	.239	.238
8	.070	.059	.081	.041	.081	.070	.081	.058	.086	.073	.081	.065
9	.113	.117	.160	.080	.132	.137	.160	.115	.139	.144	.160	.128
10												

TABLE 19 ***Freshman demand distributions for a 650 SAT student under alternative coefficient estimates***

Y_i	*$6,000*				*$12,000*				*$18,000*			
A_i	*650*				*650*				*650*			
Estimates for γ	−1.031	−1.031	.0000	−2.185	−1.031	−1.031	.0000	−2.185	−1.031	−1.031	.0000	−2.185
Estimates for α	.0211	.0294	.0294	.0294	.0211	.0294	.0294	.0294	.0211	.0294	.0294	.0294
Column	(1)	(2)	(3)	(4)	(5)	(6)	(7)	(8)	(9)	(10)	(11)	(12)
1	.015	.005	.004	.008	.013	.004	.004	.005	.012	.004	.004	.005
2	.031	.015	.011	.020	.027	.013	.011	.015	.025	.012	.011	.014
3	.102	.080	.059	.106	.090	.069	.059	.080	.086	.065	.060	.073
4	.184	.184	.140	.237	.164	.161	.140	.186	.157	.154	.140	.170
5	.022	.011	.011	.010	.023	.011	.011	.011	.023	.011	.011	.011
6	.087	.068	.059	.076	.083	.064	.059	.069	.081	.062	.059	.066
7	.158	.157	.140	.171	.152	.149	.140	.158	.150	.146	.140	.153
8	.048	.034	.041	.027	.054	.038	.041	.034	.056	.039	.041	.036
9	.084	.073	.088	.057	.094	.081	.088	.073	.097	.083	.088	.078
10	.269	.373	.448	.289	.301	.411	.448	.368	.312	.423	.448	.395

make this coefficient positive. Now it is entirely possible that higher education could become a "superior" good in the sense that more would be desired if its price were higher, but we believe a zero cost-income coefficient, indicating completely inelastic cost and income elasticities, sufficiently illustrates our objectives.

For the 375 SAT student the main effect of the shifts occurs in going or not going to college. At all income levels the probability of enrollment in an institution of higher education rises with a diminished (less negative) academic-interaction coefficient and with a diminished (less negative) cost-income coefficient. In the case where the interaction coefficient diminishes and the economic coefficient rises (becomes more negative), the net effect (compare columns [1] and [4], [5] and [8], and [9] and [12]) is an increased attendance probability increasing with income.

The magnitude of the probability changes is fairly substantial. Depending on the direction of its movement, the interaction coefficient shift increases higher education attendance by between 3 and 6 percent. For the 575 SAT student, the principal effects of the coefficient shifts are to relocate him or her between institutional types. When only the academic-interaction coefficient rises, enrollment probability rises in the high-quality/low- and medium-cost options: about 4 percent in the state university within commuting distance and about 3½ percent in the state university away from home. When both coefficients shift positively and cost is no object (since the cost-income coefficient is zero), enrollment rises in the high-cost/medium-quality options by between 2 and 5 percentage points. Increasing the negative magnitude of the economic coefficient while increasing the positive magnitude of the achievement coefficient leads to a significant rise in attendance at the local state university—between 5 and 7½ percent—and to a curtailed enrollment in the higher-priced options.

For the 650 SAT student, coefficient shifts dramatically alter enrollment rates in the high-cost/high-quality options. The achievement shift alone causes about an 11 percent enrollment rise. Diminishing the economic coefficient causes an additional increase of between 2½ and 7½ percentage points (larger shifts accompany lower incomes). The combined effect of an increased achievement coefficient and a negatively increased economic coefficient results in an enrollment rise of between 2 and 8½ percent for the high-cost/high-quality option (proportional to income).

Enrollment rates in other school types diminish almost uniformly when only the achievement coefficient shifts—medium-quality and medium-cost options taking their share. Enrollment in the local state university diminishes roughly between 2 and 4½ percent when the economic factor is no longer relevant, but increases again when the economic coefficient rises by roughly the same number of percentage points.

Throughout the reporting of these findings we have illustrated the probabilities of typical students, defined by their ability, their family income, and their feasible sets. In concluding this section, we shall present estimates of the joint probability distribution of postsecondary school choices, together with the corresponding estimates of the number of freshman students by option type.

Three sets of assumptions are required to compute an expected jointly distributed demand for higher education: first, an assumption about the joint distribution of the variables of the model, family income, and student academic ability, over the population; second, a set of assumptions about the coefficients of the model; and third, a set of assumptions about the distribution of the feasible choices throughout the nation.

Regarding the first, we have assumed that family income and student academic ability are bivariate normally distributed. Thus five statistics are necessary to determine this distribution completely—the mean and variance of both variables and the zeroth-order correlation between them.

The Educational Testing Service (College Entrance Examination Board, 1971) reports the following scores for all high school seniors:

	Males		*Females*	
	Verbal	*Math*	*Verbal*	*Math*
Mean	390	422	393	382
Standard deviation	122	130	118	117

Assuming equal numbers of males and females, the mean combined test score is 397, and the mean standard deviation is 121.85. For the record, the mean estimated SAT score for the SCOPE sample was 427.10, and the mean estimated SAT standard deviation was 119.53. For the purposes of the expected demand calculation, we assumed a population SAT mean of 400, with a standard deviation of 120 points.

SCOPE's family-income-reporting population, 1,402 out of 4,434 families, had a mean family income of $14,685.70 and a standard deviation of $15,036.25. We assumed these statistics in the expected demand calculations.

A review of the literature on the relationship between socioeconomic class and ability, reported in Flanagan and Cooley (1966, App. E), shows correlations between variations of the income and ability variables as ranging from .20 to .47. For Project TALENT data, Flanagan and Cooley reported zeroth-order correlations between 25 social-class measures and 14 ability test scores. The correlation values range from less than .10 to a maximum of .35. Their reported correlation between family income and the closest tests in Project TALENT to the SAT tests are .11 for their English total and .14 for their mathematics total. Family income here is a student-answered, multiple-choice, income-range question. Our analysis of the SCOPE data, as we reported earlier in Chapter 3, led us to be skeptical of family-income data secured in this manner, but as will become evident later, this skepticism is unwarranted with respect to correlations.

Further evidence is cited by Jewett (1971), who reports references to the College Scholarship Service's correlations between socioeconomic class and ability in the .35-to-.40 range.

The SCOPE parent reporters in our sample had a correlation of .10 between average SAT and family income and a correlation of .17 between average SAT and predicted income.

We decided to explore the consequences of two correlation values in the expected demand calculations: a minimum value of .10, which should reflect the actual income-ability correlation, and a maximum value of .40, which might reflect the maximum possible social-class–ability correlation. To anticipate, results were hardly affected by the alternative possibilities.

TABLE 20 ***Coefficients used in demand projections***

Case	*1*		*2*		*3*		*4*	
Evaluation points	γ	α	γ	α	γ	α	γ	α
	Cost-income	*Academic-interaction*	*Cost-income*	*Academic-interaction*	*Cost-income*	*Academic-interaction*	*Cost-income*	*Academic-interaction*
300,375	−3.592	−.0328	−3.592	−.01762	−1.405	−.01762	−5.779	−.01762
425	−2.450	−.00244	−2.450	−.001762	−.09583	−.001762	−3.942	−.001762
475	−2.407	−.00285	−2.407	.0000	−.09414	.0000	−4.476	.0000
525	−2.364	−.00325	−2.364	.00294	−.09246	.00294	−5.010	.00294
575,625	−1.031	.0211	−1.031	.0294	.0000	.0294	−2.185	.0294

A second set of assumptions is concerned with which coefficients should be used in the demand model. In the preceding pages we have presented alternative sets of coefficients for the lowest and highest ability groups, to which we shall hereafter refer by the following four case numbers: (1) the estimated values, (2) a set containing the estimated cost-income coefficients and positively shifted academic-interaction coefficients, (3) a set in which all coefficients are positively shifted, and (4) a set containing negatively shifted cost-income coefficients and positively shifted academic-interaction coefficients. As part of our sensitivity analysis we shall compute the estimated expected demand for all four sets of coefficients. Thus two values for the correlation coefficients and four values for the demand coefficients will result in eight sets of expected demand distribution estimates.

To account for shifts in the coefficients for the medium-low and medium-high ability groups, additional assumptions were necessary. We assumed that the academic-interaction coefficients for the medium-low and medium-high ability groups would be one order of magnitude less in absolute value than the corresponding coefficients of the low and high groups, respectively. We also assumed that the 475 SAT person, an individual midway between the two groups, would have a zero academic-interaction coefficient. All the academic-interaction coefficient shifts contain these values.

In case 3, where the cost-income coefficients shift positively, we assumed that the intermediate ability groups' shifts were proportional to the lowest ability group's cost-income coefficient shift. In case 4, where the cost-income coefficients shift negatively, we assumed that the shifts of the coefficients for the intermediate ability groups were proportional to those of the highest ability group.

Demand was evaluated at seven ability levels. Table 20 indicates the coefficient values at each level for each case.

In addition, demand was evaluated at 10 income levels, making 70 ability-income "regions" in all. Figure 8 indicates the income- and ability-variable ranges and their points of evaluation in the demand function.

Finally, we shall consider our assumptions about the national distribution of the alternative IHEs available to the population. It should be noted that our results derive from samples in which

FIGURE 8 ***Evaluation points for 70 achievement-income regions***

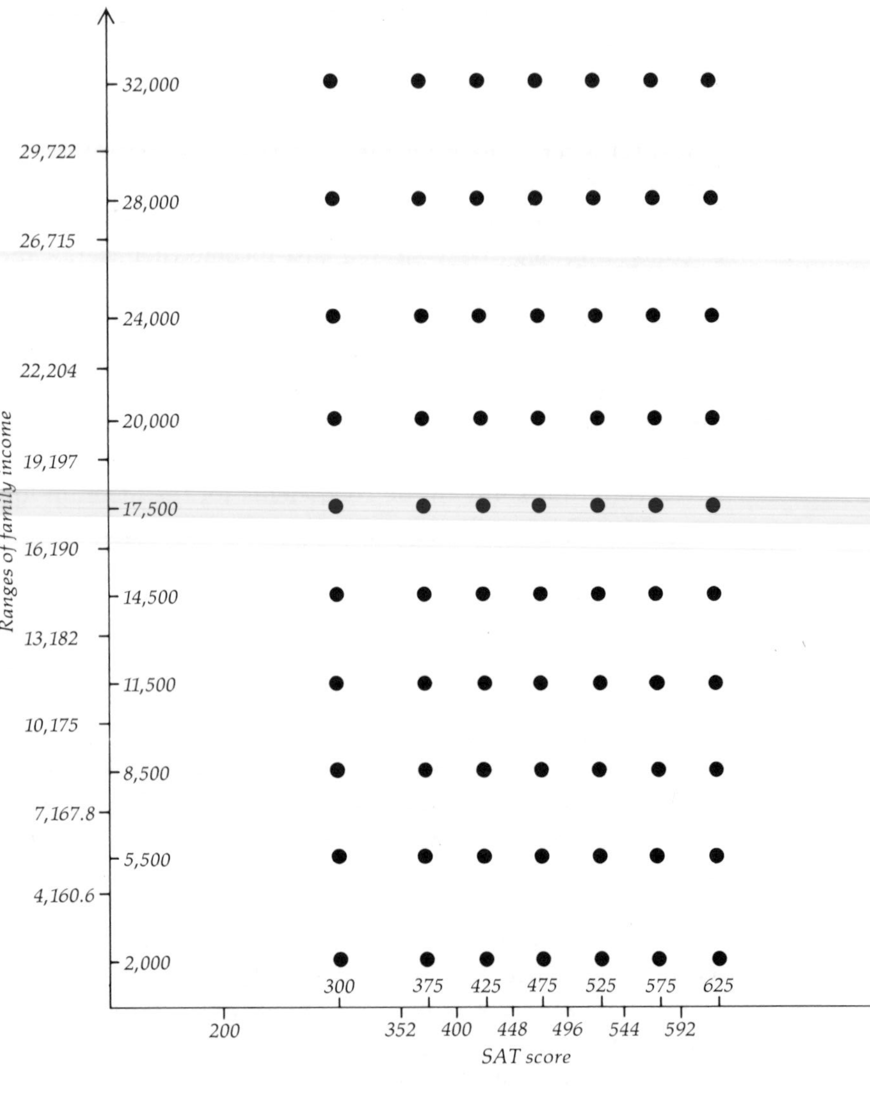

over 95 percent of the students had local community college options in their feasible choice sets. Consequently, our demand characteristics reflect a population already meeting the Carnegie Commission's recommendation that by 1980, 95 percent of all Americans be within commuting distance of a community college (Carnegie Commission on Higher Education, 1972).

Following the 1970 census (U.S. Bureau of the Census, 1971

Part A, Table 4, pp. 1–43), we assumed that the 31.5 percent of the population living in urban areas had the three public quality options in their feasible sets and that the 26.8 percent of the population living in urban-fringe areas had state college and community college options in their feasible sets. The remaining rural population was divided into two groups. Incorporating the Carnegie Commission's recommendation that 95 percent of the population be within commuting distance of a community college by 1980, we divided the remaining 41.7 percent of the population into a 36.7 percent semirural group having a community college within commuting distance of their homes and a 5 percent rural group without any public IHEs within commuting distance of their homes.

We computed the distribution of the expected demand in the following manner:

1. We evaluated the model at every ability, income, and regional specification. These demand distributions were weighted by the regional population weights and regionally summed to yield a regionally weighted distribution by ability and income.
2. These regionally weighted ability-income demand distributions were then weighted by the income-ability density function and were then summed to yield a population-weighted demand distribution.
3. This distribution was then normalized to yield what we have called the *expected value of demand.*

The four cases of alternative demand coefficients and the two cases of alternative zeroth-order correlations result in eight sets of expected demand probability distributions. These results appear in Table 21.

Very little variation in the expected demand probability distribution is introduced by increasing the correlation between income and ability from .10 to .40; since this correlation assumption proves not to be critical, further discussion will be restricted to cases 1 through 4, where the income-ability interaction correlation is .10.

All positive shifts in coefficients result in increased enrollment. The positive shift in the academic-interaction coefficient alone increased enrollment by 11 percent (compare case 2 and case 1), and the combined positive shifts increased enrollment by a total of 27 percent (compare case 3 and case 1). It appears

TABLE 21 ***Expected demand probability distributions***

Case		1	2	3	4
		Coefficient description			
	γ	*Estimates*	*Estimates*	*Positive shift*	*Negative shift*
	α	*Estimates*	*Positive shift*	*Positive shift*	*Positive shift*
Type $\rho Y,A=.1$					
1		.401	.358	.292	.401
2		.207	.222	.202	.225
3		.048	.049	.039	.053
4		.012	.013	.011	.015
5		.115	.121	.165	.098
6		.068	.070	.073	.065
7		.038	.045	.044	.044
8		.044	.044	.068	.035
9		.049	.052	.077	.042
10		.019	.025	.028	.022

that a shift in the academic-interaction coefficient is about as enrollment effective as a shift in the cost-income coefficient (given the estimates and their standard errors). It is not surprising, then, that when the two shifts are placed in opposition, as in case 4, the net result of the increase in enrollment caused by the interaction coefficient's shift and the decrease in enrollment caused by the economic coefficient's shift was to cancel each other out (compare case 4 and case 1).

The largest enrollment shift caused by the academic coefficient shift alone was from not going to enrolling in a local junior college, a shift of 1½ percentage points. Increases in the medium-cost/low- and high-quality options, and the high-cost/high-quality options were all on the order of ½ percentage point as well. The principal result of adding the positive shift in the cost-income coefficient onto the already positively shifted academic coefficient was to shift enrollment from the low-cost options

Case		5	6	7	8
		Coefficient description			
	γ	*Estimates*	*Estimates*	*Positive shift*	*Negative shift*
	α	*Estimates*	*Positive shift*	*Positive shift*	*Positive shift*
Type $\rho Y,A=.4$					
1		.401	.359	.296	.400
2		.203	.219	.203	.219
3		.046	.048	.039	.051
4		.011	.013	.011	.014
5		.111	.115	.159	.094
6		.069	.071	.073	.067
7		.038	.045	.044	.044
8		.048	.048	.068	.039
9		.053	.057	.078	.047
10		.020	.027	.028	.025

to the high-cost options. For example, in the low-cost/low- and medium-quality options, enrollment decreased by 2 and 1 percent, respectively, and in the medium-cost/low-quality and high-cost/low- and medium-quality options, increased by 4½, 2½, and 2½ percentage points, respectively (compare case 3 and case 2).

The reallocative effects of the negative shift in the economic coefficient can be ascertained by comparing case 2 with case 4. This comparison shows that enrollment in the medium- and high-cost/low- and medium-quality options declined by a total of about 5 percentage points and the not-going option gained by about 5 percentage points.

The multiplication of these expected demand probability distributions by a projection of the potential United States college attenders results in projected expected enrollment distributions for the postsecondary school options. In Table 22

TABLE 22 ***Projected freshman demand for United States higher education (in thousands)***

1975 3,435.7 high school graduates

Case	*1*	*2*	*3*	*4*
		Coefficient description		
γ	*Estimates*	*Estimates*	*Positive shift*	*Negative shift*
α	*Estimates*	*Positive shift*	*Positive shift*	*Positive shift*
Type				
1	1,377.7	1,230.0	1,003.2	1,377.7
2	711.2	762.7	694.0	773.0
3	164.9	168.3	134.0	182.1
4	41.2	44.7	37.8	51.5
5	395.1	415.7	566.9	336.7
6	233.6	240.5	250.8	223.3
7	130.6	154.6	151.2	151.2
8	151.2	151.2	233.6	120.2
9	168.3	178.7	264.5	144.3
10	65.3	85.9	96.2	75.6

1980 3,602.6 high school graduates

Case	*1*	*2*	*3*	*4*
		Coefficient description		
γ	*Estimates*	*Estimates*	*Positive shift*	*Negative shift*
α	*Estimates*	*Positive shift*	*Positive shift*	*Positive shift*
Type				
1	1,444.6	1,289.7	1,052.0	1,444.6
2	745.7	799.8	727.7	810.6
3	172.9	176.5	140.5	190.9
4	43.2	46.8	39.6	54.0
5	414.3	435.9	594.4	353.1
6	245.0	252.2	263.0	234.2
7	136.9	162.1	158.5	158.5
8	158.5	158.5	245.0	126.1
9	176.5	187.3	277.4	151.3
10	68.4	90.1	100.9	79.3

TABLE 22 (continued)

1985 3,135.2 high school graduates

Case		1	2	3	4
			Coefficient description		
	γ	*Estimates*	*Estimates*	*Positive shift*	*Negative shift*
	α	*Estimates*	*Positive shift*	*Positive shift*	*Positive shift*
Type					
1		1,257.2	1,122.4	915.5	1,257.2
2		649.0	696.0	633.3	705.4
3		150.5	153.6	122.3	166.2
4		37.6	40.8	34.5	47.0
5		360.5	379.4	517.3	307.2
6		213.2	219.5	228.9	203.8
7		119.1	141.1	137.9	137.9
8		137.9	137.9	213.2	109.7
9		153.6	163.0	241.4	131.7
10		59.6	78.4	87.8	69.0

1990 3,305.4 high school graduates

Case		1	2	3	4
			Coefficient description		
	γ	*Estimates*	*Estimates*	*Positive shift*	*Negative shift*
	α	*Estimates*	*Positive shift*	*Positive shift*	*Positive shift*
Type					
1		1,325.5	1,183.3	965.2	1,325.5
2		684.2	733.8	667.7	743.7
3		158.7	162.0	128.9	175.2
4		39.7	43.0	36.4	49.6
5		380.1	400.0	545.4	323.9
6		224.8	231.4	241.3	214.9
7		125.6	148.7	145.4	145.9
8		145.4	145.4	224.8	115.7
9		162.0	171.9	254.5	138.8
10		62.8	82.6	92.6	72.7

TABLE 22 (Continued)

1995 3,736 high school graduates

Case		1	2	3	4
			Coefficient description		
	γ	*Estimates*	*Estimates*	*Positive shift*	*Negative shift*
	α	*Estimates*	*Positive shift*	*Positive shift*	*Positive shift*
Type					
1		1,498.1	1,337.0	1,090.9	1,498.1
2		773.4	829.4	754.7	840.6
3		179.3	183.1	145.7	198.0
4		44.8	48.6	41.1	56.0
5		429.6	452.1	616.4	366.1
6		254.0	261.5	272.7	242.8
7		142.0	168.1	164.4	164.4
8		164.4	164.4	254.0	130.8
9		183.1	194.3	287.7	156.9
10		71.0	93.4	104.6	82.2

2000 4,172.1 high school graduates

Case		1	2	3	4
			Coefficient description		
	γ	*Estimates*	*Estimates*	*Positive shift*	*Negative shift*
	α	*Estimates*	*Positive shift*	*Positive shift*	*Positive shift*
Type					
1		1,673.0	1,493.6	1,218.3	1,673.0
2		863.6	926.2	842.8	938.7
3		200.3	204.4	162.7	221.1
4		50.1	54.2	45.9	62.6
5		479.8	504.8	688.4	408.9
6		283.7	292.0	304.6	271.2
7		158.5	187.7	183.6	183.6
8		183.6	183.6	283.7	146.0
9		204.4	216.9	321.3	175.2
10		79.3	104.3	116.8	91.8

we present such results. To produce this table, we multiplied the expected probability demand distributions for cases 1 through 4, presented in the previous table, by Haggstrom's projections of the number of United States high school graduates (see Chapter 11, Tables 93A–93C). The calculations have been performed for the years 1975 through 2000 at five-year intervals. Case 1 projections, those based on the estimated coefficients, are appropriate for 1966 estimates. A rereading of the earlier arguments of this section should suggest that, in our opinion, the more time that elapses since 1966, the further the demand model should move from the case 1 projections toward the case 3 projections. The rate of movement is of course speculative.

5. *Alternative Specifications of Demand*

The two preceding chapters focused on the implications of our demand estimates based on the best specifications and economic data available to us. In this chapter we present estimates based on other demand specifications and data. In Chapter 3 we went into considerable detail reporting the estimates of the cost-income and academic-interaction coefficients for a sample of SCOPE students whose parents reported their incomes. Here we shall present estimates for a sample of SCOPE students whose parents did not report their incomes. This group of students will be referred to as sample I, and the group of students whose families reported income will be referred to as sample II. We also include in this chapter a comparison of the alternative results and a brief discussion of our experiments with alternative measures of the cost-income variable.

5.1. PREDICTED INCOME

Our economic data were incomplete. The population that reported their family income tested higher in achievement and had higher family incomes than the population that did not report their family income. (Chapter 3 and Miller and Radner, 1975, report this condition in greater detail.) We thought that the very fact that parents responded to the SCOPE questionnaire probably indicated greater average interest on the part of the parents in their children's educational career, and we believed that this interest resulted in a higher demand for postsecondary schooling for their children. That is, the demand estimates reported in Chapter 3 are higher than the demand for higher education that actually exists in the whole population. This concern led us to decide to estimate demand for both the income-reporting families and the families that failed to report their income.

Since we believed that income was a major explainer of higher education demand, we needed an estimate of income for the nonreporting population. Analysis of the income biases had already convinced us that the student self-reported estimate was unreliable (see Chapter 3, Tables 2 and 3).

We began the determination of the income predictor with a rather simple linear income model in mind. The observations would be the 1,402 out of 4,434 families (31.6 percent) that responded to the parent follow-up questionnaire. As a dependent variable, the parent-reported income would be used. Information contained in the twelfth-grade questionnaire would be used for the independent variables. Since this information was available for all the observations, a predictor equation, coupled with this questionnaire information, would yield an estimated income for the entire sample.

The independent-variable information was in multiple-choice format. Consequently, the linear predictor model was amenable to the statistical methods of the analysis of variance. But, because the regression and the analysis-of-variance model can be made equivalent[1] and because it was computationally more convenient for us to use a regression specification, we did indeed treat the linear predictor problem as a regression analysis problem. The distributional ranking of the parent-reported income was eventually used as the dependent variable in the predicted-income model. It took continuous values. The independent data used in the prediction were:

1. Parents' occupations
2. Parents' education within occupational categories
3. Parents' employment status within occupational categories
4. Students' self-reporting of their family income

We were able to explain 45 percent of the variance in percentile ranking, and given the distribution of reported income, we were able to convert predicted percentile ranking into predicted dollar income, which is denoted *YH* in the demand results to follow.

Although an R^2 of .45 compares very favorably with a similar

[1]This equivalence of models is discussed in the context of the detailed procedures and results in Miller and Radner (1975).

type of investigation conducted by Morgan et al. (1962), it is difficult to judge the quality of the predictor model on the basis of the R^2 statistic alone. More appropriate statistics for judging the quality of the model are presented in the table below, which includes the sample's mean and standard deviation of the linear model's predicted errors, for both the entire sample and the lower 90 percent of the sample, in percentile-ranking values and in dollar values.

Comparison of the sample's statistics with the linear model's statistics indicates that the linear model's estimate of percentile ranking has a standard deviation 6½ points lower than the sample's value. Or, to put it another way, using the linear model for estimating income percentile reduces the sample's variance by roughly 25 percent over using the sample's mean value for the income-percentile estimate. What do these figures mean in dollar terms? When the entire sample is considered and the predicted percentile rank has been converted into dollar terms, the predicted dollar value understates the reported value by a little over $2,000 on the average. It does this with considerable variation, as its standard deviation is over $13,000. If we exclude that portion of the sample with the greatest anticipated variation, namely, the upper 10 percent of the income distribution ($25,000 and over), the predicted dollar value overstates the reported value by only about $450, on the average, and the

TABLE 23 ***Percentile distribution of SCOPE reported family income***

Percentile rank	*Reported family income*
0	0
10	5,503
20	7,412
30	8,979
40	10,103
50	11,348
60	12,621
70	14,857
80	17,825
90	24,940
100	160,000

FIGURE 9 ***Log reported income versus income percentile ranking***

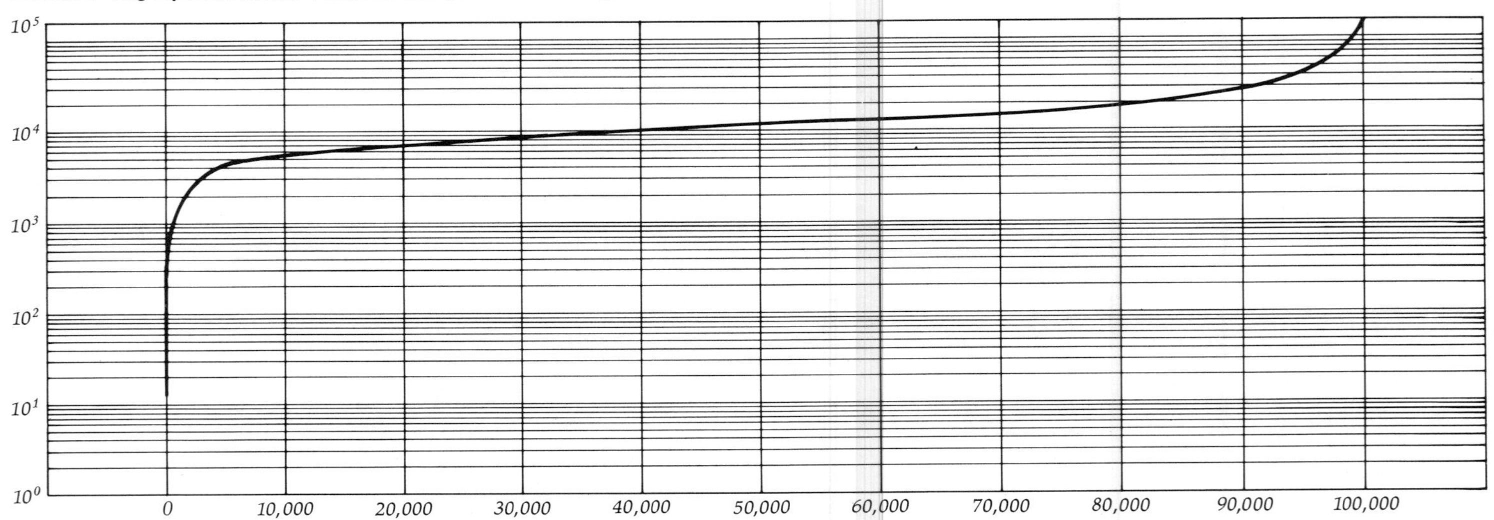

SOURCE: Table 23.

standard deviation of this predicted dollar value is reduced to only 20 percent of the dollar range being considered, a little over $5,000.

Summary statistics

	Percentile	*Dollars*
Sample mean	50.03	
Sample standard deviation	28.87	
Expected error of linear predictor	−.28	2,181.89
Standard deviation of linear predictor	22.29	13,180.23
Expected error of linear predictor excluding top 10% (dollar values $25,000 and greater)	−2.98	−442.54
Standard deviation of same observations	20.91	5,310.08

5.2. SPECIFICATION VARIATION

Two variations of our original cost-income ratio were also tried. First, rather than use either income or predicted income in the cost-income ratio, we developed a simplified measure of a family's discretionary income, a concept like that used by the College Scholarship Service (C.S.S.) to estimate the financial ability of families to pay for higher education. We based these measures on an estimate of the family size of each student and the C.S.S. published tables.

When we reported our first results, we were often criticized by our colleagues for using a measure of direct cost rather than one of total cost—that is, direct plus opportunity cost. In trying to attend to this objection, we found that, on the one hand, it was impossible to estimate each individual's separate opportunity cost. On the other hand, we agreed that the real cost differences, especially between the collection of choices that represented going on to college and not going, were inadequately represented in our formulation. Attempting to rectify this deficiency, we added $3,000 to the cost of each higher education choice for each person in our demand samples.

It is interesting to note that these more complicated formulations of the cost-income ratio, basically representing the ability of a student to pay for higher education, did *not* do a better job of explaining higher education choice than the more direct cost-income or cost/predicted-income measure. A complete exposition of the estimates of these exploratory cost-income specifications appears in Miller and Radner (1975).

5.3. RESULTS AND COMPARISONS

With four ability groups, two samples, and two ways of measuring income in sample II, we had 12 possible two-variable specifications of the demand function. The estimates of the cost-income coefficients were negative in all 12 cases and were statistically different from zero in 10 of them. The estimates of the academic-interaction coefficients were enlightening. In both samples, these estimates were (1) negative and statistically significant for the lowest ability group, (2) positive and significant for the highest ability group, and (3) sometimes positive, sometimes negative, sometimes significant, and sometimes not significant for the two intermediate ability groups.[2] These results appear in Table 24.

The observed relative frequencies of the choice types are compared with the predicted relative frequencies from the 12 demand models in Tables 25 through 28. Unfortunately, statistical tests of significance were not available for comparing predicted and observed relative frequencies in this situation. Nevertheless, the tables do give some idea of whether the predicted probability distributions resemble the observed relative frequencies.

One interesting point is that we anticipated that sample II would have a higher demand for higher education than sample I. This anticipation seems to be confirmed in every achievement group.

In the tables to follow, estimates based on sample II demand models with reported income are denoted IIR, and estimates based on sample II demand models with predicted income are denoted IIP. The sample I models obviously use predicted income, and estimates based on them are denoted IP.

To measure the relative ability of the 12 models to predict the corresponding observed relative frequencies, we computed chi-squared goodness-of-fit statistics using somewhat aggregated feasible choice sets. These figures are reported in Table 29. The

[2]In extrapolations of our demand model to other populations, there might not be sufficient information about all the variables included in our basic specification. For this reason, we included in Chap. 3 the estimates of coefficients in various single-variable demand specifications, for sample II. The corresponding estimates for sample I are reported in Miller and Radner (1975).

TABLE 24 ***Demand coefficient estimates by academic-ability group***

	Sample	Academic interaction	C/Y	C/YH
	II	$-.328 \times 10^{-1}$*	−3.592†	
SAT < 400		($.774 \times 10^{-2}$)	(1.116)	
162 observations	II	$-.503 \times 10^{-1}$†		−.392
		($.660 \times 10^{-2}$)		(.537)
	I	$-.438 \times 10^{-1}$)*		−9.593†
		($.119 \times 10^{-1}$)		(2.460)
	II	$-.244 \times 10^{-2}$	−2.450†	
SAT ⩾ 400		($.557 \times 10^{-2}$)	(.907)	
SAT < 475	II	$.130 \times 10^{-1}$†		−9.431†
84 observations		($.673 \times 10^{-2}$)		(1.874)
	I	$-.460 \times 10^{-1}$†		$.551 \times 10^{-1}$
		($.575 \times 10^{-2}$)		(.536)
	II	$-.325 \times 10^{-2}$	−2.364†	
SAT ⩾ 475		($.476 \times 10^{-2}$)	(1.037)	
SAT < 550	II	$.289 \times 10^{-2}$)		−6.514†
72 observations		($.515 \times 10^{-2}$)		(1.894)
	I	$.148 \times 10^{-1}$*		−9.704*
		($.514 \times 10^{-2}$)		(.125)
	II	$.211 \times 10^{-1}$*	−1.031†	
		($.423 \times 10^{-2}$)	(.589)	
SAT ⩾ 550	II	$.232 \times 10^{-1}$*		−3.873†
57 observations		($.451 \times 10^{-2}$)		(1.735)
	I	$.224 \times 10^{-1}$*		−8.787*
		($.486 \times 10^{-2}$)		(2.319)

*Significant at the .01 level.

†Significant at the .05 level.

TABLE 25 ***Observed and predicted relative frequencies, high academic-ability group***

	Sample II			*Sample I*	
Type	*Observed relative frequency*	*Predicted relative frequency with reported income*	*Predicted relative frequency with predicted income*	*Observed relative frequency*	*Predicted relative frequency with predicted income*
1	.0877	.0294	.0292	.1739	.0673
2	.0877	.0559	.0622	.1304	.0999
3	.0877	.0715	.0779	.0435	.1453
4	.0000	.0435	.0572	.0217	.0842
5	.0351	.0584	.0571	.0217	.0710
6	.1579	.1336	.1404	.1739	.1090
7	.1404	.2035	.2268	.1304	.2095
8	.0175	.0006	.0004	.0000	.0000
9	.0526	.1751	.1458	.0217	.1014
10	.3333	.2285	.2031	.2826	.1124

TABLE 26 ***Observed and predicted relative frequencies, medium-high academic-ability group***

	Sample II			*Sample I*	
Type	*Observed relative frequency*	*Predicted relative frequency with reported income*	*Predicted relative frequency with predicted income*	*Observed relative frequency*	*Predicted relative frequency with predicted income*
1	.1806	.2398	.2432	.2836	.176
2	.2500	.1692	.1905	.1194	.1772
3	.0556	.0700	.0945	.0296	.1535
4	.0556	.0201	.0311	.0149	.0294
5	.1806	.1676	.1492	.1045	.0995
6	.1667	.1288	.1216	.1343	.1527
7	.0417	.0519	.0643	.1791	.1020
8	.0278	.0021	.0013	.0000	.0000
9	.0139	.1314	.0901	.0597	.0884
10	.0278	.0191	.0142	.0746	.0208

TABLE 27 ***Observed and predicted relative frequencies, medium-low academic-ability group***

	Sample II			*Sample I*	
Type	*Observed relative frequency*	*Predicted relative frequency with reported income*	*Predicted relative frequency with predicted income*	*Observed relative frequency*	*Predicted relative frequency with predicted income*
1	.2024	.2641	.2705	.5544	.5175
2	.3452	.1831	.2241	.1957	.1729
3	.0595	.0872	.1542	.0217	.0178
4	.0119	.0028	.0056	.0109	.0001
5	.1786	.1501	.1109	.0978	.1862
6	.1310	.1455	.1379	.0544	.0504
7	.0119	.0084	.0121	.0000	.0001
8	.0119	.0027	.0011	.0326	.0034
9	.0238	.1499	.0799	.0326	.0510
10	.0238	.0063	.0037	.0000	.0007

TABLE 28 ***Observed and predicted relative frequencies, low academic-ability group***

	Sample II			*Sample I*	
Type	*Observed relative frequency*	*Predicted relative frequency with reported income*	*Predicted relative frequency with predicted income*	*Observed relative frequency*	*Predicted relative frequency with predicted income*
1	.5617	.5134	.4940	.7744	.6828
2	.1728	.2304	.2050	.1281	.2046
3	.0370	.0160	.0103	.0122	.0120
4	.0000	.0002	.0001	.0000	.0000
5	.1420	.1549	.1925	.0366	.0729
6	.0309	.0384	.0374	.0366	.0192
7	.0000	.0001	.0001	.0000	.0000
8	.0247	.0028	.0066	.0061	.0003
9	.0247	.0433	.0537	.0061	.0083
10	.0062	.0005	.0003	.0000	.0000

TABLE 29 ***Goodness of fit of alternative models, chi-squared statistics***

Ability group	*IIR*	*IIP*	*IP*	*Degrees of freedom*	*Aggregation of choice sets*
High	16.815	18.513	29.415	6	4 7 10
	(.01)				3 6 9
					1 2 5 8
Medium-high	8.819	6.226	14.895	6	4 7 10
	(.10)	(.30)	(.02)		3 6 9
					1 2 5 8
Medium-low	19.335	15.172	5.685	5	4 7 10
	(.001)	(.01)	(.30)		3 6 9
					1 2 5 8
Low	2.256	3.897	7.514	3	4 7 10
	(.50)	(.20)	(.05)		3 6 9
					1 2 5 8

NOTE: ( ) denotes α level of χ^2. These significance levels are those which would be appropriate if the standard chi-squared goodness-of-fit test were appropriate. There is no theoretical justification for this in the present case. Therefore, the indicated chi-squared statistics and their accompanying significance levels are to be interpreted as rough guides for the relative goodness of fit of the models.

significance levels accompanying these chi-squared statistics are those which would be appropriate if the standard chi-squared goodness-of-fit test were appropriate. For example, the chi-squared statistic of 16.815 (with 6 degrees of freedom) for the high-ability IIR demand model would normally indicate that there was only 1 chance in 100 that the IIR demand model was the true demand model for the high ability group. There is no theoretical justification for this interpretation in the present case. Therefore, the chi-squared statistics or their accompanying significance levels are to be interpreted as rough guides for the relative goodness of fit of the three competing models in each ability group.

No sample dominates in its ease of explanation. Nor, for that matter, does any model prove to be always superior to the others. The best model varies by ability group. In the high, medium-high, and low ability groups the observed data are better described in sample II. In the medium-low ability group the fit is best in sample I. In the highest and lowest ability groups the reported-income model is superior to the predicted-income model, while in the two middle ability groups the predicted-income models are superior. To summarize, the IIR model is best for the high ability group, the IIP model is best for the medium-high ability group, the IP model is best for the medium-low ability group, and the IIR model is best for the low ability group.

In Tables 30 through 32 we have used the demand models to predict the probability distributions of choices for representative types of high school seniors. Twelve types are depicted in the tables. The tables illustrate three income levels—$6,000, $12,000, and $18,000—and for each income level, four student ability levels are illustrated. More specifically, students with Scholastic Aptitude Test scores of 375, 475, 575, and 650 are illustrated. The specific demand models we used are straightforward for all but the 475 students; that is, the 375 SAT students use the lowest academic-ability group's models, etc. The 475 students use a demand model that averages the coefficient estimates for the two middle ability groups. Statistical significance was not considered here.

As was true in the case of the observed relative frequencies, the predicted choice probability for a sample II senior is always greater than the predicted choice probability for a sample I senior. The two sample II distributions are remarkably similar.

One begins to wonder how the various distributions depend on variations in the variables of the specifications. For example, it seems, from Tables 30 through 32, that the IIP models are more sensitive to variations in income levels. For a more exacting appreciation of the relative sensitivity of changes in the demand for the various options to changes in the determinants of demand, we include Tables 33 through 36, which contain the calculated elasticities of the probability of each of the choices with respect to changes in the models' variables for a $12,000-family-income student.

Table 33 contains the ability elasticities. Nine demand models are illustrated in the table—the IIR, the IIP, and the IP samples and the four ability models within each sample. Repulsion from better-quality schools due to individual gains in academic ability among the lower ability group appears most strongly in the IIP models and least strongly in the IP models. The results of the 475 SAT students' elasticities are somewhat

TABLE 30 ***Sample probability comparison, \$6,000 income***

	Sample II, R				*Sample II, P*				*Sample I, P*			
Y	*\$6,000*											
A	*375*	*475*	*575*	*650*	*375*	*475*	*575*	*650*	*375*	*475*	*575*	*650*
Estimates for γ	-3.592	-2.407	-1.031	-1.031	$-.392$	-7.972	-3.873	-3.873	-9.593	-4.820	-8.787	-8.787
Estimates for α	$-.0328$	$-.0028$	$.0211$	$.0211$	$-.0503$	$.00795$	$.0232$	$.0232$	$-.0438$	$-.0156$	$.0224$	$.0224$
1	.642	.260	.026	.015	.609	.305	.037	.024	.792	.486	.073	.055
2	.271	.214	.049	.031	.208	.256	.064	.046	.199	.254	.098	.082
3		.182	.142	.102		.310	.196	.166		.120	.262	.255
4			.239	.184			.326	.298			.381	.399
5	.086	.100	.035	.022	.183	.020	.019	.014	.009	.055	.006	.005
6		.127	.121	.087		.094	.109	.093		.058	.070	.068
7			.205	.158			.182	.167			.102	.107
8		.061	.070	.048		.007	.025	.020		.015	.003	.003
9		.057	.113	.084		.008	.042	.037		.011	.006	.006
10				.269				.134				.020

TABLE 31 ***Sample probability comparison, \$12,000 income***

	Sample II, R				*Sample II, P*				*Sample I, P*			
A	*375*	*475*	*575*	*650*	*375*	*475*	*575*	*650*	*375*	*475*	*575*	*650*
Estimates for γ	*−3.592*	*−2.407*	*−1.031*	*−1.031*	*−.392*	*−7.972*	*−3.873*	*−3.873*	*−9.593*	*−4.820*	*−8.787*	*−8.787*
Estimates for α	*−.0328*	*−.0028*	*.0211*	*.0211*	*−.0503*	*.00795*	*.0232*	*.0232*	*−.0438*	*−.0156*	*.0224*	*.0224*
1	.581	.212	.023	.013	.599	.209	.026	.015	.722	.393	.043	.029
2	.268	.185	.045	.027	.207	.213	.050	.032	.229	.231	.071	.053
3		.160	.131	.090		.278	.159	.118		.114	.205	.180
4			.223	.164			.277	.223			.331	.313
5	.151	.126	.038	.023	.194	.060	.027	.017	.050	.107	.017	.013
6		.134	.121	.083		.153	.119	.089		.080	.106	.093
7			.206	.152			.207	.167			.171	.162
8		.094	.081	.054		.040	.050	.036		.043	.021	.018
9		.089	.132	.094		.047	.085	.066		.032	.035	.031
10				.301				.237				.108

TABLE 32 ***Sample probability comparison, $18,000 income***

	Sample II, R				*Sample II, P*				*Sample I, P*			
Y	*$18,000*											
A	*375*	*475*	*575*	*650*	*375*	*475*	*575*	*650*	*375*	*475*	*575*	*650*
Estimates for γ	*−3.592*	*−2.407*	*−1.031*	*−1.031*	*−.392*	*−7.972*	*−3.873*	*−3.873*	*−9.593*	*−4.820*	*−8.787*	*−8.787*
Estimates for α	*−.0328*	*−.0028*	*.0211*	*.0211*	*−.0503*	*.00795*	*.0232*	*−.0232*	*−.0438*	*−.0156*	*.0224*	*.0224*
1	.556	.195	.022	.012	.596	.172	.023	.013	.683	.355	.034	.021
2	.264	.174	.043	.025	.206	.187	.045	.027	.233	.217	.060	.042
3		.152	.127	.086		.249	.145	.103		.109	.179	.145
4			.217	.157			.257	.196			.299	.261
5	.180	.135	.039	.023	.198	.080	.030	.018	.084	.130	.024	.017
6		.135	.120	.081		.168	.120	.084		.086	.116	.094
7			.206	.150			.212	.162			.193	.168
8		.107	.086	.056		.067	.062	.042		.059	.036	.028
9		.102	.139	.097		.078	.105	.077		.044	.060	.050
10				.312				.278				.173

TABLE 33 ***Ability elasticities for a $12,000-family-income student***

	Sample II, R				Sample II, P				Sample I, P			
Y	*$12,000*											
A	*375*	*475*	*575*	*650*	*375*	*475*	*575*	*650*	*375*	*475*	*575*	*650*
Estimates for α	−.0328	−.0028	.0211	.0211	−.0503	.00795	.0232	.0232	−.0438	−.0156	.0224	.0224
1	.289	.117	−1.872	−2.555	.423	−.342	−2.09	−2.43	.213	.426	−1.98	−2.45
2	4.400	.041	−1.192	−1.786	−.633	−.131	−1.35	−1.68	−.534	.013	−1.26	−1.63
3		−.079	−.113	−.566		.205	−.160	−.491		−.646	−.114	−.336
4			.433	.051			.440	.109			.466	.319
5	−.400	.041	−1.193	−1.786	−.633	−.131	−1.35	−1.68	−.534	.013	−1.26	−1.63
6		−.079	−.113	−.566		.205	−.160	−.491		−.646	−.114	−.336
7			.433	.051			.440	.109			.466	.319
8		−.053	−.343	−.826		.134	−.413	−.745		−.505	−.359	−.612
9		−.107	.142	−.278		.285	.120	−.211		−.802	.157	−.30
10				.888				.923				1.21

TABLE 34 ***Income elasticities for a $12,000-family-income student***

	Sample II, R				Sample II, P				Sample I, P			
Y	*$12,000*											
A	*375*	*475*	*575*	*650*	*375*	*475*	*575*	*650*	*375*	*475*	*575*	*650*
Estimates for γ	*−3.592*	*−2.407*	*−1.031*	*−1.031*	*−.392*	*−7.972*	*−3.873*	*−3.873*	*−9.593*	*−4.820*	*−8.787*	*−8.787*
1	−.123	−.233	−.120	−.167	−.016	−.505	−.378	−.534	−.141	−.278	−.646	−.836
2	−.036	−.173	−.096	−.142	−.006	−.312	−.285	−.441	.091	−.161	−.433	−.624
3		−.151	−.086	−.133		−.239	−.249	−.405		−.117	−.353	−.543
4			−.074	−.121			−.204	−.360			−.250	−.440
5	.536	.210	.068	.022	.056	.957	.332	.176	1.618	.606	.965	.775
6		.029	−.009	−.056		.359	.041	−.115		.244	.306	.116
7			.003	−.043			.087	−.069			.409	.219
8		.410	.154	.108		1.62	.655	.499		1.01	1.70	1.507
9		.410	.154	.108		1.62	.655	.499		1.01	1.70	1.507
10				.108				.499				1.507

TABLE 35 ***Cost elasticities for a $12,000-family-income student***

	Sample II, R				Sample II, P				Sample I, P			
Y	*$12,000*											
A	*375*	*475*	*575*	*650*	*375*	*475*	*575*	*650*	*375*	*475*	*575*	*650*
Estimates for γ	*−3.592*	*−2.407*	*−1.031*	*−1.031*	*−.392*	*−7.972*	*−3.873*	*−3.873*	*−9.593*	*−4.820*	*−8.787*	*−8.787*
1	0	0	0	0	0	0	0	0	0	0	0	0
2	−.064	−.047	−.024	−.024	−.008	−.152	−.089	−.091	−.179	−.090	−.197	−.201
3		−.607	−.030	−.031		−.192	−.109	−.114		−.142	−.233	−.240
4			−.036	−.039			−.126	−.135			−.275	−.272
5	−.559	−.386	−.182	−.185	−.058	−1.374	−.691	−.698	−1.67	−.789	−1.58	−1.59
6		−.226	−.098	−.102		−.731	−.370	−.382		−.480	−.851	−.863
7			−.098	−.105			−.369	−.387			−.874	−.883
8		−.582	−.253	−.260		−2.04	−.981	−.996		−1.23	−2.29	−2.301
9		−.585	−.239	−.249		−2.03	−.945	−.965		−1.24	−2.26	−2.27
10				−.192				−.788				−2.09

TABLE 36 ***Selectivity elasticities for a $12,000-family-income student***

	Sample II, R				Sample II, P				Sample I, P			
Y	*$12,000*											
A	*375*	*475*	*575*	*650*	*375*	*475*	*575*	*650*	*375*	*475*	*575*	*650*
Estimates for α	*−.0328*	*−.0028*	*.0211*	*.0211*	*−.1503*	*−.00795*	*.0232*	*.0232*	*−.0438*	*−.0156*	*.0224*	*.0224*
1	−1.927	−.398	4.43	5.06	−2.83	1.12	4.86	5.56	−1.71	−1.68	4.61	5.29
2	−3.87	−.474	4.98	5.74	−6.43	1.28	5.45	6.28	−5.45	−2.45	5.15	5.93
3		−.589	5.47	6.48		1.42	5.82	6.90		−3.40	5.31	6.20
4			5.316	6.47			5.44	6.61			5.06	5.64
5	−4.49	−.508	5.018	5.76	−6.54	1.53	5.58	6.37	−6.71	−2.85	5.44	6.18
6		−.607	5.535	6.53		1.66	6.10	7.13		−3.54	5.98	6.85
7			5.43	6.56			5.98	7.08			6.02	6.88
8		−.612	5.57	6.49		1.81	6.34	7.27		−3.55	6.30	7.15
9		−.665	5.69	6.71		1.94	6.59	7.61		−3.87	6.71	7.62
10				5.99				7.19				8.12

dubious. These elasticities are based on averages of the two middle ability group estimates. For example, the average academic-interaction coefficient is positive for the 475 SAT IIP model and negative for the 475 SAT IIR and IP models. Consequently, repulsion from better-quality schools is present in the IIR and IP elasticities, but is not present in the IIP elasticities.

The income elasticities are displayed in Table 34. Increases in family income raise the propensity to spend money on higher education. Thus the probabilities of attending the lower-cost options diminish, and the probabilities of attending the higher-cost options increase. Over all the ability groups, the IIP model seems to represent the more typical response to income increases. The IIR sample's response diminishes as ability increases, and the IP sample's response increases as ability increases.

The cost elasticities are displayed in Table 35. The response patterns are rather simple here. Sample I is more responsive to cost increases than sample II, and the IIP specifications are more cost-responsive than the IIR specifications.

The final set of elasticity measurements, displayed in Table 36, are for institutional selectivity. Since the sign on the academic-interaction coefficient changes from negative to positive as the group's academic-ability level increases, the direction of the probability response changes accordingly, as was the case with the individual ability elasticities. All the models have negative responses to improved student ability for the 375 SAT students, and they all have positive responses to improved student ability for the 575 and 650 SAT students. As was previously discussed, the 475 SAT IIR model has a positive response. The differential response character of the 475 SAT models is perhaps disconcerting. One can take some consolation in the fact that their positive responses are not as positive as the high ability group's responses. Nor are they as negative as the low ability group's responses.

We conclude this chapter with a presentation of our sample I treatment of the qualitative information—what we have formerly called the "other explanatory factors." The treatment discussed here parallels the presentation of other factor results for the sample II model appearing in Section 3.5. The indices and categories of qualitative responses listed in Table 10 are applicable to this section. So too are all the procedural operations required to compute the effects of these other factors. The 10 original options were aggregated into 8 option types because too few observations were often observed in individual cells when indices had many categories. This operation resulted, to review, in no postsecondary school as option type 1 and, in terms of the three-by-three classification of cost versus selectivity, the new option types 2 through 8 described by the following typology:

		Cost		
		Low	*Medium*	*High*
Selectivity	*High*	4 (Low–Medium)		8
	Medium	3	6	7 (Medium–Low)
	Low	2	5	

The second adjustment in our prediction procedure, also discussed in Section 3.5, involved making an overall correction in predicted choice frequencies. *Correction constants,* denoted by k_j (for each option type j), were added to the sample I models' predicted relative frequencies, for each type, so that the predicted relative frequencies equaled the observed relative frequencies. Similar predictions would have been obtained if the conditional logit specification had included a constant term for each option type. These constant-corrected predicted probabilities, the sum of the model's predicted probability for each option type and the correction constant for that type, for each student i and for each type in i's feasible set, are called *corrected choice probabilities.* Table 37 displays the calculation of these correction constants.

As before, *response residuals* for option type j and individuals in category c, denoted a_j^c, were calculated in each index category by subtracting the *predicted* frequencies (computed from the corresponding model) from the corresponding *observed* relative choice frequencies. Note, then, that a positive response residual means that the observed frequencies are actually higher than the constant-corrected model would predict. Adding the response residuals to the predicted probabilities improves the distribution of the predicted demand *beyond what can be predicted from the explanatory variables in the sample I conditional logit model.*

TABLE 37 ***Differences between observed and predicted frequencies, by option type***

Type (j)	(1) Observed numbers	(2) Predicted numbers	(3) Observed relative frequencies	(4) Average predicted relative frequencies	(5) Correction constants, k_j (3)–(4)
1	208.0000	176.4025	.5637	.4781	.0856
2	53.0000	65.1246	.1436	.1765	−.0329
3	8.0000	20.5756	.0217	.0558	−.0341
4	21.0000	22.3369	.0569	.0605	−.0036
5	20.0000	37.9099	.0542	.1027	−.0485
6	28.0000	23.0234	.0759	.0624	.0135
7	13.0000	16.9878	.0352	.0460	−.0108
8	18.0000	6.6308	.0488	.0180	.0308
TOTAL	369.0000	368.9910	1.0000	1.0000	.0000

With only slight variation, the sample I response residuals for the students' academic aspirations (index 8), their high school curricula (index 11), and their academic expectations (index 12) had the same additional explanatory power as the sample II response residuals. There were also similarities between the sample I and sample II response residuals for index 19, parents' desires for higher education for their offspring. Lesser desires were associated with less higher education attendance. The diminution in demand came from option 2, junior colleges, and option 8, high-cost/high-selectivity schools. Greater parental desires had exactly the opposite effect.

While students' perceptions of parents' concerns about their current education (index 6) had not offered any additional explanatory power in the sample II analysis, they did in the sample I analysis. Lesser concern (category 11) was associated with higher option 2 attendance, junior colleges, and lower option 8 attendance. Greater concern (category 12) was associated with lower option 2 and higher option 8 attendance.

Sample I response residuals associated with career and future labor-market expectations were somewhat more attenuated than sample II response residuals. For example, while the educational requirements for preferred jobs (index 15) affected both junior college and high-cost/high-selectivity options in sample II, only the junior college attendance was similarly affected in sample I. The measure of indifference and uncertainty about jobs with high educational requirements (index 16) increased junior college attendance at the cost of no HE for low indifference or uncertainty and decreased junior college attendance in favor of no HE for high indifference or uncertainty for the sample II observations. But no sample I responses were observed for this index. The later the postsecondary option was chosen in sample I (categories 35 through 40—lower category numbers are associated with later choices, with the exception that category 40 is ''I don't know''), the more the high school graduates allocated themselves away from the high-cost/high-selectivity schools. But in sample I no other options went up significantly. For example, no HE went up in sample II response residuals. Earliest choices, on the other hand, raised option 8 and option 6 and lowered option 1 in sample I, but had raised only option 8 in sample II.

In contrast to sample I's diminished career and labor-market expectation response residuals, the residuals associated with the eight-category response to ''What do you think will give you the most satisfaction in life?'' (index 13) were increased. Similar responses, higher public junior college attendance, were observed for both samples for those who chose ''leisure time and recreational activities'' (category 31). In addition to the increased option 6 attendance for sample II, sample I also had a significant negative residual associated with no HE for those who chose ''religious beliefs or activities'' (category 32). Additionally, sample I had a significant negative residual associated with option 8 for those who answered ''making things better for (category 27), had a significant positive residual associated with option 8 for those who answered ''making things better for other people'' (category 33), and had a significant positive residual associated with option 4, public universities, for those who answered ''literature, art, or music'' (category 34).

The format of Table 38, which lists the computed *response residuals* for sample I, is identical to that of Table 12. Each of the 54 categories is represented as a column in Table 38 (corresponding indices can be determined from Table 10). The rows of Table 38 correspond to the different option types and are organized as follows: With each option are associated three

TABLE 38 ***Response residuals, chi-squared, and percentage of observed relative frequency***

	1	2	3	4	5	6	7	8	9
1	−.0196 .6031 −.0410	.0152 .6030 .0241	−.0256 1.9738 −.0531	.0405 1.9737 .0584	−.0064 .1056 −.0107	.0081 .1055 .0158	−.0265 .6620 −.0423	.0132 .6620 .0248	.0206 1.0270 .0328
2	.0264 1.4723 .1702	−.0205 1.4727 −.1520	.0248 2.4947 .1599	−.0391 2.4953 −.3110	−.0032 .0352 −.0213	.0040 .0351 .0300	.0005 .0004 .0031	−.0003 .0004 −.0021	−.0081 .2157 .0566
3	−.0007 .0031 −.0189	.0005 .0031 .0565	−.0085 1.1776 −.2739	.0134 1.1773 1.9174	.0125 1.5953 .6454	−.0158 1.5956 −.6454	.0314* 5.6916 1.2888	−.0157* 5.6921 −.7733	.0070 .4924 .3541
4	−.0166 1.6263 −.2969	.0128 1.6260 .2226	−.0150 3.5541 −.2421	.0237 3.5538 .4841	−.0077 .5624 −.2251	.0097 .5622 .1125	−.0139 1.1111 −1.7071	.0069 1.1110 .0853	.0027 .0663 .0680
5	.0029 .0257 .0462	−.0022 .0258 −.0463	.0062 .2473 .0996	−.0098 .2477 −.2325	.0084 .3622 .1448	−.0107 .3628 −.2173	−.0077 .1258 −.1904	.0039 .1255 .0634	−.0017 .0135 −.0335
6	−.0210 2.1518 −.3070	.0162 2.1509 .1986	.0059 .3975 .0631	−.0093 .3979 −.1893	−.0063 .3182 −.0991	.0079 .3179 .0858	.0314 3.8066 .3514	−.0157 3.8075 −.2274	−.0081 .5186 −.1259
7	−.0007 .0029 −.0137	.0005 .0028 .0219	−.0059 .5392 −.1485	.0093 .5390 .3342	.0039 .1586 .1148	−.0049 .1587 −.1340	.0126 .8042 .3872	−.0063 .8044 −.1721	.0055 .3049 .1593
8	.0293** 14.8226 .3141	−.0227** 14.8227 −1.5707	.0182** 18.3160 .2421	−.0288** 18.3161 −4.1151	−.0013 .0523 −.0341	.0017 .0523 .0273	−.0279** 15.5526 −3.4359	.0140** 15.5526 .2021	−.0179** 9.1441 −.9063

TABLE 38 (*continued*)

	10	*11*	*12*	*13*	*14*	*15*	*16*	*17*	*18*
	−.0249	.0190	−.0193	.0485*	−.0499*	.1349**	−.1562**	.1044**	−.0892**
1	1.0271	.7240	.7240	4.7997	4.7998	42.5730	42.5735	18.3424	18.3427
	−.0514	.0301	−.0387	.0756	−.1031	.1713	−.5138	.1455	−.2063
	.0098	.0478*	−.0486*	.0028	−.0029	−.0420*	.0487*	−.0225	.0193
2	.2155	6.2170	6.2179	.0216	.0216	5.5392	5.5384	1.1559	1.1555
	.0683	.2470	−.5230	.0187	−.0210	−.3618	.2774	−.1742	.1236
	−.0085	−.0078	.0079	.0020	−.0021	.0000	−.0000	−.0043	.0036
3	.4926	.5249	.5248	.0360	.0360	.0000	.0000	.1399	.1399
	−.3541	−.7216	.2405	.1893	−.0631	.0081	−.0012	.0000	.0907
	−.0033	−.0130	.0132	−.0150	.0154	−.0131	.0152	−.0269*	.0230*
4	.0664	1.3781	1.3778	1.8639	1.8636	1.4816	1.4814	5.2838	5.2832
	−.0418	−.4824	.1507	−.4676	.1870	−1.2990	.1367	−2.2907	.2411
	.0020	−.0139	.0141	−.0131	.0135	−.0126	.0146	−.0146	.0125
5	.0134	.7959	.7951	.7228	.7220	.7517	.7510	.7457	.7450
	.0334	−.3683	.1982	−.3070	.2045	−.3126	.2083	−.4134	.1771
	.0098	.0026	−.0026	−.0101	.0104	−.0353**	.0409**	−.0199	.0170
6	.5181	.0443	.0444	.6905	.6900	9.0848	9.0831	2.2721	2.2712
	.1091	.0368	−.0319	−.1718	.1111	−1.7470	.2911	−.4222	.1689
	−.0067	−.0106	.0108	−.0113	.0116	.0017	−.0019	−.0108	.0092
7	.3051	.9699	.9696	1.1091	1.1088	.0261	.0261	.8686	.8683
	−.1858	−.6580	.1974	−.5273	.2343	.0828	−.0368	−.6132	.1839
	.0217**	−.0241**	.0245**	−.0038	.0040	−.0336**	.0389**	−.0053	.0046
8	9.1441	15.4228	15.4228	.3978	.3978	30.3670	30.3669	.6554	.6554
	.2589	−1.4959	.2992	−.0899	.0720	.0000	.3694	−.1299	.0826

TABLE 38 (*continued*)

	19	20	21	22	23	24	25	26	27
1	−.0337 2.9386 −.0655	.0445 2.9385 .0708	.0571 2.0876 .0772	−.0859** 12.6434 −.2592	.0869* 5.5027 .1116	−.0784** 28.1983 −.1825	.1504** 7.7125 .1739	.2500** 16.5464 .2670	−.0892 .3036 −.1338
2	.0158 .8768 .1040	−.0209 .8772 −.1585	−.0161 .2327 −.1107	.0256 1.5104 .1734	−.0268 .7185 −.1990	.0433** 11.7468 .2421	−.0834 3.4447 −1.2303	−.1375* 6.4127 −3.2303	.1599 1.0277 .4798
3	.0043 .2131 .1505	−.0057 .2132 −.4516	.0240 2.4323 1.1511	−.0208 2.9039 −.7020	.0116 .6071 1.2079	−.0045 .6410 −.1475	.0073 .1438 .0000	.0159 .7077 .0000	−.0101 .0190 .0000
4	.0043 .2054 .0597	−.0056 .2055 −.1492	.0151 1.3963 .7236	−.0033 .0641 −.0292	−.0086 .4514 .0000	.0057 1.1723 .0717	−.0071 .2470 .0000	−.0231 1.2815 .0000	−.0236 .1468 .0000
5	.0162 1.4067 .2435	−.0214 1.4078 −.5684	−.0381 2.0208 −1.8289	.0156 .8295 .2027	.0098 .1696 .2042	.0091 .9006 .1328	−.0315 .8062 −1.8575	−.0114 .0926 −.5338	.0150 .0424 .0000
6	.0042 .1566 .0487	−.0055 .1568 −.0878	−.0133 .6040 −.4269	.0347* 6.2690 .2446	−.0441* 6.2902 −4.5902	.0111 2.7450 .1121	−.0109 .2411 −.3211	−.0483 3.4994 .0000	−.0155 .5138 .0000
7	−.0165 3.0633 −.8662	.0218 3.0629 .3849	.0040 .0654 .1937	.0008 .0043 .0136	−.0050 .1150 −.5239	.0003 .0028 .0066	.0073 .1529 .4293	−.0108 .2619 .0000	−.0057 .0121 .0000
8	.0054 1.1355 .0865	−.0071 1.1355 −.2250	−.0326** 23.3555 .0000	.0332** 21.0440 .3296	−.0238** 11.8663 −2.4750	.0134** 23.6783 .1960	−.0321** 19.9841 .0000	−.0348** 13.1084 .0000	−.0308** 24.9136 .0000

TABLE 38 (*continued*)

	28	*29*	*30*	*31*	*32*	*33*	*34*	*35*	*36*
	.0318	.0898	.0091	−.0568	−.2671*	−.1003	.0416	.0557	.0532
1	.5903	1.5552	.1370	.5002	4.8455	1.7236	.0791	.8225	2.2709
	.0520	.1146	.0164	−.1278	−.8012	−.2609	.0831	.0845	.0802
	−.0046	−.0323	−.0233	.1531*	.0428	.0042	−.0268	.0417	−.0026
2	.0166	.2835	1.2293	4.3988	.1908	.0034	.0395	.6382	.0072
	−.0324	−.2394	−.2177	.4593	.2568	.0276	−.2144	.2294	−.0166
	.0079	.0411	−.0102	.0338	−.0001	−.0390	−.0402	−.0201	−.0061
3	.1710	3.4230	.7320	.6227	.0000	.7932	.2568	.4963	.1480
	.3377	1.5203	−.5705	.4560	.0000	.0000	.0000	.0000	−.6698
	.0191	−.0103	−.0161	.0304	−.0392	−.0132	.1988**	.0066	.0021
4	.9608	.3080	1.7140	.7428	.2190	.0711	7.7774	.0634	.0189
	.2711	.0000	−.3377	.4103	−.4701	−.1721	.7951	.1456	.0573
	−.0255	−.0463	.0254	−.0505	−.0059	.0455	−.0273	−.0334	.0004
5	.7563	1.0293	2.1668	.8489	.0086	.8027	.0896	.6102	.0002
	−.7234	.0000	.2843	.0000	.0000	.5913	.0000	−1.4686	.0066
	−.0190	−.0189	.0003	−.0733	.2590**	.0586	−.0358	−.0166	−.0323
6	.8072	.4546	.0004	2.9966	15.0320	1.3383	.0836	.3038	3.1381
	−.4048	−.7007	.0033	.0000	.7771	.3807	−.2864	−.3642	−.8893
	−.0197	−.0172	.0186	−.0176	.0470	−.0168	−.0529	.0059	.0109
7	1.0512	.4246	2.4516	.1527	.6212	.1315	.3851	.0382	.4897
	−1.6783	.0000	.3469	−.4745	.5635	−.4376	.0000	.1307	.3010
	.0100	−.0058	−.0037	−.0191	−.0365	.0610*	−.0573	−.0399**	−.0256**
8	.7443	.4221	.2998	.6776	2.9549	5.3793	1.1821	8.9338	12.7250
	.1702	−.2155	−.0784	−.5146	.0000	.5290	.0000	.0000	−2.8200

TABLE 38 (*continued*)

	37	38	39	40	41	42	43	44	45
	−.0126	−.0292	−.1987**	.0139	.0503*	−.0563*	−.0121	.0086	.0101
1	.1213	.2514	10.4397	.0414	5.6685	5.6687	.2061	.2061	.2194
	−.0211	−.0613	−1.2318	.0278	.0715	−.1381	−.0228	.0145	.0193
	−.0145	.0311	−.0090	−.0324	−.0117	.0131	.0153	−.0108	−.0048
2	.2260	.3705	.0246	.2750	.4125	.4123	.4425	.4427	.0667
	−.1100	.1952	−.0934	−.2753	−.0785	.0948	.0973	−.0805	−.0369
	.0173	−.0067	−.0472	.0434	.0142	−.0160	−.0080	.0056	−.0035
3	1.1497	.0461	1.1910	1.2338	1.8676	1.8679	.3654	.3653	.1183
	.6124	−.2961	.0000	.4922	.9255	−.5554	−.3046	.3046	−.1130
	.0050	.0540	−.0525	−.0528	−.0080	.0089	.0206	−.0146	−.0065
4	.1079	1.9375	.8365	1.6467	.5419	.5418	2.3367	2.3370	.3861
	.1317	.3394	−.5421	−1.7967	−.5187	.0864	.2420	−.3932	−.0967
	.0134	−.0461	.0557	.0090	.0003	−.0004	.0011	−.0008	.0020
5	.2867	1.2466	1.2973	.0342	.0005	.0005	.0033	.0033	.0182
	.0782	.0000	.5753	.1532	.0071	−.0059	.0203	−.0137	.0390
	−.0037	.0062	.1189*	.0212	−.0111	.0124	.0103	−.0073	−.0048
6	.0385	.0313	5.8978	.2367	.8893	.8888	.4873	.4877	.1677
	−.0561	.0686	.5263	.1798	−.2164	.1202	.1128	−.1129	−.0576
	.0158	−.0198	−.0296	−.0397	−.0082	.0092	−.0140	.0099	−.0088
7	.8999	.3941	.4540	1.2342	.6167	.6165	1.1477	1.1475	.7215
	.3347	−.8712	−.9179	.0000	−.8011	.1456	−.5368	.2385	−.2405
	−.0207*	.0106	.1624**	.0374	−.0259**	.0290**	−.0132	.0093	.0163**
8	6.2635	.2818	13.6683	3.4627	18.1477	18.1476	3.2781	3.2781	7.8093
	−1.0990	.1554	.5594	.4239	−2.5230	.3154	.4024	.1548	.2232

TABLE 38 (*continued*)

	46	*47*	*48*	*49*	*50*	*51*	*52*	*53*	*54*
	−.0110	−.0080	.0056	.1493**	−.1332**	.1051**	−.0879**	.0272	−.0276
1	.2194	.0904	.0904	39.0356	39.0360	18.0997	18.1000	1.4899	1.4900
	−.0182	−.0156	.0093	.1856	−.3820	.1391	−.2181	.0477	−.0496
	.0052	−.0062	.0043	−.0632**	.0563**	−.0270	.0226	.0221	−.0224
2	.0666	.0728	.0727	9.4420	9.4409	1.6041	1.6037	1.3226	1.3230
	.0329	−.0494	.0276	−.6464	.3052	−.1971	.1511	.1367	−.1784
	.0038	−.0174	.0122	.0031	−.0027	.0033	−.0027	−.0099	.0101
3	.1182	1.7127	1.7125	.0750	.0751	.0815	.0815	.8590	.8587
	.3390	−1.3197	.4399	.5352	−.0765	.5506	−.0787	−.6147	.3688
	.0071	.0188	−.0132	−.0118	.0105	−.0123	.0103	−.0067	.0068
4	.3859	1.8020	1.8023	1.0663	1.0662	1.1305	1.1303	.3731	.3730
	.1571	.1906	−.4765	−1.0240	.1078	−1.0355	.1090	−.1137	.1251
	−.0022	−.0140	.0098	−.0257	.0229	−.0216	.0180	−.0372*	.0378*
5	.0183	.5514	.5507	2.4205	2.4192	1.6096	1.6085	5.7524	5.7505
	−.0392	−.3037	.1634	−1.1184	.2795	−.9058	.2264	−.9882	.5320
	.0052	.0203	−.0142	−.0131	.0117	−.0079	.0066	.0142	−.0145
6	.1674	1.8231	1.8239	1.0336	1.0330	.3564	.3561	1.3539	1.3546
	.0767	.1927	−.2570	−.2842	.1136	−.1472	.0697	.1891	−.1891
	.0095	−.0021	.0015	−.0055	.0049	−.0065	.0054	−.0105	.0106
7	.7213	.0250	.0249	.2381	.2380	.3199	.3197	.9508	.9506
	.2806	−.0529	.0453	−.4774	.0868	−.5472	.0995	−.3249	.2784
	−.0177**	.0085	−.0060	−.0332**	.0296**	−.0331**	.0277**	.0008	−.0008
8	7.8094	1.2685	1.2685	28.3824	28.3823	27.9692	27.9691	.0179	.0179
	−.7814	.1437	−.1437	.0000	.3210	.0000	.3094	.0170	−.0170

NOTE. Response residuals that are significant at least at the 5 percent level are marked with one asterisk, and those which are significant at the 1 percent level are marked with two asterisks.

rows, i.e., three entries in a column; the first entry is the *response residual,* the second is a corresponding chi-square statistic (1 degree of freedom), and the third is the ratio of the response residual to the corresponding observed frequency. Chi-square statistics that are significant at least at the 5 percent level are marked with one asterisk, and those which are significant at least at the 1 percent level are marked with two asterisks.

6. Faculty-Student Ratios: Introduction and Historical Trends

6.1. INTRODUCTION AND SUMMARY

It usually requires no special effort to interest academicians in the subject of faculty-student ratios, at least at the level of faculty-club or cocktail-party conversation. We feel threatened by any decrease in the faculty-student ratio, and we consider any increase to be a sign of increasing quality. On the other hand, if the ratio is low, we can boast to the legislature of our "efficiency."

An interest in forecasting the demand for teachers leads naturally to an interest in the patterns of variation of student-teacher ratios among institutions and through time. More generally, it leads to an interest in the relations between inputs and outputs in higher education or, as the production economist might put it, in the "technological possibilities" that have been observed within the education sector. Of course, there are many nonhuman inputs into the educational process, but the human ones are probably still the most important. In any case, the everyday mythology of education suggests that the relations between the human inputs and outputs have remained at the heart of the educational process since at least the time of Socrates and may even have changed very little from his day to ours!

On the other hand, the measurement of the "quality" of inputs and outputs may not have advanced much either during the past 2,500 years, nor shall we here contribute to the solution of this important problem. We, like most other educators, cling to the hypothesis that an educational institution *can* do more to increase the quality of its output than merely select students with higher initial ability. But quantitative confirmation of this hypothesis still seems to elude those who have studied the question carefully (see, for example, Astin, 1968).

Relative to the magnitude of the various problems to which

we have referred, the goal of the present study is quite modest. We shall try to explain the variation in numbers of faculty, both among institutions of higher education and through time, as a function of numbers of students enrolled and in terms of several other institutional variables, such as ratings of graduate schools, faculty salaries, size, and type of control.

Although our data are crude and subject to considerable error, some conclusions may be ventured. During the period 1950–1967 there was a clear downward trend in faculty-student ratios, except in the private universities and the two-year colleges. This trend appears both in aggregate data and in data on a fixed sample of institutions (Section 6.2). For the private universities, the aggregate data show an upward trend from 1955 to 1963, with a downward trend thereafter, whereas the data on the fixed sample show a steady downward trend from 1954 to 1966. The aggregate data indicate an overall reduction in the faculty-student ratio in two-year colleges during the period 1953–1967, but the data do not exhibit a smooth trend. (Our fixed sample did not include two-year colleges.)

The variation in faculty-student ratios among institutions is striking, even within each major category of institution. This variability declined somewhat in the undergraduate categories, but remained relatively stable in the universities. A major part of our study, reported in Chapter 7, is devoted to an attempt to relate this variation to the variation in other institutional variables by means of a cross-sectional analysis of a 1966 sample of institutions. The results of that analysis are summarized at the beginning of Chapter 7.

6.2. RECENT HISTORICAL TRENDS

We first consider estimates of student-faculty ratios calculated from statistics on numbers of faculty and students published by the U.S. Office of Education. For these estimates, institutions have been grouped in six categories, based on a two-way classification:

1 Public, private

2 Universities, other four-year colleges, two-year colleges

For seven years, 1953, 1955, 1957, 1959, 1963, 1966, and 1967 and for each of the six categories, we have estimated the ratio of total full-time equivalent faculty to total full-time equivalent students. The results are presented in Table 39 and Figure 10. It should be emphasized that these estimates may be subject to considerable error because of the noncomparability of statistics in different years and the difficulties of estimating full-time equivalents. The comparability problem is particularly severe before 1957. Table 39 indicates that faculty-student ratios decreased in all categories except that of private universities; in this last category the ratio increased from 1953 to 1963 and then decreased a little between 1963 and 1967. In interpreting Table 39 and subsequent tables, it may be useful to have in mind some sample numbers relating faculty-student ratios to student-faculty ratios:

Faculty-student ratio	.04	.05	.06	.07	.08	.09
Student-faculty ratio	25.0	20.0	16.7	14.4	12.5	11.1

Appendix A of this chapter describes the method used to calculate the faculty-student ratios in Table 39, and Appendix B lists the data sources.

We consider next a sample of 382 colleges and universities taken from a larger set of more than 900 institutions for which

TABLE 39 ***Faculty-student ratios, 1953–1967, from U.S. Office of Education statistics***

	Universities		*Four-year colleges*		*Two-year colleges*	
	Public	*Private*	*Public*	*Private*	*Public*	*Private*
1953	.0736	.0816	.0733	.0827	.0567	.0853
1955(1)	.0688	.0810	.0664	.0755	.0486	.0746
1955(2)	.0688	.0810	.0663	.0754	.0490	.0783
1957	.0769	.0850	.0654	.0773	.0526	.0819
1959	.0719	.0855	.0629	.0752	.0541	.0725
1963	.0649	.0952	.0588	.0741	.0515	.0666
1966	.0596	.0893	.0569	.0690	.0443	.0556
1967	.0601	.0888	.0560	.0688	.0462	.0564
Percentage change, 1957–1967	21.85	4.47	14.37	11.00	12.17	21.14

NOTE: See Apps. A and B to this chapter for the method of calculation and data sources.

FIGURE 10 ***Faculty-student ratios, 1953–1967, from U.S. Office of Education statistics***

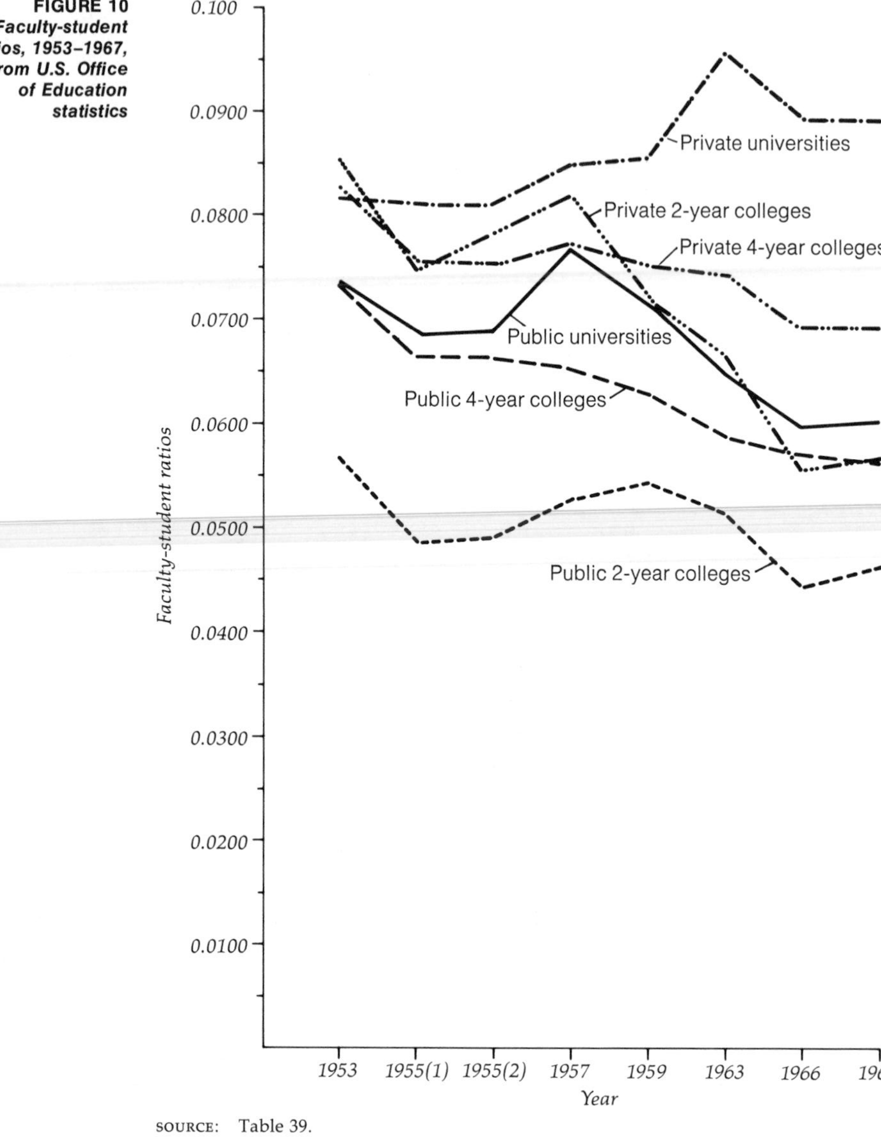

SOURCE: Table 39.

data were available[1] on numbers of faculty and students for the years 1950, 1954, 1958, 1962, and 1966. These 382 institutions included all those in the larger set that either (1) were purely undergraduate institutions or (2) had substantial graduate

[1]American Council on Education (1952, 1956, 1960, 1964, 1968). Numbers for faculty and students are "head counts" and not full-time equivalents.

enrollment in each of the five years mentioned above, but were neither purely graduate schools nor primarily religious or professional schools. In this chapter these two groups will be called "undergraduate schools" and "universities," respectively; there are 269 undergraduate schools and 113 universities. With a few exceptions, we had data on numbers of faculty and students for each of the 382 schools for each of the four years. Thus we were able to avoid the problems of possible changes in numbers and classification of institutions. On the other hand, our sample is not random, and it may well not be representative. We shall call this our "ACE sample."

After further subdividing the undergraduate schools and universities into public, private nonsectarian (hereafter called "private"), and private sectarian (hereafter called "sectarian"), we calculated the average and the standard deviation of the faculty-student ratio for each of the resulting six groups for each of the five years in our observation period (1950–1966). The results are presented in Table 40.

The mean faculty-student ratio clearly fell in each of the undergraduate groups, with the greatest decline (31 percent) in the public schools and the smallest decline (18 percent and 21 percent) in the private and sectarian schools. The mean faculty-student ratio also fell in the public universities (21 percent decline), but rose in the other universities (5 percent and 49 percent increases in the private and sectarian universities, respectively). However, for the private universities, Table 40 shows a sharp increase from 1950 to 1954 and then a steady decline, totaling 10 percent, from 1954 to 1966. This pattern for the private universities is somewhat different from that derived from the aggregate U.S. Office of Education statistics, as shown in Table 39. In both undergraduate institutions and universities, the private institutions ended the period with the highest ratios, and the public institutions with the lowest.

The variability of the faculty-student ratios, as well as their means, declined in the undergraduate groups but remained relatively stable in the university groups. On the whole, there was considerable variation in the ratios, with the means roughly two to four times the standard deviations. In 1966 the private and sectarian universities had the lowest ratios of mean to standard deviation (2.1 and 2.4, respectively), whereas the private and sectarian undergraduate institutions had the highest (4.6 and 4.1).

TABLE 40 ***Faculty-student ratios, 1950–1960, from ACE sample***

	Undergraduate schools			*Universities*		
	Public	*Private nonsectarian*	*Private sectarian*	*Public*	*Private nonsectarian*	*Private sectarian*
Mean						
1950	.0946	.1009	.1016	.0777	.1112	.0823
1954	.0843	.0937	.0964	.0758	.1297	.0807
1958	.0732	.0934	.0850	.0761	.1230	.1023
1962	.0670	.0885	.0804	.0692	.1202	.1132
1966	.0655	.0830	.0800	.0663	.1163	.1224
Percentage change, 1950–1966	−.3076	−.1774	−.2125	−.1467	.0458	.4872
Standard deviation						
1950	.0344	.0312	.0345	.0226	.0670	.0389
1954	.0390	.0271	.0314	.0247	.0750	.0336
1958	.0275	.0314	.0227	.0359	.0710	.0720
1962	.0276	.0235	.0189	.0229	.0640	.0667
1966	.0243	.0179	.0196	.0248	.0560	.0880
Numbers of institutions in groups						
1950	42	53	173	43	41	15
1954	42	51	174	47	40	15
1958	42	53	173	49	41	16
1962	42	53	173	49	40	16
*1966**	34	49	168	50	41	16

*In 1966 many of the undergraduate schools were beginning to offer graduate work; thus the numbers of institutions in each group decreased compared with those of the previous years.

FIGURE 11 ***Faculty-student ratios, 1950–1960, from ACE sample***

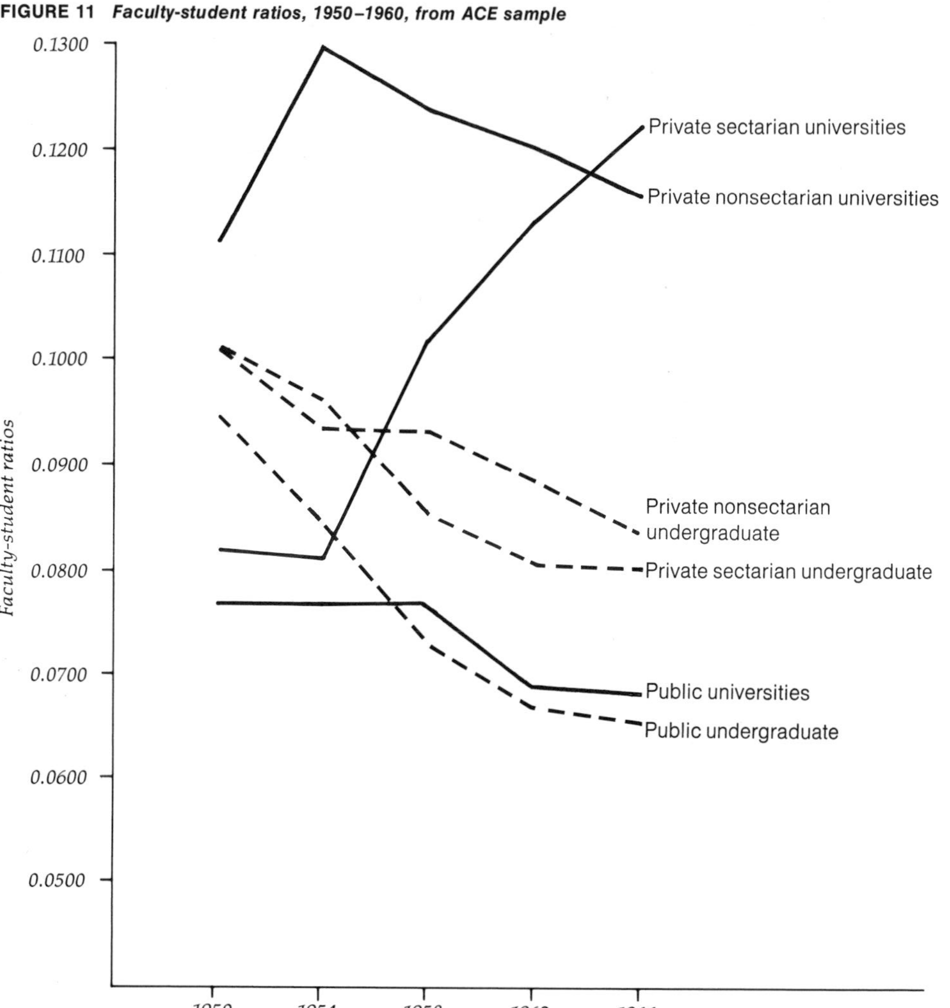

SOURCE: Table 40.

All in all, we have a picture of declining faculty-student ratios in undergraduate schools and in public universities and of fluctuating or increasing ratios in private sectarian and nonsectarian universities. The downward pressure on the faculty-student ratios seems most pronounced in the case of the public schools, both undergraduate and universities. Within each of the groups there is considerable variation in the faculty-student ratio.

Appendix A: Method of Calculation of Student-Faculty Ratios for Table 39

$$\frac{\text{Faculty}}{\text{Student}}\text{ ratio} = \frac{\text{Number of full-time equivalent (FTE) faculty}}{\text{Number of full-time equivalent (FTE) students}}$$

Calculation of FTE students

A student is defined as a resident undergraduate, first professional degree, or graduate student enrolled in a course creditable toward a bachelor's or higher degree. Excluded are extension, correspondence, summer session, and non-degree-credit students.

The data report the number of full-time students and the number of part-time students. To obtain the FTE of part-time students, we multiplied the number of part-time students by .333. For graduate students, we first calculated the percentage of total graduate students who were part-time in order to obtain the number of full-time and part-time graduate students.

Total FTE students:

(number of full-time undergraduate and first professional degree students) + (number of part-time undergraduate and first professional degree students)(.333) + (number of graduate students [head count])[(percentage part-time)/100](.333) + (number of graduate students [head count]) [(100 − percentage part-time)/100]

Calculation of FTE faculty

Faculty is defined as senior resident instructional staff (department heads, professors, instructors) for degree-credit courses. Excluded are teaching and research assistants as well as persons engaged in organized research.

The Office of Education questionnaire requested institutions to report the FTE of part-time faculty as well as the number of full-time faculty.

Total FTE faculty:

(number of full-time faculty) + (FTE of part-time faculty)

The institutions included in our categories are classified as:

- *Universities:* "Institutions which give considerable stress to graduate instruction, which confer advanced degrees as well as bachelor's degrees in a variety of liberal arts fields, and which have at least two professional schools that are not exclusively technological"[10][2]
- *Four-year colleges:* Liberal arts colleges, teachers colleges, technological schools, theological schools, schools of art, and other professional schools
- *Two-year institutions:* Institutions which offer two or more years of work but less than a bachelor's degree (degree-credit courses)

Calculations for individual years

1953 and 1955(1) The Office of Education questionnaire requested faculty and student data on numbers enrolled in "college-grade" courses. A number of technical institutes (primarily two-year institutions) were included in the 1953 and 1955 figures [1,2]; however, college-grade courses did not necessarily mean courses creditable to a bachelor's or higher degree.

For the years 1953 and 1955(1), separate figures for full-time and part-time graduate students were not available; therefore, these were calculated for the different sectors and types of schools within the sectors individually using percentage distributions for full-time and part-time graduate students given for 1959 [9].

1955(2) and 1957 In 1957, 50 technical institutes that had previously reported enrollment and faculty for college-grade courses were reclassified as giving non-degree-credit courses [4]. The 1955 data were also reworked to take into account the new classification [3]. This accounts for the discrepancy between 1955(1) and 1955(2) figures. The 1955(2) calculations correspond to the figures for the later years.

[2]References in this appendix refer to data sources used in calculating student-faculty ratios. They are listed in App. B to this chapter.

For the years 1955(2) and 1957, separate figures for full-time and part-time graduate students were not available; therefore, these were calculated for the different sectors and types of schools within the sectors individually using percentage distributions for full-time and part-time graduate students given for 1959 [9].

1959 [5,8,9]

1961 Enrollment figures for universities and other four-year colleges were grouped together [5]. We were therefore unable to calculate faculty-student ratios for our categories.

The percentage distributions of full-time and part-time graduate student enrollments were calculated for 1961 data [7] and found not to vary significantly from those calculated from 1959 data [9]. It was assumed, therefore, that these percentage distributions were fairly stable, and the 1959 figures used in the FTE graduate student calculations for 1953, 1955(1), 1955(2), and 1957 figures were not available for those years.

1963 Whereas earlier years had grouped undergraduates and first professional degree students together, giving full-time and part-time figures, in 1963 full-time and part-time figures for undergraduates were given, while only a head count of first professional degree students was reported [10,11]. Therefore, we used 1967 data [6] to calculate the percentage of first professional degree students who were part-time, and we then applied this percentage (calculated for the different sectors and types of schools within the sectors individually) to the total enrollment of first professional degree students in each type of school. Finally this number was multiplied by .333 to obtain the FTE of part-time first professional degree students.

FTE first professional degree students:

(number of first professional degree students)(percentage part-time/100)(.333) + (number of first professional degree students)(100 − percentage part-time)/100

1966 and 1967 The data were simplified [12,13,14,15]. The U.S. Office of Education categories were:

- Universities
- Other four-year institutions
- Two-year institutions

The FTE of total full-time and part-time enrollment was given for these years as well as the FTE of part-time faculty.

Appendix B: Data Sources Used in Calculating Student-Faculty Ratios in Table 39

1 U.S. Office of Education: "Statistics of Higher Education: Faculty, Students and Degrees, 1953–54," *Biennial Survey of Education in the United States, 1952–54,* chap. 4, sec. 1.

Table 2: *Faculty, Enrollment and Degrees, by Type and Control of Institution: Aggregate United States, 1953–54.*

2 U.S. Office of Education: "Statistics of Higher Education: Faculty, Students and Degrees, 1955–56," *Biennial Survey of Education in the United States, 1954–56,* chap. 4, sec. 1

Table V: *Faculty, Students and Degrees, by Type and Control of Institution: Aggregate United States, 1955–56.*

3 U.S. Office of Education: "Statistics of Higher Education: Faculty, Students and Degrees, 1957–58," *Biennial Survey of Education in the United States, 1956–58,* chap. 4, sec. 1.

Table 11: *Faculty and Other Professional Staff, by Type of Position, and Type of Control of Institution: Aggregate U.S., First Term, 1957–58, and Percent Change from November 1955.*

4 U.S. Office of Education: "Statistics of Higher Education: Faculty, Students and Degrees, 1957–58," *Biennial Survey of Education in the United States, 1956–58,* chap. 4, sec. 1.

Table 21: *Students by Type of Enrollment and Type and Control of Institution: Aggregate United States, First Term, 1957–58, and Percent Change from November 1955.*

5 U.S. Office of Education: *Comprehensive Report on Enrollment in Higher Education, 1961–62,* Circular 743.

6 United States National Center for Educational Statistics: *Students Enrolled for Advanced Degrees: Part A—Summary Data, Fall 1967.*

Table 2: *Enrollment for First-Professional Degrees in Selected Fields, by Level of Enrollment, Attendance Status, Sex of Student, Level of Institution, and Institutional Control: Aggregate United States, Fall 1967.*

7 U.S. Office of Education: *Enrollment for Advanced Degrees: Fall 1963,* Circular 786.

Table 12: *Enrollment for Advanced Degrees by Level of Study, Attendance, Status, Type of Institution, and Institutional Control: Aggregate United States, Fall 1963.*

8 U.S. Office of Education: *Faculty and Other Professional Staff in Institutions of Higher Education, First Term, 1959–60,* Circular 714.

Table 11: *Faculty and Other Professional Staff, by Type of Position, and Control and Type of Institution: Aggregate United States, First Term, 1959–60.*

9 U.S. Office of Education: *Enrollment for Advanced Degrees, Fall 1960,* Circular 674.

Table 6: *Enrollment in Degree Credit Courses in Four-Year Institutions by Level, Full-time and Part-time Status, and Type of Institution and Control: Fall 1959.*

10 *Resident and Extension Enrollment in Institutions of Higher Education, Fall 1963,* Circular 776.

Table 2: *Resident and Extension Students in Institutions of Higher Education, by Type of Enrollment, Level and Type of Institution, and Institutional Control: Aggregate United States, Fall 1963.*

11 U.S. Office of Education: *Faculty and Other Professional Staff in Institutions of Higher Education, First Term, 1963–64,* Circular No. 794.

Table 8: *Positions for Faculty and Other Professional Staff by Type of Institution, Type of Position, and Institutional Control: Aggregate United States, Fall 1963.*

12 *Numbers and Characteristics of Employees in Institutions of Higher Education, Fall 1966.*

Table I—*B,C,D,: Estimated Number of Professional Employees by Control, Employment Status, and Primary Function: Aggregate United States, Fall 1966.*

13 U.S. Office of Education: *Opening Fall Enrollment in Higher Education, 1966.*

Table 2: *Opening Enrollment of Students, by Enrollment Category, Level of Institution, and Institutional Control: Aggregate United States, Fall 1966.*

14 *Numbers and Characteristics of Employees in Institutions of Higher Education, Fall 1967.*

Table IIB: *Professional Employees in Universities, by Control, Employment Status, and Primary Function: Aggregate United States, Fall 1967.*

Table IIC: *Professional Employees in Other Four-Year Institutions, by Control, Employment Status, and Primary Function: Aggregate United States, Fall 1967.*

Table IID: *Professional Employees in Two-Year Institutions, by Control, Employment Status, and Primary Function: Aggregate United States, Fall 1967.*

15 U.S. Office of Education: *Opening Fall Enrollment in Higher Education, 1967.*

Table 2: *Opening Enrollment of Students, by Enrollment Category, Level of Institution, and Institutional Control: Aggregate United States, Fall 1967.*

7. Faculty-Student Ratios: A Cross-Sectional Study

7.1. INTRODUCTION

In the course of examining recent trends in faculty-student ratios (Chapter 6), we noted the considerable variability of these ratios within each group of institutions in the ACE sample. In the present chapter we shall discuss the statistical relationships between faculty-student ratios and other variables for a sample of 650 institutions in 1966.

Our basic hypothesis is that the number of faculty in an institution depends on the number of undergraduate and graduate students, but that the coefficients in this relationship depend on various institutional variables, in particular (1) the size of the institution, measured by the number of students; (2) the average faculty salary; (3) the fraction of the faculty who hold the Ph.D. degree; and (4) an index of the quality of the graduate program.

To provide a framework for discussion, we may imagine that there are two "activities" in any institution, educating undergraduates and educating graduate students. (Indeed, each of these activities is itself made up of a group of a large number of activities. Furthermore, many activities, such as research, do not fall neatly into either of these two groups. For a discussion of this, see Chapter 1.) We measure the level of each activity by the number of students involved (undergraduate and graduate students, respectively), and we suppose that there is a "faculty input coefficient" for each activity. Algebraically, we can represent this relationship as

$$F = a_u U + a_g G, \qquad (1)$$

where F, U, and G are the full-time equivalent numbers of faculty, undergraduates, and graduate students, respectively, and a_u and a_g are the two faculty input coefficients. Thus each faculty input coefficient is a faculty-student ratio for that particular activity. In the case of purely undergraduate institutions, $G = 0$, and the faculty input coefficient is just the faculty-student ratio. Actually, we were not successful in estimating separate input coefficients for undergraduate and graduate education in the two M.A.-granting categories, so that in these two cases the numbers of undergraduate and graduate students were aggregated, and the institutions were in effect treated in the same way as the undergraduate institutions.

Even if equation (1) adequately represented the relationship between the numbers of faculty and students for a given institution, one would not expect the input coefficients to be the same for all institutions. Furthermore, for a given institution, the input coefficients might themselves depend on the number of students. Therefore, we divided our sample of institutions into subgroups, and for each subgroup we assumed that the input coefficients depended upon the four institutional variables listed above. We call this the *variable input coefficient model.* The resulting relationship can be estimated by standard methods of regression analysis, and we present the results of such analyses in this chapter. Our data are taken mainly from Higher Education General Information Survey or HEGIS (U.S. Office of Education, 1966), but we were able to use only about one-fourth of the institutions covered by HEGIS. Table 41 shows the classification and numbers of institutions covered by our statistical analysis.

In Sections 7.2 and 7.3 we discuss the problems that arise in the estimation of equation (1) from time-series and cross-sectional data. In Section 7.4 we describe our sample, and in the remaining sections of the chapter we present and discuss the results of our statistical analyses of the variable input coefficient model. Those results are somewhat complicated and are subject to numerous qualifications. At the risk of oversimplification, we shall now briefly summarize them.

We first turn to nonuniversities, i.e., non-Ph.D.-granting institutions. For these institutions, equation (1) reduces to

$$F = aS, \tag{2}$$

where S is the number of full-time equivalent students, and the input coefficient a itself depends on (1) the size of the institu-

TABLE 41 ***Classification and numbers of institutions***

	Two-year	*Four-year*	*M.A.-granting*	*Ph.D.-granting*
Public	185	51	134	55
Private	34	44* 47†	62	38

*Average salary less than $8,000.

†Average salary greater than, or equal to, $8,000.

tion, measured by the number of students, (2) the average faculty salary, and (3) the fraction of the faculty who hold a Ph.D. degree.

To understand the relationship between faculty and size, it is useful to look at the *marginal input coefficient*. For a given size of institution, consider the increment in faculty associated with an increment in size (number of students). The ratio of these two increments (for small increments) will be called the *marginal input coefficient*.[1] If, in equation (2), the input coefficient actually depends on the size of the institution, then the marginal input coefficient will not equal the faculty-student ratio (at all sizes). If there are *increasing returns to scale* in faculty inputs, then the marginal input coefficient will be smaller than the faculty-student ratio. If there are *decreasing returns to scale*, this relationship will be reversed. If the marginal input coefficient equals the faculty-student ratio, then one has *constant returns to scale*.

Table 42 shows, for each of the five undergraduate categories, the average number of students, the number of faculty, the faculty-student ratio, and the marginal input coefficient. The table lists the groups in the order of increasing size and also shows, in the last column, the ratio of the marginal input coefficient to the faculty-student ratio (averages for each group). One sees that the larger the average size of institutions in the category, the closer to 1 is the ratio of the marginal input coefficient to the faculty-student ratio. This relationship can be seen even more clearly in Figure 12, in which the ratio of the marginal input coefficient to the faculty-student ratio (vertical axis) is plotted against average size on a logarithmic scale (horizontal axis). A straight line fitted to these five points

[1]Some authors call this the *incremental input coefficient*.

TABLE 42 ***Returns to scale in undergraduate categories***

Category	*Mean S*	*Mean (F/S)*	a^*	$a^*/(F/S)$
Private two-year	842	.066	.049	.74
Private four-year, high-salary	972	.063	.050	.78
Private four-year, low-salary	1,091	.078	.068	.86
Public four-year	1,849	.056	.050	.89
Public two-year	2,213	.049	.045	.91

NOTE: S = full-time equivalent number of students; F = full-time equivalent number of faculty; a^* = marginal input coefficient, calculated at the sample means of the explanatory variables in each category.

suggests that the point of constant returns to scale would be reached at a size of about 3,700 FTE students; i.e., this is the point at which the marginal input coefficient would just equal the faculty-student ratio.

In summary, our data suggest that, for undergraduate institutions, there are increasing returns to scale for faculty inputs as a function of size (enrollment) up to an enrollment of between 3,000 and 4,000 FTE students. This conclusion is roughly consistent with the Carnegie Commission's analysis of cost data (1972, p. 41).

On the other hand, our analysis of the 93 universities in our sample revealed no evidence of either increasing or decreasing returns to scale. Our sample of universities included only those with substantial graduate enrollments, and the average size in both the public and private categories was about 11,000 FTE students.

Of the two M.A.-level categories, the private group seemed to conform closely to the relationship shown in Figure 12, whereas the public group did not. It should be emphasized that in the private M.A.-granting category there are many of the so-called high-prestige liberal arts colleges, since these typically give some beginning graduate work. The evidence on returns to scale for all categories is discussed in more detail in Sections 7.5 through 7.7.

The two variables—average faculty salary and fraction of the faculty who hold the Ph.D. degree—relate to the quality of faculty inputs. A conventional view of higher education is that high faculty salaries, a high fraction of the faculty with the

FIGURE 12
Returns to scale in undergraduate categories

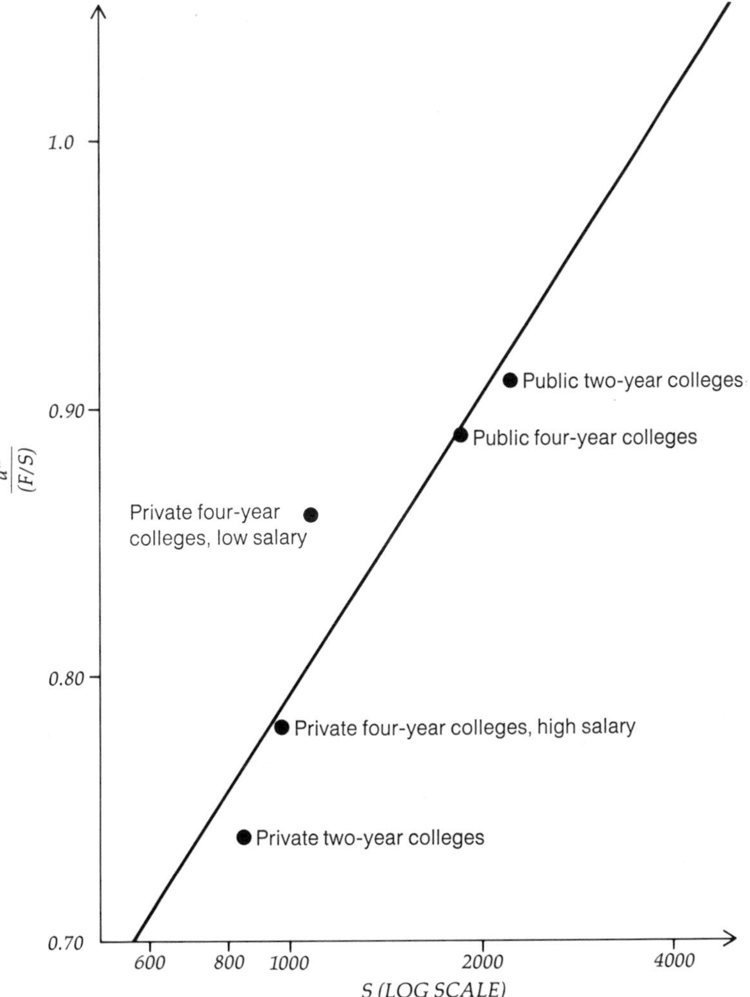

SOURCE: Table 42.

Ph.D., and low faculty-student ratios are characteristic of high-prestige institutions. A further elaboration of this view is that if an institution obtains additional resources, it will try to improve all three of these attributes. We might call this the "prestige model" of an institution. The prestige model would predict that after controlling for the effect of other variables, there would be a positive association between the faculty input coefficients and the two faculty quality variables.

A second model postulates that the quality of faculty inputs can be substituted for quantity; we might call this the "substitution" model. The substitution model would predict that after controlling for the effect of other variables, there would be an *inverse* association between faculty input coefficients and the two faculty quality variables.

Unfortunately, in order to discriminate between these two models empirically, it would be necessary to control for the level of resources available to the individual institutions, and we did not feel we could measure this variable adequately for the institutions in our sample. Indeed, our analysis does not show uniform behavior across all our categories. The universities, the public four-year and private M.A.-granting groups, and (in part) the public M.A.-granting institutions seem to follow the prestige model, whereas the two-year and high-salary private four-year groups show evidence of substitution of quantity for one of the faculty quality variables. The low-salary private four-year institutions do not show a significant effect of either salary or fraction of Ph.D.'s on the faculty input coefficient.

For the universities, we had a third quality variable, namely, an index of the quality of the graduate program. Of the three quality variables, only faculty salary and quality of graduate program were significantly associated with the faculty input coefficients; faculty salary was associated positively with both coefficients a_u and a_g in equation (1), and quality of graduate program was associated positively with a_g, the coefficient for graduate education. If we measure the "importance" of an association by the percentage variation in the faculty input coefficient associated with a one-standard-deviation change in the quality variable, then the association between the quality of the graduate program and the graduate input coefficient a_g was considerably more important than that for the faculty salary. Also, the association between salary and the *undergraduate* input coefficient a_u was more important than that between salary and the *graduate* input coefficient.

Our variable input coefficient model enabled us to make separate estimates of faculty input coefficients for undergraduate and graduate education in the universities. Table 43 shows estimates of the *marginal* faculty input coefficients, a^*_u and a^*_g, for public and private universities, as well as the marginal faculty input coefficients a^* for the M.A.-level categories (all coefficients were calculated at the sample means for the respec-

TABLE 43
Marginal faculty input coefficients for Ph.D.-granting and M.A.-granting categories

Category	Marginal input coefficients		
	a^*_u	a^*_g	a^*
Public Ph.D.-granting	.060	.012	
Private Ph.D.-granting	.058	.020	
Public M.A.-granting			.053
Private M.A.-granting			.067

tive categories). Recall that separate graduate and undergraduate coefficients were not calculated for the M.A.-level institutions. Comparison of Tables 42 and 43 shows that the faculty input coefficients for undergraduate education in the universities were lower than the input coefficients in two other categories: high-salary private four-year and private M.A.-granting institutions. The input coefficient for the public M.A.-granting category was roughly 10 percent less than the input coefficients for undergraduate education in the universities. Finally, we note that the (marginal) input coefficient for graduate education in the private universities was about 67 percent higher than that in the public universities. To put it another way, the marginal (or incremental) student-faculty ratio for *graduate* education in the private universities was estimated to be about 5 to 1, and that in the public universities about 8.3 to 1, so that the public university ratio was about 66 percent higher than the private one. On the other hand, the marginal student-faculty ratios for *undergraduate* education were (on the average) approximately the same in the two groups of universities, namely, equal to about 17 to 1.

7.2. UNDERGRADUATES AND GRADUATES: THE FIXED COEFFICIENT MODEL AND ITS DIFFICULTIES

A simple fixed coefficient model It is generally believed that graduate students take up more faculty time, per student enrolled, than do undergraduates. In the language of activity analysis, we might say that the training of undergraduates and the training of graduate students are two different activities with different (faculty) input coefficients. This suggests the simple linear relationship,

$$F = a_u U + a_g G, \qquad (3)$$

where, for a given institution, at a given date:

F = the number of (full-time equivalent) faculty

U,G = the numbers of enrolled (full-time equivalent) undergraduate and graduate students, respectively

a_u,a_g = the faculty input coefficients for undergraduate and graduate teaching, respectively

If observations were available on a given school for several points in time, during a period in which the input coefficients remained constant but the ratio of undergraduate to graduate students was changing, then the input coefficients could be estimated from, say, a regression of F on U and G. Which particular regression would be appropriate would depend on the particular stochastic specification of the relationship (3). Alternatively, if observations were available at a given point of time on each of a set of schools believed to have common input coefficients, then the coefficients could be estimated from a cross-sectional regression.

The situation we are considering is illustrated in Figure 13, which is based on a simple transformation of equation (3) into a

FIGURE 13 ***Locus of (U*,G*) pairs for constant input coefficients***

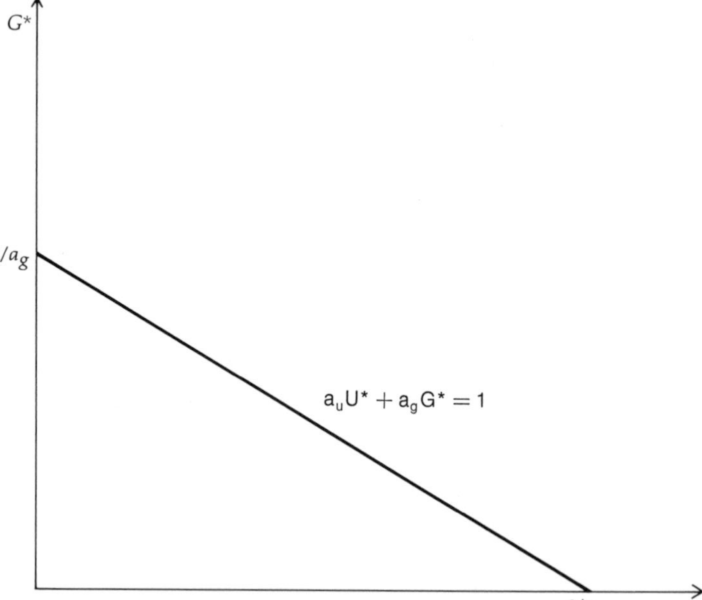

relationship involving student-faculty ratios. Define

$$U^* = \frac{U}{F}, \qquad G^* = \frac{G}{F}.$$

Then dividing both sides of equation (3) by F gives

$$1 = a_u U^* + a_g G^*. \tag{4}$$

All (non negative) pairs (U^*,G^*) satisfying equation (4) would lie on a single line, as in Figure 13. The line might be thought of as the "output transformation locus" per unit teacher input. The slope of that line would equal the negative of the ratio a_u/a_g, and the intercepts on the U^* and G^* axes would be $1/a_u$ and $1/a_g$, respectively. The figure represents a situation in which a_g is greater than a_u.

Problems in the use of time-series data Observations on a single school at different points of time would yield (U^*,G^*) pairs all lying on the same line, if the input coefficients remained constant during the period and if there were neither "disturbances" in the input-output relationship nor errors in the measurement of the variables. However, suppose there were a time trend in the input coefficients. A smooth trend would produce a situation such as that illustrated in Figure 14. Successive solid lines in the figure represent different transformation loci and

FIGURE 14
The case of a smooth trend in the input coefficients

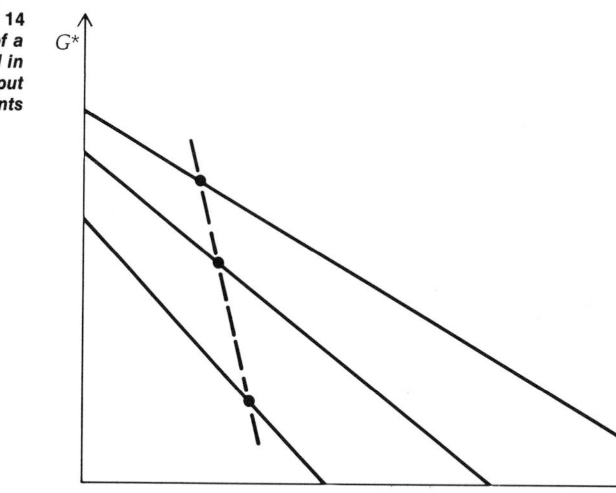

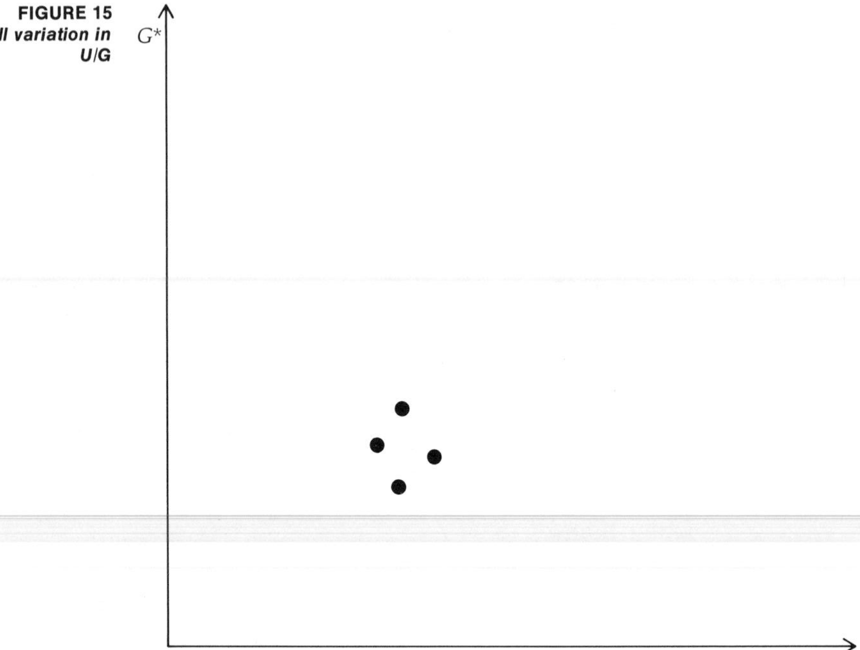

FIGURE 15
Small variation in U/G

correspond to successive pairs (a_u,a_g), but we have only one observation on each line (one observation for each point of time). In the situation depicted by the figure, the ratio of graduates to undergraduates (equal to G^*/U^*) is also increasing smoothly. The result is that observed (U^*,G^*) pairs appear to fall on a single (dotted) line, which corresponds to a (a_u,a_g) pair that is a very poor (indeed biased) estimate of the true average (a_u,a_g) pair over the period of the observation.

Even if the input coefficients remain constant during the observation period, random disturbances (or errors of measurement) may obscure the underlying relationship. It is clear that for a given variability of the disturbances, the greater the variation in the undergraduate-graduate ratio, the easier it will be to estimate the input coefficients. This is illustrated in Figures 15 and 16. In Figure 15, the undergraduate-graduate ratio is practically constant over the observation period, and it is impossible to get a good estimate of the input coefficients (i.e., it is impossible to estimate the relationship [4]). In Figure 16, there is a great variation in the undergraduate-graduate ratio, so that the relationship can be reliably estimated in spite of the random disturbances.

Unfortunately, a school that is experiencing large changes in

FIGURE 16
Large variation in U/G

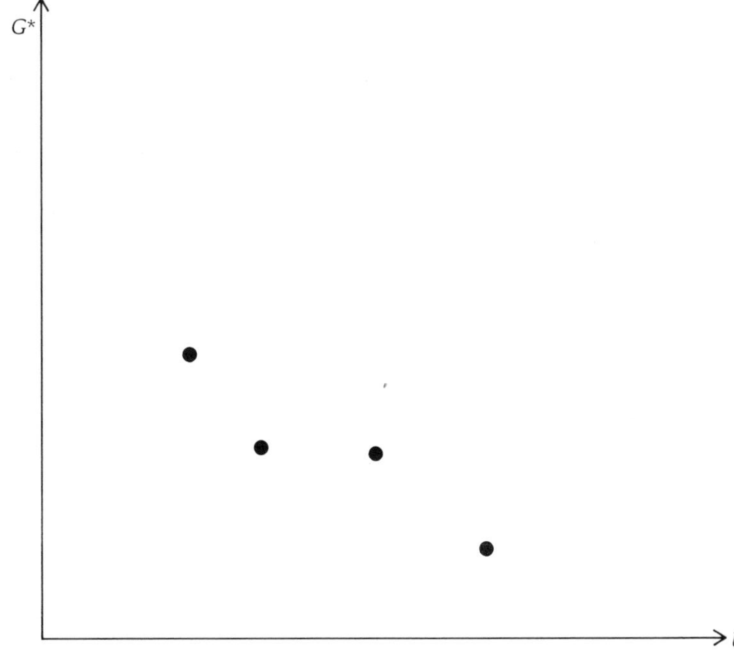

its undergraduate-graduate ratio is also likely to be experiencing "structural" or quality changes that will affect its input coefficients. Therefore, in the presence of random disturbances, we are likely to face a dilemma in which either the input coefficients are stable but we cannot estimate them, or they are not stable but we cannot identify the pattern of change.

Examination of the data reveals that we are indeed faced with this dilemma, as we shall now show. First, we note that for a least-squares fit of relation (4), the appropriate measure of stability (i.e., lack of variation) of the undergraduate-graduate ratio in a set of observations $[U^*(t),G^*(t)]$ is the coefficient

$$r = \frac{\sum U^*(t)\, G^*(t)}{\left[\sum U^*(t)^2 \sum G^*(t)^2\right]^{1/2}}.$$

Note that r has the form of a correlation coefficient, except that the moments are around zero instead of around the means of the variables. If $r = 1$, then all the pairs $[U^*(t),G^*(t)]$ lie on a common ray through the origin; the greater the variation of the undergraduate-graduate ratio in the sample, the closer r will be to zero.

In our sample of 113 universities, r ranged from 1.0 to .80 and was at least .88 in all but five cases. Figure 17 shows the scatter diagram of (U^*,G^*) observations for five selected universities, with r ranging from .88 to .999. In all but one of these cases (South Carolina State College), there is clearly no possibility of estimating the individual input coefficients from the observations. Even in the case of South Carolina State College, a line fitted to the four points would imply that the undergraduate faculty input coefficient is larger than the graduate coefficient. These selected schools are typical, and an examination of the observations for the entire set of schools shows that in most of the cases there is no clear basis for estimating the input coefficients because the variation of the random disturbances is too large, because there have been changes in the coefficients, or for both these reasons. We are, of course, handicapped by the smallness of the sample, but even with more observations during this 12-year period, it seems unlikely that reliable estimation would be feasible.

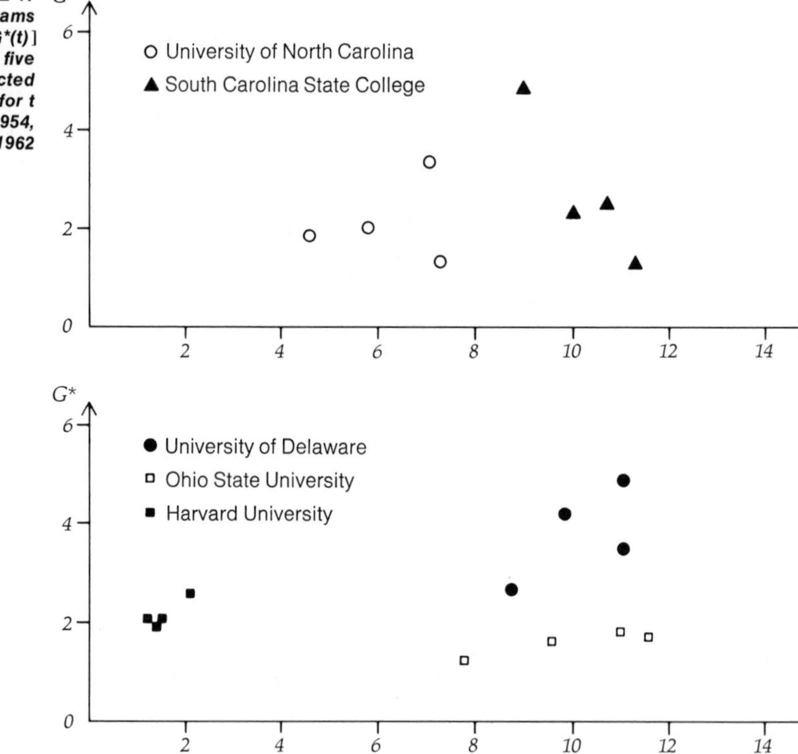

FIGURE 17 ***Scatter diagrams of [$U^*(t),G^*(t)$] pairs for five selected universities, for t = 1950, 1954, 1958, and 1962***

Problems with the use of cross-sectional data As already noted above, one could estimate equation (3) or (4) from a cross section of universities at a given point of time, provided one had a set of institutions that were approximately homogeneous with respect to input coefficients.

For this purpose, we looked at HEGIS data for 1966. Our sample included 55 public universities and 38 private universities. (We eliminated a number of universities covered by HEGIS from our sample because they did not have substantial "standard" graduate programs or because data on other variables, used in the analysis discussed in Section 7.4, were not available. (For definitions of the data and sources, see the appendixes to Chapter 6.)

To see how well the data might fit equation (4), we plotted a scatter diagram of (U^*,G^*) pairs for each of the two groups of universities, public and private. (Recall that $U^* = U/F$ and $G^* = G/F$.) The two scatter diagrams are shown in Figures 18 and 19, respectively. These figures reveal tremendous variation in the pairs (U^*,G^*), even among institutions with the same undergraduate-graduate ratio. (Recall that institutions with the same U/G ratio will lie on the same ray through the origin.) It is clear that equation (4) does not fit either of the scatter diagrams (with a line like that of Figure 13).

Of course, one expects the input coefficients to vary among institutions and to be related more or less to various institutional characteristics. This is confirmed in a rough and informal way by an examination of Figures 18 and 19. In each figure, if we compare those institutions at or near the "southwest" boundary of the scatter diagram with those near the "northeast" boundary, we find that the first set has a higher concentration of prestige institutions than the second. An attempt to relate the input coefficients to other institutional variables will be described in the next section.

7.3. A VARIABLE INPUT COEFFICIENT MODEL

In the previous section we saw that variations in student-faculty ratios were far from explained by variations in the undergraduate/graduate student mix, but that for schools with the same mix the ratios appeared to be related to other school characteristics. In the context of the activity analysis model, this could be expressed by saying that the "crude" numerical input-output coefficients, in terms of numbers of faculty, undergradu-

FIGURE 18 ***Scatter diagram of (U/F, G/F) for public universities***

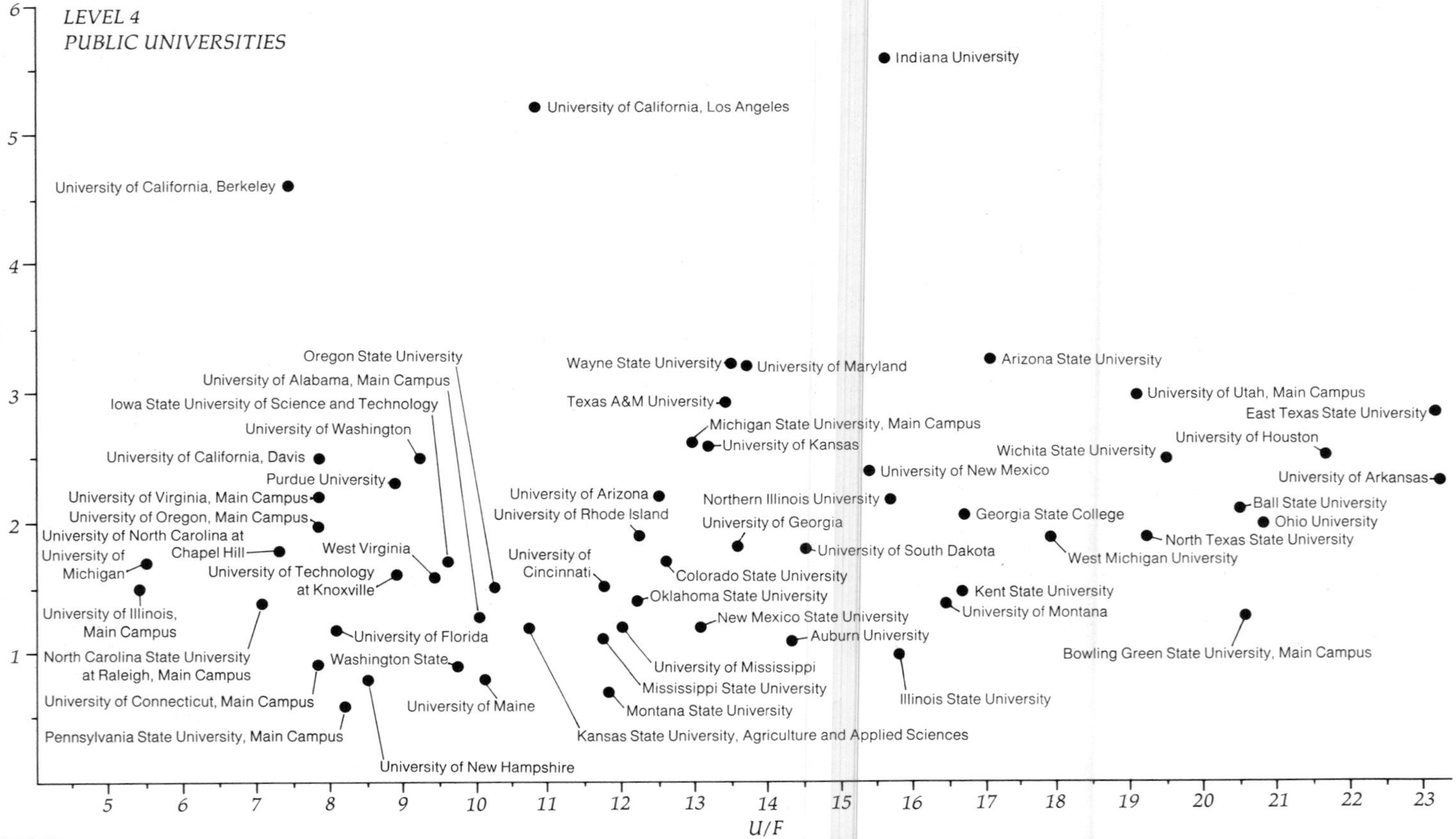

LEVEL 4
PUBLIC UNIVERSITIES

Indiana University
University of California, Los Angeles
University of California, Berkeley
Oregon State University
University of Alabama, Main Campus
Iowa State University of Science and Technology
University of Washington
University of California, Davis
Purdue University
University of Virginia, Main Campus
University of Oregon, Main Campus
University of North Carolina at Chapel Hill
University of Michigan
West Virginia
University of Technology at Knoxville
University of Illinois, Main Campus
North Carolina State University at Raleigh, Main Campus
University of Florida
Washington State
University of Connecticut, Main Campus
University of Maine
Pennsylvania State University, Main Campus
University of New Hampshire
Wayne State University
University of Maryland
Texas A&M University
Michigan State University, Main Campus
University of Kansas
University of New Mexico
University of Arizona
University of Rhode Island
Northern Illinois University
University of Georgia
University of Cincinnati
University of South Dakota
Colorado State University
Oklahoma State University
New Mexico State University
Auburn University
University of Mississippi
Mississippi State University
Montana State University
Kansas State University, Agriculture and Applied Sciences
Illinois State University
Arizona State University
University of Utah, Main Campus
East Texas State University
University of Houston
Wichita State University
University of Arkansas
Ball State University
Ohio University
Georgia State College
North Texas State University
West Michigan University
Kent State University
University of Montana
Bowling Green State University, Main Campus

G/F: 1, 2, 3, 4, 5, 6

U/F: 5, 6, 7, 8, 9, 10, 11, 12, 13, 14, 15, 16, 17, 18, 19, 20, 21, 22, 23

FIGURE 19 *Scatter diagram of (U/F, G/F) for private universities*

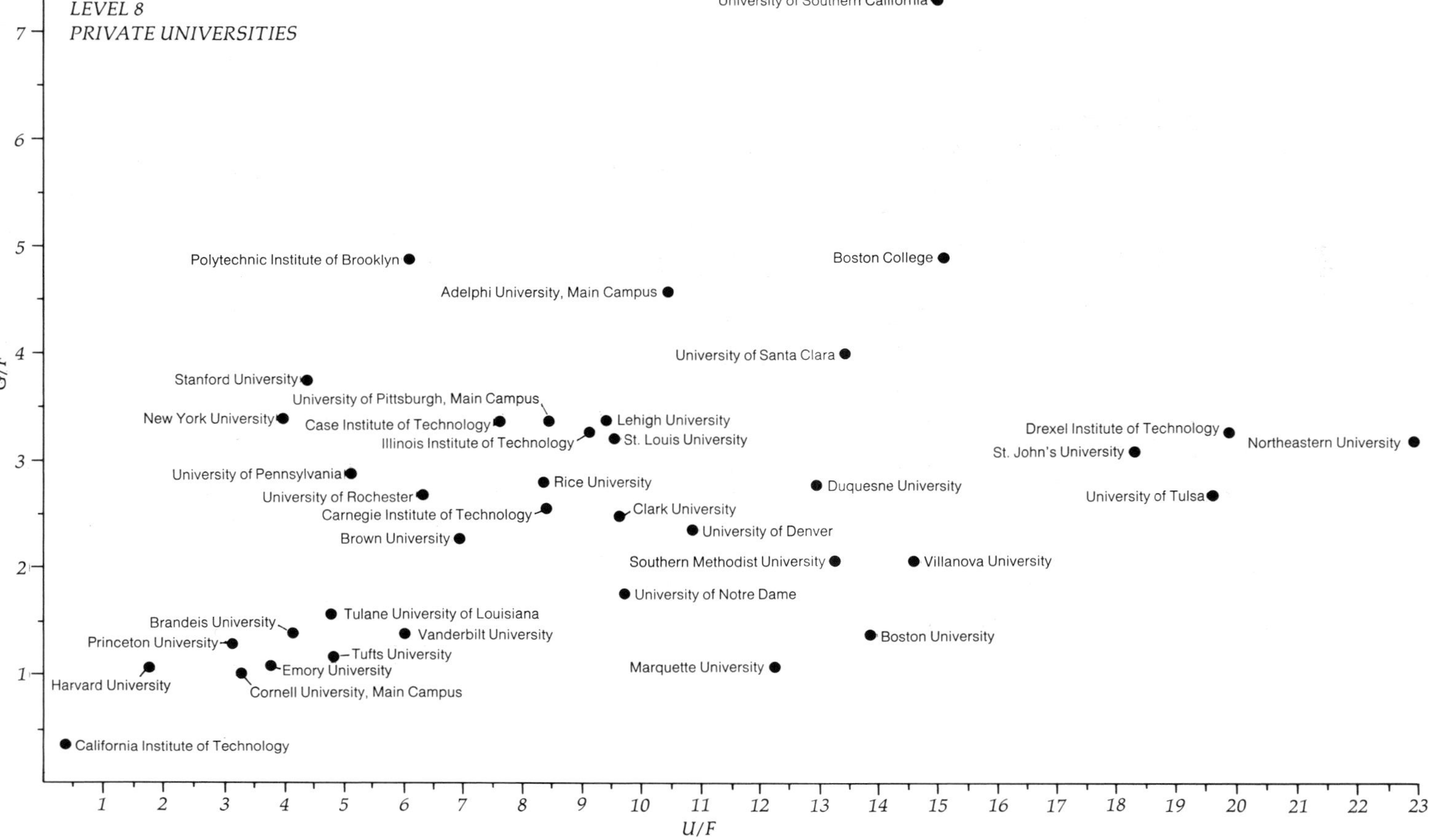

ates, and graduates, depend on the quality of the inputs and outputs, and possibly on other school characteristics as well. Why not try to relate these input-output coefficients directly to these other variables?

Unfortunately, there are few, if any, accepted measures of the quality of inputs and outputs, nor do we have available data on many of the more promising measures. However, many people have found it reasonable to suppose that institutions with the same average faculty salaries, percentage of faculty with the Ph.D. degree, etc., tend to have the same quality of inputs and outputs, or at least that the variation in quality among institutions that are similar in these characteristics is less than that which exists among the set of all institutions.

Consider again the linear relationship

$$F = a_u U + a_g G, \tag{5}$$

where F, U, and G represent the full-time equivalent numbers of faculty, undergraduate students, and graduate students, respectively. For each institution, let W and Z be two vectors of measurements of institutional characteristics (there may be some characteristics common to both vectors) and assume that the input coefficients are related to these characteristics, as follows:

$$a_u = h_0 + h \cdot W, \qquad a_g = k_0 + k \cdot Z, \tag{6}$$

where h_0 and k_0 are parameters, h and k are vectors of parameters, and

$$h \cdot W = \sum_j h_j W_j, \qquad k \cdot Z = \sum_j k_j Z_j. \tag{7}$$

Combining equations (6) and (7) and adding a constant term c yields the equation

$$F = c + (h_0 + h \cdot W)U + (k_0 + k \cdot Z)G. \tag{8}$$

The constant term c, if different from zero, could reflect the presence of increasing or decreasing returns to scale (if c is positive or negative, respectively). An alternative measure of returns to scale could be obtained by setting $c = 0$, but including a measure of "size" in the vectors W and Z.

Finally, it should be noted that equation (8) could be applied to purely undergraduate institutions to examine how variation in the faculty-student ratio a_u is related to institutional characteristics.

Equation (8) can easily be fitted by least squares, since the equation is linear in the parameters to be estimated. However, if the vectors W and Z contain measurements in common, problems of multicollinearity may arise (they may, and do, arise in any case, for other reasons!).

For the components of the vector W we have taken the variables:

PHD = fraction of the faculty holding a Ph.D. degree
SAL = average faculty salary
U = FTE undergraduates

For the components of the vector Z we have taken:

$QUAL$ = measure of the quality of the graduate program (see below)
SAL = average faculty salary
G = FTE graduate students

The variable $QUAL$ is an index derived from two measures: (1) an overall index derived from the departmental ratings in the 1966 ACE report on quality of graduate education in the United States, the so-called Cartter report,[2] and (2) the number of Woodrow Wilson and National Science Foundation fellows elected to go to a given institution. Unfortunately, we were not able to obtain a comparable measure of quality of undergraduate programs.

With these "explanatory variables," equation (8) takes the form

$$F = c + h_0U + h_1(SAL)(U) + h_2(PHD)(U) + h_3U^2 + k_0G + k_1(SAL)(G) + k_2(QUAL)(G) + k_3G^2. \qquad (9)$$

[2]See Cartter (1966).

In the regressions that we shall report, two restrictions were imposed. First, we did not include both the constant term c and the size variables U^2 and G^2 in the same regression. Second, we found that the two variables $(SAL)(U)$ and $(SAL)(G)$ were too highly correlated to permit reliable estimation of their coefficients separately; therefore, we imposed the restriction that $h_1 = k_1$, which is equivalent to replacing the two above variables by the single variable $(SAL)(STUD)$, where $STUD = U + G$.

7.4. THE SAMPLE

For our cross-sectional analysis, we used a sample of institutions for which HEGIS data were available for 1966. These institutions were grouped in a two-way classification, by control (public or private) and by highest degree granted (two-year, bachelor's, master's, or Ph.D.). Actually, for the second classification we used the following corresponding terms: two-year, four-year, M.A.-granting, and Ph.D.-granting (or university). For all institutions except the universities, "private" means "private nonsectarian." The private universities include both nonsectarian universities and those sectarian universities that did not have primarily religious programs of education. We did not include all institutions of higher education covered by the HEGIS data. In particular, we did not include (1) institutions with fewer than 300 undergraduates, (2) institutions beyond the two-year level that were very specialized or were primarily vocational, or (3) institutions for which the data on some of our variables were missing or were obviously in error. In some cases we supplemented our main body of data with material from other sources. Finally, the category "private four-year" was divided into two groups, according to whether the average faculty salary was above or below $8,000 per year.

Table 41 shows the classification of institutions and the number of institutions in each category.

The variables used were those described in Section 7.3. They are listed here again, together with the corresponding scaling factors, where applicable. (See Miller and Radner, 1975, for a complete description.)

F = full-time equivalent number of faculty $\times 10^{-2}$

U = full-time equivalent number of undergraduates $\times 10^{-3}$

G = full-time equivalent number of graduate students $\times 10^{-3}$

$STUD = U + G$ ($STUD = U$ for levels 1, 5, 2, and 6)

PHD = fraction of the faculty who hold the Ph.D. degree

$QUAL$ = an index of the quality of the graduate program (see Section 7.3)

SAL = average nine-month (or nine-month equivalent) faculty salary $\times 10^{-4}$

Tables 44 and 45 show the means and standard deviations, respectively, of the variables for each level. The statistics for the mean faculty-student ratios are also shown. In interpreting these statistics, the reader must keep in mind the scaling factors. In addition, in comparing the mean faculty-student ratios with those reported in Table 39, one must keep in mind that Table 44 gives the means of faculty-student ratios of individual institutions, whereas the ratios reported in Table 39 are ratios of total faculty to total students in a given category of institution. We see that the mean faculty-student ratios for 1966 in Table 44 are generally lower than the *corresponding* ratios for 1962 reported in Table 40, thus suggesting an extension of the downward trend. On the other hand, the fact that the mean ratios for

TABLE 44 ***Sample means***

Level	Variable / Scaling factor	F ($x\,10^{-2}$)	U ($x\,10^{-3}$)	G ($x\,10^{-3}$)	$STUD$ ($x\,10^{-3}$)	$\frac{F}{STUD}$ ($x\,10$)	PHD	$QUAL$	SAL ($x\,10^{-4}$)
1.	*Public two-year*	.935	2.213	.000	2.213	.489	.041		.835
5.	*Private two-year*	.464	.842	.000	.842	.661	.039		.715
2.	*Public four-year*	.963	1.849	.000	1.849	.556	.243		.815
6L.	*Private four-year*	.566	.972	.000	.972	.634	.263		.705
6H.	*Private four-year*	.747	1.091	.000	1.091	.783	.447		.951
3.	*Public M.A.-granting*	2.382	3.891	.359	4.249	.588	.356		.924
7.	*Private M.A.-granting*	1.379	1.872	.166	2.038	.753	.457		.937
4.	*Public Ph.D.-granting*	10.085	11.290	1.909	13.200	.742	.513	.581	1.048
8.	*Private Ph.D.-granting*	9.027	5.869	1.998	7.869	1.492	.589	.896	1.121

NOTE: Figures in parentheses under variable names indicate the scaling factors.

SOURCE: HEGIS (1966).

TABLE 45 ***Sample standard deviations***

Level	F $(x\,10^{-2})$	U $(x\,10^{-3})$	G $(x\,10^{-3})$	$STUD$ (10^{-3})	$\frac{F}{STUD}$ $(x\,10)$	PHD	$QUAL$	SAL $(x\,10^{-4})$
1. *Public two-year*	.864	2.549	.000	2.549	.131	.055		.154
5. *Private two-year*	.265	.601	.000	.601	.294	.063		.096
2. *Public four-year*	.591	1.355	.000	1.355	.115	.102		.134
6L. *Private four-year*	.264	.578	.000	.578	.146	.106		.086
6H. *Private four-year*	.336	.883	.000	.883	.192	.182		.170
3. *Public M.A.-granting*	1.752	2.548	.607	2.989	.193	.126		.128
7. *Private M.A.-granting*	.842	1.286	.281	1.455	.287	.173		.138
4. *Public Ph.D.-granting*	7.370	5.161	1.610	6.583	.253	.079	.602	.075
8. *Private Ph.D.-granting*	9.340	3.965	1.974	5.334	2.669	.146	.662	.175

NOTE: Figures in parentheses under variable names indicate the scaling factors.
SOURCE: HEGIS (1966).

1966 are generally higher than the (total) ratios for 1967 reported in Table 40 probably is more a reflection of difference in the method of averaging than a reflection of any trend (although other information suggests that the downward trend has indeed continued beyond 1966).

7.5. RESULTS OF THE REGRESSION ANALYSES FOR THE UNDERGRADUATE- AND MASTER'S-LEVEL INSTITUTIONS

For each of the categories other than the two Ph.D. levels (public and private universities), we fitted by least squares the following two regression equations:

$$F = h_0 STUD + h_1(SAL)(STUD) + h_2(PHD)(STUD) + h_3(STUD)^2 \qquad (10)$$

$$F = c + h_0 STUD + h_1(SAL)(STUD) + h_2(PHD)(STUD) \qquad (11)$$

Generally, we found that the specification without the constant term, equation (10), gave a slightly better fit, although the differences in fit were not very great. In each category, the fit was quite good; in the set of seven categories the multiple correlation (R^2) ranged between .904 and .986.

In Table 46 the estimates of the regression coefficients are given for specification (10). In order to conserve space, we have reported only one set of estimates for each category of institu-

TABLE 46 ***Regressions for nonuniversity groups***

	STUD times						
Level	*1*	*SAL*	*PHD*	*STUD*	*n*	R^2	a^*_{STUD}†
1. *Public two-year*	.667	−.197		−.013	185	.956	.446
5. *Private two-year*		1.062	−1.443*	−0.126	34	.904	.491
2. *Public four-year*	.291	.279*	.336*	−0.028	51	.986	.496
6L. *Private four-year, SAL < 8,000*	.760			−0.137	44	.967	.496
6H. *Private four-year, SAL > 8,000*	1.075	−.495	.657	−.101	47	.979	.677
3. *Public M.A.-granting*	.174*	.435		−.006*	134	.969	.525
7. *Private M.A.-granting*		.394	.852	−.022*	62	.947	.668

NOTE: Regression coefficients for the corresponding variable in the regression equation

$$F = h_0 STUD + h_1 (SAL)(STUD) + h_2 (PHD)(STUD) + h_3 (STUD)^2.$$

Except as noted, all coefficients are significant at the .005 level or lower. Coefficients marked with an asterisk are significant at the .05 level or lower. For two-year and four-year colleges, *STUD* means undergraduates only. For M.A.-granting colleges, $STUD = U + G$. All variables are scaled as in table 44.
† a^* *STUD* is the derivative of the regression equation with respect to *STUD*, evaluated at the sample means of the explanatory variables.

tion. In selecting the set of estimates to present for each particular category, we restricted ourselves to specifications that included only "explanatory" variables yielding statistically significant coefficients, and among such specifications we chose the one that gave the best fit. Since the correlations between some of the explanatory variables were rather high, we had in some instances problems of multicollinearity; these problems are discussed in Section 7.8, where we also present some examples of regressions with coefficients that are statistically not significant. In any case, in none of the specifications reported in Table 46 could the fit be significantly improved by adding more variables.

Table 46 also shows the corresponding estimates a^*_{STUD} of the derivative of the regression equations with respect to the variable *STUD*, i.e., $a^*_{STUD} = dF/dSTUD$; this derivative has been evaluated at the sample means of the explanatory variables. Thus a^*_{STUD} is the marginal input coefficient. Notice that a^*_{STUD} is not in general equal to the input coefficient a_{STUD}, since the input coefficient itself depends on the variable *STUD*. Indeed, since by equation (10)

$$a_{STUD} = h_0 + h_1 SAL + h_2 PHD + h_3 STUD,$$
$$a^*_{STUD} = h_0 + h_1 SAL + h_2 PHD + 2h_3 STUD, \qquad (12)$$

the two coefficients are related by

$$a^*_{STUD} = a_{STUD} + h_3 STUD.$$

We see from Table 46 that h_3, the coefficient of $STUD^2$, is significant in every case and negative. This indicates that in each of the nonuniversity categories there was a measurable effect of *increasing returns to scale* to the faculty input. We see, too, that this effect was more pronounced in the case of the private institutions than in the case of the public ones. This is no doubt related to the fact that the average enrollments in the public groups were consistently higher than those in the corresponding private groups (see Table 44).

If we compare the marginal input coefficients of Table 46 with the mean faculty-student ratios of Table 44, we see that the marginal coefficients are consistently lower than the average coefficients. This is, of course, consistent with the effect of increasing returns to scale. The ranking of the seven nonuniversity groups is roughly the same by the marginal as by the average coefficients, but the exceptions to this are revealing. Table 47 gives the two rankings, with the number "1" corresponding to the largest coefficient. The most obvious discrep-

TABLE 47 Rankings of nonuniversity groups by marginal and average input coefficients

	Ranking by:	
	Marginal input coefficient	*Average input coefficient*
Public two-year	7	7
Private two-year	6	3
Public four-year	4–5	6
Private four-year, low-salary	4–5	4
Private four-year, high-salary	1	1
Public M.A.-granting	3	5
Private M.A.-granting	2	2

ancies in the two rankings occur in the case of the private two-year and the public M.A.-granting groups. Table 44 shows, however, that these two groups have the lowest and highest mean enrollments, respectively, of the seven groups. Thus it would appear that although the private two-year institutions have relatively low marginal input coefficients, their average coefficient is high because of their small average size. An analogous, but reverse, argument would seem to apply to the public M.A.-granting group.

Before studying the "effects" of salary and of percentage of faculty with the Ph.D., we might speculate on some a priori models. The first, which might be called the "prestige model," postulates that high faculty-student ratios, high salaries, and high percentage of faculty with the Ph.D. are all trappings of a high-prestige institution, so that one would expect the coefficients h_1 and h_2 to be positive. The second model, which might be called the "substitution model," postulates that salary and percentage of Ph.D.'s are measures of quality and that quality of faculty inputs can be substituted for quantity, so that one would expect h_1 and h_2 to be negative. Of course, in the substitution model one would want to control for the quality of output, which we have not been able to do here.

Table 46 does not show any consistency among the groups in the signs of h_1 and h_2. Public four-year, private M.A.-granting and (in part) public M.A.-granting institutions seem to follow the prestige model, whereas the two-year and the high-salary private four-year institutions show evidence of substitution, with respect to one of the variables. It should be pointed out that most of the so-called high-prestige liberal arts colleges fall into the private M.A.-granting group, since they typically give some beginning graduate work. The low-salary private four-year institutions do not show a significant effect of either salary or percentage of Ph.D.'s on the input coefficient.

7.6. RESULTS OF THE REGRESSION ANALYSES FOR THE UNIVERSITIES

For each of the two university categories we fitted by least squares the following two regression equations:

$$\begin{aligned} F = {} & h_1(SAL)\,(U + G) \\ & + h_0U + h_2(PHD)(U) + h_3U^2 \\ & + k_0G + k_2(QUAL)(G) + k_3G^2 \end{aligned} \tag{13}$$

$$\begin{aligned} F = {} & c + h_1(SAL)(U + G) \\ & + h_0U + h_2(PHD)(U) \\ & + k_0G + k_2(QUAL)(G) \end{aligned} \tag{14}$$

Again, we found in general that the specification without the constant term (13) gave a slightly better fit. The fits for the universities were not quite as good as those for the other groups, but were still quite good.

In Table 48 the estimates of the regression coefficients are given for specification (13). For each group we have given more than one set of estimates in order to illustrate some of the problems that we face.

Recall that, for the case of the universities, one of the tasks we set ourselves was to estimate the separate effects of U and G on the numbers of faculty. Thus we aim not only to get a good fit but also to get reasonable estimates of the marginal input coefficients a^*_u and a^*_g. (See Sections 7.2 and 7.3. The marginal input coefficients are defined just as in equation [12].)

Examination of Table 48 shows that, although each regression equation shown gives a reasonably good fit, not all the specifications lead to sensible values for the marginal input coefficients. For example, the second specification for each of the two groups is the same as equation (3), i.e.:

$$F = a_uU + a_gG \tag{15}$$

The resulting estimates of a_u and a_g are reasonable for the public universities, but not for the private universities. The *first* specification for each of the two groups *does* lead to reasonable estimates of the marginal input coefficients:

	a^*_u	a^*_g
Public universities	.596	1.166
Private universities	.575	1.983

However, one would have expected a^*_u to be larger for the private than for the public universities; it is generally believed that classes are smaller, teaching loads are lighter, etc., in

TABLE 48 ***Regressions for the universities***

Level	*U times* 1	*SAL*	*PHD*	*U*	*G times* 1	*SAL*	*QUAL*	*G*	*n*	R^2	a^*_u	a^*_g
4. Public Ph.D.-granting		.569				.569	.982		55	.907	.596	1.166
	.497				2.330				55	.887	.497	2.330
8. Private Ph.D.-granting		.513				.513	1.572		38	.782	.575	1.983
	.217***				3.416				38	.702	.217	3.416
		2.395	−3.358*	−.0.039**		2.395			38	.808	.249	2.685

NOTE: The regression equation is given by (13). Significance levels are indicated as follows: unmarked—.005 or lower; *—.05 or lower; **—.10 or lower; ***—not significant at .10 level.

private universities than in public universities. These faculty input coefficients for undergraduate education are somewhat smaller than the coefficients for the private M.A.-granting and high-salary private four-year groups, but are larger than those for the other groups. It should be emphasized that the data on faculty did not include teaching assistants, teaching associates, or teaching fellows; to that extent the input coefficients underestimate the instructional inputs. On the other hand, the data for faculty include faculty in organized research units.

We do not find evidence of significantly increasing returns to scale in either undergraduate or graduate education at the mean values of the explanatory variables (except in the case of the third regression for the private universities, which does not in any case yield sensible values of the input coefficients).

If we accept the first regression in each of the two university groups as valid, then the universities appear to fit the prestige model quite well. The variable *QUAL* represents the combined judgments of faculty peers and prospective graduate students concerning the quality of the faculty in graduate programs, and therefore would seem to be a measure of the quality of faculty input. (It should not be necessary to insist here on the uncertainties surrounding the meaning of this measure!)

7.7 AN ANALYSIS OF ELASTICITIES

Although the regression coefficients discussed in Sections 7.5 and 7.6 give a fairly good qualitative idea of the relationships between the input coefficients and the explanatory variables, it is difficult to interpret their numerical magnitudes. For this reason we calculated the *elasticities* of the input coefficients with respect to each explanatory variable in the appropriate regression equation. Recall that the elasticity of an input coefficient—say, a—with respect to a variable—say, X—is defined by:

$$\text{Elasticity} = \frac{d \log a}{d \log X} = \frac{X}{a} \cdot \frac{da}{dX} \tag{16}$$

Thus, for small changes, the elasticity equals the percentage change in the input coefficient associated with a 1 percent change in the explanatory variables.

Table 49 shows the elasticities of a^*_{STUD} with respect to the explanatory variables *SAL*, *PHD*, and *STUD* in the regression

TABLE 49 ***Elasticity, coefficient of variation, and probable percentage variation: nonuniversities***

Level	1. Elasticity of a^*_{STUD} with respect to:			2. Coefficient of variation			3. Probable percentage variation of a^*_{STUD} with respect to:		
	SAL	*PHD*	*STUD*	*SAL*	*PHD*	*STUD*	*SAL*	*PHD*	*STUD*
1. *Public two-year*	−.368		−.129	.184		1.152	−.068		−.149
5. *Private two-year*	1.546	−.114	−.432	.134	1.598	.715	.207	−.182	−.309
2. *Public four-year*	.458	.165	−.209	.164	.419	.733	.075	.069	−.153
6L. *Private four-year*			−.537			.594			−.319
6H. *Private four-year*	−.695	.434	−.325	.178	.408	.809	−.124	.177	−.263
3. *Public M.A.-granting*	.766		−.097	.138		.703	.106		−.068
7. *Private M.A.-granting*	.553	.583	−.134	.147	.379	.714	.081	.221	−.096

TABLE 50 ***Elasticity, coefficient of variation, and probable percentage variation: universities***

	1. Elasticity of:			2. Coefficient of variation		3. Probable percentage variation		
	a^*_u w.r.t.	a^*_g	w.r.t.			a^*_u	a^*_g	
Level	*SAL*	*SAL*	*QUAL*	*SAL*	*QUAL*	*SAL*	*SAL*	*QUAL*
4. *Public Ph.D.-granting*	1.000	.511	.489	.072	1.036	.072	.037	.507
8. *Private Ph.D.-granting*	1.000	.290	.710	.156	.739	.156	.045	.525

equations determined by the coefficients in Table 46, taking the estimates of a^*_{STUD} from the same table and taking the variables at their sample means. Table 50 shows the corresponding elasticities for the two university groups using the first regression for each group in Table 48.

In nonuniversity groups, the elasticities of the input coefficients with respect to *STUD* are largest (in magnitude) for the private two-year and four-year institutions and lowest for the public M.A.-granting and two-year institutions. Indeed, although the regression coefficient for *STUD* is statistically significant in the case of the public M.A.-granting group, the corresponding elasticity is rather small in magnitude. It is interesting that with regard to the variable *PHD*, the private two-year group has the largest regression coefficient but the smallest elasticity (in magnitude). Generally, the elasticities with respect to *SAL* are larger in magnitude than those with respect to *PHD*.

In the two university groups, the graduate input coefficient is about equally elastic with respect to *SAL* and *QUAL* in the public universities, but almost 2½ times as elastic with respect to *QUAL* than *SAL* in the private universities.

Further insight into the relative importance of the explanatory variables can be obtained by taking account of the dispersion of the explanatory variables in the sample. To measure the relative dispersion of a variable, we used the *coefficient of variation,* equal to the ratio of the standard deviation to the mean. For the nonuniversity groups (see Table 49), the overall picture is that *STUD* had the largest coefficients of variation, and *SAL* the smallest. In the universities, the coefficient of variation was considerably larger for *QUAL* than for *SAL*.

To "correct" the elasticities for differences in relative dispersion, we measure the "probable percentage variation," defined by:

$$\text{Probable percentage variation} = (\text{elasticity}) \times (\text{coefficient of variation}) \tag{17}$$

This last measure can be interpreted as an approximation to the percentage change in the input coefficient associated with a change in the explanatory variable equal to 1 percent of its standard deviation. The figures for probable percentage variation are also given in Tables 49 and 50. It is interesting to note in Table 50 that, when measured by the probable percentage variation, the association of *QUAL* with the graduate input coefficient is considerably more "important" than that of *SAL*. Also, the probable percentage variation of the undergraduate input coefficient with respect to *SAL* is larger than that of the graduate input coefficient.

7.8. MULTICOLLINEARITY AND OTHER SPECIFICATION PROBLEMS

The pattern of correlations among the variables is such that in many instances it is not evident which selection of explanatory variables is best. Examples of this are shown in Table 51.

In the first example (private Ph.D.-granting), the coefficient of (*STUD*)(*SAL*) is not very significant (statistically) when introduced in addition to (*G*)(*QUAL*); but if the variable (*U*)(*PHD*) is then introduced, the coefficient of (*STUD*)(*SAL*) becomes more significant, and the coefficient of (*G*)(*QUAL*) loses its significance. Similar problems arise in the other examples.

For each group of institutions, we tried quite a few different regression specifications. In choosing the ones we have presented here, we considered not only the criterion of goodness of fit but also the plausibility of the resulting estimates of the input coefficients. We have already alluded to this in the discussion of the regression estimate of equation (15).

One may wonder how it is that the regression estimate of equation (15) for the public universities could give plausible results, whereas the scatter diagram in Figure 18 is so diffuse. Related to this is the fact that regressions of *F/STUD* on the

TABLE 51 ***Examples of the effects of multicollinearity***

Level	*U times*				*G times*			Constant term	R^2
	1	*SAL*	*PHD*	*U*	1	*SAL*	*QUAL*		
							2.574	3.898	
							(.00)	(.00)	
*8. Private Ph.D.-granting**		.372				.372	1.989	1.770	
		(.07)				(.07)	(.00)	(.29)	
		1.623	−3.199			1.623	.978	2.893	
		(.02)	(.06)			(.02)	(.17)	(.10)	.819
		.529				.529	1.891		
		(.00)				(.00)	(.00)		
8. Private Ph.D.-granting†		1.459	−2.206			1.459	1.151		
		(.04)	(.17)			(.04)	(.11)		
		1.790	−2.319	−.028		1.790	.727		
		(.02)	(.16)	(.26)		(.02)	(.36)		.811
	.406							.171	
	(.00)							(.00)	
6L. Private B.A.-granting‡	.189	.283						.183	
	(.32)	(.25)						(.00)	
	.203	.241	.107					.173	
	(.44)	(.34)	(.49)					(.00)	.965
		1.004			−4.432	1.004	2.375		
		(.00)			(.00)	(.00)	(.00)		
4. Public Ph.D.-granting§	1.149	−.094			−3.441	−.094	2.809		
	(.06)	(.87)			(.02)	(.87)	(.00)		.928

NOTE: In each cell, the first number is the regression coefficient, and the second number is the corresponding significance level.
*Correlation between *(G) (QUAL)* and *(U) (PHD)* is .398.
†Correlation between *(STUD) (SAL)* and *(U) (PHD)* is .913; correlation between U^2 and *(G) (QUAL)* is .202.
‡Correlation between *U* and *(U) (SAL)* is .986.
§Correlation between *U* and *(STUD) (SAL)* is .976.

other variables invariably gave poor fits (for all groups of institutions). This suggests that in the regressions in which F is the independent variable, those institutions in each group that have relatively large numbers of faculty and students may have a disproportionate influence on the results. However, we have not yet sufficiently explored this problem to come to a conclusion.

Finally, we should mention that treating undergraduate and graduate students separately in the M.A.-granting institutions did not give good results. It would appear that in this group of institutions it is not possible, with these data, to obtain reliable estimates of a_u and a_g separately.

8. The American Stock of Degreed Manpower and Womanpower

8.1. INTRODUCTION

Since the pioneering work of Solow, Denison, and others,[1] the attention of economists has shifted from a focus on the quantities of economic factors as a source of economic growth to consideration of their qualities. Examples of this attention are the vintage models of the physical-capital factor and the return-on-investment models of the human-capital factor.

With respect to human capital, attention has been almost exclusively on the *level* of educational attainment, with the result that there has been a rather striking gap in our information about the composition of the stock of degreed manpower and womanpower by educational specialty. We do, it is true, have an occupational disaggregation of the labor force, but these data cannot be used to answer certain questions because of the continual educational upgrading of the majority of occupational categories. For example, unless one is willing to assume that the educational characteristics of job-holders have remained constant, an occupational characterization of persons at a given degree level will not reliably characterize their human capital.

A considerably more stable characterization of human capital is that afforded by educational labels, e.g., bachelor's in psychology or master's in chemical engineering. One source of this stability is the fact that the set of educational labels corresponding to academic departments has stayed virtually the same for half a century. Another is that, with each type of department a national institution having its own professional society and external constituencies, students are attracted, selected, and educated so that the typical graduates of each department dis-

[1]See, for example, Solow (1957) and Denison (1964).

play certain characteristic skills and traits. The recognition of educational labels as a reasonable characterization of human capital, of course, does not imply uniformity within each educational group, nor does it suggest that the characteristic skills and traits of each educational group are nonsubstitutable for those of other groups.

For certain purposes, a vintage characterization of human capital may be desirable. Kuhn (1970) and Johnson (1971) have emphasized that revolutions in scientific thought and in the focal area of policy concern require an extensive adjustment process, "neural reprogramming,"[2] which older scholars do not always achieve. One might expect that the steady advance of knowledge in more settled times also does not bring as many older graduates to the frontier as younger. Simple human aging, with its sociological, gerontological, and existential aspects, is another vintage factor to be considered.

In line with these considerations, this study attempts to partially fill the gap in our characterization of human capital by estimating the number of persons in the United States labor market holding degrees from American universities, by 44 educational specialties, by degree of highest attainment, by sex, and by age, annually for the period 1930–1970.

Among the conclusions of the analysis are the following:

1. Degreed manpower and womanpower now comprise 10 percent of the population aged 19 through 70.
2. The overall stock grew at over 5 percent per year between 1930 and 1971, with administration, education, and psychology pacing and health lagging.
3. Twenty-four percent of the stock is qualified at the second level, and 2.5 percent at the doctorate level.
4. Current advancement probabilities are that more than half of the men bachelor's degree recipients and more than a third of the women bachelor's degree recipients will receive advanced degrees. The probability is greater than 60 percent for men bachelor's degree recipients in 17 specialties out of the 38 specialties that are not primarily graduate specialties and in 9 such specialties for women.
5. The time lapse between degrees is typically longer for women than for men at all degree levels.

[2]The quoted term is from Kuhn (1970).

6 The variances of the time-lapse distributions are surprisingly high.

7 Although there was some measure of quantitative sexual equalization at the second level, this appears to have been a consequence of the shift in specialty proportions away from the male-dominated professions rather than a general tendency toward equalization at the specialty level. Qualitative developments were not in the direction of greater equality.

8 The median age of the overall stock—37 in 1971—stayed relatively constant over the period 1930–1971, as did the median age of the doctorate segment—42 years in 1971. The bachelor's level (1971 median—34 years) aged, however, and the second level (1971 median—41 years) became younger.

The methods used to construct these estimates, and an evaluation of their quality, are discussed in detail in Adkins (1975). Basically, the methods involved:

1 Developing degree-conferral estimates for the period 1879–1971 for 44 analysis categories

2 Eliminating the double counting of persons, i.e., deleting from the degree series all but one degree for a given person, the highest he or she attained

3 Deleting degrees granted to emigrating foreign citizens

4 Producing stock estimates from the degree estimates by imposing age distributions, applying appropriate survival rates, and cumulating

Ideally, we would like to evaluate a set of estimates by (1) having a good estimate of their joint error distribution and (2) comparing them with other independently produced, accurate estimates. In this, as in most actual cases, our ability to evaluate the errors in our estimates is severely limited. Rather than have a good estimate of the distribution of our estimators, we are limited to a judgmental assessment of the quality of our data inputs and methodology. Rather than have accurate comparative estimates, we usually have not strictly comparable estimates produced by methodologies of questionable quality. Our evaluation, therefore, can be at best suggestive.

With regard to the quality of data inputs, the principal evaluative conclusions here are that (1) the aggregate stock estimates are reasonably good for the whole post-1930 period, (2) doctorate specialty stock estimates and certain professional specialty stock estimates are of like quality for the whole period, and (3) bachelor's and master's specialty stock estimates are of reasonably good quality after 1960, except for a few slowly growing specialties, but are of uncertain quality prior to that.

Our estimates of stocks can also be compared in certain respects with partial or more aggregated estimates available from the U.S. Bureau of the Census and from studies by Wolfle (1954) and Schwartz (1965). In order to achieve even a minimum of comparability, we had to make a number of substantial adjustments, and these adjustments did not remove all discrepancies. Nevertheless, taken as a whole, the evidence from these other sources appears to be strongly supportive of our own estimates.

8.2. THE SIZE AND GROWTH OF THE STOCK OF DEGREED MANPOWER AND WOMANPOWER

Table 52 presents estimates of the stock of degreed manpower and womanpower by degree level for the years 1930–1971. Tables 53 through 56 disaggregate the stock by 44 academic specialties for the years 1930, 1950, 1960, and 1970. Tables 76A–76C disaggregate Table 52 every fifth year by age and sex. Tables 77A through 78J present the same for a conventional 10-category disaggregation, and Table 79 presents the same for the full 44-category disaggregation. (Because of their length, Tables 76 through 79 appear at the end of this chapter.)

TABLE 52 ***Stock of persons in the United States holding academic degrees from United States universities, by highest degree attained, 1930–1971 (in thousands)***

	Bachelor's			*Second-level*		
Year	*Male*	*Female*	*Total*	*Male*	*Female*	*Total*
1930	454.1	461.5	915.7	456.6	57.3	513.8
1931	488.5	501.3	989.7	471.2	63.2	534.5
1932	525.1	543.0	1,068.1	487.7	69.9	557.6
1933	562.5	584.5	1,147.0	502.9	76.4	579.3
1934	600.5	625.5	1,226.0	506.8	82.6	599.4
1935	640.2	668.0	1,308.3	530.2	88.8	619.0
1936	682.0	712.0	1,393.9	543.1	95.0	638.1
1937	727.3	758.7	1,487.1	556.8	191.9	658.7
1938	776.7	811.7	1,588.4	571.4	109.6	681.0
1939	830.1	867.4	1,697.5	587.0	118.0	705.0
1940	887.8	926.9	1,814.7	603.5	127.4	730.9

In 1971, over 12 million persons aged 70 or under in the United States possessed academic degrees conferred by United States colleges and universities, about 10 percent of the total population aged 19 to 70.[3] Of these, just short of three-quarters (73.0 percent) had received the bachelor's degree but no higher degree, one-quarter (24.5 percent) had received a second-level degree (master's or professional) but not a doctorate, and a mere 2.5 percent had received a doctorate degree.

The sex distribution of the total stock was 58-42 percent men-women in 1971, a distribution that had moved only halfway to equality from the 64-36 percent distribution of 1930. The stock was almost equally split at the bachelor's attainment level—but was male-dominated at higher attainment levels. At the second level the distribution was 70-30; at the doctorate level it was 88-12. About the only important change in any of these distributions since 1930 was that the sex distribution of the second-level stock changed from 89-11 in 1930, to 77-23 in 1950, and then to 70-30 in 1970.

The stock of degreed persons grew rapidly throughout the

[3]An urgent caveat: All figures reported in this chapter are estimates, which are reliable or unreliable to a greater or lesser extent. The methodology of the construction of the estimates and an assessment of their reliability are discussed in some detail in Adkins (1975).

Doctorate			*All levels*		
Male	*Female*	*Total*	*Male*	*Female*	*Total*
17.9	2.8	20.6	928.5	521.6	1,450.1
19.6	3.1	22.8	979.3	567.6	1,547.0
21.4	3.5	24.9	1,034.2	616.4	1,650.7
23.3	3.8	27.1	1,088.7	664.7	1,753.4
25.2	4.1	29.4	1,142.5	712.3	1,854.8
27.0	4.5	31.5	1,197.5	761.3	1,854.8
28.9	4.8	33.7	1,253.9	811.8	2,065.7
30.7	5.1	35.8	1,314.8	866.8	2,181.6
32.6	5.5	38.1	1,380.7	926.8	2,307.5
34.6	5.8	40.4	1,451.7	991.2	2,442.9
36.8	6.2	43.0	1,528.2	1,060.4	2,588.6

TABLE 52 (continued)

	Bachelor's			*Second-level*		
Year	*Male*	*Female*	*Total*	*Male*	*Female*	*Total*
1941	944.0	988.3	1,932.3	618.1	136.9	755.0
1942	998.7	1,051.6	2,050.3	631.1	146.3	777.4
1943	1,035.5	1,110.3	2,145.8	637.2	154.2	791.3
1944	1,057.4	1,164.5	2,221.9	639.2	160.8	800.0
1945	1,079.8	1,221.2	2,301.0	642.6	168.2	810.8
1946	1,100.9	1,280.4	2,381.4	648.3	176.7	825.0
1947	1,166.7	1,345.9	2,512.6	663.8	187.3	851.1
1948	1,263.5	1,417.0	2,680.4	696.1	200.3	896.4
1949	1,431.4	1,492.5	2,923.9	737.2	215.0	952.1
1950	1,652.5	1,568.0	3,220.5	784.5	230.6	1,015.1
1951	1,817.8	1,643.4	3,461.2	836.2	247.5	1,083.7
1952	1,937.3	1,717.6	3,654.9	883.2	265.1	1,148.4
1953	2,034.2	1,790.5	3,824.7	926.6	282.7	1,209.3
1954	2,122.7	1,862.4	3,985.1	965.3	300.4	1,265.6
1955	2,207.5	1,932.1	4,139.6	1,003.6	318.3	1,321.9
1956	2,306.6	2,008.2	4,314.8	1,042.0	336.8	1,378.8
1957	2,424.1	2,088.8	4,512.9	1,082.9	355.6	1,438.5
1958	2,555.1	2,173.3	4,728.5	1,127.1	374.8	1,501.9
1959	2,691.4	2,263.4	4,954.8	1,174.8	394.7	1,569.6
1960	2,824.5	2,360.2	5,184.6	1,225.4	415.9	1,641.3
1961	2,953.6	2,461.5	5,415.1	1,277.9	437.3	1,715.3
1962	3,081.9	2,571.8	5,653.7	1,333.6	460.6	1,794.2
1963	3,215.3	2,693.5	5,910.8	1,393.0	485.9	1,878.9
1964	3,364.0	2,840.4	6,204.4	1,457.3	514.4	1,971.7
1965	3,521.2	2,996.3	6,517.5	1,527.4	546.8	2,074.2
1966	3,678.3	3,152.2	6,830.6	1,608.7	586.3	2,195.0
1967	3,845.4	3,315.4	7,160.8	1,698.2	632.1	2,330.3
1968	4,032.4	3,507.0	7,539.4	1,797.7	685.7	2,483.4
1969	4,260.2	3,731.9	7,992.1	1,902.9	747.2	2,650.1
1970	4,522.4	3,967.7	8,490.1	2,008.2	818.4	2,826.5
1971	4,792.8	4,215.2	9,008.0	2,125.4	898.4	3,023.8

SOURCE: Estimates by the author (Adkins, 1975). See Section 3 for a description of the methodology of their construction. These estimates are a revision of an earlier set of estimates which appear in Adkins (1973) and incorporate two more years of degree data and a number of minor changes in methodology.

Doctorate			All levels		
Male	*Female*	*Total*	*Male*	*Female*	*Total*
39.4	6.5	45.8	1,601.4	1,131.6	2,733.0
41.7	6.8	48.5	1,671.4	1,204.8	2,876.2
43.2	7.2	50.4	1,715.9	1,271.7	2,987.6
44.4	7.5	51.9	1,741.0	1,332.8	3,073.8
45.2	7.8	53.0	1,767.5	1,397.2	3,164.7
46.1	8.1	54.2	1,795.3	1,465.3	3,260.6
47.8	8.4	56.2	1,878.3	1,541.6	3,419.8
50.4	8.8	59.1	2,009.9	1,626.1	3,636.0
54.1	9.2	63.3	2,222.7	1,716.7	3,939.4
59.0	9.7	68.6	2,496.0	1,808.2	4,304.0
64.5	10.2	74.6	2,718.4	1,901.1	4,619.5
70.1	10.7	80.9	2,890.7	1,993.5	4,884.1
76.3	11.3	87.6	3,037.1	2,084.5	5,121.6
83.0	11.9	95.0	3,171.0	2,174.7	5,345.7
89.5	12.6	102.1	3,300.6	2,263.0	5,563.5
95.9	13.2	109.2	3,444.5	2,358.2	5,802.8
102.1	13.9	116.1	3,609.0	2,458.4	6,067.4
108.4	14.7	123.0	3,790.6	2,562.8	6,353.4
114.9	15.4	130.3	3,981.2	2,673.5	6,654.7
121.8	16.1	137.9	4,171.7	2,792.2	6,963.9
129.1	17.0	146.1	4,360.6	2,915.8	7,276.4
137.2	17.9	155.1	4,552.7	3,050.3	7,602.9
146.2	18.9	165.1	4,754.5	3,200.3	7,954.8
156.5	20.1	176.7	4,977.7	3,375.0	8,352.7
168.3	21.5	189.7	5,216.9	3,564.5	8,781.5
181.3	23.2	204.5	5,468.3	3,761.7	9,230.0
196.1	25.2	221.2	5,739.7	3,972.7	9,712.4
212.6	27.6	240.2	6,042.7	4,220.4	10,263.0
231.4	30.5	261.9	6,394.5	4,509.5	10,904.0
253.0	33.8	286.8	6,783.5	4,819.9	11,603.4
275.9	37.7	313.7	7,194.1	5,151.4	12,345.5

TABLE 53 ***Stock of persons in the United States holding academic degrees from United States universities, by highest degree attained, 1930, by academic specialty***

Specialty	*Bachelor's*	*Second-level*	*Doctorate*	*All levels*
1. *Mathematics and statistics*	35,138	4,945	612	40,695
2. *Computer and information science*	0	0	0	0
3. *Library science*	5,749	1,015	0	6,764
4. *Philosophy (not including scholastic philosophy)*	3,309	277	109	3,695
5. *Chemistry*	31,223	7,658	3,596	42,477
6. *Earth sciences*	15,761	2,315	613	18,689
7. *Physics*	8,490	2,669	1,117	12,276
8. *Physical science, n.e.c.*	2,711	755	99	3,565
9. *Architecture*	7,674	500	0	8,174
10. *Chemical-materials engineering*	20,600	2,461	206	23,267
11. *Civil and other heavy engineering*	23,547	1,109	17	24,673
12. *Electrical-electronic engineering*	25,283	2,190	34	27,507
13. *Geological-mining engineering*	5,872	266	0	6,138
14. *Mechanical-equipment engineering*	37,151	1,643	81	38,875
15. *Engineering and other technical specialties, n.e.c.*	8,842	426	30	9,298
16. *Biological sciences*	29,489	4,782	3,012	37,283
17. *Agriculture*	44,464	8,577	351	53,392
18. *Dentistry*	—	64,266	0	64,266
19. *Medicine*	—	142,092	46	142,138
20. *Nursing, therapy, and dental hygiene*	29,367	1,292	2	30,661
21. *Physical education*	21,520	2,248	142	23,910
22. *Health professions, n.e.c.*	23,147	7,753	440	31,340
23. *Anthropology and archaeology*	142	68	62	272
24. *Economics and agricultural economics*	25,066	1,393	1,086	27,545
25. *History*	51,762	6,008	1,204	58,974
26. *Political science*	4,642	575	538	5,755
27. *Sociology and social psychology*	13,666	594	349	14,609
28. *Social science, n.e.c.*	3,048	462	159	3,669
29. *Journalism and communications*	22,874	929	7	23,810
30. *Business administration*	56,328	3,751	67	60,146
31. *Administration, other than business administration*	5,613	10,476	855	16,944

TABLE 53 (continued)

Specialty	Bachelor's	Second-level	Doctorate	All levels
32. Law	0	139,627	506	140,133
33. Social work	2,079	2,652	38	4,769
34. Social science professions, n.e.c.	284	13	18	315
35. Psychology	8,613	1,336	1,165	11,114
36. Education—primary, preprimary, exceptional	44,344	5,641	17	50,002
37. Education—secondary, adult, specialized teaching fields	31,611	5,487	125	37,223
38. Education, n.e.c.	811	12,466	547	13,824
39. Home economics	47,507	1,390	29	48,926
40. English literature, dramatic arts, and speech	102,076	10,693	1,188	113,957
41. Art and music	60,322	6,016	248	66,586
42. Western European languages and literatures	38,551	5,037	880	44,468
43. Non-Western European languages and literatures	330	96	21	447
44. Religion and scholastic philosophy	16,673	39,878	1,002	57,553
ALL FIELDS	915,679	513,827	20,618	1,450,124

NOTE: N.e.c. = not elsewhere classified in this and later tables.

period 1930–1970, during years of depression and nondepression, and during years of war and peace. Considering all degree levels together, the annual rates of growth of the stock, calculated over the four decades 1930–1970, were:

Year	Percentage
1930–1940	7.1
1940–1950	5.9
1950–1960	4.9
1960–1970	5.1

Calculated over the full 1930–1970 period, the annual rate of increase was 5.3 percent. These rates may be compared with the

TABLE 54 ***Stock of persons in the United States holding academic degrees from United States universities, by highest degree attained, 1950, by academic specialty***

Specialty	*Bachelor's*	*Second-level*	*Doctorate*	*All levels*
1. *Mathematics and statistics*	75,465	10,927	2,024	88,416
2. *Computer and information science*	0	0	0	0
3. *Library science*	13,474	8,174	25	21,673
4. *Philosophy (not including scholastic philosophy)*	8,634	680	394	9,708
5. *Chemistry*	82,593	15,031	11,581	109,205
6. *Earth sciences*	30,227	4,992	1,426	36,645
7. *Physics*	24,365	7,119	3,342	34,826
8. *Physical science, n.e.c.*	5,488	1,462	346	7,296
9. *Architecture*	19,039	1,435	4	20,478
10. *Chemical-materials engineering*	51,641	7,354	1,222	60,217
11. *Civil and other heavy engineering*	69,568	4,618	187	74,373
12. *Electrical-electronic engineering*	81,692	7,472	356	89,520
13. *Geological-mining engineering*	15,423	845	16	16,284
14. *Mechanical-equipment engineering*	117,717	6,696	485	124,898
15. *Engineering and other technical specialties, n.e.c.*	35,506	2,268	281	38,055
16. *Biological sciences*	102,318	12,885	10,147	125,350
17. *Agriculture*	104,457	20,498	1,938	126,893
18. *Dentistry*	—	69,263	2	69,265
19. *Medicine*	—	170,343	79	170,422
20. *Nursing, therapy, and dental hygiene*	53,015	3,034	27	56,076
21. *Physical education*	117,567	15,532	656	133,655
22. *Health professions, n.e.c.*	42,151	14,320	859	57,330
23. *Anthropology and archaeology*	1,377	495	427	2,299
24. *Economics and agricultural economics*	106,078	6,110	2,746	114,934
25. *History*	136,770	15,611	3,607	155,988
26. *Political science*	33,142	3,734	1,535	38,412
27. *Sociology and social psychology*	70,880	3,153	1,255	75,288
28. *Social science, n.e.c.*	31,349	3,487	465	35,301
29. *Journalism and communications*	60,428	2,598	24	63,050
30. *Business administration*	401,915	32,561	486	434,962
31. *Administration other than business administration*	29,151	57,396	3,273	89,820
32. *Law*	0	208,024	676	208,700

TABLE 54 (continued)

Specialty	*Bachelor's*	*Second-level*	*Doctorate*	*All levels*
33. *Social work*	6,850	17,995	75	24,920
34. *Social science professions, n.e.c.*	3,001	173	32	3,206
35. *Psychology*	52,105	7,832	3,334	63,292
36. *Education—primary, preprimary, exceptional*	323,906	43,042	152	367,100
37. *Education—secondary, adult, specialized teaching fields*	202,125	44,305	881	247,311
38. *Education, n.e.c.*	3,907	70,160	3,757	77,824
39. *Home economics*	124,364	4,210	102	128,676
40. *English literature, dramatic arts, and speech*	272,601	28,692	3,917	305,210
41. *Art and music*	169,966	18,816	791	189,573
42. *Western European languages and literatures*	85,140	11,303	2,962	99,405
43. *Non-Western European languages and literatures*	1,318	303	128	1,749
44. *Religion and scholastic philosophy*	53,836	50,140	2,627	106,603
ALL FIELDS	3,220,450	1,015,109	68,649	4,304,208

rates of increase of the general population,[4] aged 20 to 69, which were as follows over the four decades:

Year	*Percentage*
1930–1940	1.3
1940–1950	1.3
1950–1960	.8
1960–1970	1.4
1930–1970	1.2

Thus the growth of the stock of degreed persons was faster than the growth of the general population and resulted in a rapid accumulation of human capital per capita.

As shown in the last line of Table 57, all three degree levels

[4]Population data from U.S. Bureau of the Census (1930–1972).

TABLE 55 ***Stock of persons in the United States holding academic degrees from United States universities, by highest degree attained, 1960, by academic specialty***

Specialty	*Bachelor's*	*Second-level*	*Doctorate*	*All levels*
1. *Mathematics and statistics*	106,034	17,732	3,994	127,760
2. *Computer and information sciences*	11	10	1	22
3. *Library science*	17,618	18,756	103	36,477
4. *Philosophy (not including scholastic philosophy)*	14,466	1,394	1,053	16,913
5. *Chemistry*	110,946	21,146	19,627	151,719
6. *Earth sciences*	43,832	9,405	2,679	55,916
7. *Physics*	39,992	12,043	7,451	59,486
8. *Physical science, n.e.c.*	8,254	2,502	682	11,528
9. *Architecture*	31,372	3,253	43	34,668
10. *Chemical-materials engineering*	69,560	11,974	3,031	84,565
11. *Civil and other heavy engineering*	106,792	11,747	761	119,300
12. *Electrical-electronic engineering*	127,256	17,308	1,607	146,171
13. *Geological-mining engineering*	22,775	1,757	76	24,608
14. *Mechanical-equipment engineering*	176,318	15,853	1,380	193,551
15. *Engineering and other technical specialties, n.e.c.*	61,378	6,836	997	69,211
16. *Biological sciences*	152,789	23,981	17,734	194,504
17. *Agriculture*	146,154	34,468	5,316	185,938
18. *Dentistry*	—	79,995	24	80,019
19. *Medicine*	—	202,139	268	202,407
20. *Nursing, therapy, and mental hygiene*	106,713	7,852	152	114,717
21. *Physical education*	188,159	27,408	1,337	216,904
22. *Health professions, n.e.c.*	77,394	23,835	1,685	102,914
23. *Anthropology and archaeology*	3,195	1,096	818	5,109
24. *Economics and agricultural economics*	154,569	11,825	4,773	171,167
25. *History*	197,701	24,139	5,982	227,822
26. *Political science*	66,172	7,557	2,869	76,598
27. *Sociology and social psychology*	118,499	6,265	2,709	127,473
28. *Social science, n.e.c.*	88,366	12,018	1,650	102,034
29. *Journalism and communications*	75,672	4,518	79	80,269
30. *Business administration*	757,525	82,165	1,468	841,158
31. *Administration other than business administration*	58,111	109,935	5,697	173,743
32. *Law*	0	259,674	796	260,470

TABLE 55 ***(continued)***

Specialty	*Bachelor's*	*Second-level*	*Doctorate*	*All levels*
33. *Social work*	7,317	33,005	212	40,534
34. *Social science professions, n.e.c.*	9,813	1,443	59	11,315
35. *Psychology*	88,214	15,525	9,151	112,890
36. *Education—primary, preprimary, exceptional*	628,981	91,707	798	721,486
37. *Education—secondary, adult, specialized teaching fields*	344,605	99,526	2,847	446,978
38. *Education, n.e.c.*	7,762	149,036	9,383	166,181
39. *Home economics*	153,498	6,832	272	160,623
40. *English literature, dramatic arts, and speech*	381,493	48,697	7,787	437,977
41. *Art and music*	228,793	35,162	1,650	265,605
42. *Western European languages and literatures*	101,692	16,387	4,022	122,101
43. *Non-Western European languages and literatures*	2,675	888	333	3,896
44. *Religion and scholastic philosophy*	102,172	72,386	4,571	179,129
ALL FIELDS	5,184,638	1,641,291	137,927	6,963,856

also grew rapidly in each period. The range of annual growth rates calculated over the decade-long periods is from a low of about 3.5 percent for the second-level stock in the 1930s and 1940s to a high of about 7.5 percent for doctorates in the 1930s and 1960s. The others lie in between. It should be noted that annual rates calculated year by year generally conform stably to those calculated for the four decades except for the wartime deceleration during 1943–1946 and the veterans' acceleration during the periods 1948–1951, 1949–1953, and 1950–1956, for the bachelor's, second-level, and doctorate stocks, respectively.

It is interesting to note not only that the stocks of degree-holders expanded steadily during the whole period, a phenomenon that will occur as long as the flow of new entrants exceeds the attrition, but also that degree *output* expanded fairly steadily. It would not be surprising from a certain point of view[5] to

[5]See Adkins (1973 and 1975) for a discussion of various theories of human-capital formation.

TABLE 56 ***Stock of persons in the United States holding academic degrees from United States universities, by highest degree attained, 1970, by academic specialty***

Specialty	*Bachelor's*	*Second-level*	*Doctorate*	*All levels*
1. *Mathematics and statistics*	215,445	51,291	10,303	277,039
2. *Computer and information science*	2,782	3,791	261	6,834
3. *Library science*	20,165	53,651	262	74,078
4. *Philosophy (not including scholastic philosophy)*	29,834	4,023	2,740	36,597
5. *Chemistry*	155,515	30,601	31,465	217,581
6. *Earth sciences*	49,186	15,023	5,385	69,594
7. *Physics*	61,207	25,056	16,278	102,541
8. *Physical science, n.e.c.*	10,037	5,002	1,297	16,336
9. *Architecture*	47,288	7,312	94	54,694
10. *Chemical-materials engineering*	82,471	18,696	7,096	108,263
11. *Civil and other heavy engineering*	131,966	27,143	3,555	162,664
12. *Electrical-electronic engineering*	173,619	42,614	6,580	222,803
13. *Geological-mining engineering*	22,712	2,922	418	26,052
14. *Mechanical-equipment engineering*	223,059	36,224	4,831	264,114
15. *Engineering and other technical specialties, n.e.c.*	102,319	19,128	4,475	125,922
16. *Biological sciences*	281,085	48,815	33,709	363,529
17. *Agriculture*	180,984	48,421	9,902	239,307
18. *Dentistry*	—	92,796	53	92,849
19. *Medicine*	—	238,099	593	238,692
20. *Nursing, therapy, and dental hygiene*	182,216	17,467	516	200,199
21. *Physical education*	293,716	48,287	2,376	344,379
22. *Health professions, n.e.c.*	117,818	35,412	2,693	155,923
23. *Anthropology and archaeology*	14,280	3,464	1,795	19,539
24. *Economics and agricultural economics*	232,644	23,920	9,255	265,819
25. *History*	368,954	49,454	10,648	429,056
26. *Political science*	171,629	17,689	5,544	194,862
27. *Sociology and social psychology*	242,872	13,148	5,344	261,364
28. *Social science, n.e.c.*	196,731	38,080	4,420	239,231
29. *Journalism and communications*	95,404	8,383	222	104,009
30. *Business administration*	1,268,813	192,943	4,681	1,466,437
31. *Administration other than business administration*	82,439	178,834	11,816	273,089
32. *Law*	2,991	322,199	853	326,043

TABLE 56 (continued)

Specialty	*Bachelor's*	*Second-level*	*Doctorate*	*All levels*
33. *Social work*	15,089	63,927	709	79,725
34. *Social science professions, n.e.c.*	18,266	7,982	419	26,667
35. *Psychology*	202,326	34,767	19,532	256,625
36. *Education—primary, preprimary, exceptional*	1,191,954	190,662	3,192	1,385,809
37. *Education—secondary, adult, specialized teaching fields*	533,783	193,677	7,619	735,079
38. *Education, n.e.c.*	17,377	284,424	21,298	323,099
39. *Home economics*	175,965	10,602	574	187,141
40. *English literature, dramatic arts, and speech*	646,230	105,426	16,044	767,700
41. *Art and music*	309,345	61,300	3,738	374,383
42. *Western European languages and literatures*	176,209	36,796	6,484	219,489
43. *Non-Western European languages and literatures*	7,632	4,085	832	12,549
44. *Religion and scholastic philosophy*	135,834	112,991	6,904	255,729
ALL FIELDS	8,490,111	2,826,527	286,806	11,603,444

find that new investment in degreed human capital should suffer the same sort of acceleration under the impact of the economic cycle as new investment in physical capital. Such has not been the case, however, in the period under consideration. Except for war- and veteran-related developments, the only instances of declining degree output occurred as a result of the Great Depression, and here the declines were conspicuously mild compared with the declines in physical investment. Table 58 compares the annual rates of change in gross domestic investment and in degree output. Rates of change on the order of plus or minus 100 percent occurred in physical investment, whereas for human investment in academic degrees, no annual or cumulative decline from the previous peak occurred that exceeded 10 percent, except for women Ph.D.'s in the period 1933–1934. By contrast, degree output declined 35 percent under the impact of World War II between 1940 and 1944. But even this decline did not produce declines either in the total

TABLE 57 ***Annual growth rates of the stocks of persons in the United States holding academic degrees from United States universities, classified by their highest degree: 10-year compound rates, 1930–1970 (in percentages)***

	Bachelor's				*Second-level*				*Doctorate*			
Specialty	*1930–1940*	*1940–1950*	*1950–1960*	*1960–1970*	*1930–1940*	*1940–1950*	*1950–1960*	*1960–1970*	*1930–1940*	*1940–1950*	*1950–1960*	*1960–1970*
1. *Mathematics and statistics*	4.3	3.5	3.5	7.3	4.3	3.8	5.0	11.2	7.9	4.5	7.0	9.9
2. *Computer and information science*	—	—	—	73.9	—	—	—	81.1	—	—	—	74.4
3. *Library science*	5.1	3.6	2.7	1.4	13.1	9.0	8.7	11.1	—	10.8	15.2	9.8
4. *Philosophy (not including scholastic philosophy)*	5.6	4.3	5.3	7.5	4.9	4.3	7.4	11.2	5.6	7.7	10.3	10.0
5. *Chemistry*	5.0	4.9	3.0	3.4	3.2	3.7	3.5	3.8	7.2	4.9	5.4	4.8
6. *Earth sciences*	3.6	3.0	3.8	1.2	4.0	3.9	6.5	4.8	5.8	2.8	6.5	7.2
7. *Physics*	5.4	5.4	5.1	4.3	4.5	5.6	5.4	7.6	6.8	4.5	8.3	8.1
8. *Physical science, n.e.c.*	3.1	4.1	4.2	2.0	3.5	3.2	5.9	6.8	7.2	5.7	7.0	6.6
9. *Architecture*	4.9	4.4	5.1	4.2	5.2	5.6	8.5	8.4	—	—	26.8	8.1
10. *Chemical-materials engineering*	5.1	4.3	3.0	1.7	5.6	5.7	5.0	4.6	11.0	7.6	9.5	8.9
11. *Civil and other heavy engineering*	5.6	5.5	4.4	2.1	6.1	8.7	9.8	8.7	14.2	11.3	15.1	16.7
12. *Electrical-electronic engineering*	5.7	6.4	4.5	3.2	6.2	6.4	8.8	9.4	14.1	10.9	16.3	15.1
13. *Geological-mining engineering*	5.4	4.5	4.0	.0	5.9	6.0	7.6	5.2	—	12.3	16.9	18.6
14. *Mechanical-equipment engineering*	5.7	6.2	4.1	2.4	6.1	8.5	9.0	8.6	11.4	7.4	11.0	13.3
15. *Engineering and other technical specialties, n.e.c.*	6.6	7.8	5.6	5.2	6.7	10.8	11.7	10.8	13.8	9.9	13.5	16.2
16. *Biological sciences*	6.4	6.5	4.1	6.3	3.9	6.3	6.4	7.4	8.6	4.0	5.7	6.6
17. *Agriculture*	4.6	4.1	3.4	2.2	4.5	4.4	5.3	3.5	9.1	8.8	10.6	6.4
18. *Dentistry*	—	—	—	—	.5	.3	1.5	1.5	—	—	28.2	8.2
19. *Medicine*	—	—	—	—	.8	1.0	1.7	1.7	3.2	2.3	13.0	8.3
20. *Nursing, therapy, and dental hygiene*	1.3	4.7	7.2	5.5	2.7	6.0	10.0	8.3	14.9	12.9	18.9	13.0

Field												
21. *Physical education*	12.5	5.3	4.8	4.6	14.5	6.0	5.8	5.8	10.3	5.7	7.4	5.9
22. *Health professions, n.e.c.*	1.4	4.7	6.3	4.3	1.1	5.2	5.2	4.0	2.8	4.0	7.0	4.8
23. *Anthropology and archaeology*	10.8	13.2	8.8	16.2	12.1	8.7	8.3	12.2	14.8	5.7	6.7	8.2
24. *Economics and agricultural economics*	8.1	6.8	3.8	4.2	7.4	8.0	6.8	7.3	5.9	3.6	5.7	6.8
25. *History*	5.6	4.4	3.8	6.4	4.7	5.1	4.5	7.4	7.4	3.9	5.2	5.9
26. *Political science*	10.0	10.7	7.2	10.0	7.3	12.4	7.3	8.9	6.6	4.1	6.5	6.8
27. *Sociology and social psychology*	9.1	8.1	5.3	7.4	8.4	9.0	7.1	7.7	7.7	5.5	8.0	7.0
28. *Social science, n.e.c.*	12.0	12.8	10.9	8.3	10.8	10.5	13.2	12.2	5.3	5.7	13.5	10.4
29. *Journalism and communications*	5.9	4.1	2.3	2.3	5.7	4.8	5.7	6.4	8.6	4.1	12.7	10.9
30. *Business administration*	11.4	9.2	6.5	5.3	12.0	10.8	9.7	8.9	14.1	6.8	11.7	12.3
31. *Administrative specialties other than business administration*	6.2	11.0	7.1	3.6	11.8	6.0	6.7	5.0	9.1	4.8	5.7	7.6
32. *Law*	—	—	—	—	2.9	1.1	2.2	2.2	3.0	–.1	1.6	0.7
33. *Social work*	5.8	6.5	.7	7.5	12.4	7.7	6.3	6.8	4.3	2.6	11.0	12.8
34. *Social science professions, n.e.c.*	11.9	13.2	12.6	6.4	13.2	14.4	23.6	18.7	4.5	1.3	6.3	21.7
35. *Psychology*	9.7	9.1	5.4	8.7	8.9	9.7	7.1	8.4	6.2	4.6	10.6	7.9
36. *Education—primary, preprimary, exceptional*	14.1	6.9	6.9	6.6	15.0	6.6	7.9	7.6	14.2	9.0	18.0	14.9
37. *Education—secondary, adult, specialized teaching fields*	13.2	6.3	5.5	4.5	15.4	6.8	8.4	6.9	12.2	8.3	12.4	10.3
38. *Education, n.e.c.*	11.6	4.9	7.1	8.4	12.1	6.1	7.8	6.7	12.0	8.2	9.6	8.5
39. *Home economics*	5.6	4.2	2.1	1.4	5.8	5.6	5.0	4.5	6.6	6.4	10.3	7.8
40. *English literature, dramatic arts, and speech*	5.6	4.5	3.4	5.4	5.0	5.1	5.4	8.0	7.9	4.4	7.1	7.5
41. *Art and music*	5.8	4.8	3.0	3.1	5.6	6.1	6.5	5.7	7.8	4.1	7.6	8.5
42. *Western European languages and literatures*	4.8	3.3	1.8	5.7	4.2	4.0	3.8	8.4	9.5	3.1	3.1	4.9
43. *Non-Western European languages and literatures*	7.2	7.2	7.3	11.1	4.5	7.4	11.4	16.5	12.8	6.2	10.0	9.6
44. *Religion and scholastic philosophy*	6.6	5.5	6.6	2.9	.4	1.9	3.7	4.6	5.1	4.8	5.7	4.2
ALL FIELDS	7.1	5.9	4.9	5.1	3.6	3.3	4.9	5.6	7.6	4.8	7.2	7.6

TABLE 58 ***Annual rates of change in gross investment in physical capital and in degreed human capital, 1930–1940 (in percentages)***

Years	Gross private domestic investment (in billions of 1954 dollars)	Degree output					
		Bachelor's*		Second-level*		Doctorate	
		Male	Female	Male	Female	Male	Female
1930–1931	−36.0	+7.4	+5.8	+7.8	+10.9	+12.9	+14.4
1931–1932	−74.0	+7.3	+5.8	+8.4	+11.0	+.3	+11.8
1932–1933	+2.6	+.2	−.9	−3.3	−2.6	+4.6	−9.9
1933–1934	+85.0	+.2	−.9	−3.4	−2.7	+6.3	−6.7
1934–1935	+117.6	+3.0	+3.0	−.6	+.4	−5.3	+3.7
1935–1936	+30.4	+3.1	+3.0	−1.0	+.3	+1.8	+3.1
1936–1937	+28.6	+7.6	+8.6	+4.4	+9.8	+.6	−3.2
1937–1938	−42.6	+7.5	+8.6	+4.7	+9.9	+5.0	+11.1
1938–1939	+39.4	+7.3	+7.1	+4.4	+9.7	+5.4	−2.1
1939–1940	+34.3	+7.1	+7.1	+4.8	+9.9	+8.5	+1.9

*Since the bachelor's and second-level degree data were collected in even years only, the single-year rates for these degrees are based on interpolations. For doctorates, we used annual National Research Council data.

SOURCES: U.S. Bureau of the Census (1960, p. 143); U.S. Office of Education (1918–1946); and Harmon and Soldz (1963).

degreed population at any level or in its male components. Thus the process of degreed human-capital formation in the United States has historically been one of steady growth.

8.3. THE SPECIALTY COMPOSITION OF THE STOCK AND ITS BEHAVIOR OVER TIME

This section describes the specialty composition of the stock of degreed persons at three levels of aggregation and its behavior over time. Estimates of the absolute number of persons in each specialty stock are presented in Tables 53 through 56 and 77 through 79.

The specialty composition of the stock of degreed manpower and womanpower is, naturally, a major area of scientific interest. Those investigators who favor what we have termed the "technogenic model" of human-capital formation[6]—that is, the theory that changes in the stocks of human resources of various kinds are ultimately determined by changes in the scale and composition of final output and by technological develop-

[6]See Adkins (1973 and 1975) for a discussion of alternative theories of human-capital formation.

ments—would expect to find the strongest evidence at the specialty level. With adequate data, technogenic effects might be demonstrated in the determination of either the absolute level of a given specialty stock or its relative share of the total stock.[7]

A sciences-technologies-arts disaggregation As a first cut in considering specialty composition, we may look at a tripartite disaggregation of degreed persons into those with their highest degree, respectively, in sciences, technologies, and arts.[8] Since these are aggregations of U.S. Office of Education degree categories, we are of course not able to completely separate all scientists from technologists. A number of sciences (e.g., chemistry) contain large applied sections which have not been spun off as separate technologies, and certain technology departments may offer studies of a substantially scientific nature (e.g., the management science specialty taught in business administration departments). One might also question the absence of a residual "other" category, an absence that necessitates categorizing every specialty as a science, a technology, or an art. Thus history becomes a (social) science, and law a (social) technology. Nevertheless, the tripartite classification serves to highlight a number of interesting observations.

First, if we look at data on degree-holders as categorized by the specialty of their highest degree level, we can observe great stability over time in the proportions in sciences, technologies, and arts. The proportion of persons with their highest degree in a technology stayed virtually constant at approximately 60 per-

[7]Efforts by the authors to explain post-World War II changes in both the absolute and relative size of two highly vocational specialty stocks (elementary education and chemical engineering), by means of stock adjustment models which are not autoregressive in form, have not been successful to date. It would take a pronounced effect indeed, however, to surmount the combination of paucity of data and the requirement of long lag specifications.

[8]For the purpose of this aggregation, a specialty is judged to be a science or technology if a large and essential part of its theoretical underpinning is scientific knowledge. Otherwise it is judged to be an art. Technologies are distinguished from sciences on the basis of their degree of applications orientation. Certain borderline cases are classified as follows: mathematics, science; philosophy, art; history, science; and law, technology. A listing of how all 44 specialties were classified precedes Table 77.

Estimates of the numbers of persons in the three categories by age and by sex are presented in Tables 77A–77C.

cent over the whole 1930–1970 period. Sciences gained slightly over the period at the expense of arts, increasing from 19 to 23 percent, as arts dropped from 19 to 14 percent. When we consider that the total stock of degreed persons doubled between Sputnik (1956) and the present (1971) and increased eight times during the whole 1930–1970 period, this stability is astonishing.

An example will serve to illustrate that this need not be so. The slowest-growing specialty of this study's 44 is dentistry, which grew at an annual rate of 0.9 percent over the 1930–1970 period. In contrast, the stock of all degree-holders grew at 5.3 percent per annum over the same period. From a technogenic point of view a growth differential of this magnitude between arts and the overall stock would not be thought strange, had it actually occurred. Arts might be expected to grow with the population, say, while sciences and technologies might be expected to grow with the economy, with perhaps an extra push from the demands of social and technological change. But if over the 40-year period a growth differential equal to that between dentistry and the overall stock had been maintained between arts and the overall stock, the share of arts by 1970 would have dropped to 18 percent of its share in 1930. (Dentistry did drop from 4.4 percent of the overall stock in 1930 to 0.8 percent in 1970.) In actual fact, all three major components grew rapidly over the period 1930–1970, with arts growing only a little less rapidly (4.6 percent per annum) than sciences (6.2 percent) and technologies (5.1 percent).

A second observation is that, while the 1970 proportion of arts was about the same for all three levels (one-eighth), the proportions of the degreed stock in sciences and technologies were considerably different at the three levels:

	Sciences	*Technologies*
Bachelor's	$\frac{1}{4}$	$\frac{3}{5}$
Second-level	$\frac{1}{8}$	$\frac{3}{4}$
Doctorate	$\frac{1}{2}$	$\frac{1}{3}$

Technologies as a group dominate the second level even more than the bachelor's level, but drop to second place at the doctorate level. Over time, comparing the 1930 stock with the 1970 stock, there was some tendency to make the distribution between sciences and technologies more uniform for the three degree levels; the proportion of technology specialties increased at the bachelor's level from about 50 to about 60 percent at the expense of arts, decreased slightly at the second level in favor of sciences, and doubled at the doctorate level mainly at the expense of sciences.

A 10-category disaggregation For a second cut at the specialty composition of the degreed manpower stock, we can look at a 10-category disaggregation into the following fairly conventional aggregation categories:[9]

1. Mathematics and physical sciences
2. Engineering (including computer and information sciences)
3. Biological and agricultural sciences
4. Health specialties
5. Social sciences and technologies (other than administration)
6. Administration (business and other)
7. Psychology
8. Education (not including educational administration)
9. Arts and humanities
10. Other (library science and home economics)

Of the 10 specialty stocks, education[10] ranked first in size in 1970 by a good margin with 25 percent of the entire stock of degreed manpower and womanpower. The education stock was about 1½ times as large as the social sciences and technologies, administration, and arts and humanities stocks, which had about 15 percent each. Categories 1 through 4 had 5 to 8 percent each, and psychology and other both had 2 percent (see Table 59).

The 1970 bachelor's-level distribution was much the same as

[9]Estimates of the numbers of persons in the 10 categories by age and sex are presented in Tables 78A–78J. The list in Table 78 defines these categories in terms of the 44 categories of this study that have been aggregated to form them. In turn, these categories are defined in Table 80 in terms of their constituent U.S. Office of Education categories.

[10]Not including educational administration, which is included in administration.

TABLE 59 ***The specialty distribution of the stock of degreed persons, by level and sex, 1970 (in percentages)***

Specialty	*Bachelor's*	*Second-level*	*Doctorate*	*All levels*
Both sexes				
Mathematics and physical sciences	6	5	23	6
Engineering	9	6	10	8
Biological and agricultural sciences	5	3	15	5
Health specialties	4	14	1	6
Social sciences and technologies	16	19	14	17
Administration	16	13	6	15
Psychology	2	1	7	2
Education	24	25	12	24
Arts and humanities	15	12	13	14
Other	2	2	0	2
Men				
Mathematics	8	5	24	8
Engineering	17	8	11	14
Biological and agricultural sciences	7	4	15	7
Health specialties	2	17	1	6
Social sciences and technologies	18	22	14	19
Administration	26	16	6	22
Psychology	2	1	6	2
Education	11	16	11	13
Arts and humanities	9	10	12	10
Other	0	1	0	0
Women				
Mathematics and physical sciences	4	3	10	4
Engineering	1	0	1	1
Biological and agricultural sciences	3	2	14	3
Health specialties	5	5	2	5
Social sciences and technologies	14	12	13	14
Administration	4	7	4	5
Psychology	3	2	11	3
Education	39	47	23	40
Arts and humanities	22	15	21	21
Other	5	6	2	5

that of the overall stock, with engineering a bit higher and health specialties a bit lower. At the second level, the proportion of the stock in health specialties was considerably higher than at the other levels. It was 14 percent versus 4 percent at the bachelor's level, 1 percent at the doctorate level, and 6 percent overall. It is also true that, in actual numbers, somewhat more than half of all degreed persons in health were at the second level. The share of education and social sciences and technologies was also somewhat higher at the second level than at the bachelor's level. The other seven specialty categories maintained much the same relative ratio to one another at the second level as in the overall stock, but their share was scaled down to accommodate the increase in health specialties, social sciences and technologies, and education.

At the doctorate level, the pattern changes. The shares of scientific specialties all increased, while the shares of most applied studies decreased. For instance, 7 percent of persons in the doctorate stock had their degree in psychology, versus 2 percent and 1 percent in psychology at the bachelor's and second level, respectively. And, conversely, 12 percent of the doctorate stock was in education, versus about 25 percent at both lower levels. While the share of social sciences and technologies was lower at the doctorate level than at the second level (14 percent versus 20 percent), the dip took place entirely in the technology (law) component, with the science share rising from 5 percent of the second-level stock to 13 percent of the doctorate stock. Thus it did not constitute an exception. Also conforming to the rule, health almost disappeared at the doctorate level,[11] and biological and agricultural sciences increased. While engineering did not conform to the rule that its share at the doctorate level should be lower than at the two preceding levels, its share of the doctorate stock was 10 percent, and its share of the second-level stock was 6 percent. It may be noted that, for men alone, the share of engineering at the doctorate level was markedly lower than at the bachelor's level

[11]For example, Ph.D.'s in cardiology, neurology, etc.; D.P.H. (Doctor of Public Health); and Ph.D.'s in nursing. A perhaps realistic extension of the "doctorate-level" concept might be to include in it completed residencies for some or all medical specialties. At present there is a probability of less than .5 percent that an M.D. will get a Ph.D. in medicine. Small though it is, the stock of Ph.D.'s in medicine grew rapidly during the 1960s from a tiny base.

(11 percent versus 17 percent). Mathematics and physical sciences, on the other hand, had a share of 22 percent of the doctorate stock, four times their share of the lower two levels.

At the 10-category level of aggregation, in contrast to the situation at the higher sciences-technologies-arts level of aggregation, there were markedly different specialty distributions for men and women. For the bachelor's-level stock, in only two of the 10 specialties—social sciences and technologies, and psychology—did the proportion of bachelor's-level men in the specialty approximately equal the proportion of bachelor's-level women in the specialty. In the others the proportions differ substantially. Most dramatically, 43 percent of bachelor's-level men have their degree in engineering or administration, in contrast to 5 percent of the women. Equally dramatically, 61 percent of the bachelor's-level women have their degree in education or arts and humanities, in contrast to 20 percent of the men. At the second level, specialization for women is even more narrowly focused on education, with 47 percent of women in education alone and 62 percent in education and arts and humanities combined. At the second level, in contrast, men are more evenly spread out than women. The highest proportion, 22 percent in social sciences and technologies, reflects the law curriculum. Not far behind are health, administration, and education, with about 16 percent each. At the doctorate level the specialty distributions for men and women are more similar to each other than at lower degree levels, but, nevertheless, 35 percent of men are in mathematics and physical sciences and engineering versus 10 percent of women, and 54 percent of women are in psychology, education, and arts and humanities versus 29 percent of men. Keeping in mind the shift over time of women from arts and humanities to education, this kind of sexual specialization persisted throughout the whole 1930–1971 period.

Looking at how the 10 categories grew over time, the key phenomenon is that administration, psychology, and education were the fastest-growing elements in the stock at all three degree levels throughout the 1930–1970 period. (Table 60 presents annual growth rates for each of the 10 categories for the period 1930–1970 and for 1960–1970.) Taking all levels together, the three specialties grew half again as fast as the total stock, with the result that their share increased from 15 percent in 1930

TABLE 60 ***Annual growth rates of specialty stocks in the 10-category disaggregation, 1930–1970 and 1960–1970 (in percentages)***

Specialty	Bachelor's		Second-level		Doctorate		All levels	
	1930–1970	1960–1970	1930–1970	1960–1970	1930–1970	1960–1970	1930–1970	1960–1970
1. Mathematics and physical sciences	4.2	4.7	5.0	7.3	6.1	6.5	4.5	5.3
2. Engineering	4.6	2.8	7.5	8.7	11.4	13.2	5.0	3.8
3. Biological and agricultural sciences	4.7	4.4	5.1	5.2	6.6	6.6	4.8	4.7
4. Health specialties	4.5	5.0	1.5	2.0	5.3	6.1	2.4	3.2
5. Social sciences and technologies	6.2	6.5	3.3	4.3	5.9	7.0	5.0	5.8
6. Administration	8.0	5.2	8.5	6.8	7.5	8.7	8.1	5.5
7. Psychology	8.2	8.7	8.5	8.4	7.3	7.9	8.2	8.6
8. Education	7.9	5.7	8.7	6.9	9.8	9.2	8.1	6.0
9. Arts and humanities	4.5	4.6	4.2	6.4	6.1	6.6	4.5	5.0
10. Other	3.3	1.4	8.6	9.6	8.8	8.3	3.9	2.9
ALL FIELDS	5.7	5.1	4.4	5.6	6.8	7.6	5.3	5.2

to 33 percent in 1950 and to 41 percent in 1970. At the bachelor's level the share of the three specialties increased over the period 1930–1970 from 18 to 42 percent, at the second level it increased from 8 to 30 percent, and at the doctorate level it increased from 14 to 25 percent. Thus, because they were maintained over a long period of time, the relatively small differentials in growth rates that favored these specialties produced the large segment of certified administrative, educational, and psychological talent which now exists in the degreed stock. In the 1960s, at the bachelor's level, the growth rate differential for administration and education vanished, but it persisted more narrowly at the graduate levels. For psychology the growth differential continued undiminished during the 1960s.

Another striking development was the extremely rapid expansion of the second-level and doctorate engineering stocks over the period. The doctorate engineering stock, in fact, was the fastest-growing segment of the entire stock of degreed persons, increasing at a compound annual rate of over 11 percent for the 40-year period 1930–1970 and increasing at an even higher rate in the 1960s. At the bachelor's level, however, engineering had the second lowest growth rate of any of the 10 specialty categories during the 1960s. Only the other category had a lower growth rate at the bachelor's level, indicating primarily that women were gradually abandoning home economics. In contrast to engineering, the reverse phenomenon occurred in social sciences and technologies. Its share increased at an above-average rate at the bachelor's level but at below-average rates at the graduate level.

While the growth prize goes to the engineering doctorate stock, the stagnation award goes to the second-level health stock, which grew at less than 2 percent per annum throughout the period. Health was 42 percent of the second-level stock in 1930, but only 14 percent by 1970. Considering the overall stock, health dropped from 18 percent to 6 percent over the period.

A 44-category disaggregation Turning now to the 44-category disaggregation, the detail is too rich to attempt a comprehensive description. Instead, we shall attempt a presentation of the highlights. Table 61 presents the distribution of the stock over 44 specialties. The distribution is such that, at all levels, the stock is well spread out over the 44 degree categories, with about one-third of the specialty categories having less than 1 percent of a given sex-level stock and up to three specialties having 10 percent or more. For men the specialties with 10 percent or more are bachelor's level—business administration (24 percent); second level—medicine (11 percent) and law (15 percent); and doctorate level—chemistry (12 percent) and biological sciences (12 percent). For women the specialties with 10 percent or more are bachelor's level—elementary, etc., education (28 percent) and English literature, dramatic arts, and speech (12 percent); second level—elementary, etc., education (18 percent), secondary, etc., education (11 percent), and education, n.e.c. (17 percent); and doctorate level—biological sciences (14 percent), education n.e.c. (13 percent), and English literature, dramatic arts, and speech (11 percent). When all levels and sexes are taken together, only business administration (13 percent) and elementary, etc., education (12 percent) remain in the 10-percent club.

Individual specialties grew at widely varying rates during the

TABLE 61 ***Percentage which each specialty stock is of the total stock of degreed persons by degree level and sex, 1970 (in percentages)***

	Bachelor's			Second-level			Doctorate			All levels		
Specialty	*Male*	*Female*	*Total*	*Male*	*Female*	*Total*	*Male*	*Female*	*Total*	*Male*	*Female*	*Total*
1. *Mathematics and statistics*	2.8	2.2	2.5	1.9	1.6	1.8	3.8	2.2	3.6	2.6	2.1	2.4
2. *Computer and information science*	.1	*	*	.2	*	.1	.1	*	.1	.1	*	.1
3. *Library science*	.1	.4	.2	.6	5.1	1.9	.1	.2	.1	.2	1.2	.6
4. *Philosophy (not including scholastic philosophy)*	.4	.3	.4	.2	.1	.1	1.0	.8	1.0	.4	.2	.3
5. *Chemistry*	2.3	1.3	1.8	1.2	.8	1.1	11.7	5.6	11.0	2.3	1.2	1.9
6. *Earth sciences*	1.0	.1	.6	.7	.1	.5	2.1	.4	1.9	1.0	.1	.6
7. *Physics*	1.3	.1	.7	1.2	.2	.9	6.3	1.3	5.7	1.4	.1	.9
8. *Physical science, n.e.c.*	.2	*	.1	.2	.1	.2	.5	.1	.5	.2	.1	.1
9. *Architecture*	1.0	.1	.6	.3	.1	.3	*	*	*	.7	.1	.5
10. *Chemical-materials engineering*	1.8	*	1.0	.9	*	.7	2.8	.1	2.5	1.6	*	.9
11. *Civil and other heavy engineering*	2.9	*	1.6	1.3	*	1.0	1.4	*	1.2	2.4	*	1.4
12. *Electrical-electronic engineering*	3.8	*	2.0	2.1	*	1.5	2.6	.1	2.3	3.3	*	1.9
13. *Geological-mining engineering*	.5	*	.3	.1	*	.1	.2	*	.1	.4	*	.2
14. *Mechanical-equipment engineering*	4.9	*	2.6	1.8	*	1.3	1.9	*	1.7	3.9	*	2.3
15. *Engineering and other technical specialties, n.e.c.*	1.9	.4	1.2	.8	.3	.7	1.7	.3	1.6	1.6	.4	1.1

TABLE 61 *(continued)*

Specialty	*Bachelor's*			*Second-level*			*Doctorate*			*All levels*		
	Male	*Female*	*Total*	*Male*	*Female*	*Total*	*Male*	*Female*	*Total*	*Male*	*Female*	*Total*
16. *Biological sciences*	3.3	3.3	3.3	1.7	1.9	1.7	11.5	13.9	11.8	3.1	3.1	3.1
17. *Agriculture*	3.9	.1	2.1	2.3	.2	1.7	3.8	.5	3.5	3.4	.1	2.1
18. *Dentistry*	—	—	—	4.6	.1	3.3	*	*	*	1.4	*	.8
19. *Medicine*	—	—	—	11.1	1.9	8.4	.2	.2	.2	3.3	.3	2.1
20. *Nursing, therapy, and dental hygiene*	.3	4.3	2.1	*	2.1	.6	.1	.9	.2	.2	3.9	1.7
21. *Physical education*	4.0	2.9	3.5	1.8	1.6	1.7	.7	1.9	.8	3.2	2.6	3.0
22. *Health professions, n.e.c.*	1.6	1.1	1.4	1.5	.7	1.3	1.0	.8	.9	1.5	1.1	1.3
23. *Anthropology and archaeology*	.1	.2	.2	.1	.2	.1	.6	1.1	.6	.1	.2	.2
24. *Economics and agricultural economics*	4.4	.8	2.7	1.1	.3	.8	3.5	1.4	3.2	3.4	.7	2.3
25. *History*	4.5	4.2	4.3	1.6	2.1	1.7	3.7	3.9	3.7	3.6	3.8	3.7
26. *Political science*	2.7	1.2	2.0	.7	.4	.6	2.0	1.4	1.9	2.1	1.1	1.7
27. *Sociology and social psychology*	1.8	4.1	2.9	.4	.6	.5	1.7	2.7	1.9	1.4	3.5	2.3
28. *Social science, n.e.c.*	2.2	2.4	2.3	1.3	1.3	1.3	1.5	1.6	1.5	1.9	2.2	2.1
29. *Journalism and communications*	1.3	.9	1.1	.3	.3	.3	.1	.1	.1	1.0	.8	.9
30. *Business administration*	24.4	4.2	14.9	9.2	1.0	6.8	1.8	.4	1.6	19.1	3.6	12.6
31. *Administration other than business administration*	1.8	.1	1.0	6.4	6.1	6.3	4.2	3.7	4.1	3.2	1.1	2.4

32. *Law*	.1	*	*	15.3	1.7	11.4	.3	.1	.3	4.6	.3	2.8
33. *Social work*	.1	.3	.2	1.1	5.0	2.3	.2	.7	.2	.4	1.1	.7
34. *Social science professions, n.e.c.*	.3	.1	.2	.4	.1	.3	.1	.2	.1	.3	.1	.2
35. *Psychology*	2.2	2.6	2.4	1.0	1.9	1.2	6.2	11.0	6.8	2.0	2.6	2.2
36. *Education—primary, preprimary, exceptional*	2.0	27.8	14.0	2.0	18.3	6.7	.9	3.1	1.1	2.0	26.0	11.9
37. *Education—secondary, adult, specialized teaching fields*	4.9	7.9	6.3	5.3	10.7	6.9	2.4	4.7	2.7	4.9	8.4	6.3
38. *Education, n.e.c.*	.1	.3	.2	7.4	16.7	10.1	6.7	13.2	7.4	2.5	3.2	2.8
39. *Home economics*	*	4.4	2.1	*	1.3	.4	.1	1.2	.2	*	3.9	1.6
40. *English literature, dramatic arts, and speech*	4.0	11.7	7.6	2.3	7.3	3.7	4.9	10.5	5.6	3.5	11.0	6.6
41. *Art and music*	2.0	5.0	3.6	1.8	3.1	2.2	1.2	2.0	1.3	1.9	5.1	3.2
42. *Western European languages and literatures*	.8	3.5	2.1	.7	2.8	1.3	1.8	5.8	2.3	.8	3.4	1.9
43. *Non-Western European languages and literatures*	.1	.1	.1	.1	.3	.1	.3	.5	.3	.1	.1	.1
44. *Religion and scholastic philosophy*	2.0	1.1	1.6	5.0	1.5	4.0	2.6	1.2	2.4	2.9	1.2	2.2
ALL FIELDS	100.0	100.0	100.0	100.0	100.0	100.0	100.0	100.0	100.0	100.0	100.0	100.0

*Less than .05 percent.

TABLE 62 ***The fastest- and slowest-growing specialties at the 44-category level of aggregation, 1960–1970: compound annual growth rates by degree level and sex[a] (in percentages)***

Fastest-growing		*Slowest-growing*	
	Bachelor's—men[b]		
Political science	10.4	*Nursing, therapy, and dental hygiene*	–.8
Psychology	10.1	*Geological-mining engineering*	.0
Philosophy	9.5	*Earth sciences*	1.1
Sociology	8.4	*Chemical-materials engineering*	1.7
Mathematics	8.3	*Journalism and communications*	2.0
	Bachelor's—women[c]		
Anthropology and archaeology	16.9	*Home economics*	1.4
Social science, n.e.c.	9.4	*Chemistry*	1.5
Political science	9.0	*Library science*	1.7
Education, n.e.c.	9.0	*Religion*	2.6
Nursing, therapy, and dental hygiene	6.2	*Art and music*	2.6
	Second-level—men[d]		
Computer and information science	46.8[e]	*Dentistry*	1.5
Social science professions, n.e.c.	18.2	*Medicine*	1.6
Social science, n.e.c.	12.5	*Law*	2.2
Engineering and other technical specialties, n.e.c.	11.6	*Chemistry*	3.3
Mathematics	11.4	*Agriculture*	3.3
	Second-level—women[f]		
Non-Western European languages and literatures	19.1	*Law*	1.1
Anthropology and archaeology	12.8	*Medicine*	2.0
Social science, n.e.c.	11.6	*Administration other than business administration*	3.2
Library science	11.5	*Religion*	3.2
Agriculture	10.6	*Home economics*	4.3
	Doctorate—men[g]		
Geological-mining engineering	18.4	*Law*	.7
Civil and other heavy engineering	16.6	*Religion*	4.3
Engineering and other technical specialties, n.e.c.	16.4	*Western European languages and literatures*	4.7
Electrical-electronic engineering	15.1	*Health professions, n.e.c.*	4.7
Elementary, etc., education	14.0	*Chemistry*	4.7

TABLE 62 (continued)

Fastest-growing		*Slowest-growing*	
	Doctorate—women[h]		
Elementary, etc., education	17.1	*Religion*	3.1
Social science professions, n.e.c.	15.9	*History*	4.9
Social work	14.9	*Earth sciences*	5.2
Non-Western European languages and literatures	12.9	*Western European languages and literatures*	5.4
Philosophy	11.8	*Health professions, n.e.c.*	5.6

[a]This list in each case contains the five fastest- and the five slowest-growing specialties which exceeded .2 percent of the sex-level total involved. The specialties excluded for smallness, which otherwise would have made the list, are given in the footnotes.

[b]Specialties excluded for smallness: fast—computer and information science, anthropology and archaeology, non-Western European languages and literatures; slow—library science, home economics.

[c]Specialties excluded for smallness: fast—computer and information science, non-Western European languages and literatures, social science professions, n.e.c.; slow—geological-mining engineering, mechanical-equipment engineering, chemical-materials engineering, architecture, earth sciences, electrical-electronic engineering, physical science, n.e.c., civil and other heavy engineering, administration other than business administration.

[d]Specialties excluded for smallness: fast—home economics, non-Western European languages and literatures, anthropology and archaeology, philosophy; slow—nursing, therapy, and dental hygiene.

[e]Average of the rates of increase from 1969 to 1970 and from 1970 to 1971.

[f]Specialties excluded for smallness: fast—computer and information science, social science professions, n.e.c., civil and other heavy engineering, electrical-electronic engineering; slow—dentistry, geological-mining engineering.

[g]Specialties excluded for smallness: fast—computer and information science, social science professions, n.e.c., nursing, therapy, and dental hygiene; slow—none.

[h]Specialties excluded for smallness: fast—civil and other heavy engineering, chemical-materials engineering, journalism and communications, electrical-electronic engineering, mechanical-equipment engineering, dentistry; slow—geological-mining engineering, law.

last several decades. Table 57 (above, p. 190) gives annual compound rates of increase for all specialties for each of the last four decades. To highlight the notable features of this mass of percentages, it will be helpful to list (in Table 62) the five fastest- and the five slowest-growing specialties at each degree level and for each sex, for the period 1960–1970. Specialties which did not have at least 0.2 percent of the total in 1970 are not included in the list, but mention is made of them in the footnotes.

What is immediately apparent is that there is great diversity in the list of fast-growing and slowly growing specialties. There is little consistency across the sexes or across degree levels. What few generalizations seem indicated are as follows:

1. Traditional social sciences (except economics) and psychology were among the fastest-growing at the bachelor's level.
2. There was no across-the-board attempt on the part of members of one sex to invade the specialty preserves of the other; in fact, some of the slowest-growing bachelor's specialties for men were nursing, etc., home economics, and library science, and for women they were various engineering specialties.
3. Mathematics was a fast-growing specialty across the board (except for women doctorates).
4. At the second level, minor and new social sciences and technologies and minor and new engineering specialties were fast growers for men.
5. Also at the second level, the professions and certain traditional specialties like religion for women and agriculture for men grew slowly. It is interesting to note that agriculture made the top five for women and the bottom five for men, the only specialty where there was a strong indication of sexual equalization.
6. Traditional engineering fields grew rapidly for Ph.D.'s of both sexes.
7. Ph.D.'s in elementary, etc., education grew rapidly for both sexes.

8.4. THE DEGREE STRUCTURE OF THE STOCK AND THE PROBABILITY OF DEGREE RECIPIENTS' RECEIVING HIGHER DEGREES

From a static point of view, the degree structure of the stock of degree-holders can be expressed as the set of percentages which the stock at each degree level is of the total stock. Tables 63 through 66 give these percentages for the four levels of aggregation for the period 1930–1970. From a dynamic point of view, the stock can also be characterized by the set of probabilities that its members will make a transition to another level and specialty at particular future times. Since changes in these probabilities will determine changes in the equilibrium degree structure of the stock, we shall term these probabilities the *dynamic structure.*[12]

Clearly, the stock of degreed human capital underwent a process of capital widening;[13] it expanded eightfold over the 1930–1970 period. A question we can address in this section is

[12]Although the term "estimated frequencies" would be a more accurate description for events which have occurred, "probabilities" is used throughout since to calculate 25-year frequencies even for 1947 degree recipients requires degree projections beyond the data. See the section on construction of the estimates for a description of the methodology of obtaining the probabilities.

[13]"Capital widening" refers to the quantitative expansion of all components for a given type of capital—in this case, degreed human capital.

TABLE 63 ***Degree structure of the stock of degreed persons, 1930: percentage which the stock at each degree level is of the total stock, by specialty and sex, aggregation levels 1 to 3***

	Bachelor's			*Second-level*			*Doctorate*		
	Male	*Female*	*Total*	*Male*	*Female*	*Total*	*Male*	*Female*	*Total*
Aggregation level 1									
Total all fields	49	89	63	49	11	35	1.9	.5	1.4
Aggregation level 2									
1. *Sciences*	75	93	83	17	6	12	8.0	1.3	4.9
2. *Technologies*	44	82	52	56	18	47	.5	.2	.4
3. *Arts*	46	93	77	51	7	22	2.9	.4	1.2
Aggregation level 3									
1. *Mathematics and physical sciences*	72	92	79	20	7	16	7.4	1.0	5.1
2. *Engineering*	94	95	94	6	5	6	.3	.1	.3
3. *Biological and agricultural sciences*	79	92	82	17	5	15	4.0	2.6	3.7
4. *Health specialties*	10	72	20	90	28	80	.2	.1	.2
5. *Social sciences*	29	86	44	70	14	54	1.7	.6	1.4
6. *Administration*	84	76	80	17	23	19	1.4	.4	1.2
7. *Psychology*	59	89	78	20	7	12	20.7	4.3	10.5
8. *Education*	72	84	79	27	16	21	1.2	.3	.7
9. *Arts and humanities*	46	93	77	51	7	22	2.9	.4	1.2
10. *Other*	84	96	96	16	4	4	0	.1	.1

TABLE 64 ***Degree structure of the stock of degreed persons, 1970: percentage which the stock at each degree level is of the total stock, by specialty and sex, aggregation levels 1 to 3***

	Bachelor's			*Second-level*			*Doctorate*		
	Male	*Female*	*Total*	*Male*	*Female*	*Total*	*Male*	*Female*	*Total*
Aggregation level 1									
Total all fields	67	82	73	30	17	24	3.7	.7	2.5
Aggregation level 2									
1. *Sciences*	76	89	81	15	9	13	8.2	1.6	5.7
2. *Technologies*	63	78	69	35	21	30	1.9	.4	1.3
3. *Arts*	65	87	78	31	12	20	4.5	.7	2.2
Aggregation level 3									
1. *Mathematics and physical sciences*	67	85	72	21	13	19	12.1	1.8	9.5
2. *Engineering*	81	95	81	16	14	16	2.9	.8	2.8
3. *Biological and agricultural sciences*	73	86	77	18	11	16	8.1	3.1	7.2
4. *Health specialties*	20	84	44	79	16	56	.7	.3	.6
5. *Social sciences*	62	85	70	35	15	28	2.7	.7	2.0
6. *Administration*	78	74	78	21	26	21	1.0	.6	.9
7. *Psychology*	74	84	79	14	13	14	11.9	3.0	7.6
8. *Education*	58	80	73	39	20	26	3.1	.4	1.2
9. *Arts and humanities*	65	87	78	31	12	20	4.5	.7	2.2
10. *Other*	22	79	75	76	21	25	2.1	.2	.3

TABLE 65 ***Degree structure of the stock of degreed persons, 1930: percentage which the stock at each degree level is of the total stock, by specialty and sex, aggregation level 4***

	Bachelor's			Second-level			Doctorate		
Specialty	*Male*	*Female*	*Total*	*Male*	*Female*	*Total*	*Male*	*Female*	*Total*
1. *Mathematics and statistics*	78	93	86	19	7	12	3.0	.4	1.5
2. *Computer and information science*	—	—	—	—	—	—	—	—	—
3. *Library science*	78	87	85	22	13	15	—	—	—
4. *Philosophy (not including scholastic philosophy)*	74	95	90	19	3	8	7.3	1.3	2.9
5. *Chemistry*	63	93	74	25	6	18	12.3	1.6	8.5
6. *Earth sciences*	84	92	84	13	6	12	3.4	2.3	3.3
7. *Physics*	68	75	69	22	21	22	9.9	3.8	9.1
8. *Physical science, n.e.c.*	75	85	76	22	15	21	3.0	—	2.8
9: *Architecture*	93	96	94	7	4	6	—	—	—
10. *Chemical-materials engineering*	89	91	89	11	9	11	.9	.6	.9
11. *Civil and other heavy engineering*	95	100	95	5	—	5	.1	—	.1
12. *Electrical-electronic engineering*	92	100	92	8	—	8	.1	—	.1
13. *Geological-mining engineering*	96	100	96	4	—	4	—	—	—
14. *Mechanical-equipment engineering*	96	95	96	4	5	4	.2	—	.2
15. *Engineering and other technical specialties, n.e.c.*	95	92	95	4	8	5	.3	.2	.3
16. *Biological sciences*	66	92	79	20	6	13	13.6	2.7	8.1

TABLE 65 (*continued*)

Specialty	*Bachelor's*			*Second-level*			*Doctorate*		
	Male	*Female*	*Total*	*Male*	*Female*	*Total*	*Male*	*Female*	*Total*
17. *Agriculture*	83	97	83	16	3	16	.7	.3	.7
18. *Dentistry*	—	—	—	100	100	100	—	—	—
19. *Medicine*	—	—	—	100	100	100	*	.1	*
20. *Nursing, therapy, and dental hygiene*	99	93	96	1	7	4	—	*	*
21. *Physical education*	88	93	90	11	7	9	.8	.4	.6
22. *Health professions, n.e.c.*	63	85	74	35	15	25	2.6	.2	1.4
23. *Anthropology and archaeology*	40	68	52	31	17	25	28.8	14.7	22.8
24. *Economics and agricultural economics*	91	94	91	5	4	5	4.2	2.3	3.9
25. *History*	76	93	88	18	7	10	5.6	.6	2.0
26. *Political science*	73	94	81	13	4	10	13.6	1.7	9.3
27. *Sociology and social psychology*	80	98	94	11	2	4	9.2	.3	2.4
28. *Social science, n.e.c.*	74	92	83	19	7	13	7.9	1.0	4.3
29. *Journalism and communications*	95	99	96	5	1	4	*	—	*
30. *Business administration*	93	97	94	7	3	6	.1	—	.1
31. *Administration other than business administration*	39	15	33	55	84	62	6.2	1.7	5.0
32. *Law*	—	—	—	99	99	99	.4	.2	.4

33. *Social work*	42	44	44	56	56	56	2.8	—	.8
34. *Social science professions, n.e.c.*	89	97	90	5	—	4	6.1	2.8	5.7
35. *Psychology*	59	89	78	20	7	12	20.7	4.3	10.5
36. *Education—primary, preprimary, exceptional*	83	90	89	17	10	11	.1	*	*
37. *Education—secondary, adult, specialized teaching fields*	84	86	85	15	14	15	.5	.1	.3
38. *Education, n.e.c.*	5	7	6	90	90	90	4.9	2.4	4.0
39. *Home economics*	99	97	97	1	3	3	—	.1	.1
40. *English literature, dramatic arts, and speech*	75	94	90	21	6	9	3.7	.3	1.0
41. *Art and music*	77	95	91	22	5	9	1.1	.2	.4
42. *Western European languages and literatures*	66	91	87	25	8	11	8.4	.6	2.0
43. *Non-Western European languages and literatures*	64	85	74	29	13	21	7.4	1.9	4.7
44. *Religion and scholastic philosophy*	16	82	29	82	17	69	1.9	1.1	1.7
ALL FIELDS	49	88	63	49	11	35	1.9	.5	1.4

*Less than .05 percent.

TABLE 66 ***Degree structure of the stock of degreed persons, 1970: percentage which the stock at each degree level is of the total stock, by specialty and sex, aggregation level 4***

Specialty	Bachelor's			Second-level			Doctorate		
	Male	*Female*	*Total*	*Male*	*Female*	*Total*	*Male*	*Female*	*Total*
1. *Mathematics and statistics*	73	86	78	22	13	18	5.5	.7	3.7
2. *Computer and information science*	39	58	40	57	41	55	4.2	.8	3.8
3. *Library science*	18	29	27	80	70	72	1.2	.1	.4
4. *Philosophy (not including scholastic philosophy)*	78	90	81	12	8	11	10.0	2.2	7.5
5. *Chemistry*	66	86	71	15	11	14	18.8	3.1	14.5
6. *Earth sciences*	71	72	71	21	24	22	7.9	4.1	7.7
7. *Physics*	59	66	60	24	27	24	16.5	6.7	15.9
8. *Physical science, n.e.c.*	61	65	61	30	33	31	9.0	1.7	7.9
9. *Architecture*	86	90	87	14	10	13	.2	.1	.2
10. *Chemical-materials engineering*	76	72	76	17	23	17	6.6	5.4	6.6
11. *Civil and other heavy engineering*	81	58	81	17	37	17	2.2	4.7	2.2
12. *Electrical-electronic engineering*	78	65	78	19	30	19	2.9	4.8	3.0
13. *Geological-mining engineering*	87	78	87	11	14	11	1.6	8.2	1.6
14. *Mechanical-equipment engineering*	85	72	85	14	25	14	1.8	2.9	1.8
15. *Engineering and other technical specialties, n.e.c.*	80	87	81	16	12	15	4.0	.6	3.6

16. *Biological sciences*	71	86	77	16	10	13	13.6	3.1	9.3
17. *Agriculture*	76	77	76	20	20	20	4.2	2.7	4.1
18. *Dentistry*	—	—	—	100	99	99	*	.9	.1
19. *Medicine*	—	—	—	99	99	99	.2	.4	.2
20. *Nursing, therapy, and dental hygiene*	95	91	91	3	9	9	1.6	.2	.3
21. *Physical education*	83	89	85	16	10	14	.8	.5	.7
22. *Health professions, n.e.c.*	70	87	76	28	12	23	2.3	.5	1.7
23. *Anthropology and archaeology*	63	82	73	22	14	18	14.7	3.9	9.2
24. *Economics and agricultural economics*	87	91	87	9	7	9	3.8	1.4	3.5
25. *History*	83	90	86	13	9	12	3.8	.7	2.5
26. *Political science*	87	92	88	10	7	9	3.5	.9	2.8
27. *Sociology and social psychology*	86	97	93	9	3	5	4.7	.5	2.0
28. *Social science, n.e.c.*	76	89	82	20	10	16	2.9	.5	1.8
29. *Journalism and communications*	90	95	92	10	5	8	.3	.1	.2
30. *Business administration*	85	95	86	14	5	13	.4	.1	.3
31. *Administration other than business administration*	37	4	30	59	94	66	4.8	2.3	4.3
32. *Law*	1	1	1	99	99	99	.3	.3	.3
33. *Social work*	12	22	19	86	77	80	1.7	.5	.9
34. *Social science professions, n.e.c.*	68	73	68	31	26	30	1.6	1.6	1.6
35. *Psychology*	74	84	79	14	13	13	11.9	3.0	7.6
36. *Education—primary, preprimary, exceptional*	68	88	86	31	12	14	1.6	.1	.2

TABLE 66 ***(continued)***

Specialty	Bachelor's			Second-level			Doctorate		
	Male	*Female*	*Total*	*Male*	*Female*	*Total*	*Male*	*Female*	*Total*
37. Education—secondary, adult, specialized teaching fields	66	78	73	32	22	26	1.8	.4	1.0
38. Education, n.e.c.	4	7	5	86	90	88	9.8	2.9	6.6
39. Home economics	70	94	94	17	6	6	12.9	.2	.3
40. English literature, dramatic arts, and speech	76	88	84	19	11	14	5.2	.7	2.1
41. Art and music	70	89	83	27	10	16	2.3	.3	1.0
42. Western European languages and literatures	66	85	80	26	14	17	8.2	1.2	3.0
43. Non-Western European languages and literatures	57	65	61	33	33	33	10.7	2.7	6.6
44. Religion and scholastic philosophy	46	78	53	50	22	44	3.2	.8	2.7
ALL FIELDS	67	82	73	30	17	24	3.7	.7	2.5

*Less than .05 percent.

whether it also underwent a process of capital deepening. In the present context, capital deepening would occur if higher degree levels expanded relative to lower degree levels in the same specialty. Capital deepening may also be the result of changes in the specialty composition of the stock described in the previous section; since there is no agreed-upon hierarchy of skills, however, this latter point will not be pursued.

The static structure As noted in Section 8.1, the total stock of degreed persons in 1971 was just enough short of 75 percent bachelor's level and 25 percent second level to fit in 2.5 percent at the doctorate level. Somewhat surprisingly, the proportion at the bachelor's level has *increased* from 63 percent in 1930 to its level of 73 percent in 1971. The proportion at the second level has correspondingly decreased from 35 percent to 24 percent over the same interval. It would be more precise to locate this shift in time between 1930 and 1947, when approximately the present proportions were attained, and to identify it as strictly a male phenomenon related to the relatively slow growth of the major second-level professions (dentistry, medicine, law, and theology). The proportions of males at the bachelor's level and at the second level changed in percentage from 49-49 to 67-30, while for females the percentages changed from 88-11 to 82-17.

The increase in the percentage of the degreed stock at the doctorate level, which changed from 1.4 percent in 1930 to 2.5 percent in 1971, is also almost entirely ascribable to the change in the doctorate percentage in the male stock. This changed from 1.9 percent in 1930 to 3.8 percent in 1971. Women doctorate-holders, on the other hand, hardly increased the .5 percent share of the female stock which they had in 1930. It was still only .7 percent in 1971.

At the sciences-technologies-art level of disaggregation, we find that sciences has both the highest bachelor's proportion and the highest doctorate proportion and that arts has the next highest proportion at both levels. This is true of both sexes and has persisted since 1930. The same ordering of the three categories also exists with respect to the doctorate/second-level ratio.

At the 10-category disaggregation level, the relative emphasis on the second level for technologies and the relative deemphasis on the second level for sciences carry over in each case,[14] with arts and humanities having a doctorate/second-level ratio less than all sciences and greater than all technologies except engineering.

It could be that the adoption by engineering of a degree structure more like that of the sciences is a precursor of similar changes in the structure of other technology stocks. In engineering the ratio of doctorate to second-level rose steadily from 5 percent in 1930 to 17 percent in 1970, as did the ratio of doctorate to bachelor's, which also rose steadily, from .3 percent in 1930 to 3 percent in 1970. Both of these events constitute a substantial deepening of the engineering stock. Looked at in a certain way, there was also substantial deepening in the health stock. Although the health doctorate/second-level ratio increased by a factor of 5 from 1930 to 1970, doctorates were still only 2 percent of second-level degrees in 1970. If, however, we consider that medical residencies and the passing of medical specialty board examinations constitute effective qualification at the level of the Ph.D., then the proportion of M.D.'s holding Ph.D.-level qualifications not only grew rapidly but also reached a significant level. Thus there was a deepening in biological technology corresponding to that which occurred in physical technology.

In the case of social and psychological technology stocks, however, there has not been any substantial deepening during the 1930–1970 period. Administration as a whole, for example, experienced a decline in the doctorate/second-level ratio during the period from 6 percent to 4 percent. This was composed of a small increase for business administration and a small decrease for other administration.

If the deepening of the engineering and health stocks is a precedent for other technology stocks, then administration, law, and education stocks would seem to be far from their future equilibrium. One might argue that outside the natural science area, it is possible that the deepening of technology took place formally within the educational bounds of the relevant sciences (e.g., within psychology for education). But

[14]For this the two components of social sciences and technologies are considered separately.

though this did happen, it also happened to a certain extent in the natural sciences (e.g., in organic chemistry, solid-state physics, and pharmacology), and there it did not prevent the concurrent deepening of the engineering and health stocks. Nor is there any particular reason to suppose that social and psychological technology would be uniquely resistant to spillover effects from the social and psychological sciences. It would seem, therefore, that if substantial deepening should occur, it would be likely to occur for the technologies in question in the regular academic credential system and be reflected in increases in their doctorate/second-level ratios.

A formal residency system in law does not seem likely as a response to pressures for deepening, although it has been proposed; more likely would be the revivification of J.S.D. programs or the establishment of substantial Ph.D. programs in law schools. In education and business administration, the established Ph.D. programs may be supplemented, under the impact of the coming academic buyer's market for Ph.D.'s, by a revitalization of practitioner doctorate programs.

At the 44-category level of aggregation, there is substantial diversity in degree structure. (See Tables 65 and 66 for the 1930 and 1970 structures.) The proportion at the bachelor's level ranges up to 93 and 94 percent, respectively, for sociology and home economics and down to 5 and 19 percent, respectively, for education, n.e.c., and social work (not considering dentistry, medicine, and law in this comparison).

At the second level the range is from 99 percent for dentistry, medicine, and law and 88 percent for education, n.e.c., down to 5 and 8 percent, respectively, for sociology and journalism. The nursing, economics, and political science stocks are also at the low end of the range with only 9 percent at the second level.

At the doctorate level the high specialties are chemistry (15 percent), physics (16 percent), biology (9 percent), and anthropology (9 percent). The low specialties are elementary, etc., education (.2 percent), law (.3 percent), business administration (.3 percent), journalism (.2 percent), medicine (.2 percent), and dentistry (.1 percent).

There was also substantial diversity in the amount of human capital deepening in the various specialty stocks. As measured by the ratio of the doctorate share in 1970 to that in 1930, the leaders were architecture, civil and other heavy engineering, electrical-electronic engineering, and geological-mining engineering. Other specialties experiencing substantial deepening were chemistry, earth sciences, philosophy, and agriculture. Most of the social and psychological sciences experienced a shallowing over the period, as they became more popular undergraduate majors. The most severe shallowing was for anthropology, which dropped its doctorate share from 23 to 9 percent.

The dynamic structure We turn now to the dynamic structure of the stock of degreed persons; it should be noted that the estimates reported in this section, of the historical probabilities of degree recipients subsequently receiving advanced degrees, are considerably higher than those which might be derived through casual empiricism. Casual empiricism could err because of two phenomena connected with the dispersion of the distribution of time between degrees. First, impressions formed from data could be considerably on the low side if the size of the current advanced degree cohort is compared with the size of the *current* bachelor's degree cohort, rather than with the sizes of the 25 or so previous bachelor's degree cohorts. Second, impressions formed from faculty experience could also be on the low side because professors tend to lose track of that large fraction of their bachelor's students who do ultimately enroll for and receive advanced degrees, but who do so at relatively distant future times, in other universities, or in other specialties. Casual empirical observation of student transitions may therefore be quite misleading.

Impressions of transition distributions may also err through the confusion of *forward* and *backward* distributions. We may define the *backward* distribution of elapsed time between the bachelor's degree and an advanced degree as the probability that an advanced degree recipient received his bachelor's t years earlier, and the *forward* distribution as the probability that a bachelor's recipient will receive an advanced degree t years later. It would seem to be often the case that impressions of forward time-lapse distributions, based either on data or on experience with students, are in fact impressions of the corresponding backward distributions. It is the contention here that many observers with impressions of backward distributions, based on either data or experience with students, implicitly use these backward distributions as if they were forward distributions.

That this mistake can have a substantial effect can be illustrated by using an exponential distribution. If the forward distribution should be proportional to a simple exponential distribution with parameter λ and if the size of bachelor's degree cohorts should grow at rate r, the backward distribution would be

$$p(t) = \frac{\lambda + r}{\lambda} e^{-rt} \lambda e^{-\lambda t} \quad \lambda > 0, \qquad t \geq 0.$$

It can also be shown that the median of the forward distribution m_f would be related to the median of the backward distribution m_b by

$$m_f = m_b\left(1 + \frac{r}{\lambda}\right).$$

With a positive growth rate, the median of the forward distribution would be greater than the median of the backward distribution, and, under realistic assumptions, it could be considerably greater.

With this as an introduction, the estimated probabilities that bachelor's and second-level degree recipients have received or will receive advanced degrees for selected years are given in Table 67. What is absorbing about these estimates is that they assert that getting a graduate degree is no longer the preserve of a clear minority of American bachelor's recipients and, indeed, that this has not been the case for men for two generations. The estimate of this study is that 46 percent of all 1965 bachelor's recipients, and over half (54 percent) of the men, will go on to get graduate degrees at some time in the future. It is also the case that men bachelor's recipients who will go on to get a doctorate (over 9 percent in 1965) no longer constitute the tiny minority they did in 1930. Those 1965 women bachelor's recipients who have received or will receive a doctorate still consti-

TABLE 67 ***Probabilities that bachelor's and second-level degree recipients in selected years have received or will receive advanced degrees, by sex (in percentages)***

(1) *Earlier degree*	(2) *Later degree*	(3) *Year*	(4) *Men*	(5) *Women*	(6) *All*	(7) *Ratio men to women**
		1930	45	20	34	2.3
Bachelor's	*Second-level*	1955	42	26	36	1.6
		1965†	52	36	45	1.5
		1930	4	1	3	4.5
Bachelor's	*Doctorate*	1955	6	2	4	3.7
		1965†	9	3	7	3.3
		1930	46	20	34	2.3
Bachelor's	*Advanced*	1955	43	26	37	1.6
		1965†	54	36	46	1.5
		1930	8	6	7	1.3
Second-level	*Doctorate*	1955	13	5	11	2.5
		1965†	20	8	17	2.4

*Calculated using the unrounded percentages whose rounded forms are cols. (4) and (5) of this table.

†1965 was chosen as the most recent date for which a case can be made that its probabilities are substantially based on recent data and near-term, high-quality projections. Most of the advancement probabilities are sensitive to no more than 12 years of degree conferrals. For 1965, this would cause the probabilities to be based on 6 years of data and 6 years of projections. For comparison, the probabilities for 1960 and 1970 bachelor's degree recipients receiving an advanced degree are 41 and 45 percent, respectively. Degree-conferral projections were made by the author, for academic specialties based on aggregate degree-conferral projections by Haggstrom (1971*a*, 1971*b*).

tute a very small minority (3 percent), however. Women bachelor's recipients came a long way in the period 1930–1965; their probability of reaching the second level doubled, and their probability of reaching the doctorate tripled. Nevertheless, these 1965 probabilities for women bachelor's recipients did not quite equal the corresponding 1930 probabilities for men bachelor's recipients.

With respect to particular specialties, the estimates for 1965 are that in the following specialties (not considering specialties which are primarily graduate specialties like law or social work), more than 60 percent of either men or women or both will eventually receive an advanced degree:

A 1965 advancement probability over 60 percent is indicated by (x)		
	Men	*Women*
Mathematics and statistics	x	x
Computer and information science	x	x
Philosophy	x	x
Chemistry	x	
Physics	x	x
Physical science, n.e.c.	x	x
All engineering specialties except engineering and technical specialties, n.e.c.		x
Biological sciences	x	
Anthropology	x	x
History	x	
Political science	x	
Social science, n.e.c.	x	
Social science professions, n,e.c.	x	x
Psychology	x	
Elementary, etc., education	x	
English literature, dramatic arts, and speech	x	
Western European languages and literatures	x	
Non-Western European languages and literatures	x	x

Thus in a large number of specialties, particularly in the sciences and arts, it is now the norm for bachelor's degree recipients to obtain one or more graduate degrees. (See Tables 68 and 69 for the advancement probabilities for the 44 individual specialties for 1955 and 1965.)

On the other hand, there are a few specialties where the 1965 probability of a bachelor's degree recipient's receiving an advanced degree is below one-third for both sexes: architecture, agriculture, nursing, therapy and dental hygiene, physical education, journalism and communications, and business administration. For women, a number of additional specialties—notably elementary, etc., education and secondary, etc.,

TABLE 68 ***Probabilities that 1955 bachelor's and second-level degree recipients have received or will receive advanced degrees, by earlier degree specialty and sex (in percentages)***

Earlier degree:	Bachelor's				Second-level			
Later degree:	Second-level		Doctorate		Advanced*		Doctorate	
Earlier degree specialty	Men	Women	Men	Women	Men	Women	Men	Women
1. *Mathematics and statistics*	54	44	10	2	57	44	29	8
2. *Computer science and information science*	—	—	—	—	—	—	—	—
3. *Library science*	12	24	32	1	19	24	3	1
4. *Philosophy (not including scholastic philosophy)*	†	46	26	9	†	48	†	35
5. *Chemistry*	52	34	15	4	60	36	37	13
6. *Earth sciences*	40	†	9	4	42	†	29	17
7. *Physics*	47	51	20	11	56	54	40	22
8. *Physical science, n.e.c.*	†	†	14	21	†	†	39	36
9. *Architecture*	22	13	§	¶	22	13	5	2
10. *Chemical-materials engineering*	34	†	7	37	36	†	27	48
11. *Civil and other heavy engineering*	30	†	3	26	30	†	16	40
12. *Electrical-electronic engineering*	40	†	5	31	40	†	21	60
13. *Geological-mining engineering*	23	63	3	8	24	65	10	¶
14. *Mechanical-equipment engineering*	28	†	3	30	28	†	15	51

15. *Engineering and other technical specialties, n.e.c.*	29	21	6	2	30	21	39	7
16. *Biological sciences*	†	31	11	3	†	32	49	21
17. *Agriculture*	22	10	5	14	23	14	18	27
18. *Dentistry*	—	—	—	—	—	—	¶	¶
19. *Medicine*	—	—	—	—	—	—	1	1
20. *Nursing, therapy, and dental hygiene*	18	30	4	1	20	30	†	4
21. *Physical education*	22	14	4	1	23	14	6	6
22. *Health professions, n.e.c.*	35	19	7	1	37	19	9	5
23. *Anthropology and archaeology*	†	68	36	11	†	71	56	27
24. *Economics and agricultural economics*	37	15	4	2	38	16	34	17
25. *History*	58	32	6	2	60	32	31	9
26. *Political science*	63	25	6	2	64	25	39	19
27. *Sociology and social psychology*	50	21	9	1	49	21	48	21
28. *Social science, n.e.c.*	†	38	7	2	†	39	27	8
29. *Journalism and communications*	15	11	2	1	16	11	16	2
30. *Business administration*	21	9	1	§	21	9	5	4
31. *Administrative specialties other than business administration*	62	†	7	8	63	†	10	3
32. *Law*	—	—	—	—	—	—	§	§
33. *Social work*	†	75	3	1	†	75	5	1
34. *Social science professions, n.e.c.*	†	71	5	4	†	72	34	31
35. *Psychology*	69	38	22	6	74	39	66	24
36. *Education—primary, preprimary and exceptional*	68	24	7	1	68	24	12	2
37. *Education—secondary, adult, specialized teaching fields*	51	28	5	1	52	28	11	4

TABLE 68 (*continued*)

Earlier degree:	*Bachelor's*				*Second-level*			
Later degree:	*Second-level*		*Doctorate*		*Advanced**		*Doctorate*	
Earlier degree specialty	*Men*	*Women*	*Men*	*Women*	*Men*	*Women*	*Men*	*Women*
38. *Education, n.e.c.*	†	†	†	42	†	†	14	4
39. *Home economics*	54	11	†	§	75	11	†	7
40. *English literature, dramatic arts, and speech*	54	31	10	2	55	31	35	9
41. *Art and music*	45	21	5	1	46	21	16	5
42. *Western European languages and literatures*	61	36	14	2	64	36	31	10
43. *Non-Western European languages and literatures*	†	†	37	8	†	†	76	28
44. *Religion and scholastic philosophy*	40	14	5	2	40	14	7	6
ALL FIELDS	42	26	6	2	43	26	13	5

*Advanced degree denotes "either second-level or doctorate." Simply adding the probabilities for second-level and doctorate does not produce this probability since those doctorates who have second-level degrees would be counted twice.

†In the case of very small specialties (e.g., *male* bachelor's in home economics), the estimation method sometimes produced a number higher than 80 percent. But since 80 percent is regarded here as the highest believable value, any such probability was scaled to 80 percent for use in further calculations.

§Between .25 and .5 percent.

¶Less than .25 percent.

TABLE 69 ***Probabilities that 1965 bachelor's and second-level degree recipients have received or will receive advanced degrees, by earlier degree specialty and sex (in percentages)***

Earlier degree:	*Bachelor's*						*Second-level*	
Later degree:	*Second-level*		*Doctorate*		*Advanced**		*Doctorate*	
Earlier degree specialty	*Men*	*Women*	*Men*	*Women*	*Men*	*Women*	*Men*	*Women*
1. *Mathematics and statistics*	70	61	13	3	74	62	30	9
2. *Computer and information science*	70‡	61‡	68	37	†	69	33	11
3. *Library science*	20	40	46	2	28	40	3	1
4. *Philosophy (not including scholastic philosophy)*	†	66	31	14	†	70	†	49
5. *Chemistry*	50	49	22	8	62	53	47	18
6. *Earth sciences*	46	†	14	10	50	†	36	23
7. *Physics*	59	72	28	21	71	80	46	29
8. *Physical science, n.e.c.*	†	†	23	32	†	†	55	54
9. *Architecture*	32	27	¶	¶	32	27	5	3
10. *Chemical-materials engineering*	48	†	14	69	52	†	40	†
11. *Civil and other heavy engineering*	44	†	8	46	45	†	27	58
12. *Electrical-electronic engineering*	56	†	9	56	58	†	30	69
13. *Geological-mining engineering*	34	†	9	14	36	†	30	¶
14. *Mechanical-equipment engineering*	40	†	8	55	42	†	27	51
15. *Engineering and other technical specialties, n.e.c.*	44	24	13	3	47	25	57	13

TABLE 69 ***(continued)***

Earlier degree:	*Bachelor's*						*Second-level*	
Later degree:	*Second-level*		*Doctorate*		*Advanced**		*Doctorate*	
Earlier degree specialty	*Men*	*Women*	*Men*	*Women*	*Men*	*Women*	*Men*	*Women*
16. *Biological sciences*	76	41	15	7	†	43	64	30
17. *Agriculture*	21	20	8	29	23	29	25	32
18. *Dentistry*	—	—	—	—	—	—	¶	¶
19. *Medicine*	—	—	—	—	—	—	§	2
20. *Nursing, therapy, and dental hygiene*	21	34	12	1	25	34	†	6
21. *Physical education*	27	19	6	2	28	20	8	8
22. *Health professions, n.e.c.*	39	25	8	2	41	26	12	7
23. *Anthropology and archaeology*	†	†	34	14	†	†	60	39
24. *Economics and agricultural economics*	47	23	6	5	48	24	40	28
25. *History*	64	44	7	3	65	45	35	13
26. *Political science*	63	31	6	4	64	32	42	28
27. *Sociology and social psychology*	50	25	10	2	52	26	57	31
28. *Social science, n.e.c.*	†	45	8	2	†	45	28	10
29. *Journalism and communications*	20	19	3	1	21	19	25	5
30. *Business administration*	28	11	2	1	27	11	7	8

31. *Administration other than business administration*	67	†	9	10	69	†	12	3
32. *Law*	63	31	¶	¶	63	31	¶	§
33. *Social work*	†	†	3	1	†	†	7	2
34. *Social science professions, n.e.c.*	†	†	7	4	†	†	35	27
35. *Psychology*	71	45	21	9	76	47	69	34
36. *Education—primary, preprimary, and exceptional*	74	29	9	1	74	29	15	3
37. *Education—secondary, adult, specialized teaching fields*	53	32	6	1	54	32	14	4
38. *Education, n.e.c.*	†	†	†	53	†	†	20	6
39. *Home economics*	†	15	†	1	†	15	†	9
40. *English literature, dramatic arts, and speech*	63	44	12	3	65	44	39	13
41. *Art and music*	55	30	9	1	56	30	23	
42. *Western European languages and literatures*	72	54	17	4	76	55	35	14
43. *Non-Western European languages and literatures*	†	†	41	11	†	†	72	29
44. *Religion and scholastic philosophy*	37	17	5	2	37	18	6	7
ALL FIELDS	52	36	9	3	54	36	20	8

*Advanced degree denotes "either second-level or doctorate." Simply adding the probabilities for second-level and doctorate does not produce this probability since those doctorates who have second-level degrees would be counted twice.

†In the case of very small specialities (e.g., *male* bachelor's in home economics), the estimation method sometimes produced a number higher than 80 percent. But since 80 percent is regarded here as the highest believable value, any such probability was scaled to 80 percent for use in further calculations.

‡Footnote † applies, but instead the probabilities for mathematics were substituted.

§Between .25 and .5 percent.

¶Less than .25 percent.

education—can be added to the list. If we simply remove business administration for men and elementary and secondary education for women from consideration, the revised probabilities of getting advanced degrees for male and female bachelor's recipients increase to 60 and 40 percent, respectively.

It should be clear from what has already been presented that sex makes a pronounced difference in the likelihood of transition from lower to higher levels of the stock. In 1965 this was true at the aggregate level, where men have substantially greater advancement probabilities than women: 1.5 times greater for bachelor's to second-level, 3.3 times greater for bachelor's to doctorate, and 2.4 times greater for second-level to doctorate. (See the last column of Table 67.) While not denying the direction of the aggregate effect, one might hypothesize that the magnitude was dependent on the specialty composition of degree output. Table 70 shows that this is not the case; if anything, the effect goes in the opposite direction. In order to analyze this, we selected 14 specialties which are not untypical for either sex according to the criterion that the specialty is ranked among the top 22 specialties with respect to the number of persons in the bachelor's-level stock. The result is that, for all transitions, the average ratio of specialty male-to-female advancement probabilities was equal to, or greater than, the aggregate ratio of advancement probabilities. (See the last two lines of Table 70.) This effect tends to rule out the existence of significant sectors of the stock where men and women have approximately the same likelihood of advancing to higher degree levels.

It is interesting to compare the static and dynamic degree structures of the overall stock of degreed persons. Whereas in 1965 only 26 percent of persons in the stock were qualified beyond the bachelor's level, the 1965 probability that bachelor's recipients would receive an advanced degree was 46 percent. If we ignore considerations of age structure and time lapse between degrees, this would result in a no-growth equilibrium structure of 32 percent advanced degrees.[15] But such is the

[15] A ratio of 46 advanced degrees to 100 bachelor's degrees can be expressed as 46 advanced degrees to 146 total degrees or 32 percent. To go the other way, 26 percent advanced degrees converts to a 35 to 100 ratio of advanced to bachelor's degrees.

TABLE 70 ***Ratios of male to female probabilities that 1965 bachelor's and second-level degree recipients have received or will receive advanced degrees, selected specialties****

Earlier degree: / *Later degree:* / *Earlier degree specialty*	*Bachelor's* / *Second-level*	*Bachelor's* / *Doctorate*	*Second-level* / *Doctorate*
Mathematics	1.1	4.3	3.3
Chemistry	1.0	2.8	2.6
Biological sciences	1.9	2.1	2.1
Economics	2.0	1.2	1.4
History	1.5	2.3	2.7
Political science	2.0	1.5	1.5
Sociology and social psychology	2.0	5.0	1.8
Social sciences, n.e.c.	1.8	4.0	2.8
Business administration	2.5	2.0	.9
Psychology	1.6	2.3	2.0
Elementary, etc., education	2.6	9.0	5.0
Secondary, etc., education	1.7	6.0	3.5
English literature, dramatic arts, and speech	1.4	4.0	3.0
Religion	2.2	2.5	.9
Simple unweighted average of the above specialties	1.9	3.5	2.4
All specialties†	1.5	3.3	2.4

*Those specialties which are in the top half according to size for both sexes were selected. This eliminates from consideration those specialties which have small representation from one or both sexes and which are therefore not typical.

†Derived from the last line of Table 69.

inertia in the system that, on the basis of projections that will be reported elsewhere, 32 percent advanced degrees in the stock is not likely to be attained before the year 2000.

The discrepancy between the static and dynamic structures is even more pronounced in the case of doctorates. In the static structure, doctorates were 2.2 percent of the overall stock in 1965; in the dynamic structure, the 7 percent probability of bachelor's recipients' getting a doctorate converts (under the simplifying assumptions used above) into an equilibrium static structure of 6 percent doctorates in the overall stock. Thus the implication of the present dynamic structure is a static structure sometime after the year 2000 of:

- 69 percent bachelor's level
- 26 percent second level
- 6 percent doctorate level

Time-Lapse Distributions

In addition to contemplating the total probability of getting advanced degrees, we may consider the distribution of this probability over time (the forward distribution referred to earlier). Figures 20 and 21 give estimates of this distribution by sex and degree level for 1965. A presentation of the full distribution for each individual specialty would for 1965 be too voluminous. Table 71 therefore gives the median number of years between degrees for each specialty.

Each of the sex-transition distributions presented in Figures 20 and 21 is unimodal, is substantially skewed (with the exception of the female bachelor's-to-doctorate distribution), and has a long tail which would extend beyond 25 years had it not been truncated for the purpose of this study. One is not particularly surprised to find the long tail, since classrooms are occasionally graced even by the presence of a septuagenarian. What is notable in these distributions, however, is how fat the tails are. The upper quartile for the bachelor's-to-second-level transition is 8.0 years for men and 9.0 years for women. For the bachelor's-to-doctorate transition the upper quartile is 12.1 years for men and 14.2 years for women. And for the second-level-to-doctorate transition the upper quartile is 9.6 years for men and 9.9 years for women. Thus large numbers of degreed persons are attaining higher degree levels only after exceptionally long periods.

8.5. THE SEX DISTRIBUTION

The sex distribution of the stock of degreed persons has certain striking characteristics. While in 1970, for the overall stock, it was not so very different from that which would occur by random selection—the distribution was 58-42 percent male-female—any disaggregation by degree level and specialty reveals a structure which is more highly sex-linked than the overall distribution. Tables 76A through 79 contain sex distri-

FIGURE 20 ***Time-lapse distribution: for 1965 male degree recipients, the probability of receiving a subsequent degree in each succeeding year***

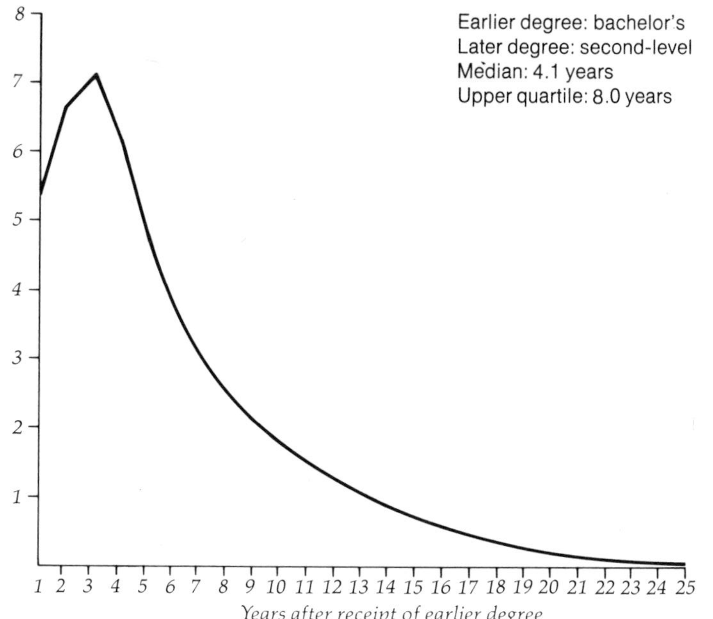

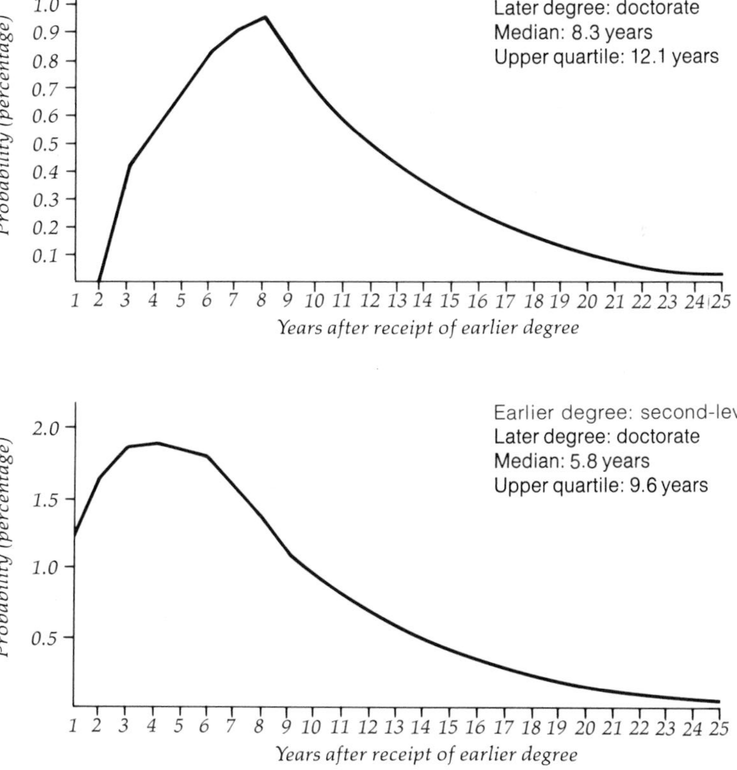

FIGURE 21 ***Time lapse distribution: for 1965 female degree recipients, the probability of receiving a subsequent degree in each succeeding year***

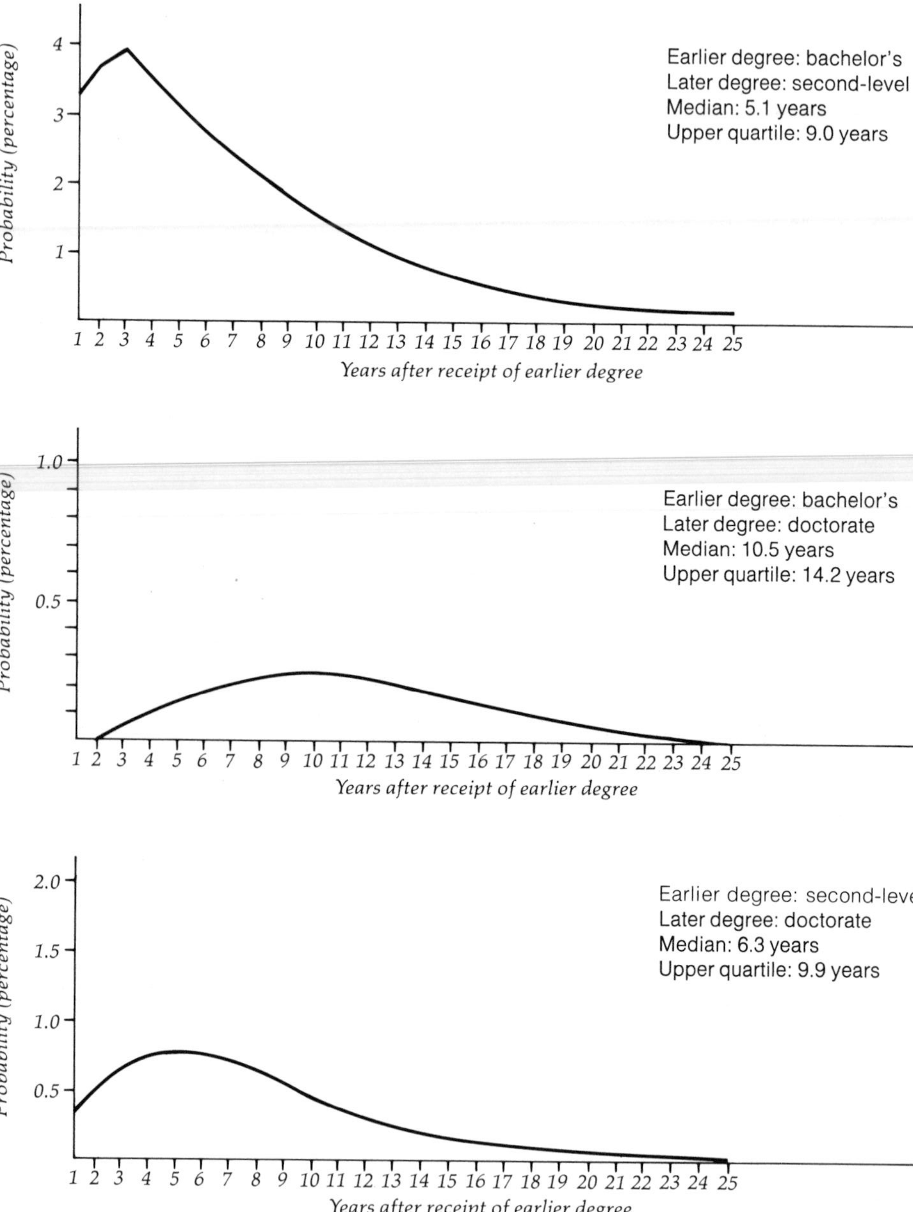

TABLE 71 ***Median number of years between degrees, by earlier degree specialty and sex, for 1965 earlier degree recipients***

Earlier degree:	*Bachelor's*		*Bachelor's*		*Second-level*	
Later degree:	*Second-level*		*Doctorate*		*Doctorate*	
Earlier degree specialty	*Men*	*Women*	*Men*	*Women*	*Men*	*Women*
1. *Mathematics and statistics*	3.8	4.5	7.3	8.3	5.1	5.1
2. *Computer and information science*	*	*	*	*	*	*
3. *Library science*	1.3	4.2	6.4	11.0	7.7	7.7
4. *Philosophy (not including scholastic philosophy)*	4.5	4.0	10.0	9.3	7.0	5.3
5. *Chemistry*	3.2	3.9	5.9	6.7	3.7	4.2
6. *Earth sciences*	3.5	4.6	7.5	7.1	4.7	4.5
7. *Physics*	3.2	3.5	7.0	7.3	4.5	4.4
8. *Physical science, n.e.c.*	3.5	4.9	8.4	10.5	7.1	10.4
9. *Architecture*	4.1	3.6	6.9		6.7	6.2
10. *Chemical-materials engineering*	3.6	4.4	6.6	9.0	3.8	5.6
11. *Civil and other heavy engineering*	3.8	4.3	7.1	7.8	5.1	4.3
12. *Electrical-electronic engineering*	3.8	4.3	7.7	8.6	5.6	6.8
13. *Geological-mining engineering*	3.8	4.2	7.5	7.9	4.4	—
14. *Mechanical-equipment engineering*	3.7	3.7	7.6	7.9	5.9	4.7
15. *Engineering and other technical specialties, n.e.c.*	4.3	4.5	7.3	7.5	6.3	4.9
16. *Biological sciences*	3.7	3.9	7.4	7.3	4.4	4.5
17. *Agriculture*	3.3	3.5	6.8	7.2	3.9	4.6
18. *Dentistry*	—	—	—	—	8.6	—
19. *Medicine*	—	—	—	—	4.0	7.4
20. *Nursing, therapy, and dental hygiene*	2.5	10.8	6.3	12.3	6.3	6.3
21. *Physical education*	4.9	5.2	11.5	11.7	7.1	6.3
22. *Health professions, n.e.c.*	9.9	6.4	9.4	10.6	4.4	4.6
23. *Anthropology and archaeology*	5.2	5.8	10.0	10.2	5.5	5.6
24. *Economics and agricultural economics*	3.8	3.8	7.9	7.8	5.5	4.8
25. *History*	4.0	4.1	9.1	9.6	5.9	5.4
26. *Political science*	4.3	5.1	9.1	9.9	5.7	6.0
27. *Sociology and social psychology*	4.3	4.0	9.5	10.0	5.2	5.0
28. *Social science, n.e.c.*	7.6	6.3	14.2	11.6	8.1	6.6
29. *Journalism and communications*	3.6	3.8	8.5	9.8	6.8	6.8
30. *Business administration*	4.9	4.8	10.3	10.1	6.7	4.6

TABLE 71 (continued)

Earlier degree:	*Bachelor's*		*Bachelor's*		*Second-level*	
Later degree:	*Second-level*		*Doctorate*		*Doctorate*	
Earlier degree specialty	*Men*	*Women*	*Men*	*Women*	*Men*	*Women*
31. *Administration specialties other than business administration*	5.9	3.3	9.5	8.3	5.8	5.3
32. *Law*	4.3	5.1	—	—	4.7	3.2
33. *Social work*	3.7	2.0	8.2	8.5	5.9	5.1
34. *Social science professions, n.e.c.*	7.0	7.7	14.9	11.8	14.8	7.1
35. *Psychology*	4.2	4.5	8.1	8.5	4.8	4.9
36. *Education—primary, preprimary, exceptional*	4.4	6.5	13.5	14.4	8.8	9.2
37. *Education—secondary, adult, specialized teaching fields*	4.1	6.0	13.2	14.2	9.3	8.6
38. *Education, n.e.c.*	4.7	7.3	11.7	13.2	7.9	7.9
39. *Home economics*	4.1	4.1	7.2	9.5	6.1	5.6
40. *English literature, dramatic arts, and speech*	3.8	4.3	9.7	11.0	6.7	6.9
41. *Art and music*	3.2	3.6	14.6	11.1	9.6	7.8
42. *Western European languages and literatures*	3.3	3.6	8.8	8.6	5.7	5.6
43. *Non-Western European languages and literatures*	5.0	5.1	11.1	10.2	8.1	7.3
44. *Religion and scholastic philosophy*	4.6	4.4	11.9	10.3	5.7	4.0
ALL FIELDS	4.1	5.1	8.3	10.5	5.8	6.3

*Because of inadequate information on the "backward frequencies" for computer and information science, no median is presented. Where needed in calculations, the median for mathematics was used.

butions for the individual specialties at the four levels of aggregation.

With advancement in degree level, the stock becomes progressively more male-dominated. At the bachelor's level the sex distribution, male-feamle, is 53-47 percent; at the second level the distribution is 71-29 percent; and at the doctorate level the distribution is 88-12 percent, with few exceptions for individual specialties. It is mildly interesting to note that a few of the most highly male-dominated specialties in 1970 are exceptions to this pattern in that they had a slightly larger percentage of women in the doctorate stock than they did in the second-level stock.[16] Medicine and dentistry are the only instances among these where the percentage female was, however, substantially higher at the doctorate level than at the second level (dentistry—9 percent versus 1 percent; medicine—10 percent versus 6 percent).

A number of specialty stocks are sexually differentiated, being almost entirely dominated by one sex or the other. The 10 fields with, respectively, the largest and smallest female participation in 1970 are listed in Table 72 according to their percentage of females. None of the specialties on the list will come as any particular surprise to the reader, since this sexual differentiation is well known and has persisted over time. It is interesting to note that only 3 of the 44 doctorate specialty stocks have a female share over half.

At the sciences-technologies-arts aggregation level, in 1970 the percentage of females in the overall stock appears to increase with distance from science:

	Percentage female, 1970			
	Bachelor's	*Second-level*	*Doctorate*	*All levels*
Sciences	41	27	10	37
Technologies	44	28	12	39
Arts	67	38	19	61

In fact, a more general rule would seem to be that, while arts are indeed less male-dominated than sciences, technologies are more male-dominated. The opposite effect at the sciences-technologies-arts level is produced by the fact that, while exceptions to the rule are small in number, they are quantitatively large enough to produce the aggregate effect.

First, a few examples of specialties that follow the hypothesized general rule that individual technology stocks will tend to be less female than the stocks of the sciences to which they are related:

[16]These specialties are architecture, geological-mining engineering, dentistry, medicine, law, and social science professions, n.e.c.

		Percentage female, 1970		
		Bachelor's	*Second-level*	*Doctorate*
I.	1. *Mathematics and physical sciences*	30	18	5
	2. *Engineering*	2	2	1
II.	1. *Biological sciences*	46	32	14
	2. *Medicine*	—	6	10
III.	1. *Economics*	14	10	5
	2. *Business administration**	13	4	3
IV.	1. *Political science*	28	21	9
	2. *Law**	6	4	5

*Business administration and law, of course, also depend on the other principal social sciences and psychology, all of which have higher percentages of females than economics and political science.

The exceptions to the rule of higher female participation in sciences than in technologies are certain technologies that are dominated by women. Only education is quantitatively notable and is responsible for the high female percentage in technologies as a whole, but nursing, therapy, and dental hygiene; social work; and home economics also have much higher female proportions than their respective sciences:

		Percentage female, 1970		
		Bachelor's	*Second-level*	*Doctorate*
I.	1. *Psychology*	52	45	19
	2. *Education*	76	54	22
II.	1. *Biological sciences*	46	32	14
	2. *Nursing, therapy, and dental hygiene*	93	97	57
III.	1. *Sociology*	67	36	17
	2. *Social work*	79	64	35
IV.	1. *Chemistry**	33	21	6
	2. *Home economics*	99	98	73

*Chemistry can perhaps be considered a basic science for food preparation. If the biological, psychological, or social sciences, which were used in the other examples, were compared with home economics, the same point would be made.

TABLE 72 ***Percentage female in certain specialty stocks, 1970, ranked according to largest and smallest participation rates in the overall stock***

Specialty	*Bachelor's*	*Second-level*	*Doctorate*	*All levels*
Largest				
1. *Home economics*	99	98	73	99
2. *Nursing, therapy, and dental hygiene*	93	97	57	93
3. *Elementary, etc., education*	92	79	32	90
4. *Library science*	86	77	28	79
5. *Western European languages and literatures*	79	61	30	75
6. *English literature, dramatic arts, and speech*	72	57	22	69
7. *Social work*	79	64	35	67
8. *Art and music*	70	42	18	65
9. *Sociology and social psychology*	67	36	17	64
10. *Secondary, etc., education*	59	45	21	55
Smallest				
1. *Mechanical-equipment engineering*	*	*	*	*
2. *Electrical-electronics engineering*	*	*	*	*
3. *Civil and other heavy engineering*	*	*	*	*
4. *Geological-mining engineering*	*	*	1	*
5. *Chemical-materials engineering*	1	1	*	1
6. *Dentistry*	—	1	19	1
7. *Agriculture*	3	3	2	3
8. *Law*	6	4	5	4
9. *Earth sciences*	5	6	3	5
10. *Physics*	7	7	3	6

*Less than .5 percent.

Considering all fields together and looking at the behavior of the sex ratio over time, the bachelor's and doctorate stocks have maintained a remarkably stable sex ratio during the period 1930–1970. In both cases the percentage of females was somewhat higher in 1930 than in 1970 (see Figure 22). The sex ratio for the bachelor's stock shows an interesting bulge in the percentage of females due to the effects of World War II, a bulge

FIGURE 22
Sex distribution of degreed persons, 1930–1971

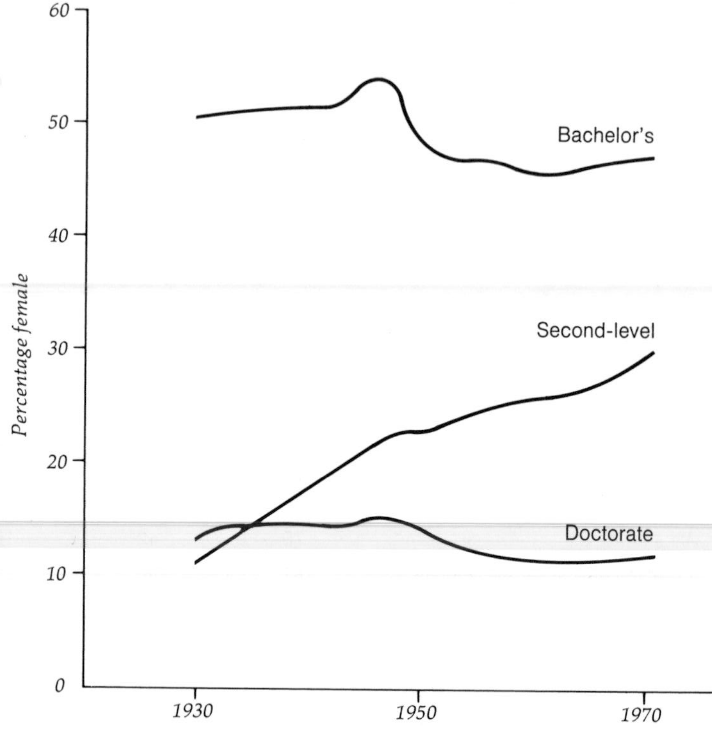

which reaches its highest point in 1946, at 54 percent. Except for this bulge, the bachelor's-level stock has been between 45 and 51 percent female throughout the period. Except for a World War II-induced bulge to 15 percent, the doctorate stock has likewise stayed in a narrow band between 11 and 14 percent female.

The percentage of females in the second-level degree stock, however, has risen over the period 1930–1970. At the sciences-technologies-arts aggregation level, second-level sciences did not experience much of an upward trend in the proportion female, but both second-level technologies and second-level arts did. (See Figures 23 and 24.) As it turns out, this is not one of the rare instances of movement in the degreed manpower economy, but is derivative of the change in specialty proportions discussed above. In fact, at the 44-category level of aggregation, the sex ratio has stayed remarkably constant for most specialties at the second level, as well as at the bachelor's and doctorate levels. A calculation was made to see what the aggregate second-level percentage-female statistics would have been in 1930 if the actual 1930 sex distribution for each specialty had obtained but if the 1970 specialty mix had occurred instead. The results strikingly demonstrate that the changes in the second-level aggregate sex ratios have been due primarily to the change in specialty proportions:

	Percentage female		
Second-level stocks in:	*1930 at actual 1930 specialty proportions*	*1930 at 1970 specialty proportions*	*1970 actual*
Technologies	09	24	28
Arts	22	38*	38

*Calculated by separating religion and scholastic philosophy into theology and a remainder.

If we address the question of whether there has been a trend toward sexual equality over the last generation or two, the answer, on balance, is probably in the negative. The slightly increased proportion of women in the degreed stock as a whole and the significantly increased proportion of women in the second-level stock would suggest a narrowing of sexual inequality. Of these, however, the significance of the first is lessened by the fact that the increase in the female share took place entirely in the 1930s, and the significance of the second is lessened by the fact that the narrowing was caused almost entirely by a shift in specialty proportions away from the male-dominated professional specialties. On the other hand, there was a slight increase in inequality over the 1930–1970 period in the highly important doctorate segment of the stock.

Perhaps most persuasive on the question, given the conflicting quantitative evidence at the aggregate level, is evidence on whether sexual differentiation along the lines of "separate but equal" increased or decreased, specialty by specialty. Certain evidence would appear to suggest that it increased somewhat. Over the period 1930–1970, a curious pattern appears to have emerged concerning those specialty stocks in which the share of women was relatively large in 1930. Two groups can be discerned: first, certain regular academic departments with a high percentage of females (e.g., history and English literature) and, second, the small number of specialties in which the women's

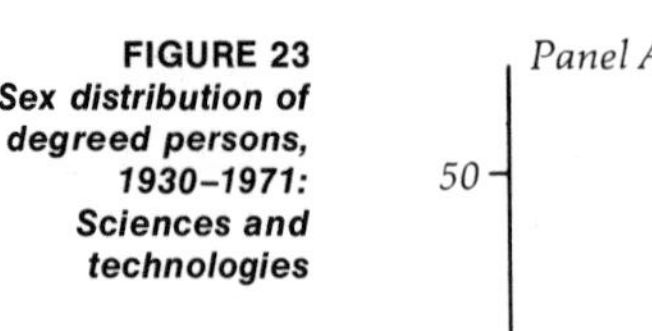

FIGURE 23
Sex distribution of degreed persons, 1930–1971: Sciences and technologies

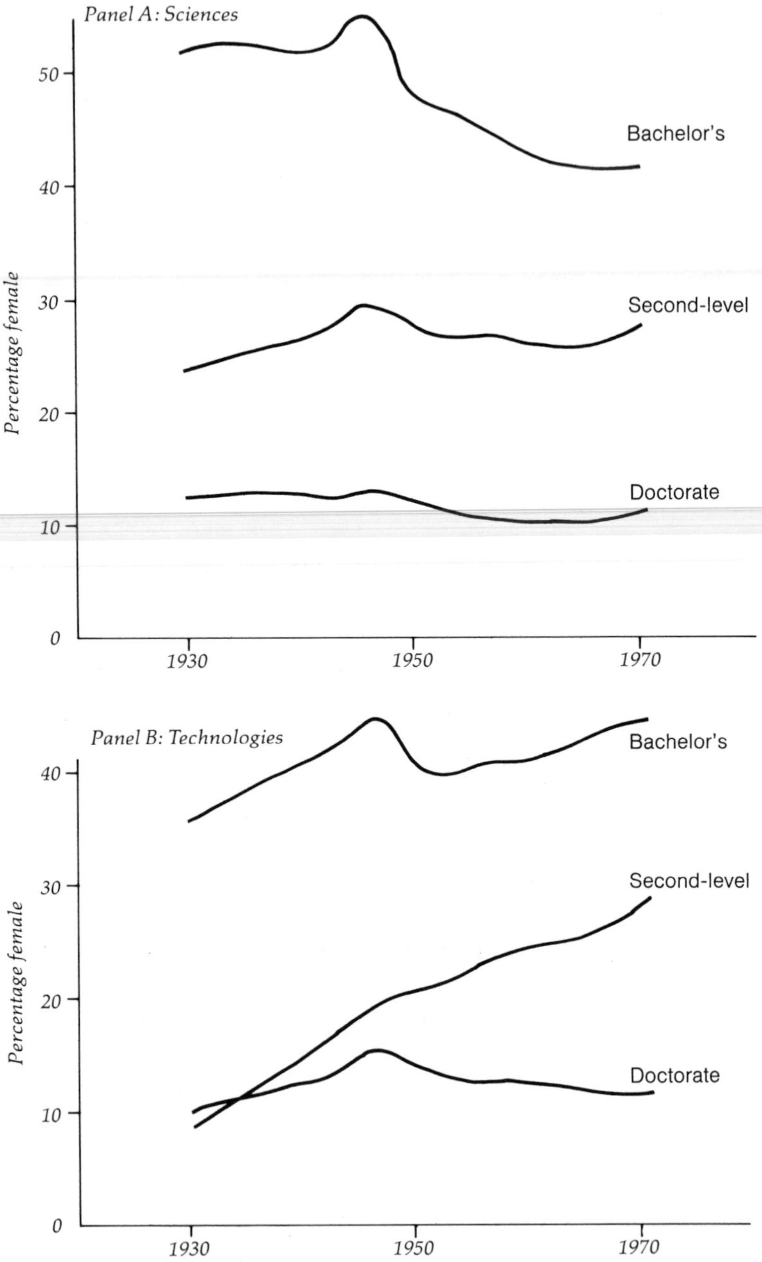

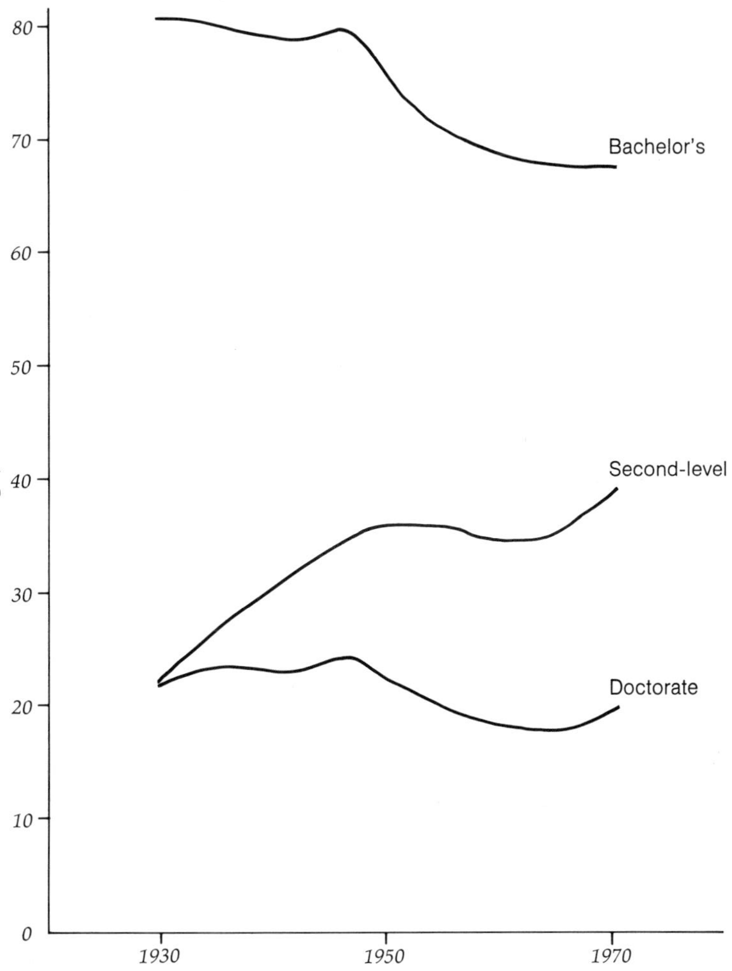

FIGURE 24
Sex distribution of degreed persons, 1930–1971: Arts

share was preponderant (e.g., elementary, etc., education and nursing, etc.). If we rank specialties by their percentage of females in 1930 and by their relative increase in the male share over the period 1930–1970, the two groups of specialties can be seen to have different responses (see Table 73.)

In the first group of regular academic specialty stocks with relatively high female proportions, the position of women at the bachelor's level slipped in the sense that the male share increased. At higher levels the effect appears to persist, but there are some exceptions, particularly at the second level. This effect does not work in reverse, however; highly male fields did not become less male to any notable extent.

TABLE 73 *Ranks of certain specialties with respect to the sex ratio and its rate of change**

Specialty	*Bachelor's*		*Second-level*		*Doctorate*	
	Rank ratio percentage male, 1970, to percentage male, 1930	*Rank percentage female, 1930*	*Rank ratio percentage male, 1970, to percentage male, 1930*	*Rank percentage female, 1930*	*Rank ratio percentage male, 1970, to percentage male, 1930*	*Rank percentage female, 1930*
Group I						
Philosophy	1	8	5	15	3	3
History	2	9	3	8	5	12
Sociology	3	5	14	11	41	19
Psychology	4	11	37	13	6	9
Western European languages and literatures	5	2	17	6	39	8
English literature	6	3	32	7	17	10
Religion and scholastic philosophy	7	17	28	32	9	17
Art and music	8	4	13	9	4	4
Mathematics and statistics	9	12	9	17	8	16
Health professions, n.e.c.	10	15	4	20	37	25
Biological sciences	11	13	36	22	11	14

Group II						
Nursing, therapy, and dental hygiene	44	16	44	2	2	2
Elementary, etc., education	43	6	43	4	38	5
Home economics	42	1	1	1	1	1
Library science	41	7	42	5	—	—
Secondary, etc., education	40	23	31	10	40	15
Education, n.e.c.	39	20	40	12	15	11
Social work	38	10	2	3	44	30

*Rank 1 is the highest, and rank 44 is the lowest.

The second group, on the other hand, is a group of what we might call "women's technologies." Here the women's position also appears to have slipped, unless an increase in women's separatism can be considered an advance, because it appears that the principal women's technologies are also the ones with the fastest-declining male role. This effect also persists at higher levels, but again there are exceptions.

The two effects together certainly do not support a conclusion of a lessening of inequality between the sexes. Together with the quantitative evidence, they suggest, rather, a qualitative move in the opposite direction.

8.6. THE VINTAGE DISTRIBUTION OF THE STOCK

The flow of economic services from the stock of degreed manpower and womanpower depends not only on the size of the stock but also on its vintage distribution. The holder of a bachelor's degree in electrical engineering who was born before World War I and received his degree in the 1930s will typically have different capabilities from those of a person who was born in 1946 and received his degree in the 1970s.

Degree-holders such as these can be characterized either by their personal vintage (their age) or by the vintage of their degrees. A case can be made that a large, perhaps preponderant, part of a person's human capital depends directly on the basic cognitive and affective skills that are inculcated by family upbringing in the context of a particular social and technical culture. This would suggest an age measure of vintage. A case can also be made that the rapidity of development of technical knowledge in a discipline is such that earlier degree cohorts cannot fully absorb new knowledge unless they have formally studied it. This would suggest a degree-date vintage characterization. Both cases are persuasive; age, however, was selected for this study, since it has importance beyond vintage considerations. The two methods would, in any case, produce similar vintage distributions.

It is in the nature of stocks and time that the individual elements of a stock should age. The distribution of ages, then, in the stock of degreed persons will change over time in response to the aging process. It will also change as given numbers of persons of given ages enter or leave the stock. The median age of a stock will decline if there is a large-enough

TABLE 74 ***Age structure of the stock of degreed persons, 1930 and 1971, by sex***

	Bachelor's		*Second-level*		*Doctorate*		*All levels*	
Age group	*1930*	*1971*	*1930*	*1971*	*1930*	*1971*	*1930*	*1971*
19–30								
Total	52	41	10	12	11	11	36	33
Men	51	40	10	13	11	11	30	31
Women	52	42	13	10	13	11	48	36
31–45								
Total	34	37	45	52	49	50	38	41
Men	36	41	43	52	49	52	40	44
Women	32	32	59	54	48	43	35	36
46–60								
Total	12	17	33	27	31	31	19	20
Men	10	15	34	27	31	30	22	19
Women	13	20	21	28	33	35	14	21
61–70								
Total	3	6	12	8	8	8	6	6
Men	2	4	13	8	9	7	8	6
Women	3	7	6	8	6	11	3	7
Median age								
Total	30.6	34.2	44.1	41.3	42.5	42.4	35.4	36.7
Men	30.7	34.0	45.0	41.2	42.5	42.2	37.3	36.7
Women	30.4	34.5	39.2	41.6	42.5	44.7	31.8	36.5

inflow of relatively young degree-holders and/or a large-enough outflow of relatively old degree-holders to overbalance the aging process.

Estimates of the age distributions of various components of the stock of degreed persons can be found in Tables 74 through 79. Five-point age distributions are given in Tables 77 through 79 for the various levels of aggregations by specialty and stock date, but not by sex. The age distribution by sex at the aggregate degree level is given in Tables 74 and 76; for specialties, however, only the age medians are given in Table 75.

TABLE 75 ***Median age of the stock of degreed persons, 1971, by specialty and sex***

Specialty	*Bachelor's*		*Second-level*		*Doctorate*		*All levels*	
	Men	*Women*	*Men*	*Women*	*Men*	*Women*	*Men*	*Women*
Aggregation level 1								
Total all fields	34.0	34.5	41.2	41.6	42.2	44.7	36.7	36.5
Aggregation level 2								
1. *Sciences*	30.6	32.7	36.6	36.8	41.3	42.1	32.4	33.7
2. *Technologies*	36.2	34.5	42.0	42.5	42.7	47.9	38.7	37.0
3. *Arts*	33.1	36.7	41.6	40.0	44.3	44.8	36.7	37.6
Aggregation level 3								
1. *Mathematics and physical sciences*	32.7	36.8	36.6	35.3	40.4	40.2	34.6	36.4
2. *Engineering*	38.4	37.1	36.5	35.5	37.5	37.8	37.8	36.7
3. *Biological and agricultural sciences*	32.9	35.9	39.9	36.0	42.4	41.7	35.3	36.2
4. *Health specialties*	37.5	32.7	45.9	42.0	43.7	43.7	43.9	34.3
5. *Social sciences and technology*	31.0	32.1	41.9	40.2	42.6	44.7	35.0	34.2
6. *Administration*	34.7	40.6	39.5	45.6	45.1	50.3	36.0	42.0
7. *Psychology*	28.4	30.0	34.3	36.7	41.0	41.0	30.3	31.7
8. *Education*	35.5	33.2	42.2	42.7	45.9	48.4	39.2	36.0
9. *Arts and humanities*	33.1	36.7	41.6	40.0	44.3	44.8	36.7	37.6
10. *Other*	44.5	44.7	39.1	39.3	42.6	48.4	39.9	43.2
Aggregation level 4								
1. *Mathematics and statistics*	30.6	31.3	34.6	34.4	37.2	39.4	32.0	32.2
2. *Computer and information science*	24.7	23.6	30.6	29.7	31.4	32.5	28.3	25.5
3. *Library science*	44.7	43.0	39.2	38.7	43.0	46.4	40.0	39.4

4. *Philosophy (not including scholastic philosophy)*	27.8	33.9	33.5	35.0	39.1	40.1	29.3	34.4
5. *Chemistry*	33.3	45.4	40.1	37.5	42.1	40.4	36.0	44.4
6. *Earth sciences*	39.7	39.2	39.8	35.2	41.5	42.6	39.9	37.4
7. *Physics*	33.3	40.4	36.2	36.7	39.3	40.0	35.2	38.9
8. *Physical science, n.e.c.*	30.6	32.1	37.3	36.1	40.4	37.8	33.6	34.7
9. *Architecture*	35.6	45.4	37.1	35.8	43.3	45.2	36.0	44.2
10. *Chemical-materials engineering*	41.0	40.8	39.2	33.2	38.7	34.8	40.4	35.9
11. *Civil and other heavy engineering*	40.3	29.0	36.9	31.2	37.0	36.4	39.3	31.1
12. *Electrical-electronic engineering*	36.7	30.6	36.3	31.8	37.4	38.5	36.6	31.9
13. *Geological-mining engineering*	43.8	49.8	40.1	31.4	36.3	35.1	43.4	45.8
14. *Mechanical-equipment engineering*	39.7	47.2	37.3	35.0	37.7	38.0	39.1	41.5
15. *Engineering and other technical specialties, n.e.c.*	33.9	35.7	34.6	38.7	36.8	39.0	34.3	36.3
16. *Biological sciences*	28.4	35.7	36.3	36.1	41.9	41.7	30.8	36.1
17. *Agriculture*	40.9	40.4	42.7	35.1	44.0	42.6	41.5	38.8
18. *Dentistry*	—	—	45.4	51.0	40.8	42.5	45.4	50.9
19. *Medicine*	—	—	46.6	48.3	42.3	42.3	46.5	48.3
20. *Nursing, therapy, and dental hygiene*	44.9	32.6	35.1	38.7	38.0	42.5	44.7	33.4
21. *Physical education*	36.0	37.5	42.0	42.6	47.7	50.0	37.3	38.4
22. *Health professions, n.e.c.*	36.0	33.3	43.2	39.8	44.9	45.5	38.1	34.5
23. *Anthropology and archaeology*	26.8	25.1	35.1	35.4	43.0	44.1	29.8	26.4
24. *Economics and agricultural economics*	36.2	41.3	37.7	37.8	42.7	42.9	36.8	41.1
25. *History*	30.3	34.8	37.8	39.5	43.6	47.3	31.8	35.9
26. *Political science*	29.0	30.0	37.2	36.3	42.4	39.8	29.9	30.7
27. *Sociology and social psychology*	30.1	31.8	37.1	39.3	43.2	47.9	31.3	32.3

TABLE 75 *(continued)*

Specialty	*Bachelor's*		*Second-level*		*Doctorate*		*All levels*	
	Men	*Women*	*Men*	*Women*	*Men*	*Women*	*Men*	*Women*
28. *Social science, n.e.c.*	28.7	29.0	36.2	36.5	40.2	41.8	30.4	30.1
29. *Journalism and communications*	41.6	41.4	39.5	36.8	39.1	39.2	41.3	40.9
30. *Business administration*	34.7	40.7	38.4	43.4	40.9	44.8	35.5	40.8
31. *Administration other than business administration*	33.8	28.8	41.3	45.9	47.0	51.0	39.0	45.6
32. *Law*	27.8	26.1	44.8	48.1	50.3	54.6	44.6	47.8
33. *Social work*	26.9	25.6	38.3	41.4	39.0	41.2	37.1	39.2
34. *Social science professions, n.e.c.*	28.6	26.7	34.7	33.8	37.0	41.7	30.8	29.7
35. *Psychology*	28.4	30.0	34.3	36.7	41.0	41.0	30.3	31.7
36. *Education—primary, preprimary, exceptional*	33.5	32.7	42.5	43.2	44.6	46.6	37.4	34.5
37. *Education—secondary, adult, specialized teaching fields*	36.3	34.3	43.3	43.9	45.5	48.0	39.7	37.4
38. *Education, n.e.c.*	26.9	24.7	41.4	41.2	46.0	48.8	41.4	40.5
39. *Home economics*	43.3	44.8	33.0	43.4	42.1	48.8	38.2	44.7
40. *English literature, dramatić arts, and speech*	31.9	34.2	38.7	39.6	43.2	43.9	34.1	35.7
41. *Art and music*	34.8	41.6	43.0	42.2	44.8	47.2	38.1	41.7
42. *Western European languages and literatures*	31.0	33.5	37.8	37.4	45.7	45.5	34.2	35.1
43. *Non-Western European languages and literatures*	27.8	25.2	35.3	34.7	42.6	41.4	31.5	28.5
44. *Religion and scholastic philosophy*	37.0	40.9	43.4	46.8	47.3	50.0	40.7	42.2

In 1971, the estimated median age of the population of degreed persons was 36.7 years, approximately the figure which has been maintained since 1930 (see Table 74). The age distribution of the 1971 stock was 33 percent age 30 or under, 41 percent age 31 through 45, 20 percent age 46 through 60, and 6 percent age 61 through 70.

The doctorate stock, not surprisingly, was the oldest of the degree-level stocks in 1971, with a median age of 42. What is somewhat unexpected is that the second-level stock was virtually as old, with a median age of 41. The bachelor's-level stock was considerably younger, with a median age of 34. Over the 1930–1970 period, there was more change in the age distributions of the bachelor's- and second-level stocks than in the aggregate. As measured by the median age, the bachelor's stock aged nearly four years, while the second-level stock became three years younger. The age of the doctorate stock, however, remained constant over the period.

In 1971, the median ages of men and women were approximately equal at all three degree levels and in the overall stock. This was not true in 1930, however. Then, the overall stock of degreed women was over five years younger than the stock of degreed men, and the second-level women were younger by almost six years. A priori, one might hypothesize that the stock of women should be older than that of men, both because of the greater longevity of women and because of time taken out for childbirth and housekeeping. While these phenomena undoubtedly have some bearing at all times and would produce a higher equilibrium median age for women than for men if a constant-volume net inflow of set age distribution were maintained for half a century, other factors affecting the stock age predominated in 1930. In particular, the rapid change in the proportion of total degrees conferred on women—from about 20 percent in 1910 to about 40 percent in 1930—resulted in about one-half of the 1930 female stock's being age 30 or under, versus about one-third of the 1930 male stock.

In passing, a small but interesting age effect, which occurred in 1971, may be noted. While women were slightly older at each degree level in that year, they were nevertheless slightly younger in the overall stock (see Table 74).

At the sciences-technologies-arts level of aggregation, the

sciences stock is considerably younger, with a median age of 33 years, than the technologies and arts stocks, with respective median ages of 38 and 37 years (see Tables 75 and 77). This effect is also true at all levels. Contributing factors are the relatively rapid growth rate of the sciences stock and the relatively high median age of second-level technology degree recipients. For the overall sciences stock, the high proportion at the bachelor's level was also a contributing factor.

At the 10-category level of aggregation (see Tables 75 and 78), for all degree levels together, the 1971 specialty age medians from highest to lowest are as follows:

Specialty	*Years*
Other	43.0
Health specialties	40.5
Engineering	37.8
Arts and humanities	37.2
Education	37.0
Administration	36.6
Biological and agricultural sciences	35.5
Mathematics and physical sciences	34.8
Social sciences and technologies	34.8
Psychology	30.8

At the 44-category level of aggregation the median ages of all overall specialty stocks[17] vary from 30 years for anthropology and architecture to 47 years for medicine and osteopathy (see Table 79). At the bachelor's level the range is from age 25 (education, n.e.c.) to age 45 (home economics); at the second level, from age 34 (philosophy) to age 47 (medicine); and at the doctorate level, from age 36 (geological-mining engineering) to age 50 (law).

[17]Not considering computer and information science, which is the youngest specialty stock because of its newness.

TABLE 76 ***Stock of persons in the United States holding academic degrees from United States universities, 1930–1971, by age and sex: aggregation level 1***

	List of subtables
76A	Total all fields
76B	Total all fields—men only
76C	Total all fields—women only

TABLE 76A ***Stock of persons in the United States holding academic degrees from United States universities, 1930–1971, by age and sex, total all fields***

Stock	*Age (percentage)*					*Median*	*Percentage*	*Total*
year	*19–30*	*31–45*	*46–60*	*61–65*	*66–70*	*age*	*female*	*number*
Highest degree attained—bachelor's								
1930	51.7	34.0	11.6	1.6	1.1	30.6	50.4	915,679
1935	49.9	36.3	11.3	1.6	.9	31.0	51.1	1,308,272
1940	46.0	39.9	11.6	1.5	1.0	31.9	51.1	1,814,663
1945	39.6	44.8	13.0	1.7	1.0	33.6	53.1	2,301,011
1950	41.4	41.9	14.0	1.7	1.0	33.3	48.7	3,220,450
1955	41.2	39.2	16.5	2.0	1.2	33.8	46.7	4,139,574
1960	35.9	42.1	18.4	2.2	1.4	34.4	45.5	5,184,638
1965	36.3	40.1	19.2	2.9	1.6	35.4	46.0	6,517,508
1970	39.5	37.5	17.6	3.4	2.0	34.5	46.7	8,490,111
1971	40.5	36.7	17.4	3.4	2.1	34.2	46.8	9,007,983
Highest degree attained—second-level								
1930	10.3	44.6	32.7	7.4	5.0	44.1	11.1	513,827
1935	9.9	49.1	29.0	6.9	5.1	42.7	14.4	619,038
1940	9.1	51.6	28.2	6.2	4.8	42.6	17.4	730,941
1945	6.6	50.6	32.4	5.9	4.6	44.0	20.7	810,838
1950	11.0	46.6	33.2	5.3	3.9	43.6	22.7	1,015,109
1955	10.8	49.5	31.1	5.2	3.4	42.4	24.1	1,321,886
1960	9.4	51.9	29.3	5.9	3.6	42.2	25.3	1,641,291
1965	10.1	51.7	28.4	5.7	4.0	42.4	26.4	2,074,216
1970	11.9	52.0	27.6	4.8	3.7	41.6	29.0	2,826,527
1971	12.0	52.4	27.3	4.6	3.6	41.3	29.7	3,023,827

TABLE 76A (*continued*)

Stock	*Age (percentage)*					*Median age*	*Percentage female*	*Total number*
	19–30	*31–45*	*46–60*	*61–65*	*66–70*			
Highest degree attained—doctorate								
1930	11.5	49.1	31.0	5.2	3.2	42.5	13.4	20,618
1935	11.5	52.4	29.0	4.3	2.8	41.5	14.2	31,498
1940	9.5	53.4	30.4	4.2	2.6	42.2	14.3	42,996
1945	6.7	50.9	34.7	4.9	2.8	43.9	14.8	53,046
1950	8.9	45.9	36.7	5.4	3.2	44.6	14.1	68,649
1955	10.8	47.2	33.9	5.0	3.1	43.3	12.3	102,067
1960	8.7	49.7	33.1	5.3	3.2	43.2	11.7	137,927
1965	9.3	49.8	32.1	5.5	3.3	43.2	11.3	189,744
1970	10.9	50.1	31.0	4.8	3.1	42.6	11.8	286,806
1971	11.0	50.4	30.9	4.6	3.1	42.4	12.0	313,680
All levels								
1930	36.5	38.0	19.3	3.7	2.5	35.4	36.0	1,450,124
1935	36.6	40.6	17.2	3.3	2.3	34.7	38.9	1,958,808
1940	35.0	43.4	16.6	2.9	2.1	35.0	41.0	2,588,600
1945	30.5	46.4	18.3	2.8	2.0	36.5	44.1	3,164,895
1950	33.7	43.1	18.9	2.6	1.7	35.9	42.0	4,304,208
1955	33.4	41.8	20.3	2.8	1.7	36.2	40.7	5,563,527
1960	29.1	44.5	21.3	3.1	1.9	36.7	40.1	6,963,856
1965	29.5	43.0	21.7	3.6	2.2	37.4	40.6	8,781,468
1970	32.1	41.3	20.4	3.8	2.4	36.9	41.5	11,603,444
1971	32.8	40.9	20.2	3.7	2.4	36.7	41.7	12,345,490

NOTE: See Adkins (1975) for a more extensive presentation of estimates of degrees conferred, 1890–1971, and of stocks of degree holders, 1930–1971.

TABLE 76B ***Stock of persons in the United States holding academic degrees from United States universities, 1930–1971, by age and sex, total all fields—men only***

Stock	*Age (percentage)*					*Median*	*Percentage*	*Total*
year	*19–30*	*31–45*	*46–60*	*61–65*	*66–70*	*age*	*female*	*number*
Highest degree attained—bachelor's								
1930	51.3	35.9	10.4	1.4	1.0	30.7	0	454,139
1935	48.8	38.7	10.2	1.4	.8	31.3	0	640,246
1940	45.9	41.5	10.4	1.3	.8	31.9	0	887,808
1945	36.7	48.4	12.4	1.5	.9	33.9	0	1,079,831
1950	44.6	40.7	12.5	1.4	.8	32.4	0	1,652,465
1955	46.0	37.5	14.1	1.5	.9	32.1	0	2,207,499
1960	37.8	43.8	15.6	1.8	1.0	33.3	0	2,824,462
1965	36.7	43.5	16.3	2.4	1.2	34.7	0	3,521,247
1970	38.7	41.7	15.3	2.7	1.6	34.2	0	4,522,366
1971	39.6	40.7	15.3	2.8	1.6	34.0	0	4,792,799
Highest degree attained—second-level								
1930	9.9	42.8	34.1	7.9	5.3	45.0	0	456,555
1935	9.6	46.7	30.4	7.6	5.6	43.5	0	530,203
1940	9.1	49.3	29.1	7.0	5.5	43.2	0	603,509
1945	6.4	48.5	33.0	6.7	5.4	44.6	0	642,602
1950	11.6	44.8	33.2	5.8	4.5	43.9	0	784,490
1955	11.6	48.5	30.6	5.4	3.8	42.2	0	1,003,566
1960	10.3	51.6	28.4	6.0	3.7	41.8	0	1,225,415
1965	11.1	51.9	27.2	5.7	4.0	42.0	0	1,527,427
1970	12.7	51.6	27.2	4.8	3.7	41.4	0	2,008,158
1971	12.8	51.8	27.2	4.6	3.6	41.2	0	2,125,386
Highest degree attained—doctorate								
1930	11.2	49.3	30.8	5.3	3.3	42.5	0	17,856
1935	11.4	53.0	28.3	4.4	2.9	41.3	0	27,027
1940	9.6	54.2	29.5	4.1	2.6	41.9	0	36,841
1945	6.7	52.0	33.9	4.7	2.8	43.6	0	45,215
1950	9.2	46.9	35.8	5.1	3.0	44.2	0	58,991
1955	11.3	48.5	32.8	4.6	2.8	42.7	0	89,505
1960	8.9	51.3	32.0	5.0	2.9	42.6	0	121,780
1965	9.5	51.2	31.1	5.1	3.0	42.8	0	168,268
1970	10.9	51.2	30.4	4.5	2.9	42.3	0	252,981
1971	10.9	51.5	30.3	4.4	2.9	42.2	0	275,935

TABLE 76B (continued)

Stock	*Age (percentage)*					*Median*	*Percentage*	*Total*
year	*19–30*	*31–45*	*46–60*	*61–65*	*66–70*	*age*	*female*	*number*
All levels								
1930	30.2	39.5	22.5	4.7	3.1	37.3	0	928,550
1935	30.6	42.6	19.6	4.2	3.0	36.4	0	1,197,476
1940	30.5	44.9	18.2	3.6	2.7	36.4	0	1,528,158
1945	24.9	48.6	20.4	3.5	2.6	37.8	0	1,767,648
1950	33.4	42.1	19.6	2.9	2.0	36.1	0	2,495,946
1955	34.6	41.1	19.7	2.8	1.8	35.7	0	3,300,570
1960	28.9	46.3	19.8	3.1	1.9	35.9	0	4,171,657
1965	28.3	46.2	19.9	3.4	2.1	37.1	0	5,216,942
1970	29.9	45.0	19.4	3.4	2.3	36.9	0	6,783,505
1971	30.6	44.4	19.4	3.4	2.2	36.7	0	7,194,120

TABLE 76C ***Stock of persons in the United States holding academic degrees from United States universities, 1930–1971, by age and sex, total all fields—women only***

Stock	Age (percentage)					Median	Percentage	Total
year	19–30	31–45	46–60	61–65	66–70	age	female	number
Highest degree attained—bachelor's								
1930	52.1	32.2	12.7	1.7	1.3	30.4	100.0	461,540
1935	51.0	34.0	12.3	1.7	1.0	30.8	100.0	668,026
1940	46.2	38.3	12.7	1.7	1.1	31.9	100.0	926,855
1945	42.1	41.5	13.5	1.8	1.1	33.3	100.0	1,221,180
1950	38.0	43.2	15.6	2.1	1.2	34.4	100.0	1,567,985
1955	35.7	41.2	19.1	2.5	1.5	35.8	100.0	1,932,075
1960	33.6	39.9	21.9	2.7	1.9	36.6	100.0	2,360,176
1965	35.8	36.1	22.7	3.5	2.0	36.5	100.0	2,996,261
1970	40.5	32.7	20.3	4.1	2.4	34.9	100.0	3,967,745
1971	41.5	32.1	19.7	4.2	2.6	34.5	100.0	4,215,184
Highest degree attained—second-level								
1930	13.3	59.2	21.1	3.7	2.7	39.2	100.0	57,272
1935	11.1	63.5	20.5	2.8	2.1	39.5	100.0	88,835
1940	9.5	62.5	23.9	2.5	1.7	40.6	100.0	127,432
1945	7.2	58.3	30.0	2.8	1.7	42.2	100.0	168,236
1950	9.0	52.6	33.1	3.5	1.8	42.8	100.0	230,619
1955	8.1	52.7	32.6	4.4	2.3	42.7	100.0	318,320
1960	6.7	52.7	32.0	5.6	3.1	43.2	100.0	415,876
1965	7.5	51.0	31.8	5.8	3.9	43.6	100.0	546,789
1970	9.9	52.9	28.7	4.9	3.6	42.0	100.0	818,369
1971	10.2	53.9	27.8	4.7	3.5	41.6	100.0	898,441
Highest degree attained—doctorate								
1930	13.1	47.8	32.6	4.2	2.3	42.5	100.0	2,762
1935	12.1	49.0	32.8	3.9	2.2	42.5	100.0	4,471
1940	9.0	48.3	35.7	4.6	2.5	43.8	100.0	6,155
1945	6.7	44.6	39.6	6.0	3.2	45.6	100.0	7,831
1950	6.6	39.8	42.1	7.2	4.3	47.1	100.0	9,658
1955	7.3	37.8	42.1	7.8	5.0	47.6	100.0	12,562
1960	6.9	38.0	41.4	8.2	5.5	47.7	100.0	16,147
1965	7.8	38.9	39.4	8.2	5.6	47.1	100.0	21,476
1970	10.7	41.9	35.8	6.7	4.8	45.1	100.0	33,825
1971	11.1	42.7	35.3	6.3	4.6	44.7	100.0	37,745

TABLE 76C (*continued*)

Stock	*Age (percentage)*					*Median*	*Percentage*	*Total*
year	*19–30*	*31–45*	*46–60*	*61–65*	*66–70*	*age*	*female*	*number*
All levels								
1930	47.6	35.2	13.8	2.0	1.5	31.8	100.0	521,574
1935	46.1	37.5	13.4	1.9	1.1	32.0	100.0	761,332
1940	41.5	41.3	14.2	1.8	1.2	33.2	100.0	1,060,442
1945	37.7	43.6	15.6	1.9	1.2	34.7	100.0	1,397,247
1950	34.1	44.4	17.9	2.3	1.3	35.7	100.0	1,808,262
1955	31.6	42.8	21.1	2.8	1.6	37.0	100.0	2,262,957
1960	29.4	41.8	23.5	3.2	2.1	38.1	100.0	2,792,199
1965	31.3	38.4	24.2	3.9	2.3	38.1	100.0	3,564,526
1970	35.1	36.2	21.8	4.3	2.7	36.9	100.0	4,819,939
1971	35.8	36.0	21.2	4.3	2.7	36.5	100.0	5,151,370

TABLE 77 ***Stock of persons in the United States holding academic degrees from United States universities, 1930–1971, by age and sex: aggregation level 2***

	List of subtables and specialties that have been aggregated to form them
77A	Sciences
	Mathematics and statistics
	Chemistry
	Earth sciences
	Physics
	Physical science, n.e.c.
	Biological sciences
	Anthropology and archaeology
	Economics and agricultural economics
	History
	Political science
	Sociology and social psychology
	Social science, n.e.c.
	Psychology
77B	Technologies
	Computer and information science
	Library science
	Architecture
	Chemical-materials engineering
	Civil and other heavy engineering
	Electrical-electronic engineering
	Geological-mining engineering
	Mechanical-equipment engineering
	Engineering and other technical specialties, n.e.c.
	Agriculture
	Dentistry
	Medicine and osteopathy
	Nursing, therapy, and dental hygiene
	Health professions, n.e.c.
	Journalism and communications
	Business administration
	Management specialties other than business administration
	Law
	Social work
	Social science professions, n.e.c.
	Education—primary, preprimary, exceptional
	Education—secondary, adult, specialized teaching fields
	Physical education
	Education, n.e.c.
	Home economics

TABLE 77 (*continued*)

77C Arts

Art and music
English literature, dramatic arts, and speech
Philosophy (not including scholastic philosophy)
Western European languages and literatures
Non-Western European languages and literatures
Religion and scholastic philosophy

TABLE 77A *Stock of persons in the United States holding academic degrees from United States universities, 1930–1971, by age and sex, sciences*

Stock	*Age (percentage)*					*Median*	*Percentage*	*Total*
year	*19–30*	*31–45*	*46–60*	*61–65*	*66–70*	*age*	*female*	*number*
Highest degree attained—bachelor's								
1930	55.0	31.8	10.8	1.4	1.0	29.7	51.6	229,752
1935	52.5	34.0	11.0	1.5	.9	30.4	52.3	309,849
1940	48.7	37.4	11.4	1.5	1.0	31.3	51.5	419,857
1945	42.6	42.2	12.4	1.7	1.1	32.9	53.6	526,778
1950	45.9	38.7	12.6	1.7	1.0	32.1	48.5	752,160
1955	44.5	37.2	15.1	2.0	1.2	32.6	45.5	939,464
1960	39.3	40.6	16.6	2.1	1.4	33.4	42.5	1,178,562
1965	42.7	37.0	16.4	2.5	1.4	33.3	40.9	1,558,061
1970	48.5	33.4	13.8	2.7	1.6	31.4	40.6	2,201,831
1971	49.6	32.8	13.4	2.7	1.6	31.1	40.6	2,367,748
Highest degree attained—second-level								
1930	19.6	51.8	22.0	4.0	2.7	38.4	23.3	33,559
1935	18.8	53.7	21.1	3.8	2.6	38.3	25.0	42,872
1940	17.7	54.3	21.8	3.6	2.6	38.8	26.1	53,049
1945	13.0	55.1	25.4	3.8	2.6	40.4	28.6	60,675
1950	23.6	48.8	22.1	3.3	2.1	37.9	27.7	92,857
1955	20.1	54.0	20.8	3.1	2.0	37.3	26.3	127,982
1960	17.9	56.2	20.4	3.4	2.1	38.2	25.8	165,324
1965	21.0	54.5	19.2	3.2	2.1	37.9	25.2	234,591
1970	23.1	54.1	18.3	2.6	1.8	36.7	26.6	356,312
1971	22.8	54.6	18.3	2.5	1.8	36.7	27.2	383,084

TABLE 77A (continued)

Stock	*Age (percentage)*					*Median*	*Percentage*	*Total*
year	*19–30*	*31–45*	*46–60*	*61–65*	*66–70*	*age*	*female*	*number*
Highest degree attained—doctorate								
1930	14.0	49.6	28.5	4.9	3.0	41.3	12.2	13,609
1935	14.1	52.9	26.1	4.2	2.7	40.3	12.7	20,277
1940	12.0	54.7	26.8	3.9	2.5	40.9	12.5	27,545
1945	8.5	53.5	31.0	4.3	2.6	42.6	12.4	33,684
1950	10.4	47.8	34.1	4.8	2.9	43.6	12.0	42,236
1955	13.2	47.3	32.1	4.6	2.8	42.4	10.4	60,766
1960	10.8	50.1	31.0	5.1	3.0	42.1	9.8	80,121
1965	11.3	50.7	29.4	5.4	3.3	42.1	9.5	106,830
1970	13.2	50.7	28.1	4.7	3.2	41.6	10.2	154,976
1971	13.4	50.9	28.0	4.6	3.1	41.4	10.4	167,802
All levels								
1930	48.7	35.1	13.0	1.9	1.3	31.4	46.3	276,920
1935	46.6	37.3	13.0	1.9	1.2	31.8	47.0	372,998
1940	43.4	40.2	13.3	1.9	1.2	32.6	46.6	500,451
1945	37.9	44.1	14.7	2.1	1.3	34.2	48.9	621,137
1950	41.9	40.2	14.6	2.0	1.2	33.2	44.6	887,253
1955	40.1	39.7	16.6	2.2	1.4	33.9	41.4	1,126,212
1960	35.3	42.9	17.8	2.4	1.6	34.5	38.7	1,424,007
1965	38.3	39.9	17.5	2.7	1.6	34.6	37.2	1,899,482
1970	43.2	37.1	15.2	2.8	1.7	33.0	37.1	2,713,119
1971	44.0	36.7	14.9	2.8	1.7	32.7	37.1	2,918,634

TABLE 77B ***Stock of persons in the United States holding academic degrees from United States universities, 1930–1971, by age and sex, technologies***

Stock	*Age (percentage)*					*Median*	*Percentage*	*Total*
year	*19–30*	*31–45*	*46–60*	*61–65*	*66–70*	*age*	*female*	*number*
Highest degree attained—bachelor's								
1930	51.9	34.9	10.8	1.4	1.0	30.6	35.5	464,668
1935	50.3	37.3	10.3	1.4	.8	30.9	38.4	703,400
1940	46.5	40.9	10.5	1.3	.8	31.8	40.5	1,013,156
1945	39.3	46.3	12.2	1.4	.8	33.6	43.5	1,304,119
1950	41.3	43.0	13.4	1.5	.8	33.3	40.2	1,876,797
1955	41.5	40.0	15.9	1.7	1.0	33.6	40.0	2,480,581
1960	36.0	43.0	17.9	2.0	1.1	34.2	40.6	3,174,785
1965	34.7	41.9	19.3	2.7	1.4	35.7	42.4	3,950,911
1970	35.6	40.5	18.7	3.3	1.9	35.7	44.0	4,983,196
1971	36.4	39.6	18.6	3.4	2.0	35.5	44.2	5,264,764
Highest degree attained—second-level								
1930	10.2	44.5	32.8	7.5	5.0	44.2	8.6	418,271
1935	9.6	49.4	28.9	7.0	5.1	42.7	11.8	506,651
1940	8.7	52.0	28.2	6.2	4.9	42.7	15.0	600,197
1945	6.1	50.5	32.9	5.8	4.6	44.2	18.4	663,724
1950	9.8	46.0	34.7	5.4	4.0	44.2	20.4	812,318
1955	10.0	48.5	32.6	5.4	3.5	43.0	22.3	1,052,378
1960	8.6	51.1	30.5	6.2	3.7	42.7	24.1	1,301,054
1965	8.8	51.1	29.6	6.2	4.3	43.0	25.4	1,611,792
1970	10.2	51.3	29.2	5.2	4.1	42.4	28.0	2,145,594
1971	10.5	51.7	28.9	5.0	3.9	42.1	28.7	2,293,104
Highest degree attained—doctorate								
1930	6.5	48.5	36.2	5.4	3.4	44.5	9.6	3,580
1935	7.0	51.2	34.8	4.3	2.7	43.6	11.4	5,913
1940	4.6	50.5	37.8	4.6	2.5	44.6	12.6	8,303
1945	3.2	45.7	42.3	5.7	3.0	46.3	14.9	10,694
1950	7.3	43.3	40.2	5.9	3.3	45.8	13.9	15,595
1955	8.0	48.7	35.3	5.0	3.0	43.8	12.5	26,400
1960	6.0	50.7	35.4	5.0	2.9	44.0	12.4	38,390
1965	7.4	49.5	35.2	5.0	2.9	44.0	11.8	57,469
1970	8.6	50.2	34.2	4.4	2.6	43.4	11.6	95,088
1971	8.5	50.6	34.1	4.3	2.6	43.3	11.7	105,804

TABLE 77B (continued)

Stock	*Age (percentage)*					*Median*	*Percentage*	*Total*
year	*19–30*	*31–45*	*46–60*	*61–65*	*66–70*	*age*	*female*	*number*
All levels								
1930	32.0	39.5	21.3	4.3	2.9	36.8	22.7	886,499
1935	33.1	42.4	18.2	3.7	2.6	35.7	27.2	1,215,964
1940	32.3	45.0	17.2	3.1	2.3	35.8	30.9	1,621,656
1945	28.0	47.7	19.3	2.9	2.1	37.2	34.9	1,978,537
1950	31.6	43.9	20.0	2.7	1.8	36.6	34.1	2,704,710
1955	32.0	42.5	20.9	2.8	1.7	36.6	34.6	3,559,359
1960	27.8	45.4	21.7	3.2	1.9	37.1	35.6	4,514,229
1965	27.0	44.6	22.4	3.7	2.2	38.0	37.2	5,620,172
1970	27.7	43.8	22.0	3.9	2.6	38.3	38.6	7,223,878
1971	28.3	43.4	21.9	3.9	2.6	38.1	39.1	7,663,672

TABLE 77C ***Stock of persons in the United States holding academic degrees from United States universities, 1930–1971, by age and sex, arts***

Stock	Age (percentage)					Median	Percentage	Total
year	19–30	31–45	46–60	61–65	66–70	age	female	number
Highest degree attained—bachelor's								
1930	47.9	34.6	14.1	2.0	1.5	31.6	80.4	221,259
1935	46.3	36.3	14.0	2.1	1.3	31.9	79.9	295,023
1940	41.8	39.9	14.6	2.2	1.4	33.1	78.7	381,650
1945	36.9	43.4	15.8	2.4	1.6	34.7	79.0	470,116
1950	35.8	42.5	17.5	2.6	1.7	35.2	75.7	591,493
1955	35.5	39.2	20.3	3.0	1.9	36.0	71.3	719,530
1960	30.6	40.6	23.1	3.3	2.3	37.0	68.6	831,291
1965	32.5	37.5	23.4	4.1	2.5	37.2	67.7	1,008,536
1970	39.3	32.9	20.2	4.7	2.9	35.5	67.4	1,305,084
1971	40.5	32.2	19.6	4.7	3.0	35.0	67.3	1,375,470
Highest degree attained—second-level								
1930	6.1	41.2	37.5	8.8	6.4	47.0	21.7	61,997
1935	6.3	44.5	34.2	8.5	6.5	45.7	26.5	69,515
1940	6.4	47.1	32.1	8.1	6.3	44.8	30.3	77,696
1945	5.5	47.7	33.1	7.6	6.1	45.0	33.5	86,437
1950	8.9	48.8	31.3	6.0	5.0	43.5	35.4	109,934
1955	7.9	53.2	29.5	5.3	4.0	42.3	35.5	141,525
1960	7.5	53.7	29.5	5.6	3.7	42.6	34.5	174,914
1965	8.7	52.9	29.4	5.2	3.8	42.6	34.7	227,833
1970	10.7	54.3	27.4	4.4	3.2	41.2	38.0	324,622
1971	10.6	55.0	27.0	4.3	3.1	41.0	38.9	347,638
Highest degree attained—doctorate								
1930	6.8	48.0	35.4	6.0	3.9	44.5	21.7	3,448
1935	6.9	51.7	33.3	4.9	3.2	43.4	23.2	5,308
1940	5.3	51.4	35.3	4.9	3.0	44.1	23.1	7,148
1945	3.6	47.3	39.9	5.9	3.4	45.8	23.7	8,668
1950	5.1	42.4	41.9	6.7	4.0	46.7	22.4	10,818
1955	5.8	44.3	39.0	6.6	4.1	45.9	19.5	14,901
1960	5.1	46.2	37.5	6.9	4.4	45.6	18.2	19,417
1965	5.5	46.5	36.4	7.0	4.5	45.4	17.7	25,445
1970	7.1	47.6	35.2	5.9	4.2	44.6	19.1	36,742
1971	7.4	48.1	34.8	5.7	4.1	44.4	19.6	40,074

TABLE 77C (*continued*)

Stock	*Age (percentage)*					*Median*	*Percentage*	*Total*
year	*19–30*	*31–45*	*46–60*	*61–65*	*66–70*	*age*	*female*	*number*
All levels								
1930	38.4	36.2	19.4	3.5	2.6	35.1	67.0	286,704
1935	38.2	38.1	18.0	3.4	2.3	34.5	69.1	369,846
1940	35.3	41.3	17.9	3.2	2.3	35.1	69.8	466,494
1945	31.6	44.1	18.8	3.2	2.3	36.5	71.2	565,221
1950	31.2	43.4	20.0	3.2	2.2	36.9	68.6	712,245
1955	30.6	41.6	22.1	3.5	2.3	37.5	64.6	875,956
1960	26.2	42.9	24.5	3.8	2.6	38.7	61.8	1,025,622
1965	27.7	40.5	24.7	4.4	2.8	38.6	60.7	1,261,814
1970	33.0	37.4	21.9	4.6	3.0	37.5	60.6	1,666,448
1971	33.8	37.1	21.4	4.6	3.1	37.2	60.6	1,763,182

TABLE 78 ***Stock of persons in the United States holding academic degrees from United States universities, 1930–1971, by age and sex: aggregation level 3***

	List of subtables and specialties that have been aggregated to form them
78A	Mathematics and physical sciences
	Mathematics and statistics
	Chemistry
	Earth sciences
	Physics
	Physical science, n.e.c.
78B	Engineering
	Computer and information science
	Architecture
	Chemical-materials engineering
	Civil and other heavy engineering
	Electrical-electronic engineering
	Geological-mining engineering
	Mechanical-equipment engineering
	Engineering and other mechanical specialties, n.e.c.
78C	Biological and agricultural sciences
	Biological sciences
	Agriculture
78D	Health specialties
	Dentistry
	Medicine and osteopathy
	Nursing, therapy, and dental hygiene
	Health professions, n.e.c.
78E	Social sciences and technologies
	Anthropology and archaeology
	Economics and agricultural economics
	History
	Political science
	Sociology and social psychology
	Social science, n.e.c.
	Journalism and communications
	Law
	Social work
	Social science professions, n.e.c.
78F	Administration
	Business administration
	Management specialties other than business administration
78G	Psychology

TABLE 78 (*continued*)

78H	Education
	Education—primary, preprimary, exceptional
	Education—secondary, adult, specialized teaching fields
	Physical education
	Education, n.e.c.
78I	Arts and humanities
	Art and music
	English literature, dramatic arts, and speech
	Philosophy (not including scholastic philosophy)
	Western European languages and literatures
	Non-Western European languages and literatures
	Religion and scholastic philosophy
78J	Other
	Library science
	Home economics

TABLE 78A ***Stock of persons in the United States holding academic degrees from United States universities, 1930–1971, by age and sex, mathematics and physical sciences***

Stock year	*Age (percentage)* 19–30	31–45	46–60	61–65	66–70	*Median age*	*Percentage female*	*Total number*
Highest degree attained—bachelor's								
1930	49.0	34.5	13.4	1.8	1.3	31.3	40.9	93,323
1935	46.0	36.2	14.6	2.1	1.2	32.0	41.9	115,102
1940	42.9	38.3	15.1	2.3	1.4	32.8	41.5	144,972
1945	38.4	41.7	15.8	2.6	1.6	34.2	43.4	173,350
1950	39.2	39.9	16.4	2.8	1.8	34.1	39.7	218,140
1955	37.5	38.4	19.0	3.1	2.0	35.2	35.9	254,342
1960	35.6	39.2	19.9	3.0	2.2	34.9	32.4	309,057
1965	40.4	35.1	19.0	3.4	2.1	34.4	30.6	394,716
1970	42.3	34.3	17.1	3.8	2.5	33.4	30.3	491,390
1971	42.4	34.2	16.9	3.9	2.6	33.3	30.1	510,911
Highest degree attained—second-level								
1930	19.5	49.7	23.6	4.3	2.9	38.9	15.3	18,341
1935	18.4	51.1	23.2	4.4	2.9	38.9	16.5	22,507
1940	17.1	51.5	24.0	4.3	3.0	39.6	17.1	26,581
1945	12.7	51.7	27.7	4.7	3.2	41.4	18.7	29,221
1950	22.1	44.8	25.8	4.4	2.9	39.6	18.0	39,531
1955	20.0	48.2	24.6	4.3	2.9	38.5	16.5	49,947
1960	19.4	50.8	22.4	4.5	2.9	38.3	16.1	62,918
1965	24.1	50.6	18.6	4.0	2.7	37.2	16.1	89,265
1970	25.0	51.9	17.6	3.2	2.4	36.3	18.1	126,974
1971	24.3	52.5	17.8	3.0	2.4	36.4	18.6	134,337
Highest degree attained—doctorate								
1930	17.0	48.8	26.7	4.7	2.8	40.3	7.0	6,036
1935	17.9	51.5	23.9	4.1	2.7	39.1	7.2	8,786
1940	15.6	54.5	23.8	3.7	2.5	39.6	6.8	11,907
1945	11.9	54.8	27.0	3.9	2.5	41.0	6.4	14,727
1950	13.6	49.9	29.8	4.1	2.5	41.9	6.0	18,719
1955	16.6	48.0	29.1	3.9	2.4	40.9	5.3	26,642
1960	13.5	50.5	29.0	4.5	2.6	40.9	4.9	34,434
1965	14.2	50.7	27.4	4.8	2.9	41.0	4.8	45,700
1970	16.3	50.2	26.0	4.5	2.9	40.5	5.0	64,728
1971	16.3	50.3	26.0	4.4	2.9	40.4	5.1	69,304

TABLE 78A (*continued*)

Stock	*Age (percentage)*					*Median*	*Percentage*	*total*
year	*19–30*	*31–45*	*46–60*	*61–65*	*66–70*	*age*	*female*	*number*
All levels								
1930	42.8	37.6	15.7	2.3	1.6	33.1	35.2	117,700
1935	40.0	39.4	16.5	2.6	1.5	33.6	35.9	146,395
1940	37.4	41.3	17.0	2.6	1.7	34.3	35.7	183,460
1945	33.1	43.9	18.1	2.9	1.9	35.8	37.6	217,298
1950	35.0	41.3	18.6	3.1	2.0	35.5	34.3	276,390
1955	33.2	40.6	20.6	3.3	2.2	36.2	30.5	330,931
1960	31.3	42.0	21.1	3.4	2.3	36.2	27.6	406,409
1965	35.4	39.1	19.7	3.6	2.3	35.7	25.9	529,681
1970	36.6	39.0	18.0	3.8	2.5	34.9	25.7	683,092
1971	36.5	39.2	18.0	3.8	2.6	34.8	25.5	714,552

TABLE 78B ***Stock of persons in the United States holding academic degrees from United States universities, 1930–1971, by age and sex, engineering***

Stock	*Age (percentage)*					*Median*	*Percentage*	*Total*
year	*19–30*	*31–45*	*46–60*	*61–65*	*66–70*	*age*	*female*	*number*
Highest degree attained—bachelor's								
1930	43.1	42.6	11.7	1.5	1.1	32.5	2.1	128,970
1935	38.9	46.1	12.5	1.6	.9	33.5	2.2	173,976
1940	34.9	47.6	14.7	1.7	1.0	34.7	2.4	222,304
1945	29.6	49.0	18.3	2.0	1.2	36.3	2.8	268,954
1950	38.5	39.9	18.4	2.1	1.1	34.5	2.7	390,586
1955	37.9	38.4	19.7	2.6	1.4	34.8	2.6	486,266
1960	30.5	44.6	19.9	3.2	1.8	35.2	2.4	595,462
1965	29.1	44.3	20.3	3.9	2.3	37.3	2.4	689,220
1970	28.1	43.7	21.0	4.2	3.0	38.5	2.7	786,216
1971	28.8	42.6	21.4	4.3	3.0	38.3	2.9	812,998
Highest degree attained—second-level								
1930	20.6	60.4	15.2	2.3	1.5	36.5	1.8	8,594
1935	18.9	60.9	16.7	2.1	1.4	37.5	1.9	11,905
1940	16.1	59.4	21.1	2.1	1.4	38.9	2.0	15,337
1945	10.7	56.7	28.4	2.7	1.5	41.1	2.5	17,656
1950	26.9	46.6	22.6	2.6	1.3	36.9	2.6	30,690
1955	22.4	54.5	18.7	2.8	1.4	36.0	2.7	46,668
1960	21.2	58.7	15.6	2.9	1.6	36.7	2.4	68,738
1965	22.6	58.8	14.7	2.3	1.6	36.6	2.1	104,992
1970	22.7	57.6	16.5	1.9	1.3	36.4	2.2	157,828
1971	22.3	57.7	16.9	1.8	1.3	36.5	2.3	169,739
Highest degree attained—doctorate								
1930	23.6	52.0	20.3	2.7	1.4	37.3	.8	369
1935	24.7	56.0	16.6	1.6	1.0	35.9	.6	793
1940	15.1	63.2	19.0	1.8	1.0	38.0	.8	1,129
1945	10.7	61.4	24.3	2.5	1.2	40.4	.6	1,455
1950	20.7	51.8	24.1	2.3	1.2	39.2	.6	2,552
1955	21.1	54.8	21.3	1.8	1.0	37.1	.7	5,001
1960	16.2	59.8	20.9	2.1	.9	38.0	.7	7,896
1965	19.3	58.1	19.4	2.2	1.0	38.0	.8	14,248
1970	19.9	58.1	19.2	1.8	1.0	37.4	.8	27,309
1971	19.2	58.6	19.5	1.7	1.0	37.5	.8	30,498

TABLE 78B (*continued*)

Stock	Age (percentage)					Median	Percentage	Total
year	*19–30*	*31–45*	*46–60*	*61–65*	*66–70*	*age*	*female*	*number*
All levels								
1930	41.7	43.7	11.9	1.6	1.1	32.8	2.1	137,933
1935	37.5	47.1	12.8	1.7	1.0	33.8	2.2	186,674
1940	33.6	48.5	15.2	1.7	1.1	35.0	2.3	238,770
1945	28.3	49.6	18.9	2.0	1.2	36.7	2.7	288,065
1950	37.5	40.5	18.7	2.1	1.2	34.8	2.6	423,828
1955	36.4	40.0	19.6	2.6	1.4	35.0	2.6	537,935
1960	29.4	46.2	19.5	3.1	1.8	35.5	2.4	672,096
1965	28.1	46.4	19.6	3.7	2.2	37.2	2.3	808,460
1970	27.0	46.4	20.2	3.8	2.6	37.9	2.6	971,353
1971	27.4	45.6	20.6	3.8	2.6	37.8	2.8	1,013,235

TABLE 78C ***Stock of persons in the United States holding academic degrees from United States universities, 1930–1971, by age and sex, biological and agricultural sciences***

Stock	*Age (percentage)*					*Median*	*Percentage*	*Total*
year	*19–30*	*31–45*	*46–60*	*61–65*	*66–70*	*age*	*female*	*number*
Highest degree attained—bachelor's								
1930	46.7	36.4	13.7	1.9	1.3	31.9	24.5	73,953
1935	43.7	39.2	13.7	2.2	1.2	32.6	26.9	94,326
1940	42.7	39.9	13.9	2.1	1.4	32.9	28.7	124,601
1945	36.9	42.7	16.6	2.3	1.5	34.7	33.3	144,992
1950	43.4	37.0	16.1	2.1	1.4	33.0	30.7	206,775
1955	42.5	35.8	17.6	2.5	1.5	33.4	28.9	253,983
1960	35.4	40.9	18.7	3.0	1.9	34.4	28.4	298,943
1965	36.7	38.7	19.0	3.5	2.2	35.5	29.2	360,856
1970	41.6	35.3	17.1	3.6	2.4	33.8	29.2	461,988
1971	42.5	34.5	17.0	3.6	2.4	33.5	29.1	486,223
Highest degree attained—second-level								
1930	16.6	53.5	21.4	4.9	3.6	38.9	8.2	13,359
1935	15.8	55.6	21.2	4.2	3.3	39.2	8.9	16,589
1940	15.9	54.3	23.4	3.6	2.8	39.7	9.6	20,348
1945	12.0	54.0	27.7	3.7	2.6	41.0	11.0	23,434
1950	20.3	48.8	25.0	3.7	2.1	39.1	12.6	33,383
1955	19.1	53.4	21.6	3.7	2.2	37.7	12.2	47,414
1960	15.0	56.9	21.6	4.0	2.5	38.8	12.7	58,449
1965	16.1	55.0	22.4	3.9	2.7	39.8	14.6	73,658
1970	18.5	51.2	24.2	3.5	2.5	39.2	17.4	97,236
1971	18.4	50.9	24.7	3.5	2.5	39.1	18.1	101,987
Highest degree attained—doctorate								
1930	12.9	52.7	27.6	4.3	2.6	41.0	15.3	3,364
1935	13.0	55.9	25.4	3.5	2.2	40.1	15.4	5,396
1940	11.0	57.0	26.7	3.3	2.0	40.8	15.2	7,700
1945	7.2	55.3	31.4	3.9	2.2	42.6	15.0	9,719
1950	8.1	48.9	35.7	4.7	2.6	44.1	14.5	12,086
1955	10.4	48.2	34.0	4.7	2.7	43.3	12.2	17,511
1960	8.5	49.9	33.2	5.3	3.0	43.2	11.2	23,050
1965	8.9	50.2	31.6	5.7	3.5	43.1	10.6	30,494
1970	10.8	50.4	30.2	5.2	3.5	42.6	11.2	43,611
1971	11.0	50.6	30.0	5.0	3.4	42.4	11.4	47,197

TABLE 78C (continued)

Stock year	Age (percentage) 19–30	31–45	46–60	61–65	66–70	Median age	Percentage female	Total number
All levels								
1930	41.0	39.6	15.3	2.4	1.7	33.4	21.8	90,676
1935	38.3	42.3	15.3	2.5	1.6	34.0	23.5	116,311
1940	37.6	42.6	15.8	2.4	1.6	34.4	25.4	152,649
1945	32.0	44.8	18.8	2.6	1.7	36.2	29.3	178,145
1950	38.6	39.2	18.2	2.4	1.5	34.5	27.5	252,244
1955	37.3	39.1	19.1	2.8	1.6	34.9	25.5	318,908
1960	30.7	43.9	20.1	3.3	2.0	35.8	24.9	380,442
1965	31.6	42.1	20.3	3.7	2.4	36.9	25.7	465,008
1970	35.7	38.9	19.2	3.7	2.5	35.8	26.0	602,835
1971	36.3	38.4	19.2	3.7	2.5	35.5	26.0	635,407

TABLE 78D ***Stock of persons in the United States holding academic degrees from United States universities, 1930–1971, by age and sex, health specialties***

Stock year	Age (percentage) 19–30	31–45	46–60	61–65	66–70	Median age	Percentage female	Total number
Highest degree attained—bachelor's								
1930	33.9	38.7	22.2	3.0	2.1	38.6	56.8	52,514
1935	27.9	37.3	28.4	4.0	2.3	39.5	58.4	56,598
1940	20.7	39.5	31.6	5.0	3.2	40.0	59.8	60,090
1945	20.5	40.7	28.1	6.7	4.0	41.7	62.5	63,815
1950	41.3	28.6	19.8	6.4	3.9	35.6	61.0	95,167
1955	52.5	23.9	15.8	4.1	3.7	30.4	60.5	140,909
1960	44.7	36.3	14.2	2.0	2.8	32.1	64.4	184,107
1965	39.9	43.4	12.3	3.0	1.4	33.6	67.8	232,558
1970	39.4	44.3	11.3	2.9	2.1	34.1	71.3	300,035
1971	40.0	43.4	11.8	2.7	2.1	34.0	71.9	317,281
Highest degree attained—second-level								
1930	7.1	36.5	39.5	10.0	6.9	48.4	5.3	215,404
1935	7.1	38.5	36.1	10.5	7.8	47.8	5.5	225,073
1940	6.9	41.0	33.5	10.2	8.4	46.8	5.7	232,081
1945	7.0	41.8	33.9	9.2	8.1	46.4	5.8	239,979
1950	7.9	41.9	34.9	8.1	7.1	46.1	6.8	256,961
1955	8.4	43.2	34.7	7.5	6.1	45.4	7.5	285,214
1960	7.8	44.4	34.0	8.1	5.7	45.2	8.0	313,821
1965	7.5	44.1	34.0	8.2	6.2	45.5	8.6	344,203
1970	8.0	43.3	34.5	7.8	6.3	45.6	10.3	383,772
1971	8.2	43.3	34.6	7.7	6.3	45.5	10.7	393,601
Highest degree attained—doctorate								
1930	6.1	42.2	37.7	8.4	5.5	46.5	7.2	488
1935	7.0	44.4	35.6	7.6	5.5	45.6	10.3	604
1940	4.1	44.2	38.2	7.7	5.7	46.5	11.1	651
1945	3.9	40.4	41.1	8.6	6.0	47.7	11.4	696
1950	10.3	41.5	35.8	7.2	5.2	45.4	13.9	967
1955	11.4	50.6	29.2	5.0	3.8	41.6	15.1	1,565
1960	7.3	55.8	28.9	4.7	3.1	41.9	13.9	2,129
1965	6.6	53.1	32.2	5.0	3.2	43.5	14.6	2,714
1970	8.5	49.4	34.4	4.6	3.1	43.8	16.5	3,855
1971	8.8	49.2	34.5	4.5	3.0	43.7	16.8	4,175

TABLE 78D (*continued*)

Stock	*Age (percentage)*					*Median*	*Percentage*	*Total*
year	*19–30*	*31–45*	*46–60*	*61–60*	*66–70*	*age*	*female*	*number*
All levels								
1930	12.3	36.9	36.1	8.6	6.0	46.3	15.4	268,406
1935	11.3	38.3	34.5	9.2	6.7	46.2	16.1	282,275
1940	9.7	40.7	33.2	9.1	7.3	45.8	16.8	292,822
1945	9.8	41.6	32.7	8.6	7.3	45.5	17.7	304,490
1950	16.9	38.3	30.8	7.6	6.2	44.1	21.4	353,095
1955	23.0	36.9	28.5	6.3	5.3	41.7	25.0	427,688
1960	21.4	41.5	26.7	5.8	4.6	40.5	28.7	500,057
1965	20.5	43.9	25.3	6.1	4.3	40.2	32.4	579,475
1970	21.7	43.7	24.4	5.7	4.5	40.6	36.9	687,662
1971	22.3	43.3	24.5	5.5	4.4	40.5	37.9	715,057

TABLE 78E ***Stock of persons in the United States holding academic degrees from United States universities, 1930–1971, by age and sex, social sciences and technologies***

Stock year	Age (percentage) 19–30	31–45	46–60	61–65	66–70	Median age	Percentage female	Total number
Highest degree attained—bachelor's								
1930	56.0	31.3	10.2	1.4	1.0	29.5	52.9	123,563
1935	53.7	34.0	10.0	1.4	.8	30.2	52.1	176,141
1940	48.4	39.0	10.4	1.4	.9	31.4	50.6	243,429
1945	41.3	44.7	11.6	1.5	.9	33.1	51.6	311,702
1950	44.4	40.9	12.3	1.5	.9	32.5	47.2	449,877
1955	43.9	38.2	15.2	1.7	1.0	32.9	44.4	574,531
1960	37.5	42.0	17.3	1.9	1.2	33.7	42.0	721,305
1965	40.0	38.8	17.4	2.5	1.3	34.1	41.0	942,005
1970	47.4	34.0	14.2	2.8	1.6	31.8	41.4	1,358,861
1971	48.9	33.0	13.7	2.8	1.6	31.3	41.5	1,474,548
Highest degree attained—second-level								
1930	12.4	48.2	29.9	6.0	3.6	42.1	6.8	152,323
1935	10.5	51.8	27.7	5.9	4.0	41.7	8.5	185,234
1940	8.9	52.4	28.8	5.7	4.2	42.6	10.2	212,737
1945	4.6	48.4	36.1	6.3	4.6	45.2	12.3	218,161
1950	11.2	41.0	37.4	6.1	4.4	45.3	13.9	261,378
1955	10.4	44.1	34.8	6.5	4.2	44.2	14.6	317,162
1960	8.8	47.1	31.4	7.9	4.8	43.6	15.2	361,540
1965	10.0	47.9	28.6	7.7	5.7	43.4	16.2	424,487
1970	13.0	48.4	27.6	5.9	5.1	42.0	18.1	548,247
1971	13.3	48.9	27.3	5.6	4.9	41.6	18.7	579,523
Highest degree attained—doctorate								
1930	8.5	47.9	33.4	6.2	4.0	43.9	11.3	3,965
1935	8.2	52.1	31.1	5.1	3.5	42.7	12.4	5,774
1940	6.5	52.3	32.9	5.0	3.3	43.5	13.0	7,432
1945	3.9	48.5	38.3	5.8	3.6	45.4	13.5	8,637
1950	6.9	43.0	39.9	6.3	3.9	46.0	13.3	10,843
1955	7.7	46.0	36.5	6.0	3.8	44.8	11.8	15,162
1960	6.8	48.6	34.3	6.3	3.9	44.1	11.2	19,948
1965	7.3	49.5	32.8	6.3	4.1	43.9	10.8	26,501
1970	9.1	50.3	31.7	5.1	3.7	43.1	11.5	39,210
1971	9.4	50.8	31.4	4.9	3.5	42.8	11.7	42,975

TABLE 78E (*continued*)

Stock	*Age (percentage)*					*Median*	*Percentage*	*Total*
year	*19–30*	*31–45*	*46–60*	*61–65*	*66–70*	*age*	*female*	*number*
All levels								
1930	31.6	40.7	21.3	4.0	2.4	36.7	27.2	279,851
1935	31.2	43.3	19.3	3.7	2.5	36.4	29.5	367,149
1940	29.6	45.3	19.2	3.4	2.4	36.8	31.4	463,598
1945	25.8	46.3	21.9	3.5	2.5	38.3	35.1	538,500
1950	31.8	41.0	21.8	3.2	2.2	37.1	34.6	722,098
1955	31.6	40.4	22.4	3.5	2.2	36.9	33.4	906,855
1960	27.6	43.8	22.2	4.0	2.4	37.3	32.7	1,102,793
1965	30.2	41.8	21.1	4.1	2.7	37.4	32.6	1,392,993
1970	36.9	38.4	18.3	3.7	2.6	35.3	34.2	1,946,318
1971	38.3	37.8	17.8	3.6	2.6	34.8	34.6	2,097,046

TABLE 78F ***Stock of persons in the United States holding academic degrees from United States universities, 1930–1971, by age and sex, administration***

Stock year	Age (percentage) 19–30	31–45	46–60	61–65	66–70	Median age	Percentage female	Total number
Highest degree attained—bachelor's								
1930	66.7	30.0	2.9	.2	.2	28.4	21.0	61,941
1935	58.9	37.4	3.4	.2	.1	29.5	21.5	107,763
1940	53.4	41.8	4.5	.2	.1	30.4	21.3	176,406
1945	43.1	49.0	7.4	.3	.1	32.4	22.5	241,319
1950	50.4	40.3	8.8	.4	.2	30.9	18.8	431,067
1955	48.8	39.1	11.3	.6	.2	31.3	17.1	615,868
1960	37.2	47.7	13.6	1.1	.4	33.3	14.8	815,637
1965	33.4	48.3	15.7	1.8	.7	35.4	13.4	1,028,656
1970	35.0	45.3	16.3	2.3	1.2	35.4	12.4	1,351,252
1971	36.1	43.8	16.5	2.4	1.2	35.2	12.3	1,441,638
Highest degree attained—second-level								
1930	23.2	64.7	10.5	1.0	.7	35.5	27.7	14,227
1935	19.8	67.5	11.5	.7	.4	36.3	28.9	27,223
1940	16.5	67.0	15.3	.8	.4	37.6	29.2	43,760
1945	10.1	65.2	23.0	1.2	.5	39.9	31.4	57,012
1950	16.2	56.5	25.0	1.7	.7	39.6	27.7	89,957
1955	15.1	58.1	23.6	2.3	.9	38.7	24.5	143,344
1960	11.4	59.3	24.7	3.2	1.5	40.0	21.9	192,101
1965	11.5	56.8	25.9	3.7	2.1	41.0	19.1	257,835
1970	13.4	54.4	26.3	3.6	2.3	40.5	15.8	371,777
1971	13.8	54.4	26.0	3.5	2.3	40.2	15.0	403,673
Highest degree attained—doctorate								
1930	3.5	51.3	38.3	4.3	2.6	44.7	7.8	922
1935	2.5	52.1	39.5	3.8	2.1	44.8	8.8	1,577
1940	2.1	48.3	42.7	4.7	2.2	45.9	9.5	2,301
1945	1.3	41.6	47.6	6.4	3.1	47.7	11.1	2,924
1950	2.3	38.1	47.7	7.7	4.2	48.6	11.3	3,759
1955	3.1	42.5	42.8	7.3	4.3	47.3	11.1	5,635
1960	2.2	42.4	42.8	7.7	4.9	47.6	10.3	7,165
1965	3.3	45.4	40.1	6.8	4.4	46.4	10.0	10,763
1970	3.7	47.5	39.2	5.7	3.9	45.7	8.5	16,498
1971	3.9	48.0	38.8	5.6	3.7	45.5	8.2	18,117

TABLE 78F (continued)

Stock	*Age (percentage)*					*Median*	*Percentage*	*Total*
year	*19–30*	*31–45*	*46–60*	*61–65*	*66–70*	*age*	*female*	*number*
All levels								
1930	57.9	36.7	4.7	.4	.3	29.7	22.1	77,090
1935	50.5	43.6	5.4	.4	.2	30.9	22.5	136,553
1940	45.7	46.8	7.0	.4	.2	31.9	22.7	222,467
1945	36.5	52.0	10.7	.6	.2	33.9	24.4	301,255
1950	44.2	43.1	11.8	.7	.3	32.5	20.3	524,783
1955	42.1	42.7	13.8	1.0	.4	33.0	18.4	764,847
1960	32.1	49.9	15.9	1.5	.6	34.5	16.1	1,014,903
1965	28.8	50.0	17.9	2.2	1.0	36.6	14.5	1,297,254
1970	30.1	47.3	18.6	2.6	1.5	36.8	13.1	1,739,527
1971	30.9	46.1	18.8	2.6	1.5	36.6	12.8	1,863,428

TABLE 78G ***Stock of persons in the United States holding academic degrees from United States universities, 1930–1971, by age and sex, psychology***

Stock year	*Age (percentage)* 19–30	31–45	46–60	61–65	66–70	*Median age*	*Percentage female*	*Total number*
Highest degree attained—bachelor's								
1930	64.6	27.1	6.9	.8	.6	27.8	71.2	8,613
1935	62.6	29.6	6.6	.8	.4	28.6	70.6	13,948
1940	58.2	33.7	6.9	.7	.4	29.4	69.1	21,727
1945	51.1	39.6	8.0	.8	.4	30.8	71.2	29,985
1950	56.7	34.6	7.6	.7	.4	29.3	64.0	52,105
1955	53.7	34.9	10.0	.9	.5	30.2	61.7	67,868
1960	44.4	42.0	11.9	1.1	.7	32.1	57.9	88,214
1965	47.5	38.0	12.4	1.4	.7	31.7	54.9	123,180
1970	56.1	31.7	9.8	1.5	.8	29.4	51.8	202,326
1971	58.0	30.3	9.3	1.5	.8	29.0	51.5	227,847
Highest degree attained—second-level								
1930	28.4	51.6	15.7	2.7	1.6	35.4	36.9	1,335
1935	28.6	54.7	13.0	2.2	1.5	34.9	37.6	2,065
1940	26.5	58.2	12.4	1.7	1.2	35.4	37.0	3,123
1945	18.9	63.0	15.4	1.6	1.1	37.1	40.0	4,118
1950	31.0	53.3	13.7	1.2	.7	35.0	42.4	7,853
1955	27.2	56.6	14.3	1.2	.7	35.1	42.5	12,138
1960	21.1	59.4	16.9	1.7	.8	36.8	44.6	15,525
1965	22.3	56.3	18.1	2.1	1.1	37.4	44.4	21,363
1970	28.3	52.0	16.5	2.0	1.2	35.6	45.1	34,767
1971	28.6	52.1	16.1	2.0	1.2	35.3	45.6	38,307
Highest degree attained—doctorate								
1930	13.6	48.2	29.7	5.2	3.2	41.9	25.8	1,165
1935	12.5	52.2	27.6	4.6	3.1	41.0	25.4	1,660
1940	9.9	53.5	29.0	4.5	3.0	41.9	26.2	2,124
1945	6.6	50.6	34.3	5.2	3.3	44.0	27.3	2,453
1950	12.6	44.7	34.3	5.2	3.2	43.7	24.4	3,334
1955	18.0	50.1	25.9	3.7	2.3	39.2	18.3	6,265
1960	12.5	57.1	24.6	3.7	2.2	39.6	16.8	9,150
1965	11.6	56.9	25.4	3.9	2.3	40.8	17.2	12,856
1970	13.5	53.7	27.2	3.4	2.2	41.1	19.1	19,532
1971	13.8	53.3	27.5	3.2	2.2	41.0	19.5	21,409

TABLE 78G (*continued*)

Stock	*Age (percentage)*					*Median*	*Percentage*	*Total*
year	*19–30*	*31–45*	*46–60*	*61–65*	*66–70*	*age*	*female*	*number*
All levels								
1930	54.9	32.3	10.3	1.5	1.0	29.8	62.3	11,113
1935	53.9	34.7	9.3	1.3	.8	30.2	62.5	17,673
1940	50.8	38.1	9.3	1.1	.7	30.8	62.0	26,974
1945	44.5	43.0	10.6	1.2	.7	32.3	64.8	36,556
1950	51.2	37.4	9.8	1.0	.6	30.7	59.3	63,292
1955	47.4	39.0	11.7	1.2	.7	31.7	55.8	86,271
1960	38.6	45.6	13.6	1.4	.8	33.3	52.8	112,889
1965	41.1	42.0	14.2	1.7	.9	33.5	50.4	157,399
1970	49.1	36.1	12.1	1.7	1.0	31.2	48.4	256,625
1971	50.8	34.9	11.6	1.7	.9	30.8	48.3	287,563

TABLE 78H ***Stock of persons in the United States holding academic degrees from United States universities, 1930–1971, by age and sex, education***

Stock	*Age (percentage)*					*Median*	*Percentage*	*Total*
year	*19–30*	*31–45*	*46–60*	*61–65*	*66–70*	*age*	*female*	*number*
Highest degree attained—bachelor's								
1930	74.8	22.4	2.4	.2	.1	26.6	59.9	98,287
1935	69.2	27.8	2.8	.1	.1	27.7	62.6	204,114
1940	60.6	35.3	3.9	.1	.1	29.1	64.7	348,020
1945	49.0	44.5	6.1	.2	.1	31.2	68.4	483,298
1950	41.0	48.8	9.6	.4	.1	33.0	68.1	647,404
1955	40.6	44.2	14.1	.8	.3	34.0	68.9	865,448
1960	40.7	39.9	17.6	1.3	.5	33.7	71.0	1,169,507
1965	41.3	36.3	19.5	2.0	.8	33.8	73.6	1,559,014
1970	40.8	36.4	18.4	2.9	1.4	33.8	75.7	2,036,829
1971	41.3	36.2	17.9	3.1	1.5	33.8	75.9	2,159,405
Highest degree attained—second-level								
1930	12.9	73.0	12.7	.9	.6	37.7	44.2	25,842
1935	10.4	73.6	15.0	.6	.3	38.6	45.5	54,968
1940	8.4	69.9	20.6	.7	.3	39.9	46.6	93,377
1945	4.7	63.4	30.1	1.4	.5	42.2	50.3	126,912
1950	5.9	54.5	36.2	2.6	.9	43.5	50.4	173,038
1955	6.8	53.9	34.0	3.8	1.5	43.0	49.9	259,543
1960	5.9	55.5	31.4	4.9	2.4	42.8	50.8	367,677
1965	5.5	54.6	31.4	5.3	3.2	43.3	51.4	492,584
1970	6.5	55.3	30.3	4.6	3.2	42.8	54.0	717,050
1971	6.8	55.9	29.8	4.4	3.1	42.5	54.8	783,545
Highest degree attained—doctorate								
1930	2.9	50.4	40.0	4.2	2.5	45.1	23.1	832
1935	2.0	51.3	41.3	3.6	1.9	45.1	24.9	1,545
1940	2.0	48.7	43.2	4.2	1.8	45.8	25.6	2,542
1945	1.4	43.7	46.9	5.5	2.5	47.2	28.4	3,678
1950	2.1	42.6	45.8	6.3	3.2	47.4	26.0	5,445
1955	2.1	46.0	42.9	5.8	3.2	46.5	23.0	9,151
1960	1.7	46.2	43.3	5.5	3.2	46.6	22.4	14,364
1965	1.7	43.5	45.3	6.2	3.4	47.2	22.2	20,482
1970	2.3	45.4	43.3	5.8	3.2	46.6	22.4	34,485
1971	2.4	46.1	42.8	5.6	3.1	46.4	22.5	38,997

TABLE 78H (*continued*)

Stock	*Age (percentage)*					*Median*	*Percentage*	*Total*
year	*19–30*	*31–45*	*46–60*	*61–65*	*66–70*	*age*	*female*	*number*
All levels								
1930	61.5	33.1	4.8	.4	.2	28.4	56.4	124,961
1935	56.4	37.6	5.6	.3	.1	29.7	58.8	260,627
1940	49.3	42.7	7.7	.3	.1	31.2	60.7	443,939
1945	39.6	48.4	11.3	.5	.2	33.5	64.4	613,888
1950	33.4	49.9	15.4	.9	.3	35.2	64.1	825,887
1955	32.5	46.5	18.9	1.5	.6	36.5	64.2	1,134,142
1960	32.1	43.6	21.1	2.2	1.0	36.8	65.7	1,551,548
1965	32.4	40.7	22.6	2.8	1.4	37.0	67.8	2,072,080
1970	31.5	41.4	21.8	3.4	1.9	37.1	69.4	2,788,364
1971	31.7	41.5	21.4	3.5	2.0	37.0	69.6	2,981,947

TABLE 78I ***Stock of persons in the United States holding academic degrees from United States universities, 1930–1971, by age and sex, arts and humanities***

Stock	Age (percentage)					Median	Percentage	Total
year	19–30	31–45	46–60	61–65	66–70	age	female	number
Highest degree attained—bachelor's								
1930	47.9	34.6	14.1	2.0	1.5	31.6	80.4	221,259
1935	46.3	36.3	14.0	2.1	1.3	31.9	79.9	295,023
1940	41.8	39.9	14.6	2.2	1.4	33.1	78.7	381,650
1945	36.9	43.4	15.8	2.4	1.6	34.7	79.0	470,116
1950	35.8	42.5	17.5	2.6	1.7	35.2	75.7	591,493
1955	35.5	39.2	20.3	3.0	1.9	36.0	71.3	719,530
1960	30.6	40.6	23.1	3.3	2.3	37.0	68.6	831,291
1965	32.5	37.5	23.4	4.1	2.5	37.2	67.7	1,008,536
1970	39.3	32.9	20.2	4.7	2.9	35.5	67.4	1,305,084
1971	40.5	32.2	19.6	4.7	3.0	35.0	67.3	1,375,470
Highest degree attained—second-level								
1930	6.1	41.2	37.5	8.8	6.4	47.0	21.7	61,997
1935	6.3	44.5	34.2	8.5	6.5	45.7	26.5	69,515
1940	6.4	47.1	32.1	8.1	6.3	44.8	30.3	77,696
1945	5.5	47.7	33.1	7.6	6.1	45.0	33.5	86,437
1950	8.9	48.8	31.3	6.0	5.0	43.5	35.4	109,934
1955	7.9	53.2	29.5	5.3	4.0	42.3	35.5	141,525
1960	7.5	53.7	29.5	5.6	3.7	42.6	34.5	174,914
1965	8.7	52.9	29.4	5.2	3.8	42.6	34.7	227,833
1970	10.7	54.3	27.4	4.4	3.2	41.2	38.0	324,622
1971	10.6	55.0	27.0	4.3	3.1	41.0	38.9	347,638
Highest degree attained—doctorate								
1930	6.8	48.0	35.4	6.0	3.9	44.5	21.7	3,448
1935	6.9	51.7	33.3	4.9	3.2	43.4	23.2	5,308
1940	5.3	51.4	35.3	4.9	3.0	44.1	23.1	7,148
1945	3.6	47.3	39.9	5.9	3.4	45.8	23.7	8,668
1950	5.1	42.4	41.9	6.7	4.0	46.7	22.4	10,818
1955	5.8	44.3	39.0	6.6	4.1	45.9	19.5	14,901
1960	5.1	46.2	37.5	6.9	4.4	45.6	18.2	19,417
1965	5.5	46.5	36.4	7.0	4.5	45.4	17.7	25,445
1970	7.1	47.6	35.2	5.9	4.2	44.6	19.1	36,742
1971	7.4	48.1	34.8	5.7	4.1	44.4	19.6	40,074

TABLE 78I (*continued*)

Stock	*Age (percentage)*					*Median*	*Percentage*	*Total*
year	*19–30*	*31–45*	*46–60*	*61–65*	*66–70*	*age*	*female*	*number*
All levels								
1930	38.4	36.2	19.4	3.5	2.6	35.1	67.0	286,704
1935	38.2	38.1	18.0	3.4	2.3	34.5	69.1	369,846
1940	35.3	41.3	17.9	3.2	2.3	35.1	69.8	466,494
1945	31.6	44.1	18.8	3.2	2.3	36.5	71.2	565,221
1950	31.2	43.4	20.0	3.2	2.2	36.9	68.6	712,245
1955	30.6	41.6	22.1	3.5	2.3	37.5	64.6	875,956
1960	26.2	42.9	24.5	3.8	2.6	38.7	61.8	1,025,622
1965	27.7	40.5	24.7	4.4	2.8	38.6	60.7	1,261,814
1970	33.0	37.4	21.9	4.6	3.0	37.5	60.6	1,666,448
1971	33.8	37.1	21.4	4.6	3.1	37.2	60.6	1,763,182

TABLE 78J ***Stock of persons in the United States holding academic degrees from United States universities, 1930–1971, by age and sex, other***

Stock	Age (percentage)					Median	Percentage	Total
year	*19–30*	*31–45*	*46–60*	*61–65*	*66–70*	*age*	*female*	*number*
Highest degree attained—bachelor's								
1930	45.4	35.3	15.5	2.2	1.6	32.5	96.6	53,296
1935	43.4	37.4	15.4	2.3	1.4	32.8	96.9	71,293
1940	38.2	41.4	16.3	2.5	1.6	34.1	97.2	91,465
1945	34.7	43.4	17.5	2.7	1.8	35.7	97.6	113,483
1950	31.5	43.4	20.1	3.0	2.0	36.9	97.7	137,838
1955	29.0	41.0	24.1	3.7	2.3	38.3	97.9	160,830
1960	21.3	42.1	29.1	4.5	3.1	41.1	97.8	171,116
1965	15.9	40.6	33.2	6.4	3.9	43.6	98.0	178,766
1970	19.6	33.9	32.8	8.3	5.4	44.6	98.1	196,130
1971	21.2	32.3	32.4	8.4	5.7	44.7	98.1	201,660
Highest degree attained—second-level								
1930	14.3	63.2	16.9	2.3	1.4	38.3	85.4	2,405
1935	12.3	65.6	18.9	1.9	1.2	38.6	83.4	3,958
1940	10.8	64.2	21.9	2.0	1.1	39.7	82.2	5,903
1945	7.9	60.9	27.5	2.5	1.3	41.3	83.2	7,907
1950	12.0	56.5	27.3	2.7	1.4	40.6	83.2	12,384
1955	10.6	58.8	25.8	3.1	1.6	40.2	81.4	18,931
1960	8.6	58.6	26.8	3.9	2.1	41.2	80.9	25,609
1965	10.4	57.1	26.3	3.8	2.4	41.1	79.7	37,996
1970	12.6	58.8	23.4	3.1	2.1	39.5	80.5	64,253
1971	12.7	59.6	22.8	3.0	2.0	39.3	80.6	71,477
Highest degree attained—doctorate								
1930	3.4	37.9	48.3	6.9	3.4	48.4	100.0	29
1935	5.7	43.4	41.5	5.7	3.8	46.3	92.5	53
1940	1.6	41.3	46.0	6.3	4.8	48.0	90.5	63
1945	3.4	38.6	45.5	8.0	4.5	48.3	92.0	88
1950	4.8	38.1	44.4	7.9	4.8	48.1	86.5	126
1955	6.4	45.7	38.5	5.6	3.8	45.3	74.4	234
1960	4.3	49.1	38.4	5.1	3.2	44.9	64.0	375
1965	3.9	47.0	40.1	5.9	3.1	45.8	62.1	541
1970	4.9	45.2	40.6	5.7	3.6	46.0	58.7	836
1971	5.2	45.6	40.1	5.6	3.5	45.8	57.2	935

TABLE 78J (continued)

Stock	Age (percentage)					Median	Percentage	Total
year	*19–30*	*31–45*	*46–60*	*61–65*	*66–70*	*age*	*female*	*number*
All levels								
1930	44.0	36.5	15.6	2.2	1.6	32.9	96.1	55,690
1935	41.8	38.9	15.6	2.3	1.4	33.2	96.2	75,304
1940	36.5	42.8	16.7	2.5	1.6	34.6	96.3	97,431
1945	32.9	44.5	18.2	2.7	1.7	36.2	96.7	121,478
1950	29.9	44.5	20.7	3.0	1.9	37.4	96.5	150,348
1955	27.0	42.8	24.3	3.6	2.2	38.6	96.1	179,995
1960	19.6	44.2	28.8	4.4	3.0	41.1	95.6	197,100
1965	14.9	43.5	32.0	5.9	3.6	43.0	94.7	217,303
1970	17.8	40.1	30.5	7.0	4.6	43.1	93.7	261,219
1971	18.9	39.4	29.9	7.0	4.7	43.0	93.5	274,072

TABLE 79 ***Stock of persons in the United States holding academic degrees from United States universities, 1930–1971; aggregation level 4:* absolute number, median age, and percentage female***

	(1) Mathematics and statistics			(2) Computer and information science		
Stock year	*Median age*	*Percentage female*	*Total number*	*Median age*	*Percentage female*	*Total number*
Highest degree attained—bachelor's						
1930	32.3	60.5	35,138			
1940	34.1	59.1	53,426			
1950	36.5	55.5	75,465			
1960	36.6	46.0	106,033	23.5	9.1	11
1970	30.7	41.2	215,445	24.4	14.8	2,782
1971	30.8	41.1	226,984	24.5	15.4	4,704
Highest degree attained—second-level						
1930	38.6	30.3	4,945			
1940	39.4	32.2	7,503			
1950	40.6	31.6	10,927			
1960	38.5	27.1	17,731	28.7	9.1	11
1970	34.3	25.7	51,291	30.3	7.8	3,791
1971	34.5	26.3	55,252	30.5	8.6	5,269
Highest degree attained—doctorate						
1930	38.6	13.7	612			
1940	38.9	13.9	1,306			
1950	42.1	12.5	2,024			
1960	39.8	8.5	3,994	29.5	0	1
1970	37.4	7.2	10,303	31.2	1.9	260
1971	37.4	7.2	11,338	31.4	2.1	378

*Forty-four specialties.

(3) Library science			(4) Philosophy (not including scholastic philosophy)		
Median age	*Percentage female*	*Total number*	*Median age*	*Percentage female*	*Total number*
33.6	78.5	5,749	30.5	77.3	3,308
34.8	81.7	9,423	31.7	71.7	5,685
37.8	83.7	13,474	32.9	64.2	8,634
40.3	83.4	17,619	31.8	46.0	14,466
43.2	85.9	20,165	28.7	35.3	29,833
43.3	86.2	20,599	28.6	34.5	31,980
36.6	65.9	1,014	38.6	32.1	277
38.5	70.0	3,467	38.1	34.4	448
40.0	75.0	8,174	38.0	33.4	680
40.7	74.1	18,756	35.3	26.7	1,394
38.9	77.0	53,651	33.6	23.8	4,023
38.8	77.5	60,068	33.7	24.3	4,360
—	—	0	44.3	32.1	109
41.4	33.3	9	42.6	25.0	188
43.9	44.0	25	40.3	14.5	394
41.2	26.2	103	39.3	8.1	1,053
43.9	28.2	262	39.5	9.5	2,740
43.8	28.3	297	39.2	9.4	3.088

TABLE 79 (continued)

	(5) Chemistry			(6) Earth sciences		
Stock year	*Median age*	*Percentage female*	*Total number*	*Median age*	*Percentage female*	*Total number*
Highest degree attained—bachelor's						
1930	29.1	45.1	31,223	35.5	8.4	15,761
1940	30.8	47.9	50,989	35.8	7.8	22,535
1950	32.1	46.8	82,593	37.5	7.7	30,227
1960	34.8	40.4	110,946	35.5	4.9	43,832
1970	36.0	33.4	155,515	39.8	5.1	49,186
1971	36.0	32.7	159,768	39.7	5.1	50,817
Highest degree attained—second-level						
1930	38.8	10.9	7,658	40.2	3.7	2,315
1940	40.1	13.0	10,469	40.4	4.3	3,416
1950	39.3	16.4	15,031	41.0	4.9	4,992
1960	39.0	17.0	21,146	38.2	4.1	9,405
1970	39.6	20.9	30,601	39.6	5.6	15,023
1971	39.5	21.4	31,718	39.6	5.9	15,792
Highest degree attained—doctorate						
1930	40.0	6.7	3,596	42.9	5.5	614
1940	39.1	6.6	7,176	42.3	4.6	1,078
1950	41.4	5.7	11,581	45.6	4.8	1,426
1960	41.6	5.2	19,627	42.4	3.2	2,679
1970	42.1	6.0	31,465	41.5	2.7	5,385
1971	42.0	6.1	33,134	41.5	2.7	5,752

(7) Physics			(8) Physical science, n.e.c.		
Median age	*Percentage female*	*Total number*	*Median age*	*Percentage female*	*Total number*
31.6	14.5	8,490	27.9	9.2	2,711
32.2	12.7	14,358	28.7	12.7	3,665
32.9	11.3	24,365	28.1	17.1	5,488
32.8	7.8	39,992	29.8	16.4	8,254
33.3	6.9	61,207	31.0	15.9	10,037
33.5	6.8	62,812	30.7	14.9	10,529
38.9	12.9	2,669	39.6	6.0	755
38.5	13.5	4,126	40.0	7.7	1,068
37.3	11.2	7,119	40.8	9.2	1,462
37.3	8.0	12,043	36.8	15.1	2,592
36.0	6.8	25,056	37.1	16.0	5,002
36.2	7.0	26,277	37.1	16.0	5,297
40.8	5.6	1,117	41.4	0	99
40.0	4.7	2,148	39.8	0	199
42.2	4.7	3,342	41.1	0	346
39.4	3.2	7,451	40.4	2.2	682
39.4	2.6	16,278	41.0	3.2	1,297
39.3	2.7	17,631	40.2	3.2	1,448

TABLE 79 (continued)

	(9)			*(10)*		
	Architecture			*Chemical-materials engineering*		
Stock year	*Median age*	*Percentage female*	*Total number*	*Median age*	*Percentage female*	*Total number*
Highest degree attained—bachelor's						
1930	36.2	18.3	7,674	32.3	.8	20,600
1940	35.2	18.9	12,403	35.0	.8	33,843
1950	36.0	17.2	19,039	36.7	.9	51,642
1960	35.0	11.8	31,372	37.6	.5	69,560
1970	37.1	8.6	47,288	40.8	.5	82,471
1971	36.3	8.9	51,085	41.0	.5	83,672
Highest degree attained—second-level						
1930	40.4	11.8	500	35.9	.6	2,461
1940	39.6	11.6	830	38.8	.7	4,228
1950	38.9	9.6	1,435	38.4	.6	7,354
1960	37.2	6.8	3,253	38.5	.6	11,974
1970	37.2	6.2	7,312	39.2	.7	18,696
1971	37.0	6.5	8,079	39.1	.8	19,471
Highest degree attained—doctorate						
1930	—	—	—	36.7	.5	206
1940	—	—	—	37.5	.3	586
1950	36.4	0	5	39.1	.2	1,222
1960	39.1	4.7	43	38.1	.2	3,031
1970	43.3	6.4	94	38.6	.4	7,095
1971	43.4	8.6	105	38.7	.4	7,653

(11) Civil and other heavy engineering			(12) Electrical-electronic engineering		
Median age	*Percentage female*	*Total number*	*Median age*	*Percentage female*	*Total number*
32.5	.2	23,547	32.2	.3	25,283
34.8	.2	40,749	34.4	.3	43,998
35.1	.3	69,568	33.5	.3	81,692
33.5	.1	106,792	34.4	.2	127,256
40.1	.1	131,966	36.6	.2	173,619
40.3	.1	134,787	36.7	.2	177,773
36.6	0	1,109	36.5	0	2,190
39.1	0	2,013	38.9	.1	4,010
35.6	.2	4,618	38.1	.2	7,472
36.3	.2	11,747	36.4	.2	17,308
36.7	.4	27,143	36.1	.3	42,614
36.8	.5	29,134	36.3	.3	45,521
36.5	0	17	38.0	0	34
38.2	0	64	38.0	0	127
38.0	0	187	38.0	0	356
37.6	.1	761	37.3	.3	1,607
36.9	.4	3,554	37.2	.3	6,580
37.0	.4	4,042	37.4	.3	7,355

TABLE 79 (*continued*)

	(13) Geological-mining engineering			(14) Mechanical-equipment engineering		
Stock year	*Median age*	*Percentage female*	*Total number*	*Median age*	*Percentage female*	*Total number*
Highest degree attained—bachelor's						
1930	32.6	.3	5,872	32.4	.4	37,151
1940	35.3	.4	9,928	34.7	.4	64,613
1950	37.0	.4	15,423	34.1	.4	117,717
1960	36.8	.3	22,775	35.4	.2	176,318
1970	43.3	.3	22,712	39.6	.2	223,059
1971	43.9	.3	22,766	39.7	.2	227,769
Highest degree attained—second-level						
1930	36.6	0	266	36.5	.5	1,643
1940	39.1	0	472	38.9	.5	2,968
1950	38.8	0	845	35.7	.6	6,696
1960	38.2	0	1,757	36.7	.4	15,853
1970	40.0	.3	2,922	37.0	.3	36,224
1971	40.0	.4	3,086	37.3	.3	38,265
Highest degree attained—doctorate						
1930	—	—	0	38.5	0	81
1940	35.2	0	5	38.9	0	238
1950	38.6	0	16	40.8	0	485
1960	37.6	0	76	39.2	.3	1,380
1970	36.1	1.4	418	37.6	.3	4,831
1971	36.3	1.2	481	37.7	.3	5,409

(15) Engineering and other technical specialties, n.e.c.			(16) Biological sciences		
Median age	*Percentage female*	*Total number*	*Median age*	*Percentage female*	*Total number*
32.3	9.9	8,842	28.5	58.6	29,489
33.9	12.3	16,767	30.0	62.4	54,724
32.3	15.9	35,506	29.9	59.3	102,318
34.0	15.6	61,378	32.4	53.2	152,789
34.7	15.5	102,319	30.2	46.2	281,005
34.1	15.5	110,443	30.1	45.5	299,010
36.0	16.9	426	37.1	22.4	4,782
37.8	20.6	816	37.8	26.7	7,004
33.9	24.5	2,268	35.9	30.7	12,885
35.0	17.8	6,836	37.3	29.0	23,981
34.8	11.8	19,128	36.2	31.9	48,815
34.9	11.4	20,913	36.3	32.8	51,749
37.5	6.7	30	40.9	17.0	3,012
38.3	6.4	109	40.7	17.0	6,864
38.8	4.6	281	44.6	17.0	10,147
38.0	4.0	997	44.0	14.1	17,734
36.7	2.5	4,475	42.1	13.9	33,709
36.8	2.5	5,072	41.9	14.2	36,606

TABLE 79 (*continued*)

	(17)			(18)		
	Agriculture			*Dentistry*		
Stock year	*Median age*	*Percentage female*	*Total number*	*Median age*	*Percentage female*	*Total number*
Highest degree attained—bachelor's						
1930	34.3	1.9	44,464			
1940	35.3	2.3	69,877			
1950	36.3	2.6	104,457			
1960	36.8	2.5	146,154			
1970	40.8	2.7	180,984			
1971	40.9	2.8	187,214			
Highest degree attained—second-level						
1930	39.9	.3	8,577	45.8	1.6	64,266
1940	40.6	.7	13,343	48.0	1.6	67,321
1950	41.2	1.2	20,499	48.9	1.6	69,263
1960	40.1	1.4	34,468	46.1	1.4	79,995
1970	42.5	2.7	48,420	45.4	1.2	92,796
1971	42.5	2.9	50,237	45.5	1.2	94,509
Highest degree attained—doctorate						
1930	41.7	.9	351			
1940	41.7	1.2	836			
1950	41.2	1.2	1,938	34.2	0	2
1960	41.1	1.6	5,316	37.7	12.5	24
1970	43.9	1.7	9,901	42.0	18.9	53
1971	44.0	1.9	10,591	41.0	14.9	67

(19) Medicine and osteopathy			(20) Nursing, therapy, and dental hygiene		
Median age	Percentage female	Total number	Median age	Percentage female	Total number
			39.6	56.7	29,367
			40.7	62.4	33,558
			36.1	74.2	53,015
			31.5	86.7	106,713
			33.4	92.8	182,216
			33.3	93.2	193,682
49.9	4.9	142,092	42.4	93.1	1,292
46.3	5.1	154,458	44.3	92.7	1,690
45.5	6.2	170,343	39.7	92.8	3,034
46.2	6.2	202,139	38.2	95.2	7,852
46.7	6.4	238,099	38.8	97.4	17,467
46.7	6.5	242,467	38.7	97.5	19,089
45.0	10.9	46	36.4	100.0	2
46.0	20.6	63	41.4	100.0	8
48.0	24.1	79	39.8	88.9	27
38.6	9.7	268	39.3	69.7	152
41.9	9.8	593	40.3	57.0	516
42.3	11.3	631	40.3	55.3	586

TABLE 79
(continued)

	(21)			(22)		
	Physical education			*Health professions, n.e.c.*		
Stock year	*Median age*	*Percentage female*	*Total number*	*Median age*	*Percentage female*	*Total number*
Highest degree attained—bachelor's						
1930	27.1	44.8	21,520	37.3	56.9	23,147
1940	30.1	44.3	69,963	39.2	56.6	26,532
1950	34.7	43.9	117,467	34.9	44.4	42,151
1960	36.5	39.0	188,159	32.6	33.5	77,394
1970	36.9	38.9	293,715	35.2	37.9	117,818
1971	36.5	39.0	312,266	35.2	38.5	123,599
Highest degree attained—second-level						
1930	35.8	31.0	2,248	45.1	29.1	7,753
1940	38.3	28.5	8,692	46.8	30.8	8,614
1950	42.3	29.4	15,532	38.7	20.7	14,320
1960	43.1	26.6	27,408	39.7	16.2	23,835
1970	42.4	26.5	48,287	42.9	17.2	35,412
1971	42.1	26.9	51,646	42.6	17.8	37,537
Highest degree attained—doctorate						
1930	45.4	28.2	142	46.7	6.4	440
1940	46.6	31.6	377	46.7	8.6	579
1950	49.1	33.2	656	45.3	10.6	859
1960	48.5	27.2	1,337	42.8	9.4	1,685
1970	48.6	27.2	2,376	45.1	10.1	2,693
1971	48.3	26.9	2,598	44.9	10.3	2,891

(23) Anthropology and archaeology			(24) Economics and agricultural economics		
Median age	Percentage female	Total number	Median age	Percentage female	Total number
27.0	55.6	142	28.1	14.8	25,066
27.4	59.7	397	30.7	15.9	54,809
26.3	57.0	1,377	32.5	16.0	106,078
28.8	53.8	3,195	35.2	14.6	154,569
25.9	57.5	14,280	37.0	13.5	232,644
25.8	57.5	17,356	36.8	13.6	241,716
35.1	29.4	68	35.8	10.3	1,393
35.0	37.7	215	36.7	9.8	2,833
36.8	41.0	495	36.1	12.2	6,110
37.9	37.3	1,095	37.9	10.7	11,825
35.4	39.5	3,464	37.7	10.4	23,920
35.2	40.8	4,072	37.7	10.6	25,439
41.1	27.4	62	43.1	8.4	1,086
41.3	28.0	246	43.2	7.6	1,927
45.3	23.7	427	46.0	7.4	2,746
45.4	20.4	818	44.3	5.7	4,773
43.5	21.6	1,795	42.8	5.1	9,255
43.2	22.2	2,008	42.7	5.2	9,968

TABLE 79 (continued)

	(25) History			(26) Political science		
Stock year	*Median age*	*Percentage female*	*Total number*	*Median age*	*Percentage female*	*Total number*
Highest degree attained—bachelor's						
1930	30.5	74.7	51,761	26.8	41.7	4,642
1940	32.0	69.4	89,229	28.1	40.0	12,046
1950	34.2	61.9	136,770	28.2	34.9	33,143
1960	35.2	51.9	197,701	30.8	30.5	66,172
1970	31.8	44.9	368,953	29.2	27.9	171,629
1971	31.5	44.3	395,060	29.2	27.4	190,504
Highest degree attained—second-level						
1930	39.8	47.0	6,008	36.6	14.6	575
1940	40.5	49.7	9,512	36.4	18.1	1,164
1950	40.4	45.5	15,611	34.2	18.8	3,734
1960	41.0	39.3	24,139	37.8	18.4	7,557
1970	38.5	35.1	49,454	37.1	20.6	17,689
1971	38.4	35.2	53,013	37.0	20.9	19,232
Highest degree attained—doctorate						
1930	43.4	19.6	1,204	43.7	6.3	538
1940	43.1	19.2	2,452	42.5	8.2	1,023
1950	46.1	18.0	3,607	44.7	9.0	1,535
1960	45.6	13.6	5,982	43.1	7.9	2,869
1970	44.3	12.3	10,648	42.6	8.7	5,544
1971	44.0	12.3	11,461	42.2	9.1	6,129

(27) Sociology and social psychology			(28) Social science, n.e.c.		
Median age	Percentage female	Total number	Median age	Percentage female	Total number
28.2	80.3	13,666	27.2	57.0	3,048
30.7	79.2	32,524	28.3	56.6	9,431
31.4	76.0	70,880	27.4	52.8	31,349
34.0	69.5	118,499	29.2	44.2	88,366
31.7	66.6	242,871	29.0	48.8	196,731
30.9	66.2	269,709	28.8	49.3	215,636
36.5	39.4	594	36.5	28.6	462
37.5	41.3	1,330	37.0	30.4	1,288
36.9	40.7	3,153	36.5	35.9	3,487
38.9	37.6	6,265	36.4	30.7	12,018
38.1	36.3	13,148	36.3	29.0	38,080
37.8	36.8	14,379	36.4	29.7	42,556
43.2	10.9	349	42.8	11.9	159
43.5	16.5	735	43.5	14.6	267
45.5	18.1	1,255	43.5	15.1	465
43.9	16.4	2,709	39.1	11.8	1,649
44.2	17.2	5,344	40.5	12.4	4,420
44.0	17.7	5,878	40.4	13.1	5,039

TABLE 79
(continued)

	(29) Journalism and communications			(30) Business administration		
Stock year	*Median age*	*Percentage female*	*Total number*	*Median age*	*Percentage female*	*Total number*
Highest degree attained—bachelor's						
1930	32.1	29.6	22,874	28.2	22.0	56,328
1940	33.9	33.1	40,470	30.4	22.1	166,153
1950	36.9	36.5	60,428	31.1	19.7	401,915
1960	40.6	37.0	75,672	33.5	15.7	757,525
1970	42.5	39.1	95,404	35.6	13.0	1,268,813
1971	41.5	38.8	103,763	35.3	12.8	1,358,271
Highest degree attained—second-level						
1930	39.8	9.6	929	35.3	10.3	3,751
1940	40.7	10.9	1,621	37.7	9.8	11,679
1950	41.7	14.3	2,598	37.0	9.6	32,561
1960	41.1	17.4	4,518	38.9	6.6	82,166
1970	40.2	24.6	8,383	38.9	4.4	192,943
1971	38.7	26.7	9,914	38.5	4.4	216,334
Highest degree attained—doctorate						
1930	38.7	0	7	38.4	0	67
1940	42.8	0	16	40.8	.8	251
1950	46.3	0	24	44.1	4.1	486
1960	41.0	6.3	79	41.8	3.9	1,468
1970	41.6	9.9	222	41.2	3.0	4,681
1971	39.1	11.0	354	41.0	3.0	5,408

(31) Management specialties other than business administration			(32) Law		
Median age	Percentage female	Total number	Median age	Percentage female	Total number
31.4	11.2	5,613			
30.4	8.5	10,252			
28.3	6.7	29,151			
31.2	3.0	58,111			
33.4	2.7	82,440	27.4	5.8	2,991
33.8	3.0	83,367	27.7	5.7	3,530
35.6	33.9	10,476	42.6	3.5	139,627
37.5	36.3	32,080	43.3	4.8	186,190
41.0	37.9	57,396	47.0	5.4	208,024
41.1	33.2	109,935	46.1	4.9	259,674
42.4	28.0	178,834	45.1	4.4	322,199
42.4	27.4	187,339	44.9	4.6	332,186
45.2	8.4	855	48.2	2.4	506
46.5	10.5	2,050	48.0	3.7	680
49.3	12.3	3,273	51.8	5.5	676
49.0	12.0	5,697	51.0	4.8	796
47.4	10.6	11,816	50.2	4.8	853
47.4	10.4	12,709	50.5	4.7	848

TABLE 79 (*continued*)

	(33) Social work			(34) Social science professions, n.e.c.		
Stock year	*Median age*	*Percentage female*	*Total number*	*Median age*	*Percentage female*	*Total number*
Highest degree attained—bachelor's						
1930	28.8	73.5	2,078	26.7	12.3	284
1940	29.9	75.8	3,653	27.9	13.0	871
1950	29.8	77.1	6,850	26.6	12.4	3,001
1960	34.6	73.8	7,317	28.3	9.8	9,813
1970	26.5	79.3	15,089	28.5	14.2	18,266
1971	25.9	78.8	17,872	28.3	14.3	19,401
Highest degree attained—second-level						
1930	35.2	72.2	2,652	34.9		13
1940	37.6	73.9	8,542	35.8	8.9	45
1950	39.7	74.5	17,994	34.1	13.9	173
1960	41.4	69.2	33,005	34.2	8.1	1,443
1970	40.6	64.3	63,927	34.5	11.6	7,982
1971	40.2	63.8	69,469	34.6	13.3	9,261
Highest degree attained—doctorate						
1930	44.2	2.6	38	42.0	5.6	18
1940	43.9	8.6	58	44.5	10.7	28
1950	46.9	10.7	75	48.6	12.5	32
1960	41.0	29.2	212	43.6	22.0	59
1970	40.0	35.0	708	37.0	13.6	419
1971	39.7	34.4	829	37.5	13.0	462

(35) Psychology			(36) Education—primary, preprimary, exceptional		
Median age	Percentage female	Total number	Median age	Percentage female	Total number
27.8	71.2	8,613	26.2	80.2	44,344
29.4	69.1	21,727	28.7	85.1	166,090
29.3	64.0	52,105	32.5	88.1	323,906
32.1	57.9	88,214	32.7	90.4	628,981
29.4	51.8	202,326	32.7	92.4	1,191,954
29.0	51.5	227,847	32.8	92.6	1,264,802
35.4	36.9	1,335	38.7	67.2	5,641
35.4	37.0	3,123	41.1	68.5	22,763
35.0	42.4	7,853	45.0	73.3	43,042
36.8	44.6	15,525	44.2	75.9	91,707
35.6	45.1	34,767	43.4	78.5	190,662
35.3	45.6	38,307	43.1	78.9	211,852
41.9	25.8	1,165	42.0	29.4	17
41.9	26.2	2,124	45.1	23.4	64
43.7	24.4	3,334	46.8	23.7	152
39.6	16.8	9,150	44.1	26.9	798
41.1	19.1	19,532	45.1	32.5	3,193
41.0	19.5	21,409	45.2	33.4	3,653

TABLE 79 (*continued*)

	(37) Education—secondary, adult, specialized teaching fields			(38) Education, n.e.c.		
Stock year	*Median age*	*Percentage female*	*Total number*	*Median age*	*Percentage female*	*Total number*
Highest degree attained—bachelor's						
1930	26.9	42.2	31,611	25.8	47.0	811
1940	29.3	47.1	109,544	26.8	51.2	2,424
1950	32.9	50.3	202,125	28.4	54.9	3,907
1960	33.9	53.3	344,605	26.4	58.7	7,762
1970	35.2	58.9	533,783	25.9	61.9	17,377
1971	35.1	59.1	561,488	25.4	62.5	20,848
Highest degree attained—second-level						
1930	38.4	40.5	5,487	37.1	37.7	12,466
1940	40.6	40.9	22,983	39.0	41.3	38,938
1950	44.2	44.5	44,305	42.3	44.8	70,160
1960	43.2	43.6	99,526	41.4	44.6	149,036
1970	43.7	45.4	193,677	41.6	48.1	284,424
1971	43.5	46.1	208,909	41.3	48.9	311,138
Highest degree attained—doctorate						
1930	44.9	16.0	125	45.2	23.2	547
1940	45.5	19.4	396	45.7	25.8	1,705
1950	47.0	20.7	881	47.3	26.1	3,757
1960	45.6	20.3	2,847	46.8	21.9	9,383
1970	46.1	20.7	7,619	46.8	21.0	21,298
1971	46.0	21.0	8,701	46.6	21.0	24,045

(39) Home economics			(40) English literature, dramatic arts, and speech		
Median age	Percentage female	Total number	Median age	Percentage female	Total number
32.3	98.8	47,507	31.5	82.0	102,076
34.0	99.0	82,041	33.0	80.5	175,750
36.8	99.2	124,364	35.2	78.0	272,601
41.1	99.5	153,498	37.1	73.1	381,493
44.8	99.5	175,965	33.8	71.9	646,230
44.8	99.5	181,062	33.3	71.7	685,125
39.8	99.7	1,390	41.0	52.3	10,693
41.8	99.5	2,436	41.8	55.6	17,471
42.1	99.1	4,210	41.9	56.0	28,692
42.7	99.3	6,853	41.5	54.0	48,697
43.7	98.0	10,602	39.3	57.0	105,426
43.1	97.9	11,409	39.2	57.7	114,444
48.4	100.0	29	43.2	23.2	1,188
49.1	98.2	55	43.2	24.5	2,537
49.1	96.1	102	46.1	25.5	3,917
46.5	78.3	272	44.3	20.8	7,787
47.0	72.6	574	43.6	22.1	16,044
46.8	70.7	638	43.4	22.7	17,601

TABLE 79 ***(continued)***

	(41)			(42)		
	Art and music			*Western European languages and literatures*		
Stock year	*Median age*	*Percentage female*	*Total number*	*Median age*	*Percentage female*	*Total number*
Highest degree attained—bachelor's						
1930	32.4	80.5	60,321	31.5	86.8	38,551
1940	33.4	79.9	106,133	33.5	86.4	61,823
1950	35.2	77.8	169,966	37.1	84.9	85,140
1960	38.1	73.3	228,793	41.1	80.8	101,692
1970	39.9	70.4	309,345	33.2	79.3	176,209
1971	39.6	70.0	325,747	32.5	79.3	185,204
Highest degree attained—second-level						
1930	42.4	44.8	6,016	39.5	61.4	5,037
1940	42.7	46.0	10,399	40.9	66.6	7,632
1950	42.1	45.2	18,816	42.1	66.2	11,303
1960	42.6	40.9	35,162	42.5	61.3	16,387
1970	43.0	41.7	61,300	37.8	61.4	36,796
1971	42.7	42.3	65,805	37.6	62.2	40,174
Highest degree attained—doctorate						
1930	46.1	31.9	248	43.9	26.6	880
1940	46.2	30.7	527	43.1	29.2	2,182
1950	48.8	27.9	791	47.6	31.0	2,962
1960	46.1	19.0	1,650	49.5	28.9	4,022
1970	45.4	18.2	3,738	46.2	30.3	6,484
1971	45.2	18.7	4,185	45.7	31.2	7,019

(43) Non-Western European languages and literatures			(44) Religion and scholastic philosophy		
Median age	Percentage female	Total number	Median age	Percentage female	Total number
30.2	55.5	330	30.6	55.9	16,673
30.2	56.7	660	32.1	50.6	31,599
30.3	57.3	1,318	33.4	44.7	53,836
29.6	50.0	2,675	33.1	32.7	102,172
26.2	53.5	7,632	37.5	31.8	135,834
26.4	53.3	8,186	37.9	31.8	139,227
39.1	30.2	96	50.3	5.0	39,878
38.0	40.9	149	48.6	9.1	41,598
36.4	45.9	303	45.4	12.9	50,140
35.6	40.3	888	43.7	12.2	72,386
34.7	50.5	4,085	43.7	10.7	112,991
35.1	51.6	4,380	43.6	10.9	118,475
41.8	19.0	21	46.4	12.0	1,002
41.5	18.6	70	46.3	10.3	1,643
44.9	16.4	128	46.8	8.1	2,627
42.6	15.0	333	46.1	6.8	4,571
42.5	20.2	832	47.5	6.1	6,904
42.3	20.0	935	47.5	5.9	7,246

TABLE 80 ***1971 U.S. Office of Education degree categories which are aggregated to form the degree categories of this study****

Codes	*Degree categories†*
1.	Mathematics and statistics
1701	*Mathematics, general*
1702	*Statistics, mathematical and theoretical*
1703	*Applied mathematics*
1799	*Other mathematics*
2.	Computer and information sciences
0701	*Computer and information sciences, general*
0702	*Information sciences and systems*
0703	*Data processing*
0704	*Computer programming*
0705	*Systems analysis*
0799	*Other computer and information sciences*
3.	Library science
1601	*Library science, general*
1699	*Other library science*
4.	Philosophy (not including scholastic philosophy)
1509	*Philosophy (not including scholastic philosophy)‡*
5.	Chemistry
1905	*Chemistry, general*
1906	*Inorganic chemistry*
1907	*Organic chemistry*
1908	*Physical chemistry*
1909	*Analytical chemistry*
1910	*Pharmaceutical chemistry*
1920	*Metallurgy*
6.	Earth sciences
1913	*Atmospheric sciences and meteorology*
1914	*Geology*
1915	*Geochemistry*
1916	*Geophysics and seismology*
1917	*Earth sciences, general*
1918	*Paleontology*
1919	*Oceanography*
1999	*Other earth sciences*
7.	Physics
1902	*Physics, general*
1903	*Molecular physics*
1904	*Nuclear physics*
1911	*Astronomy*
1912	*Astrophysics*
8.	Physical science, n.e.c.
1901	*Physical sciences, general*
1999-2	*Other physical sciences*
9.	Architecture
0201	*Environmental design, general*
0202	*Architecture*
0203	*Interior design*
0204	*Landscape architecture*
0205	*Urban architecture*
0299	*Other architecture*
10.	Chemical-materials engineering
0906	*Chemical engineering*
0914	*Metallurgical engineering*
0915	*Materials engineering*
0916	*Ceramic engineering*
11.	Civil and other heavy engineering
0903	*Agricultural engineering*
0904	*Architectural engineering*
0908	*Civil, construction, and transportation engineering*
0922	*Environmental and sanitary engineering*
12.	Electrical-electronic engineering
0909	*Electrical, electronics, communications engineering*
13.	Geological-mining engineering
0907	*Petroleum engineering*

TABLE 80 (continued)

Codes	Degree categories†
0911	*Geological engineering*
0912	*Geophysical engineering*
0918	*Mining and mineral engineering*
0924	*Ocean engineering*
14.	Mechanical-equipment engineering
0910	*Mechanical engineering*
0902	*Aerospace, aeronautical, astronautical engineering*
0923	*Naval architecture and marine engineering*
15.	Engineering and other technical specialties, n.e.c.
0901	*Engineering, general*
0905	*Bioengineering and biomedical engineering*
0917	*Textile engineering*
0919	*Engineering physics*
0920	*Nuclear engineering*
0921	*Engineering mechanics*
0925	*Engineering technologies*
0999	*Other engineering*
1303	*Clothing and textiles*
16.	Biological sciences
0401	*Biology, general*
0402	*Botany, general*
0403	*Bacteriology*
0404	*Plant pathology*
0405	*Plant pharmacology*
0406	*Plant physiology*
0407	*Zoology, general*
0408	*Pathology, human and animal*
0409	*Pharmacology, human and animal*
0410	*Physiology, human and animal*
0411	*Microbiology*
0412	*Anatomy*
0413	*Histology*
0414	*Biochemistry*
0415	*Biophysics*
0416	*Molecular biology*
0417	*Cell biology*
0418	*Marine biology*
0419	*Biometrics and biostatistics*
0420	*Ecology*
0421	*Entomology*
0422	*Genetics*
0423	*Radiobiology*
0424	*Nutrition, scientific*
0425	*Neurosciences*
0426	*Toxicology*
0427	*Embryology*
0499	*Other biological sciences*
17.	Agriculture
0101	*Agriculture, general*
0102	*Agronomy*
0103	*Soils science*
0104	*Animal science*
0105	*Dairy science*
0106	*Poultry science*
0107	*Fish, game, and wildlife management*
0108	*Horticulture*
0109	*Ornamental horticulture*
0113	*Food science and technology*
0114	*Forestry*
0115	*Natural resources management*
0116	*Agriculture and forestry technologies*
0117	*Range management*
0199	*Other agriculture and natural resources*
1218	*Veterinary medicine (D.V.M. degree)*
1219	*Veterinary medicine specialties*

TABLE 80 (continued)

Codes	*Degree categories†*
18. Dentistry	
1204	*Dentistry, D.D.S. or D.M.D. degree*
1205	*Dental specialties*
19. Medicine and osteopathy	
1206	*Medicine (M.D. degree)*
1207	*Medical specialties*
1210	*Osteopathic medicine (D.O. degree)*
20. Nursing, therapy, and dental hygiene	
1203	*Nursing*
1208	*Occupational therapy*
1212	*Physical therapy*
1213	*Dental hygiene*
1306	*Foods and nutrition*
21. Physical education	
0835	*Physical education*
22. Health professions, n.e.c.	
1201	*Health professions, general*
1209	*Optometry*
1211	*Pharmacy*
1214	*Public health*
1216	*Podiatry or podiatric medicine*
1217	*Biomedical communication*
1221	*Chiropractic*
1223	*Medical laboratory technologies*
1224	*Dental technologies*
1225	*Radiologic technologies*
1299	*Other health professions*
23. Anthropology and archaeology	
2202	*Anthropology*
2203	*Archaeology*
24. Economics and agricultural economics	
0517	*Business economics*
0111	*Agricultural economics*
2204	*Economics*
25. History	
2205	*History*
26. Political science	
2207	*Political science and government*
27. Sociology and social psychology	
2005	*Social psychology*
2208	*Sociology*
2215	*Demography*
28. Social science, n.e.c.	
0301	*Asian studies, general*
0302	*East Asian studies*
0303	*South Asian (India, etc.) studies*
0304	*Southeast Asian studies*
0305	*African studies*
0306	*Islamic studies*
0307	*Russian and Slavic studies*
0308	*Latin American studies*
0309	*Middle Eastern studies*
0310	*European studies, general*
0311	*Eastern European studies*
0312	*Western European studies*
0313	*American studies*
0314	*Pacific area studies*
0399	*Other area studies*
1505	*Linguistics*
2201	*Social studies, general*
2206	*Geography*
2210	*International relations*
2211	*Afro-American (black culture) studies*
2212	*American Indian cultural studies*
2213	*Mexican-American cultural studies*
2214	*Urban studies*
2299	*Other social studies*

TABLE 80 (*continued*)

Codes	Degree categories†
29.	Journalism and communications
0601	*Communications, general*
0602	*Journalism*
0603	*Radio/television*
0604	*Advertising*
0605	*Communication media*
0699	*Other communications*
30.	Business administration
0501	*Business and commerce, general*
0502	*Accounting*
0503	*Business statistics*
0504	*Banking and finance*
0505	*Investments and securities*
0506	*Business management and administration*
0507	*Operations research*
0508	*Hotel and restaurant management*
0509	*Marketing and purchasing*
0510	*Transportation and public utilities*
0511	*Real estate*
0512	*Insurance*
0513	*International business*
0514	*Secretarial studies*
0515	*Personnel management*
0516	*Labor and industrial relations*
0599	*Other business and management*
31.	Administration other than business administration
0110	*Agricultural and farm management*
0112	*Agricultural business*
0809	*Administration of special education*
0827	*Educational administration*
0913	*Industrial and management engineering*
1202	*Hospital and health care administration*
1215	*Medical record librarianship*
1307	*Institutional management and cafeteria management*
1801	*Military science (Army)*
1802	*Naval science (Navy, Marines)*
1803	*Aerospace science (Air Force)*
1899	*Other military sciences*
2102	*Public administration*
2103	*Parks and recreation management*
32.	Law
1401	*Law, general*
1499	*Other law*
33.	Social work
1222	*Clinical social work*
2101	*Community services, general*
2104	*Social work and helping services*
34.	Social science professions, n.e.c.
0206	*City, community, and regional planning*
2105	*Law enforcement and corrections*
2106	*International public service*
2199	*Other public affairs and services*
2209	*Criminology*
35.	Psychology
0822	*Educational psychology*
2001	*Psychology, general*
2002	*Experimental psychology*
2003	*Clinical psychology*
2004	*Psychology for counseling*
2006	*Psychometrics*
2007	*Statistics in psychology*
2008	*Industrial psychology*
2009	*Developmental psychology*
2010	*Physiological psychology*
2099	*Other psychology*

TABLE 80 (*continued*)

Codes	*Degree categories*†	*Codes*	*Degree categories*†
36.	Education—primary, preprimary, exceptional	*0899-3*	*Home economics education*
0802	*Elementary education, general*	*0899-4*	*Nursing education*
0808	*Special education, general*	38.	Education, n.e.c.
0810	*Education of the mentally retarded*	*0801*	*Education, general*
0811	*Education of the gifted*	*0824*	*Educational statistics and research*
0812	*Education of the deaf*	*0825*	*Educational testing, evaluation, and measurement*
0813	*Education of the culturally disadvantaged*	*0826*	*Student personnel*
0814	*Education of the visually handicapped*	*0828*	*Educational supervision*
0815	*Speech correction*	*0829*	*Curriculum and instruction*
0816	*Education of the emotionally disturbed*	*0821*	*Social foundations*
0817	*Remedial education*	*0837*	*Health education*
0818	*Special learning disabilities*	39.	Home economics
0819	*Education of the physically handicapped*	*1301*	*Home economics, general*
0820	*Education of the multiple handicapped*	*1302*	*Home decoration and home equipment*
0823	*Preelementary education*	*1304*	*Consumer economics and home management*
0899-2	*Education of exceptional children, n.e.c.*	*1305*	*Family relations and child development*
37.	Education—secondary, adult, specialized teaching	*1399*	*Other*
0803	*Secondary education, general*	40.	English literature, dramatic arts, and speech
0804	*Junior high school education*	*1501*	*English, general*
0805	*Higher education, general*	*1502*	*Literature, English*
0806	*Junior and community college education*	*1503*	*Comparative literature*
0807	*Adult and continuing education*	*1007*	*Dramatic arts*
0830	*Reading education*	*1506*	*Speech, debate, and forensic science*
0831	*Art education*	*1507*	*Creative writing*
0832	*Music education*	*1508*	*Teaching of English as a foreign language*
0833	*Mathematics education*	*1599*	*Other letters*
0834	*Science education*	41.	Art and music
0836	*Driver and safety education*	*1001*	*Fine arts, general*
0838	*Business, commerce, and distributive education*	*1002*	*Art*
0839	*Industrial arts, vocational, and technical education*	*1003*	*Art history and appreciation*
0899-1	*Agricultural education*	*1004*	*Music (performing, composition, theory)*
		1005	*Music (liberal arts program)*

TABLE 80 (continued)

Codes	Degree categories†	Codes	Degree categories†
1006	*Music history and appreciation*	*1111*	*Hebrew*
1008	*Dance*	*1112*	*Arabic*
1009	*Applied design*	*1113*	*Indian (Asiatic)*
1010	*Cinematography*	*1115*	*Slavic languages (other than Russian)*
1011	*Photography*	*1116*	*African languages (non-Semitic)*
1099	*Other fine and applied arts*	*1199*	*Other foreign languages*
2302	*Religious music*	44.	Religion and scholastic philosophy
42.	Western European languages and literatures	*1509*	*Scholastic philosophy*‡
1101	*Foreign languages, general*	*1510*	*Religious studies*
1102	*French*	*2301*	*Theological professions, general*
1103	*German*	*2303*	*Biblical languages*
1104	*Italian*	*2304*	*Religious education*
1105	*Spanish*	*2399*	*Other*
1109	*Latin*	**	Distributed pro rata to the categories of this study in parentheses
1110	*Greek, classical*	*4901*	*General liberal arts and sciences (4, 23–28, 40–44)*
1114	*Scandinavian languages*	*4902*	*Biological and physical sciences (1, 5–8, 16)*
1504	*Classics*	*4903*	*Humanities and social sciences (4, 23–28, 40–44)*
43.	Non-Western European languages and literatures	*4904*	*Engineering and other disciplines (2, 10–15)*
1106	*Russian*	*4999*	*Other interdisciplinary studies 1–44)*
1107	*Chinese*		
1108	*Japanese*		

*The basic Office of Education classification system can be found in U.S. National Center for Educational Statistics (1970). A few changes in the system were made in the tabulations of 1971 degree data.

†Degree categories of the Office of Education are in italics; those of this study are in nonitalics.

‡The former separate categories, "philosophy" and "scholastic philosophy," were consolidated in 1971, but are not consolidated for this study. Consequently, an estimate was made for the two categories for 1971 by a pro rata division using the 1970 proportion.

9. Academic Demand for New Ph.D.'s: 1970–1990

9.1. INTRODUCTION AND SUMMARY[1]

The future supply of, and demand for, holders of doctoral degrees is of increasing concern to national- and state-level policy makers, colleges and universities, and individuals who are present or future doctorates. The current recession in doctoral employment markets has inflicted frustration on many recent doctorates who could not find jobs appropriate to their training, and it has aroused anxieties about the future among present graduate students and their teachers. Allan Cartter, in his December 1970 paper[2] to the American Association for the Advancement of Science, drew upon and updated previous work to support the view that there is nothing temporary about this: that, indeed, the accelerating production of doctorates will probably confront a constant and then a declining academic demand for them in the years ahead, throwing an increasing proportion of new doctorates into competition for other types of employment.

In this chapter we shall test in some detail the plausibility of recent projections of academic demand for new doctorates, examine the possible contributions to this demand by each major sector of American higher education, and seek to illumine some positive policy choices in the financing and staffing standards of higher education. These choices have significant implications for the number of new doctorates who will find jobs in colleges and universities.

We shall present quantitative projections of the number of new doctorates hired in faculty positions under each of a series

[1]This chapter is based on Balderston and Radner (1971). We gratefully acknowledge the substantial research and programming assistance of Sharon C. Bush.

[2]See Cartter (1971) for a slightly revised version of this paper.

of different policy assumptions. These assumptions work in combination. The approach does not, in itself, yield a *forecast* of future academic hiring demand, although Cartter used it for this purpose by adopting a set of what he felt were "best-case" behavioral assumptions. Cartter's projections may themselves stimulate actions that vitiate their accuracy as forecasts—and, indeed, Cartter expresses the hope that the supply of new doctorates will be reduced by actions taken in response to the plausible picture of the future that he describes.

Unfortunately, we shall not be able to deal with the question of supply, nor shall we investigate prospects for employment of new doctorates in industrial and governmental research and professional work, as distinct from faculty appointment in colleges and universities. Dael Wolfle and Charles V. Kidd (1971), in "The Future Market for Ph.D.'s," summarize and interpret a great deal of recent work on both supply projections and demand analysis. Their discussion draws on documents and comments from an informal conference held on April 2, 1971, in Washington, D.C. The findings we present and discuss below in their completed form were reported in part at that meeting.

As a point of departure for this study of academic hiring demand for new doctorates from 1970 to 1990, it is useful first to summarize Cartter's approach and conclusions.

Cartter in a nutshell The essence of Allan Cartter's paper is that the academic job market for new Ph.D.'s can be expected to absorb annually only 8,000 to 10,000 new doctorates until the early 1980s, after which the net demand for new doctorates in academic positions will become negative, while the projected production rate of new doctorates is on a sharply rising trend, already above 30,000 per year and expected to reach about 68,000 per year by 1980, according to National Research Council projections, or to about 48,000 per year in 1980, according to Cartter's own most recent and more conservative projections. Historically, about half the new doctorates in all fields have gone into college and university teaching posts, and so the predicted situation is that other types of occupations will have to absorb a far larger fraction of new doctorates in the future than they have in the past.

The critical assumptions underlying Cartter's estimates and the method of estimation Cartter built up his estimate of the annual number of new doctorates for whom academic jobs would be available by:

1 Constructing an estimate of each year's total FTE enrollment from figures on the United States population, 18- to 24-year age group, and an assumed slow rise in the percentage of those who will enter post-secondary studies (and, implicitly, an assumption about the duration of stay in college of those in the 18- to 24-year population who are assumed to begin)

2 Assuming an incremental United States *full-time equivalent student/full-time faculty ratio* (25 to 1) drawn from judgments about the pattern of the late 1960s and using this to compute the number of full-time faculty required for the projected enrollment increases

3 Obtaining the total increment of number of faculty to be hired by adding to the increase of numbers a percentage of total faculty representing mortality, retirement, and a small net out-migration to nonacademic employment sectors from faculty ranks (the total assumed to be 2 percent per year)

4 Applying to the total number of faculty to be hired a percentage estimate of those who will need to be hired with doctoral training (the average over all sectors of higher education assumed to be 44 percent)

Disaggregated projections based on assumptions analogous to Cartter's Since enrollment growth forecasts, student-faculty ratios, and percentage of faculty with doctoral training vary enormously among the different sectors of higher education, we made disaggregated projections utilizing the above variables for each of the six sectors of higher education: public universities, private universities, public four-year colleges, private four-year colleges, public two-year colleges, and private two-year colleges. The method of calculation is fully described in Section 9.2. The aggregate total from our sectoral analysis can be compared with Cartter's projections as follows:

1a Enrollment: We used Cartter's aggregate enrollment series; however, it was also necessary to take the aggregate enrollment projection for each year and distribute it by some reasonable assumption over the six sectors. Tentative and judgmental estimates distributing various fractions of the expected increment from 1969 on, developed by the Carnegie Commission staff, were used to disaggregate the total enrollment series.

2a Student-faculty ratio: We calculated an average *full-time equivalent student/full-time equivalent faculty* ratio for each of the six sectors from

1967 U.S. Office of Education data; the weighted average of these six ratios is 17.3 to 1. This differs from Cartter's figure in that he used the number of *full-time faculty,* not *full-time equivalent faculty,* in calculating the ratio.

3a Rate of death, retirement, and net out-migration: The 2 percent figure that Cartter used was assumed to be constant over the six sectors analyzed.

4a Percentage of new hires having doctoral-level training: Cartter used the figure 44 percent for his projections, assuming that enough new faculty would be hired with the Ph.D. to just maintain this percentage throughout the next 20 years; however, our projections utilized sectoral percent-of-doctorate parameters from 1967 U.S. Office of Education data, and their weighted average was calculated to be 35.7 percent.

The above assumptions 1a through 4a employed in the sectoral analysis comprise our "no-change" model. Cartter's own projections are about 10 percent higher than our no-change case in predicting total hiring demand for new faculty at the doctoral level for the period 1970–1990; Cartter estimates a demand of 123,300, while our no-change model predicts that 111,500 new faculty with doctorates will be required. Figure 25 compares these two projections. The United States faculty population is large—approximately 375,000 FTE positions in 1970—and the potential number of years of service of each faculty member from the beginning of full-time teaching until death or retirement may be 30 years or more. Stock-flow situations of this kind often show high variations of the flow requirements when modest changes of assumptions are made.

Cartter's projection depends critically upon the student-faculty ratio (assumption 2a above). In Chapter 6 we have summarized the evidence concerning recent historical trends in the student-faculty ratios in each of six major sectors of United States higher education. This material will be used in making our disaggregated projections.

Alternative assumptions Cartter's method of projection is multiplicative; hence a change in any one assumption—and, to an even greater extent, a change in two or more assumptions at the same time—may have substantial effects on the number of new doctorates hired for academic work each year.

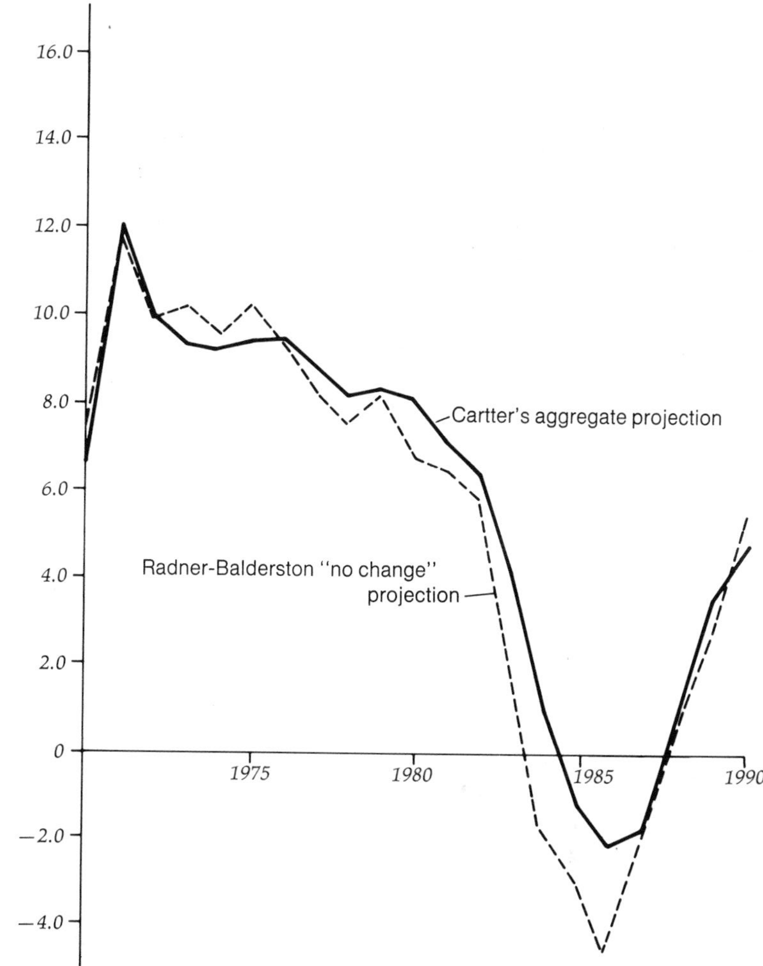

FIGURE 25 ***Projected demand for new doctoral-level faculty (TNFDL) (in thousands)***

In order to test the sensitivity of Cartter's projections to each of the assumptions, and also to show the impacts on academic hiring of doctorates if new policy standards are adopted by government and institutional decision makers, we therefore employed departures from each of the assumptions used in our no-change projections. These and other projections are fully described in Section 9.2. Some of the alternative assumptions we considered are:

1b Enrollment: As an alternative to Cartter's series, we used one of several United States enrollment projections recently made by Gus Haggstrom. These enrollments are a bit higher for each year than Cartter's—in 1980, for example, 891,000, or about 9 percent above Cartter's. Haggstrom's projections also do not show the steep fall in enrollments in the 1980s that Cartter's enrollment series does.

2b Student-faculty ratio: We utilized the fact that student-faculty ratios increased throughout the 1950s and 1960s in the various segments of United States higher education to pose the question: What if it were considered desirable, and the money were found, to permit the weighted average student-faculty ratio of 17.3 to 1 in 1967 to be reduced in regular annual decrements to a weighted average over all sectors of 15.4 to 1 in 1990?

3b Rate of death, retirement, and net out-migration: Remains the same (2 percent) as in the no-change case.

4b Percentage of new hires having doctoral-level training: Cartter assumed that enough new faculty would be hired with the Ph.D. to just maintain, throughout the next 20 years, the 1970 percentage of Ph.D.'s. However, if it is socially desirable to upgrade the level of training of new faculty, the 1967 overall percentage might be incremented to a weighted average of 65 percent by 1990.

In brief, the combined effect of assumptions 1b through 4b is very substantial—for the year 1980, about 115 percent more new doctorates would be needed for academic positions than under our no-change projection.

Sensitivity analysis of alternative projections Recalculating our no-change projection of demand for new doctoral-level faculty, with only the change in the student-faculty ratio assumption (assumption 2b instead of assumption 2a), produced about a 17 percent increase in the annual number of new faculty doctoral positions through the 1970s, and its effect is also to lessen the trough of negative-demand years in the no-change projection during the early 1980s.

The Haggstrom enrollment series (assumption 1b) also produces by itself a 17 percent increase in annual demand for new doctoral faculty through the 1970s, and it also eliminates the period of negative demand in the 1980s.

The change in assumption 4b—the percentage of new faculty hired at the doctoral level—increases the demand for new doctorates by about 30 percent through the 1970s; however, it also creates an even deeper trough of negative demand for doctorates during the 1980s.

Sector-by-sector hiring demand for new doctorates In Section 9.3, the sector-by-sector demand for new faculty with the doctorate is examined and interpreted. A sectoral analysis based on the Cartter enrollment projection and on unchanging sectoral student-faculty ratios and doctoral hiring proportions shows that the public universities' contribution to doctoral hiring demand remains slightly above one-third of total doctoral hiring into academic positions. Because private universities are thought to have low prospective enrollment growth, their share of demand for doctorates falls from 11 percent in 1970 to 4 percent in 1980. Public four-year colleges, with expected rapid enrollment increases, rise from 30 percent of the total in 1970 to 37 percent in 1980, whereas private four-year colleges decline slightly to 14 percent in 1980.

Public two-year colleges rise slightly in their hiring demand for new doctorates—from 4 percent in 1970 to 6 percent in 1980. Private two-year colleges are a tiny and static market sector.

It may seem odd that this sectoral analysis shows a very small influence of the enormous enrollment growth in public two-year colleges (forecast for the decade ahead) on hiring demand. The reason is that, historically, the two-year colleges have hired only a very small proportion of doctorates for available teaching positions, and if the future is like the past, their very large requirement for total new faculty in the 1970s will translate into a very small demand for doctorates.

We also examine, in Section 9.3, the effect in each sector of modifying both the student-faculty ratio and the percentage of new positions filled with doctorates, according to various hypotheses.

Smoothing demand for new faculty The Cartter projection, because its driving variable is enrollment and because the other assumptions are held constant throughout the interval, shows positive hiring demand for doctorates throughout the 1970s and then, in the early 1980s, *negative* hiring demand for several years, when total enrollment is expected to decline. A slow recovery of hiring demand is then shown for the last few years of the 1980s.

The Haggstrom enrollment series is a higher one and thus results in a slightly less bleak picture for the 1980s, when the projection of new doctorates hired is made using all the other no-change assumptions with the exception of the enrollment series. Nevertheless, doctoral hiring demand almost disappears from 1984 to 1986 in this projection.

We discuss this problem of peak and trough in Section 9.4, utilizing two approaches to the amelioration of what otherwise will be a grim period of adjustment. The first approach is that of averaging the total hiring demand. The second is to postulate possibilities of growth in hiring demand by various means.

Conclusions In Section 9.5 we offer concluding comments and policy observations, directed to the various types of decision makers who will be taking an interest in this problem.

9.2. ALTERNATIVE PROJECTIONS OF AGGREGATE DEMAND FOR NEW FACULTY AT THE DOCTORAL LEVEL

In this section we present six alternative projections of the number of new faculty needed at the doctoral level, for the period 1970–1990. These projections were made for each sector of higher education, as explained below, but in this section we present only the aggregate projections for all higher education; the examination of differences between the sectors is deferred to the next section.

We first explain the simple calculations on which the projections are based and then describe the various hypotheses that are combined to generate the six alternative projections. This is followed by the projections themselves, together with some brief remarks concerning the differences between them.

Calculation of projections For each sector, the calculation of the projections of the number of new faculty needed at the doctoral level involves the following variables, which are defined for each year t in the projection:

$S(t)$ = number of full-time equivalent students

$F(t)$ = number of full-time equivalent faculty

$R(t)$ = student-faculty ratio

$N(t)$ = total new faculty needed in the sector

$P(t)$ = proportion (fraction) of new faculty needed at the doctoral level

$D(t)$ = total new faculty needed at the doctoral level

For each sector, we hypothesize projections of $S(t)$, $R(t)$, and $P(t)$ and calculate the projections of $F(t)$, $N(t)$, and $D(t)$ that are implied by the following relationships (following Cartter, we assume that the rate of death, retirement, and net out-migration of faculty is 2 percent per year):

$$F(t) = \frac{S(t)}{R(t)}$$
$$N(t) = F(t) - F(t-1) + (.02)F(t-1) = F(t) - (.98)F(t-1) \quad (1)$$
$$D(t) = P(t)N(t)$$

These equations can be combined to give a single equation relating the projected values of total new faculty needed at the doctoral level to the projected values of students, student-faculty ratio, and proportion of new faculty at the doctoral level:

$$D(t) = P(t)\left[\frac{S(t)}{R(t)} - (.98)\,\frac{S(t-1)}{R(t-1)}\right] \qquad t = 1970, \ldots, 1990 \qquad (2)$$

Alternative hypotheses Two alternative projections of student enrollment are used here: (1) the projection used by Cartter in his paper and (2) one of a family of projections developed by Professor Gus Haggstrom for the Carnegie Commission on Higher Education.[3] We shall call these the "Cartter" and "Haggstrom" projections, respectively; they are given in Table 81. The Haggstrom projection is somewhat higher than the Cartter projection, especially at the end of the 1990s. However, the difference never exceeds 20 percent of the Cartter projection, and for most of the period it is less than 10 percent.

Two alternative hypotheses are considered for the student-faculty ratio. The first hypothesis assumes that the student-faculty ratio in each sector will remain at its 1967 value. The second hypothesis assumes that the student-faculty ratio in each sector will decline in the 1970s and 1980s to a value near the bottom end of the range of values experienced by that sector during the period 1953–1967 (using the ratios reported in Table 39 in Chapter 6). These lower ratios are called here the "target" values for the student-faculty ratio and are given in Tables 82A and 82B. It is assumed under the second hypothesis that during the period 1970–1990, the student-faculty ratio in each sector will decrease linearly to the target value in 1990. Given the

[3]Unpublished manuscript.

TABLE 81 ***Alternative projections of total enrollment in United States higher education, 1970–1990 (in thousands)***

Year	*Cartter*	*Haggstrom*
1970	6,303	6,697
1971	6,755	7,125
1972	7,115	7,623
1973	7,489	8,095
1974	7,831	8,526
1975	8,197	8,925
1976	8,525	9,280
1977	8,799	9,601
1978	9,050	9,918
1979	9,324	10,205
1980	9,537	10,428
1981	9,705	10,596
1982	9,834	10,661
1983	9,746	10,601
1984	9,514	10,477
1985	9,228	10,312
1986	8,862	10,175
1987	8,639	10,114
1988	8,541	10,116
1989	8,545	10,214
1990	8,674	10,378

experience of the past two decades, such target values for 1990 would not be unreasonable in a situation with an excess supply of Ph.D.'s, *if institutions of higher education were adequately financed*.

Three alternative hypotheses are considered regarding $P(t)$, the proportion of new faculty hired at the doctoral level. The first assumes that in each sector $P(t)$ will remain constant at the 1967 value. The second hypothesis assumes that in each sector $P(t)$ will increase linearly to the average value for all associate professors in that sector in 1967. The third hypothesis assumes that $P(t)$ will increase linearly to certain target values, which are higher than the average 1967 associate professor values, but still would be reasonable target values to achieve in a 20-year period

TABLE 82A ***Alternative hypotheses for student-faculty ratio***

	Public universities	*Private universities*	*Public four-year colleges*	*Private four-year colleges*	*Public two-year colleges*	*Private two-year colleges*
(1) 1967 values	16.64	11.26	17.86	14.54	21.64	17.72
(2) Target values	14.0	10.0	15.0	13.0	19.0	13.0

TABLE 82B ***Alternative hypotheses for proportion hired at the doctoral level***

	Universities	*Four-year colleges*	*Two-year colleges*
(1) 1967 average values	.543	.389	.059
(2) 1967 associate professor values	.674	.538	.149
(3) target values	.90	.75	.30

TABLE 82C ***Summary of hypotheses for alternative projections***

	Student-faculty ratio (R)	*Proportion hired at doctoral level (P)*
No-change (from 1967)	(1)	(1)
Intermediate	(2)	(2)
Adequate-finance	(2)	(3)

if a sustained effort were made to increase the percentage of new faculty at the doctoral level.

The rationale for the second hypothesis concerning *P(t)* is that the average proportion with the Ph.D. for associate professors gives a better estimate of the proportion of young faculty with doctoral-level training than the overall proportion for all faculty in a given sector does. Furthermore, the comparable figure for assistant professors is probably not appropriate because in many fields assistant professors are hired while they are still completing the last stages of their doctoral training and research.

The various hypotheses were put together in a number of different combinations, of which we have chosen six to present in this chapter. Three combinations of hypotheses regarding the student-faculty ratios and the proportion hired at the doctoral level are summarized in Table 82C; these are labeled "no-change," "intermediate," and "adequate-finance." Each of these three combinations was then combined with each of the two alternative enrollment projections, the Cartter and Haggstrom projections, given in Table 81. The resulting six projections of total new faculty needed at the doctoral level are presented in Tables 83A and 83B and in Figures 26 through 28.

Comparison of projections We first consider the effect of using the Haggstrom rather than the Cartter projection of enrollment. Although the Haggstrom projection is not more than 10 percent higher for most of the period, and never more than 20 percent higher, the *total* new faculty at the doctoral level from 1970 to 1990 is approximately 33 percent higher under the Haggstrom projection than under the Cartter projection, for each of the three cases. The time pattern of new faculty at the doctoral level is similar in both sets of projections, with peaks in the 1970s and troughs in the 1980s, but the differences between corresponding projections are generally most pronounced near the peaks and the troughs.

For any one enrollment projection, the three cases (no-change, intermediate, and adequate-finance) differ markedly in their projections of total new faculty at the doctoral level over the period 1970–1990. Thus this total is almost twice as large for the adequate-finance case as for the no-change case (for each enrollment projection).

However, all projections agree in predicting a sharp dip in new faculty at the doctoral level in 1985 or 1986, the lowest dip (to −5,840) occurring in the Cartter enrollment adequate-finance case, and the shallowest dip (to 3,480) in the Haggstrom enrollment adequate-finance case. It is not surprising that the Haggstrom enrollment adequate-finance case minimizes the dip in the 1980s, but one might be surprised by the fact that the lowest dip occurs in the Cartter enrollment adequate-finance case, rather than in the Cartter enrollment no-change case, which seems to be the least favorable. However, the lower the student-faculty ratio, the greater in magnitude will be the fluctuations in required numbers of faculty caused by any given pattern of fluctuation in enrollments; hence the greater sensitivity of required numbers of new faculty to the dip in enrollment in the adequate-finance case.

In the foregoing analysis we have concentrated on the examination of policies that would produce a demand for doctorates higher than that predicted by Cartter. However, two plausible trends in the environment of higher education could imply projections of demand for doctorates that are *lower* than the Cartter enrollment no-change model suggests:

1 A greater shift of the enrollment distribution away from the universities (public and private) and toward the two-year colleges than we have assumed

2 A more stringent fiscal environment, leading to student-faculty ratios higher, for some or all sectors, than the 1967 student-faculty ratios

In Section 9.3 below, we have shown our assumptions about the future distribution of enrollment among the sectors of United States higher education. While our assumption is that some shift away from the universities and toward the two-year colleges is expected to occur, a still more drastic shift (actuated by financing pressures on students or on institutions, particularly private institutions) is quite possible.

Fiscal pressures increasing student-faculty ratios would also give rise to lower academic hiring demand for doctorates than has been projected. If we assume that the weighted average student-faculty ratio of 17.3 to 1 to 1967 will be increased to 22.3 to 1 by 1981, then we can project a 40 percent decrease in hiring demand through 1981, as compared with that derived using the

TABLE 83A ***Alternative projections of new faculty needed at the doctoral level (TNFDL) using the Cartter projection of student enrollment (in thousands)***

Year		*No-change*	*Intermediate*	*Adequate-finance*
1970		7.16	8.40	8.82
1971		11.90	13.68	14.69
1972		9.92	11.91	13.07
1973		10.23	12.58	14.10
1974		9.56	12.17	13.91
1975		10.12	13.15	15.32
1976		9.29	12.53	14.88
1977		8.18	11.54	13.96
1978		7.66	11.21	13.80
1979		8.15	12.13	15.17
1980		6.95	10.92	13.90
1981		6.66	10.74	13.81
1982		5.88	9.97	13.01
1983		1.42	4.07	5.48
1984		−1.58	−.07	.06
1985		−2.73	−1.76	−2.21
1986		−4.48	−4.42	−5.84
1987		−1.67	−.37	−.34
1988		.79	3.34	4.81
1989		2.80	6.54	9.36
1990		5.29	10.67	15.33
	TOTAL	111.52	168.93	205.08

other assumptions of the Cartter enrollment no-change model. The results are shown in Table 84.

9.3. HIRING DEMAND FOR NEW DOCTORATES IN EACH OF THE SECTORS OF AMERICAN HIGHER EDUCATION

We have divided American higher education into six sectors for this study: the private universities; the public universities; the private two-year colleges; the public two-year colleges; all other private institutions (chiefly B.A.-granting, but including some which offer master's degrees as well); and all other public institutions (again, chiefly B.A.-granting, but including some offering postbaccalaureate degrees). The latter two sectors are referred to as "private four-year colleges" and "public four-year colleges" in our analysis. The aggregate projected enrollment

TABLE 83B ***Alternative projections of new faculty needed at the doctoral level (TNFDL) using the Haggstrom projection of student enrollment (in thousands)***

Year	*No-change*	*Intermediate*	*Adequate-finance*
1970	11.67	13.13	13.78
1971	11.48	13.30	14.27
1972	13.09	15.42	16.91
1973	12.53	15.23	17.05
1974	11.67	14.68	16.77
1975	11.03	14.33	16.70
1976	10.07	13.59	16.13
1977	9.39	13.15	15.90
1978	9.28	13.37	16.44
1979	8.65	12.94	16.19
1980	7.40	11.67	14.87
1981	6.95	11.31	14.55
1982	4.85	8.76	11.46
1983	2.27	5.42	7.26
1984	.92	3.63	4.99
1985	.06	2.47	3.48
1986	.53	3.20	4.52
1987	2.04	5.50	7.75
1988	3.28	7.52	10.64
1989	5.19	10.68	15.21
1990	6.52	13.06	18.77
TOTAL	148.87	222.35	273.65

for all higher education was distributed among the six sectors according to (assumed) percentages as shown in Table 85.

However, our assumptions concerning sectoral enrollment trends need some comment. The best information available to us was judgmental, although the Carnegie Commission staff expects forthcoming studies to produce refined estimates of sectoral enrollments. Table 85 is constructed on the hypothesis that the public universities and private universities will experience relatively slow growth in enrollment and that the latter, in particular, will have a considerable shrinkage in their market share during the next 20 years. With heavy emphasis on undergraduate enrollment growth, especially in the 1970s, the public

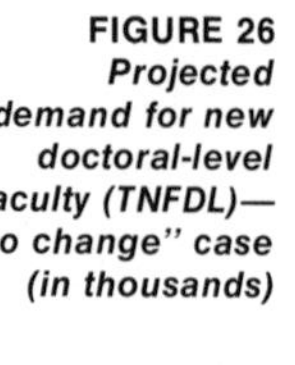

FIGURE 26 ***Projected demand for new doctoral-level faculty (TNFDL)—"no change" case (in thousands)***

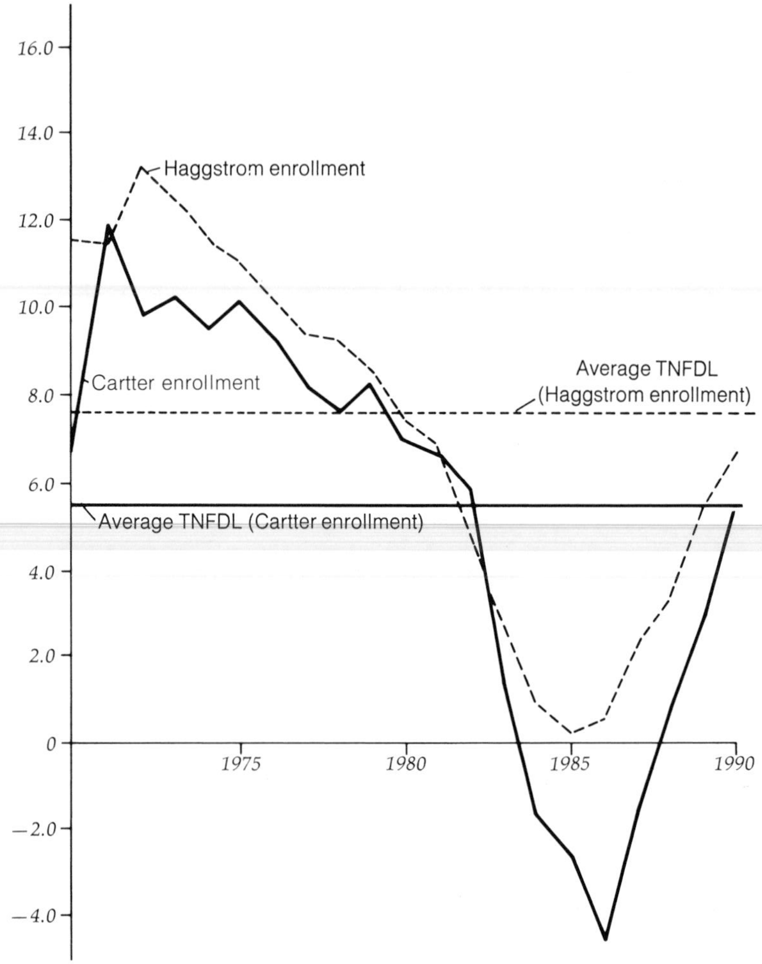

SOURCE: Tables 83A and 83B.

four-year colleges are expected to increase their percentage of total enrollment. Private four-year colleges, compelled to increase student charges, face a slowly declining market share between 1970 and 1990. Public four-year colleges, continuing the trend of the 1960s with strong political support from all levels of government that have financed their spectacular growth so far, are expected to continue that growth in the 20-year interval ahead, ending with 30 percent of total enrollment by 1990. Private two-year colleges are not expected to change in significance.

While these assumed enrollment trends seem quite plausible

FIGURE 27 ***Projected demand for new doctoral level faculty (TNFDL)—"intermediate" case (in thousands)***

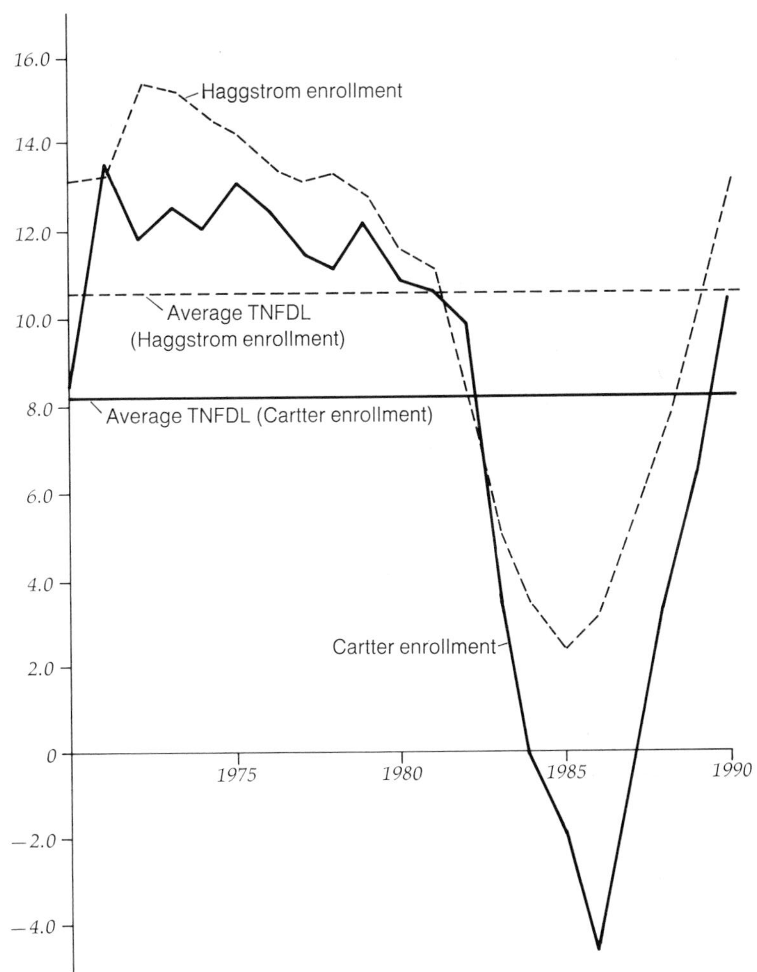

SOURCE: Tables 83A and 83B.

in the light of recent experience, numerous factors might change the trends. A substantial new program of federally financed student aid or cost-of-education allowances might improve the ability of private universities and four-year colleges to obtain enrollment growth, with consequent shifts away from their public counterparts.

The continuing relative and absolute growth assumed for public two-year colleges could be reduced by several factors. Large financial aid programs might impel some students to enter degree-granting institutions as freshmen if their main motive for attending two-year colleges now is to save money on

FIGURE 28 ***Projected demand for new doctoral-level faculty (TNFDL)—"adequate finance" case (in thousands)***

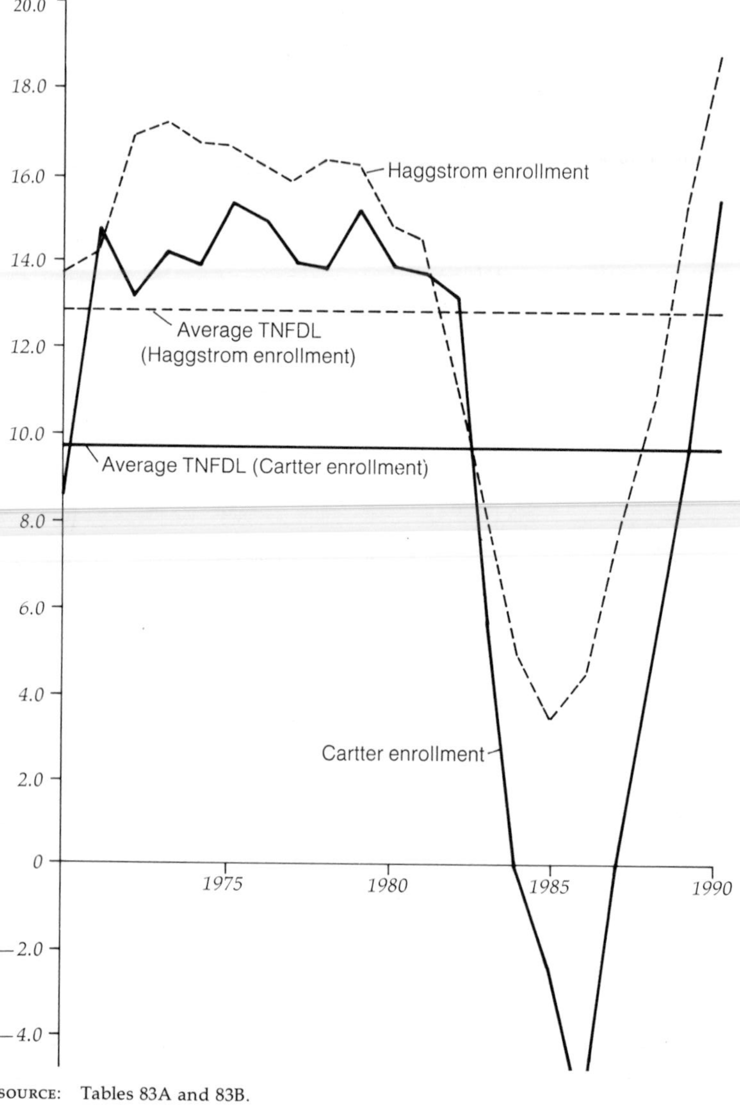

SOURCE: Tables 83A and 83B.

college attendance. Public concern may arise in the future over the very high rates of attrition from academic programs in the community colleges, causing some of them to be made into degree-granting institutions and others to experience some reduction in student preference and in financing from state sources.

In the first set of disaggregated projections, the Cartter enrollment no-change case, the sectoral student-faculty ratios and the

TABLE 84 ***Demand for new faculty at the doctoral level (TNFDL), 1970–1981, when (1) sectoral student-faculty ratios remain constant at the 1967 level and (2) sectoral student-faculty ratios increase to the 1981 level***

	Cartter enrollment no-change projection			
	(1)		*(2)*	
	*1967 student-faculty ratio**	*TNFDL, 1970–1981 (in thousands)*	*Increased 1981 student-faculty ratio†*	*TNFDL, 1970–1981 (in thousands)*
Public universities	16.64	38.42	21.16	21.76
Private universities	11.26	10.14	13.55	5.03
Public four-year colleges	17.86	34.16	21.76	22.97
Private four-year colleges	14.54	17.81	17.22	11.53
Public two-year colleges	21.64	5.01	26.83	3.38
Private two-year colleges	17.72	.30	20.49	.22
TOTAL		105.84		64.89

NOTE: The student-faculty ratio averages are weighted according to the estimated enrollment distribution in the given year.

*1967 average student-faculty ratio: 17.3 to 1.

†1981 average student-faculty ratio: 22.3 to 1.

proportions of new faculty hired were assumed to continue the historical figures derived from 1967 U.S. Office of Education data, as shown below:

	1967 student-faculty ratio	*1967 proportion of total faculty with doctorate*
Public universities	16.64	.543
Private universities	11.26	.543
Public four-year colleges	17.86	.389
Private four-year colleges	14.54	.389
Public two-year colleges	21.64	.059
Private two-year colleges	17.72	.059

SOURCE: Tables 82A through 82C.

Using these assumptions, we projected the annual number of new faculty and new faculty with the doctorate for each sector

TABLE 85 ***Assumed fractional distribution of each year's total enrollment among the six sectors of United States higher education***

Year	*Public universities*	*Private universities*	*Public four-year colleges*	*Private four-year colleges*	*Public two-year colleges*	*Private two-year colleges*
1970	.242	.082	.255	.163	.239	.020
1971	.240	.080	.256	.161	.243	.020
1972	.239	.078	.258	.159	.247	.019
1973	.238	.075	.259	.157	.252	.019
1974	.237	.073	.260	.155	.256	.019
1975	.235	.071	.261	.153	.260	.019
1976	.234	.069	.263	.151	.265	.019
1977	.233	.067	.264	.149	.269	.019
1978	.232	.065	.265	.146	.273	.018
1979	.230	.063	.267	.144	.278	.018
1980	.229	.061	.268	.142	.282	.018
1981	.227	.060	.269	.142	.284	.018
1982	.225	.059	.270	.142	.286	.018
1983	.223	.058	.271	.142	.288	.018
1984	.221	.057	.272	.142	.290	.019
1985	.219	.056	.274	.142	.291	.019
1986	.216	.056	.275	.141	.293	.019
1987	.214	.055	.276	.141	.295	.019
1988	.212	.054	.277	.141	.297	.019
1989	.210	.053	.278	.141	.299	.019
1990	.208	.052	.279	.141	.301	.019

SOURCE: Tentative estimates for selected years, by Carnegie Commission staff, interpolated and extrapolated by the authors.

from 1970 to 1990. The results for the Cartter enrollment no-change case are shown in Table 86. It is of interest that the figure for total new faculty hired before applying the proportion hired at the doctoral level is quite high in the public two-year colleges. This number approximates 7,000 annually from 1971 to 1980 before the projected enrollment declines of the 1980s begin to take hold; but in this projection, the very low percentage of faculty hired with the doctorate (5.9 percent) reduces to insig-

TABLE 86 ***Estimated total new faculty (TNF) and new faculty with the doctorate (TNFDL) hired by each sector, 1970–1990, in the Cartter enrollment no-change projection (in thousands) (disaggregated constant 1967 student-faculty ratios and proportion at the doctoral level)***

	Public universities		Private universities		Public four-year colleges		Private four-year colleges		Public two-year colleges		Private two-year colleges		Total all sectors	
	TNF	*TNFDL*	*TNF*	*TNFDL*	*TNF*	*TNFDL*	*TNF*	*TNFDL*	*TNF*	*TNFDL*	*TNF*	*TNFDL*	Σ *TNF*	Σ *TNFDL*
1970	4.80	2.61	1.50	.82	5.58	2.17	3.19	1.24	5.18	.31	.37	.02	20.62	7.17
1971	7.87	4.27	2.99	1.62	8.71	3.39	5.47	2.13	7.72	.46	.57	.03	33.33	11.90
1972	6.64	3.61	2.17	1.18	7.62	2.96	4.46	1.74	6.97	.41	.46	.03	28.32	9.93
1973	6.84	3.71	2.16	1.17	7.99	3.11	4.57	1.78	7.39	.44	.48	.03	29.43	10.24
1974	6.42	3.49	1.83	1.00	7.70	2.99	4.18	1.63	7.31	.43	.49	.03	27.93	9.57
1975	6.84	3.71	1.87	1.02	8.21	3.19	4.38	1.71	7.81	.46	.47	.03	29.58	10.12
1976	6.29	3.42	1.60	.87	7.77	3.02	3.88	1.51	7.61	.45	.43	.03	27.58	9.30
1977	5.62	3.05	1.09	.59	7.18	2.79	3.33	1.30	7.22	.43	.42	.03	24.86	8.19
1978	5.27	2.86	.86	.47	6.97	2.71	3.05	1.19	7.11	.42	.34	.02	23.60	7.67
1979	5.60	3.04	.89	.48	7.43	2.89	3.23	1.26	7.60	.45	.36	.02	25.11	8.14
1980	4.84	2.63	.54	.29	6.66	2.59	2.59	1.01	7.06	.42	.35	.02	22.04	6.96
1981	3.71	2.02	1.16	.63	6.03	2.35	3.37	1.31	5.53	.33	.42	.03	20.22	6.67
1982	3.17	1.72	.94	.51	5.47	2.13	3.09	1.20	5.10	.30	.39	.02	18.16	5.88
1983	.24	.13	−.21	−.11	2.24	.87	.99	.39	2.25	.13	.22	.01	5.73	1.42
1984	−1.70	−.92	−.95	−.52	.08	.03	−.49	−.19	.34	.02	.02	.00	−2.70	−1.58
1985	−2.43	−1.32	−1.22	−.67	−.84	−.33	−1.00	−.39	−.47	−.03	−.05	−.00	−6.01	−2.74
1986	−3.56	−1.93	−1.54	−.84	−2.23	−.87	−1.89	−.74	−1.67	−.10	−.14	.01	−11.03	−4.47
1987	−1.69	−.92	−.92	−.50	−.17	−.07	−.50	−.20	.14	.01	.00	.00	−3.14	−1.68
1988	−.11	−.06	−.32	−.17	1.73	.67	.61	.24	1.73	.10	.18	.01	3.82	.79
1989	1.15	.63	.15	.08	3.29	1.28	1.58	.61	3.15	.19	.24	.01	9.56	2.80
1990	2.69	1.46	.72	.39	5.21	2.03	2.84	1.11	4.90	.29	.37	.02	16.73	5.30

TABLE 87 ***Estimated proportion of (1) total faculty at the doctoral level (TFDL) and (2) total new faculty at the doctoral level (TNFDL) in each sector of higher education, 1970–1981, Cartter enrollment no-change projection (disaggregated constant 1967 student-faculty ratios and proportion at the doctoral level)***

	Public universities		*Private universities*		*Public four-year colleges*		*Private four-year colleges*		*Public two-year colleges*		*Private two-year colleges*	
	TFDL	*TNFDL*	*TFDL*	*TNFDL*	*TFDL*	*TNFDL*	*TFDL*	*TNFDL*	*TFDL*	*TNFDL*	*TFDL*	*TNFDL*
1970	.351	.364	.175	.114	.247	.303	.195	.173	.029	.043	.003	.003
1971	.352	.359	.172	.136	.250	.255	.193	.179	.030	.038	.003	.003
1972	.352	.363	.169	.119	.253	.299	.192	.175	.030	.041	.003	.003
1973	.353	.363	.165	.114	.256	.304	.191	.174	.031	.043	.003	.003
1974	.354	.365	.162	.104	.260	.313	.190	.170	.032	.045	.003	.003
1975	.355	.367	.158	.100	.263	.316	.189	.169	.033	.046	.003	.003
1976	.355	.368	.155	.093	.266	.325	.187	.162	.034	.048	.003	.003
1977	.356	.373	.152	.072	.269	.341	.186	.159	.034	.052	.003	.003
1978	.357	.373	.148	.061	.273	.353	.185	.155	.035	.055	.003	.003
1979	.357	.374	.144	.059	.276	.355	.184	.154	.036	.055	.003	.003
1980	.358	.378	.141	.042	.279	.372	.182	.145	.037	.060	.003	.003
1981	.356	.303	.139	.095	.282	.352	.183	.197	.037	.049	.003	.004

nificant proportions the contribution that the public two-year colleges make to total hiring demand for new doctorates.

Table 87 shows the fractional distributions of total faculty at the doctoral level and total new faculty at the doctoral level for 1970–1981. This table contrasts the distribution of future demand for new doctoral faculty with the current allocation of doctoral faculty. Private universities, in 1970, have 17.5 percent of the total doctoral faculty in all sectors but hire only 11.4 percent of total new doctoral faculty in all sectors, while public four-year colleges have only 26.0 percent of total doctoral faculty but place a demand for 31.3 percent of total new doctoral faculty.

Several policy issues and possible questions of hiring response to the supply situation suggest themselves from the difference between total new faculty hired and the computed demand for doctoral-level new faculty. First, two-year colleges may well find that their traditional aversion to hiring Ph.D.'s is replaced by a greater advantage in doing so as a number of universities prove more willing to adjust their curricula, increase their emphasis on preparation for teaching, and change their ways of placing students in jobs.

Similarly, future supply conditions may alter the historical differences between total new faculty (TNF) and total new faculty with the doctorate (TNFDL) shown in Table 86. First, every one of the four sectors that contribute significantly to doctoral hiring demand—public and private universities and public and private four-year colleges—could accommodate a significant number of doctorates in teaching positions. The total of all positions we project from the Cartter enrollment no-change assumptions *not* to be filled by candidates at the doctoral level in these four sectors from 1970 to 1980 is 11,460, or 55 percent of all new faculty positions.

As these types of institution, which already display historical hiring preference for doctorates, experience greater and greater ease of filling positions with willing applicants who possess the doctorate, the assumption of fixed doctoral hiring percentages may well prove to be wrong.

The same type of hiring response may occur in the public two-year colleges. Their total new faculty requirements for 1970–1980 are projected to be 78,890, whereas the projected number of doctorates hired is only 4,680 because of this sector's very low historical percentage of doctorates.

A plentiful supply of doctorates seeking teaching positions could alter this pattern in two-year colleges, but there is reason to be cautious about the prospects for this. Recent evidence from a study by Lucian Pugliaresi (1970) of the pattern of hiring preferences in California community colleges suggests a probable resistance to the hiring of Ph.D.'s on a wide scale. Pugliaresi found that nearly all the community college administrators he interviewed would not hire Ph.D.'s because, they said, the typical doctorate tended to be dissatisfied with heavy and diversified teaching obligations, resented the lack of opportunity to do research and scholarly work, and did not have a positive interest in the academic mission of the community college. The modal hiring preference of *all* California community colleges in a recent year, cited by Pugliaresi, was for candidates who had the master's degree and several years of prior teaching experience.

Two other qualitative observations come forward from Pugliaresi's interviews. The community college administrators did not regard experience as a teaching assistant as "real" teaching experience, and while they were antagonistic to the Ph.D., they expressed strong interest in possible hiring of people with a doctor of arts degree or, in other words, an advanced degree designed as a preparation for a purely teaching career.

Alternative sectoral enrollment distributions Our sectoral projections of both total new faculty and new doctoral-level faculty are significantly affected by the assumed trends in the sectoral composition of enrollment, and the reader should discount our projections accordingly if the assumptions about sectoral enrollment trends do not appear satisfactory to him. To test the sensitivity of our projections to assumed sectoral enrollment distributions (taken from the Carnegie Commission estimates), we developed an alternative enrollment distribution. Under an assumption that there might be some future disillusionment with two-year colleges, we held two-year college enrollments constant at the 1968 level and redistributed their projected enrollment increases to four-year colleges.

The effect on academic demand for doctorates is to increase the 20-year total to 126,000, or about a 13 percent increase, when using all other Cartter enrollment no-change assumptions, as compared with the base case. Tables 88A and 88B show these results.

The Carnegie Commission, recommending the establishment of doctor of arts degree programs as a fully parallel option to the (research-oriented) Ph.D., applied essentially the same logic to the situation. So far, only a few doctorate-producing institutions have adopted this approach, but with the prodding of the Commission's recommendations, more will undoubtedly do so in the future.

This leads us to a policy suggestion directed toward the doctorate-producing institutions, especially the public universities in regions where significant expansion of public two-year colleges will be taking place. Whether they adopt the approach of a separate type of degree or not, these institutions will need to take specific actions on several fronts if they are to expect their graduate students to be actively desired for community college teaching and their own claims for budgetary support for

TABLE 88A ***Alternative sectoral enrollment proportions—assuming two-year colleges hold at constant enrollment proportions—for selected years from 1970 to 1990***

Sector	1970	1980	1990
Public universities	.242	.229	.208
Private universities	.0816	.0609	.052
Public four-year colleges	.263	.315	.345
Private four-year colleges	.164	.145	.145
Public two-year colleges	.231	.235	.235
Private two-year colleges	.019	.015	.015

NOTE: Annual fractions were used for the disaggregated enrollment calculations, but only selected years are given here.

TABLE 88B ***Sum of total new faculty hired at the doctoral level (TNFDL) from 1970 to 1990 using (1) alternative enrollment distribution and (2) enrollment distribution from Carnegie Commission estimates—Cartter enrollment no-change projection***

Sector	(1) Using alternative enrollment distribution (in thousands)*	(2) Using Carnegie Commission estimates of enrollment distribution (in thousands)†
Public universities	37.21	37.21
Private universities	8.31	8.31
Public four-year colleges	54.98	39.91
Private four-year colleges	21.01	19.82
Public two-year colleges	4.01	5.90
Private two-year colleges	.22	.38
TOTAL (all sectors)	125.74	111.53

*From Table 88A.

†From Table 85.

advanced graduate programs to be well justified in the 1970s, including the following:

1. Overhaul of doctoral curricula for more breadth and more attention to teaching preparation
2. Specific arrangements for teaching internships and other means of developing teaching skills through supervised practice, possibly through cooperative schemes with neighboring community colleges

3 Emphasis on the respectability and desirability of the teaching career

4 Establishment of firmer lines of communication with community colleges in the placement process

9.4. SMOOTHING DEMANDS FOR NEW FACULTY

Cartter's own projection of the academic demand for doctorates shows a deep trough in the early 1980s, with *negative* demand for several years in the middle of that decade. (Because the number of faculty vacancies created by deaths, retirements, and withdrawals from academic work is assumed to be a constant percentage each year of the total stock of faculty, a negative hiring rate can be interpreted to mean that the number of vacancies created by deaths and retirements is not sufficient to adjust the total number of faculty to the available enrollment; thus some nontenured faculty positions are abolished in a year of negative demand, and the people who previously filled them are obliged to find other types of employment.)

As was shown in Section 9.2, a deep relative trough occurs during the 1980s in all the projections of new faculty hired at the doctoral level using the Cartter enrollment projections, whatever other assumptions are made. The cause is the expected downturn of enrollment, and this in turn can be forecast from the birthrate decline of the 1960s. The Haggstrom enrollment projection, being higher than Cartter's, does eliminate the years of negative academic demand that Cartter shows for 1980 through 1987, but does not eliminate the troughs.

If there were some way to achieve it, smoothing of this disastrous pattern of peak and trough would be highly desirable. Failure to do so would mean the loss to academic work, and the loss of academic career opportunity, for several years' worth of Ph.D. winners in the mid-1980s. It would mean that colleges and universities, for a long time after, would have a "hole" in the age distribution of their faculty. It could and perhaps should mean, on the supply side, either that graduate institutions would begin to sharply curtail their entering graduate classes some five to seven years before the trough or that they would take in their customary numbers of students but expect to train them for very different kinds of employment from that of college and university teaching.

As a starting point for analysis of the smoothing problem, we can estimate the size of the adjustment problem by comparing the *average* annual number of doctorates hired in all sectors over a 20-year period with the peak and the lowest annual demand in each of four projections:

Annual number of new faculty at doctoral level, 1970–1990 (in thousands)

	Average	*Peak*	*Low*
Cartter enrollment—no change	5.41	11.90	−4.48
Haggstrom enrollment–no-change	7.16	13.09	+.06
Cartter enrollment—adequate-finance	9.72	15.32	−5.84
Haggstrom enrollment—no change	12.89	17.05	3.48

The *peak* of academic demand in the first of these four cases is near the *average* of the fourth. Figures 26 through 28 also illustrate this problem.

We have made calculations showing how the student-faculty ratios in the various sectors could be adjusted to smooth the demand for new doctoral-level faculty over the 1970–1990 interval. By allowing the student-faculty ratios to rise considerably in the 1970s and then be reduced in the 1980s, the annual doctoral faculty hires could be held constant over the 20-year period. For the Cartter enrollment no-change case, adjusting the student-faculty ratios such that each sector hired only its 1970–1990 annual average number of doctorates in every year would result in the following variations of the student-faculty ratios:

	1967 ratio	*Peak ratio (year)*	*Lowest ratio (year)*
Public universities	16.64	21.2 (1980)	15.7 (1990)
Private universities	11.26	13.6 (1979)	10.7 (1990)
Public four-year colleges	17.86	21.8 (1981)	17.1 (1989)
Private four-year colleges	14.54	17.2 (1982)	13.9 (1989)
Public two-year colleges	21.64	26.9 (1980)	20.8 (1989)
Private two-year colleges	17.72	20.6 (1982)	17.1 (1989)

Adjustments could also be made by decreasing the percentage of new faculty hired with the doctorate, reducing this percentage in the 1970s, and increasing it in the 1980s; but for obvious reasons this adjustment method is inadequate, if used by itself, to distribute doctoral hiring evenly over the 20-year interval. The ample supply of new doctorates expected in the 1970s makes it very unlikely that a smoothing policy entailing a decrease in the percentage of doctorates hired in each sector will actually be the outcome of many thousands of decentralized decisions, and even a centralized manpower agency, if one existed, would no doubt avoid a policy so perverse in view of supply availability.

We also examined, for each type of projection, the effect on student-faculty ratios of smoothing the *total number of faculty* in each sector of higher education (by varying the student-faculty ratio) so that the total faculty would be held constant every year at the average for the whole period. This approach could result from budgetary controls in public agencies and institutions holding the total number of faculty positions constant. For the Cartter enrollment no-change case, the results were as follows (remember that they refer to total faculty and not to the number of new faculty hired or the number hired with the doctorate):

	No-change case		*Effect of smoothing by total faculty constant*	
	Constant student-faculty ratio	*Peak total faculty (year)*	*Peak student-faculty ratio (year)*	*Average total faculty (in thousands)*
Public universities	16.64	132.9 (1982)	19.2 (1982)	115.4
Private universities	11.26	52.4 (1977)	12.3 (1977)	48.0
Public four-year colleges	17.86	148.7 (1982)	20.9 (1982)	126.8
Private four-year colleges	14.54	96.0 (1982)	16.3 (1982)	85.7
Public two-year colleges	21.64	129.9 (1982)	26.0 (1982)	107.9
Private two-year colleges	17.72	10.1 (1983)	20.0 (1983)	8.9

If the expected 20-year average of total faculty were enforced in each sector for every year, the student-faculty ratio would peak for each sector at the level and year indicated. The annual average of total faculty required under the "smoothing" case may be compared with the total faculty required in the peak year under the Cartter enrollment no-change assumptions. In addition, it is of interest that smoothing, by holding total faculty constant, requires about 10 percent fewer total faculty over the 1970–1990 period because of the different impact of the 2 percent per year withdrawal rate (in the Cartter enrollment no-change case).

If there were centralized manpower planning and management for United States higher education—which, fortunately from other points of view, is not the case—such a manpower agency could choose a policy—one of the four sets of assumptions, let us say—and then avoid the trough of the 1980s with respect to that policy by avoiding greater-than-average hiring of doctorates in the earlier years. However, because United States higher education is really highly decentralized, it cannot be anticipated that the doctoral hiring trough of the 1980s will be entirely avoided by any likely range of policies adopted and enforced by individual institutions.

At the federal level, adoption of a steady, long-range policy of financing gradual enrichment of student-faculty ratios and a policy of substantial aid to students to bolster enrollment would both help. At the institutional level, a helpful policy would consist in some increase of student-faculty ratios in the late 1970s in anticipation of the desirability of later hiring during what otherwise would be very dry years.

All these comments are directed toward the smoothing of demand. As to the supply side, we present our comments about smoothing in the concluding section of this chapter.

9.5. CONCLUSIONS

Quantitative implications of the sensitivity analysis In Section 9.2 it was shown that academic demand for doctorates could be significantly greater than the numbers projected by Allan Cartter. Some increase will occur if total enrollments follow a more expansionary course than that used by Cartter, and the academic demand for doctorates would also be affected by both enrichments of the student-faculty ratios in the various sectors of American higher education (which will occur only if the financing base improves) and increases over historical values in the percentage of new faculty hired at the doctoral level. This last effect is likely to be induced, at least in part, by the plentiful supply of doctorates seeking college and university teaching positions.

Reduction of student-faculty ratios is often associated with conventionally defined improvements in the quality of higher education. Whether such improvements will be perceived as desirable enough in public policy terms to justify significant increases of public support remains to be seen. (We would be remiss, in this part of the argument, if we did not also comment that much public policy discussion at the present time concerns the issue of increasing the productivity of college and university faculty—which is often taken to mean that student-faculty ratios should be *increased* beyond present levels.)

Our projections of sectoral demand for doctorates (discussed in Section 9.3) are based on judgmental assumptions about the distribution of future enrollment. These projections show a declining share of academic demand for doctorates by universities and a big percentage increase by public four-year colleges. Public two-year colleges are expected to expand their total faculty numbers very substantially, but if they hire no more than the historical percentage of doctorates, their demand influence will remain very small.

The magnitude of the trough of academic demand for doctorates in the 1980s was explored in Section 9.4, with the aim of showing how demand could be smoothed over the whole 20-year interval to 1990. It was pointed out, however, that under the conditions of policy decentralization prevalent in United States higher education, demand smoothing would be very difficult to achieve. Individual institutions, facing the situation in the mid-1980s of inability to hire new young Ph.D.'s, will undoubtedly want to turn increasingly to devices for opening additional vacancies beyond those made available through normal attrition and retirement. Early retirement schemes, already being talked of for the 1970s, would have special pertinence in the 1980s as a means of avoiding a significant period of inability to add young people to faculty cadres.

Implications of the analysis for public decision makers Public decision makers—federal and state—have cause to examine carefully the issues discussed in this chapter. The most fundamental of these, of course, is the question of basic financing of higher education, either through improvement of students' ability to finance their higher education or through increases in institutional support from state and federal sources. It is beyond the scope of this chapter to address the merits of alternative approaches to higher education finance, but it is clear that the outcome of these debates will affect very substantially the academic demand for doctorates in the next two decades. Related to the question of financing are two other issues: that of quality, conventionally approached by weighing the implications of decreasing student-faculty ratios, and that of faculty productivity, often approached by exploring ways of increasing student-faculty ratios.

Public decision makers also have a major stake in the question of support of institutions responsible for conferring the doctorate. Because federal and state actions concerning such support need to be considered jointly with questions of institutional decisions by doctorate-offering universities, we shall discuss the question of governmental policies together with that of institutional decision making.

Implications of the analysis for doctorate-granting institutions and for agencies supporting doctoral education The present analysis does not purport to cover the *total* future demand for Ph.D.'s, nor does it provide information concerning the supply and demand conditions in particular fields or disciplines. Wolfle and Kidd (1971) summarize and cite various recent studies of demand for Ph.D. scientists in governmental and industrial research and professional employment, a very important component of total demand in some fields.

Academic demand for doctorates has typically accounted for widely differing proportions of the appropriate types of employment made available to new doctorates in different fields—from roughly one-third to one-half in the hard sciences to essentially the whole of suitable employment in various specialties in the humanities. Thus the analysis discussed in this chapter should be taken to provide different degrees of definition of future market conditions for new doctorates. (Also, it has not been possible for anyone, including the present authors, to do much with the question of future *student* demand for specialized study in various fields and the influence this may have on the disciplinary composition of academic demand for doctorates.)

What this study does show is that future academic demand for doctorates, without reference to fields of specialization, could vary over a wide range as a function of future policies of higher education finance and future staffing standards and hiring practices of the various types of institutions. If stringent financing conditions prevail in the 1970s, academic demand will be below the level projected in Cartter's study, whereas the demand could, under the revised assumptions we have explored, exceed his estimates by a factor of 2 or 3.

A relatively small number of universities—the AAU member institutions—have historically accounted for approximately two-thirds to three-quarters of doctorates awarded in the United States. These institutions have committed heavy capital and operating resources to the development and operation of doctoral programs. Our analysis shows that the degree of buoyancy of future demand for the educational services at the doctoral level for which these institutions are mainly responsible will be greatly affected by the financing policies of state and federal agencies regarding higher education as a whole.

Our analysis also shows quite clearly two other important demand factors:

1. The 1980s, by reason of an expected downturn in higher education enrollments, will be far worse than the 1970s.
2. The enrollment expansion of the 1970s implies a considerable expansion of total faculty positions in higher education, but the composition of this expansion—weighted toward public four-year colleges and with an even more substantial growth of two-year colleges—compels reexamination of present patterns of doctoral training for academic careers.

We have not made an independent study of the projections of future supply of doctorates. Wolfle and Kidd summarize and compare various of these. Even the most conservative of them, Cartter's and Froomkin's, show continued growth in the number of doctorates awarded each year throughout the 1970s. It can be assumed that, especially for the first half of the decade, supply pressure for academic employment of doctorates will be intense, even if studies such as Cartter's and this one are taken seriously by decision makers. This means that the problem of making more academic jobs available to doctorates and of fitting new doctorates properly for them, in terms of both motivation and training, is of high priority for the doctorate-producing institutions.

The Carnegie Commission had recommended that programs leading to a teaching doctorate, in parallel with the traditional research and scholarly orientation of the Ph.D., be widely adopted. The analysis of sectoral demand in Section 9.3 shows the cogency of this recommendation from the standpoint of many doctoral candidates and many doctorate-producing institutions. This is one very significant means of expanding the market for those who undergo training for academic careers. The projections made in Section 9.3, and other evidence, suggest that a substantial opening of positions in two-year colleges is unlikely to be achieved purely by supply pressure on the part of new Ph.D.'s whose training has not been shaped to equip them for the kinds of jobs that will need to be filled on a large scale in this expanding sector.

Implications for institutions contemplating the establishment of new doctoral programs and public agencies deciding whether to support them Manpower forecasting is a notoriously inaccurate business. It is quite possible that all the current work on both the supply and the demand sides of the doctoral equation will prove in due course to be wrong. For one thing, if the projections now being made and debated are taken seriously, actions will be taken that may invalidate the projections; and, indeed, the projections are partly for the purpose of encouraging the reexamination of policies.

What does seem quite clear, on the basis of present information, is that proposed new doctoral programs should be examined very carefully both by institutions and by funding agencies before they are approved.

Consider the institution that would like to initiate a series of new doctoral programs as soon as it can. As of 1975, it can appoint organizing committees of key faculty to design the content of curriculum. In a year or two a new program could be approved and announced. A trickle of students might be attracted to enroll. Meanwhile, efforts would be made to hire a few "star" faculty to attract other, more junior faculty and to serve also as a basis for attracting research funds from extramural sources. Along the way, perhaps at the time the new program is announced, the plans would be firm enough to show that a new building was needed for the program and to commence the planning and the effort to acquire funding for it.

Five years after this decision, a new building would actually be on stream and operating, so that a definite expansion of the doctoral program's enrollment could now occur. But it is now 1981. An enlarged class of new graduate students, entering in that year, would come on the market in 1986, a year of absolutely negative academic demand for new Ph.D.'s—*and* they would all have to wait until 1988 or 1989 to have a prayer of a chance of an academic position.

Clearly, if this is a trustworthy picture of the future, it would be very unwise for the institution to start, in 1975, with the sequence of efforts and decisions which would produce such a catastrophe for it and its students in the mid-1980s.

Many academic planners and faculty with high aspirations for entry into doctoral training will no doubt react to this as scare talk, but two points are worth keeping in mind. First, Allan Cartter did not invent the decline in the birthrate, and the 18- to 24-year-olds of 1984 are already eight years old in 1974, so that what we are talking about—an enrollment decline in the 1980s—would fail to occur only if increases in college participation rates and in duration of education were enough to overcome a quite steep, absolute, and *known* decline in the age-group population of potential college attendance. Second, many *existing* doctoral programs are small and insecure and should probably expand in order to have more reasonable unit costs and vitality; thus the net expansion potential of existing programs is probably an important factor to be considered. As of 1975, if Cartter's work is to be believed, it would be a grave mistake to start conversations about initiating a Ph.D. program in any field for which academic demand for those emerging from the program is the significant factor unless it can be shown that the field in question or the design of the program exempts it from the bleak pressure of the market that Cartter predicts will obtain. Furthermore, any existing Ph.D. program that is making a claim for a new building or other major resource expansion should, under Cartter's picture of the future, be compelled to produce similar evidence of exemption from average reality.

Implications for students who contemplate doctoral preparation for academic careers The prospective doctoral student can draw some lessons from this analysis concerning his prospects of a future academic career if he completes a doctorate. The unusually gifted student who has a vocation for academic life will not and should not be dissuaded from it by any of the data and projections here. What this study does show is that for the student who has not yet started a doctoral program, the market he or she will face in the early years of an academic career after completing a degree will be difficult—and it is most likely to be most difficult to find a rewarding post in the research-oriented universities. It is likely to be easier for students who would be happy as teachers and who can find a doctoral program that promises to equip them well and put positive effort toward effective placement in a teaching post in a four-year or two-year publicly supported college.

Finally, the doctorate will in the future turn out to be increasingly a course of training that, as law and engineering have already proved to be, serves as a base for a widening variety of career employments. Students who take steps to equip themselves flexibly for a variety of possible careers will be in a better position to compete for employment than those who pick a narrow research field and have only that string to their bow.

10. A Dynamic Input-Output Model

10.1. INTRODUCTION

The dynamics of demand and supply in higher education are influenced by two significant features of the technology of education: (1) the "durability" of the faculty, who form an important part of the capital stock of institutions of higher education, and (2) the long duration of the educational process and, in particular, the great length of time needed to produce new faculty. Thus, counting only the years of formal schooling, it typically takes more than 20 years to produce a new faculty member with a Ph.D. degree, and that faculty member may last for 40 years on the job.

In the previous chapter, we saw how durability of faculty members has the consequence that fluctuations in the *time rate of change* of the demand for total faculty (i.e., the demand for the faculty *stock*) can cause significant fluctuations in the *level* of the demand for *new* faculty (i.e., the demand for the *flow* of faculty). In that analysis, we were concerned with a situation of a potential surplus of new Ph.D.'s. A decline in the rate of increase of the demand for faculty stock will cause an absolute decline in the demand for new faculty with the Ph.D. degree—or possibly even a negative demand. On the other hand, the recent prolonged expansion of higher education has generated an increasing flow of students who aspire to a Ph.D. degree and who have expectations of obtaining academic positions.

In the face of a sharply increasing rate of change in total enrollment, the situation is reversed. The level of demand for new faculty is sharply increased, but unless the increased demand has been anticipated a number of years earlier by an increase in graduate students in the appropriate fields, this increase in demand cannot be met except by competing more strongly with nonacademic sources of demand for new Ph.D.'s, if any, or by drawing older Ph.D.'s back into academic life, if in fact qualified older Ph.D.'s in nonacademic life exist.

Of course, similar considerations apply to the dynamics of supply and demand for any highly educated group, whether they be academic or not. In the case of education, the feedback effects are particularly important because higher education must essentially "feed on itself" for its supply of human inputs. In such a situation, a *dynamic input-output model* can provide a useful tool for the analysis of the changes in inputs and outputs that would be required to effect prescribed changes in activity at different levels. The indirect as well as the direct consequences of such changes in activity can be predicted with the use of a dynamic input-output model, and this can be particularly important in the prevention of bottlenecks.

In this chapter we present a dynamic input-output model and show how it can be used to calculate the dynamic implications of changes in enrollments and of changes in faculty-student ratios. This theory is then applied in Chapter 11 to the calculation of resource requirements for alternative time paths of the introduction of the universal two-year college program, and in Chapter 12 to the calculation of the impact on higher education of alternative plans for compensatory education at the primary and secondary levels.

The reader without a knowledge of matrix algebra can still get some idea of the model from Section 10.2, which explains how the model works for a simplified, two-level system. The general model is presented in Section 10.3. Because of data and computational limitations, most planning exercises must use a finite planning horizon (e.g., 20 years), which raises a problem of how to calculate reasonable terminal conditions, since the capabilities of the system beyond the planning horizon will depend upon the stocks of faculty and students at different levels that exist at the horizon date. Section 10.4 shows how this problem can be resolved in a practical manner by making an approximation in terms of proportional growth beyond the planning horizon. The final section shows how *changes* in dynamic requirements that are implied by alternative plans can be calculated with a minimum of information about the system.

10.2. A SIMPLIFIED MODEL

It may help some readers to see a simplified, two-activity version of the model before the detailed model actually used for computation is set forth. For this purpose, imagine that there are only two levels of education in the system, called "lower" and "higher" and denoted by the index i (= 1,2). The "educational system" is made up of students and teachers. Students are of two types: those who are enrolled in level 1 and those who have completed level 1 and are enrolled in level 2. There is only one type of teacher, and in order to be a teacher, one must have completed the higher level of education (a teacher can teach either level). Assume that (1) a student who completes level 1 may either stay in the system as a student in level 2 or leave the system to join the nonteaching labor force; (2) a student who completes level 2 may either stay in the system as a teacher or leave the system to join the nonteaching labor force; (3) the faculty-student ratios at the two levels may differ from each other, but each one is constant in time; (4) each year a certain fraction of the teachers leave the system (because of death, retirement, etc.); (5) all dropping out of students from the system occurs between levels, not during the school year (thus a student who drops out during a particular level is not counted as having enrolled in that level); and (6) time is divided into discrete periods, indexed by t, and it takes one period of time to complete one level of education. Consider the following variables and parameters:

$X_1(t)$ = the number of persons in the system at the beginning of period t who have completed level 1 (these are of course the students who are beginning their studies at the second level).

$X_2(t)$ = the number of persons in the system at the beginning of period t who have completed level 2 (this is the total stock of teachers).

$Y_i(t)$ = the number of students enrolled in, and graduating from, level i during period t ($i = 1,2$).

$F_i(t)$ = the number of persons in the system who have completed level i and who leave the system at the end of period t to join the nonteaching labor force. (For $i = 1$ this can include only students currently graduating from level 1; for $i = 2$ this may include both students graduating from level 2 and teachers leaving the system to join the nonteaching labor force.) The $F_i(t)$ are also called "final demands."

m = the fraction of teachers in any period who do *not* leave the system at the end of the period because of death or retirement (this may include, however, some teachers who leave the system to join the nonteaching labor force).

a_i = the teacher-student ratio in level i ($i = 1,2$).

There are two types of relationships in the model, "accounting" and "technological." The (intertemporal) accounting relationships are:

$$Y_1(t) = F_1(t) + X_1(t+1) \tag{1}$$

$$Y_2(t) + mX_2(t) = F_2(t) + X_2(t+1) \tag{2}$$

Equation (1) states that at the end of any period, the students completing level 1 either go on to level 2 studies in the next period or leave the system to join the nonteaching labor force. In equation (2) the quantity $Y_2(t) + mX_2(t)$ is the number of persons in the education sector who have completed level 2 and are surviving into period $(t + 1)$. Equation (2) states that this number is divided between (1) the outflow from the education system to the nonteaching labor force and (2) the stock of teachers for the next period.

The technological relationships are:

$$X_1(t) = Y_2(t) \tag{3}$$

$$X_2(t) = a_1Y_1(t) + a_2Y_2(t) \tag{4}$$

Equation (3) states that there are no student dropouts during the second level, and equation (4) describes the determination of the teacher inputs in any one period in terms of the student enrollments and the teacher-student ratios at the two levels.

Notice that at the second level the model explicitly recognizes two types of inputs, namely, students who have completed the first level and teachers. At the first level, only teacher inputs appear explicitly; it is implicitly understood that the student inputs come from some pool of "uneducated" persons (e.g., five-year-olds who have not yet attended primary school).

To illustrate how the model might be used for planning or projecting, suppose that the planning interval covers the periods $t = 1, \ldots, T$ (where T is the planning horizon). The variables of the system, over time, are then:

$$\left.\begin{array}{l} X_i(1), \ldots, X_i(T+1) \\ Y_i(1), \ldots, Y_i(T) \\ F_i(1), \ldots, F_i(T) \end{array}\right\} \quad i = 1,2$$

There are therefore $2(3T + 1)$ variables in the system and $4T$ equations. In order for the system to be determinate, some of the variables must be specified exogenously. For example, one might treat the lower-level enrollments as exogenously determined by demographic forces and the final demands for higher-level graduates as determined exogenously by economic forces. If one specifies the first-level enrollments $Y_1(1), \ldots, Y_1(T)$, the second-level outflows (or final demands) $F_2(1), \ldots, F_2(T)$, and the input requirements at the beginning of the first posthorizon year $X_1(T + 1)$ and $X_2(T + 1)$, then one can solve the equations for the remaining $4T$ variables: teacher requirements; student inputs to, and outputs from, the second level; and outflows of students graduating from the first level (all for $t = 1, \ldots, T$). Indeed, it is a simple matter to solve the system of equations recursively, starting with period T and working backward to period 1. It is clear, of course, that other divisions of the variables into exogenous and endogenous groups would be possible. Also, it would be easy to allow the coefficients a_i and m to depend upon t.

Notice that no nonnegativity conditions have been imposed on any of the variables. Therefore, for some given target values of the exogenous variables, it might turn out that some of the resulting endogenous variables would be negative. This might indicate that the assumed targets were not feasible or that some additional sources of supply, or activities, should be considered besides those explicitly described by the model. It might also indicate that some nonlinearities should be introduced into the model to make it more realistic (e.g., economies of scale).

The reader may wonder how the initial posthorizon inputs $X_1(T + 1)$ and $X_2(T + 1)$ can be treated as exogenous, since the requirements for these inputs depend upon the evolution of the system after period $T + 1$ and this evolution is not described by the model. One way out of this difficulty is to make some simplifying assumption about the posthorizon evolution of the system—for example, that inputs and outputs will grow proportionately at a rate equal to the rate of growth of the population (or labor force). An exposition of this method is given in Section 10.4. In any case, numerical computation with the model indicates that the projections produced by the model for the earlier periods in the planning interval are relatively insensitive to posthorizon assumptions if the horizon is sufficiently distant.

10.3. A GENERAL DYNAMIC INPUT-OUTPUT MODEL[1]

We now present the general model actually used in Chapters 11 and 12.[1] Suppose that the educational system has n activities $(i = 1, \ldots, n)$, e.g., the 24 activities listed in Table 95 in Chapter 11. Corresponding to these n activities are n types of persons in the system; activity i produces persons of type i as its sole (new) output. For each time period t, let $X(t)$, $Y(t)$, and $F(t)$ be the vectors of inputs, outputs, and final demands, respectively. The accounting and technological relationships corresponding to equations (1) through (4) are:

$$Y(t) + MX(t) = F(t) + X(t+1) \tag{5}$$

$$X(t) = AY(t) \tag{6}$$

where A is the $n \times n$ matrix of input-output coefficients and M is a diagonal matrix of "survival coefficients." (Indeed, the diagonal elements of M will be zero for all rows and columns corresponding to student types.) For example, in our simplified, two-activity model the matrixes A and M were

$$A = \begin{bmatrix} 0 & 1 \\ a_1 & a_2 \end{bmatrix} \qquad M = \begin{bmatrix} 0 & 0 \\ 0 & m \end{bmatrix}$$

Suppose now that the n types (and activities) are partitioned into two groups such that for all types in the first group the outputs (enrollments) are given exogenously, whereas for all types in the second group the final demands are given exogenously. If the vectors and matrixes are partitioned correspondingly, then equations (5) and (6) become:

$$Y_1(t) + M_1X_1(t) = F_1(t) + X_1(t+1) \tag{7}$$

[1]The reader who is unfamiliar with matrix algebra should skip the rest of the present chapter.

$$Y_2(t) + M_2X_2(t) = F_2(t) + X_2(t+1) \tag{8}$$

$$X_1(t) = A_{11}Y_1(t) + A_{12}Y_2(t) \tag{9}$$

$$X_2(t) = A_{21}Y_1(t) + A_{22}Y_2(t) \tag{10}$$

Given the vectors $Y_1(1), \ldots, Y_1(T)$, $F_2(1), \ldots, F_2(T)$, $X_1(T+1)$, $X_2(T+1)$, one can solve equations (7) through (10) recursively as follows:

$$X_2(t) = (I_2 + A_{22}M_2)^{-1} \{A_{21}Y_1(t) + A_{22}[F_2(t) + X_2(t+1)]\} \tag{11}$$

$$Y_2(t) = F_2(t) + X_2(t+1) - M_2X_2(t) \tag{12}$$

$$X_1(t) = A_{11}Y_1(t) + A_{12}Y_2(t) \tag{13}$$

$$F_1(t) = Y_1(t) + M_1X_1(t) - X_1(t+1) \tag{14}$$

where $t = T, T-1, \ldots, 2, 1$.

10.4. COMPUTATION OF INITIAL POSTHORIZON INPUTS

We have already noted in Section 10.2 that, strictly speaking, the initial posthorizon inputs $X_i(T+1)$ cannot be treated as exogenous since the requirements for these inputs depend upon the evolution of the system after the period $T+1$. In the computations of Chapters 11 and 12 we shall compute the initial posthorizon inputs by assuming proportional growth at a constant rate after the horizon period. In practice, one can make the projections for any fixed initial segment of the planning interval relatively insensitive to the assumptions about the posthorizon evolution of the system by taking the horizon T to be sufficiently distant.

Our proportional growth assumption is, for $t \geqq T+1$,

$$X(t) = (1+g)^{(t-T-1)}X$$
$$Y(t) = (1+g)^{(t-T-1)}Y$$
$$F(t) = (1+g)^{(t-T-1)}F$$

where $X = (T+1)$ $Y = Y(T+1)$, $F = F(T+1)$, and g is the posthorizon rate of growth.

Corresponding to equations (5) and (6), we have the following equations for X, Y, and F:

$$Y + MX = F + (1+g)X \tag{15}$$

$$X = AY \tag{16}$$

Corresponding to equations (7) through (10) we have:

$$Y_1 + M_1X_1 = F_1 + (1 + g)X_1 \tag{17}$$

$$Y_2 + M_2X_2 = F_2 + (1 + g)X_2 \tag{18}$$

$$X_1 = A_{11}Y_1 + A_{12}Y_2 \tag{19}$$

$$X_2 = A_{21}Y_1 + A_{22}Y_2 \tag{20}$$

Equations (17) and (18) can be rewritten as

$$Y_1 + M^*_1X_1 = F_1, \tag{21}$$

$$Y_2 + M^*_2X_2 = F_2, \tag{22}$$

where

$$M^*_1 = M_1 - (1 + g)I_1, \tag{23}$$

and $\quad M^*_2 = M_2 - (1 + g)I_2.$

It is straightforward to solve equations (21), (22), (19), and (20) to obtain equations corresponding to equations (11) through (14):

$$X_2 = (I_2 + A_{22}M^*_2)^{-1}(A_{21}Y_1 + A_{22}F_2) \tag{24}$$

$$Y_2 = F_2 - M^*_2X_2 \tag{25}$$

$$X_1 = A_{11}Y_1 + A_{12}Y_2 \tag{26}$$

$$F_1 = Y_1 + M^*_1X_1 \tag{27}$$

We now examine how the errors in the variables at a given date t depend on an error in the initial posthorizon inputs. We shall show that the errors at t are linear functions of the errors at T and that, roughly speaking, the coefficients in these linear functions decline to zero geometrically as $(T - t)$ increases.

An inspection of equations (11) through (14) reveals that the endogenous variables at date t depend on the endogenous variables at date $(t + 1)$ through the vector $X_2(t + 1)$ and that this relationship is linear. Hence it suffices to consider the relationship between the error in $X_2(t)$ and the error in $X_2(t + 1)$. Let $\Delta X_2(t)$ and $\Delta X_2(t + 1)$ denote the errors in $X_2(t)$ and $X_2(t + 1)$, respectively. Equation (11) implies that

$$\begin{aligned} X_2(t) &= C\Delta X_2(t+1), \\ C &= (I_2 + A_{22}M_2)^{-1}A_{22}, \end{aligned} \tag{28}$$

which in turn implies that, for any nonnegative integer K,

$$X_2(t) = C^K \Delta X_2(t+K). \tag{29}$$

In particular, if we set $K = T + 1 - t$, we get

$$X_2(t) = C^{(T+1-t)} X_2(T+1). \tag{30}$$

For realistic values of the parameters of the system, i.e., for realistic matrixes A_{22} and M_2, the matrix C will have norm strictly less than unity, and therefore C^K will converge to zero geometrically.

To apply this result, it is useful to distinguish an "actual planning horizon" T_0 from the "computational horizon" T. For example, if we were interested in projections of the endogenous variables for the period 1970–1985, we would take T_0 to be 1985 and T to be, say, 1999. This means that we would have to project the exogenous variables from 1970 to 1999 and then assume proportional growth at a constant rate after the year 2000. If the year 1999 is a suitable choice for T, then the projections of the endogenous variables for the entire period 1970–1985 will be relatively insensitive to errors in the assumptions about growth beyond the year 2000. Just how large T must be can be determined by examination of the matrix C and by the size of the errors one is willing to tolerate. For example, in the computations of Chapters 11 and 12, every element of C^{14} was zero to six significant figures.

10.5. PLAN INCREMENTS

In Chapters 11 and 12 we shall examine how a particular projection is affected by changes in the projection of the exogenous variables of the input-output coefficients. Thus in Chapter 11 we shall examine the effects of altering the projection of the exogenously given enrollments $Y_1(t)$, whereas in Chapter 12 we shall examine the effects of altering the matrix A_{21} of faculty-student ratios. In each case, a sequence of changes in the exogenous variables or input-output coefficients will result in a sequence of corresponding changes in the projections of the endogenous variables. These resulting changes will be called the *plan increments*.

We shall now show how to calculate the plan increments associated with a given alteration in the projection of the enrollments $Y_1(t)$. In particular, we shall show that these plan increments depend neither on the base projection of $Y_1(t)$ nor on the projected values of the other exogenous variables. A similar analysis would be applicable to changes in any of the exogenous variables.

We shall also show how to calculate the plan increments associated with a given alteration in the projection of the matrix A_{21}. In this case, the plan increments depend on the projection of the exogenous enrollments $Y_1(t)$, but not on the projections of the other exogenous variables.

Suppose, then, that certain coordinates of the vectors $Y_1(t)$ are changed, but that the vectors $F_2(t)$ are left unchanged. We wish to calculate the induced changes in the vectors $Y_2(t)$, $F_1(t)$, $X_1(t)$, and $X_2(t)$. Since the system of equations (11) through (14) is linear, these changes are linear functions of the changes in the vectors $Y_1(t)$:

$$\Delta X_2(t) = (I_2 + A_{22}M_2)^{-1}[A_{21}\Delta Y_1(t) + A_{22}\Delta X_2(t+1)] \quad (31)$$

$$\Delta Y_2(t) = \Delta X_2(t+1) - M_2\Delta X_2(t) \quad (32)$$

$$\Delta X_1(t) = A_{11}\Delta Y_1(t) + A_{12}\Delta Y_2(t) \quad (33)$$

$$\Delta F_1(t) = \Delta Y_1(t) + M_1\Delta X_1(t) - \Delta X_1(t+1) \quad (34)$$

Notice that we need to know the changes $\Delta X_1(T+1)$ and $\Delta X_2(T+1)$ in posthorizon inputs, but *we do not need to know any of the base values of the variables as they were before the changes induced by the plan*. (This is a consequence, of course, of the linearity of the model.) Furthermore, a similar result holds for the initial posthorizon inputs. Corresponding to equations (24) through (27), we have:

$$\Delta X_2 = (I_2 + A_{22}M^*_2)^{-1}(A_{21}\Delta Y_1) \quad (35)$$

$$\Delta Y_2 = -M^*_2\Delta X_2 \quad (36)$$

$$\Delta X_1 = A_{11}\Delta Y_1 + A_{12}\Delta Y_2 \quad (37)$$

$$\Delta F_1 = \Delta Y_1 + M^*_1\Delta X_1 \quad (38)$$

Again, if the only exogenous variables changed in the posthorizon period are the coordinates of Y_1, then the increments in $X_1(T+1)$ and $X_2(T+1)$ depend only on the increment in Y_1.

Consider now the effects of an alteration of the matrix A_{21}. An inspection of equations (11) through (14) shows that the matrix A_{21} appears only in equation (11), and we have already noted (see Section 10.4) that the endogenous variables at date t depend on the endogenous variables at date $(t + 1)$ through the vector $X_2(t + 1)$. Therefore, let us replace the matrix A_{21} in equation (11) by the matrix $(A_{21} + \Delta A_{21})$; the resulting increments in the vectors $X_2(t)$ will be given recursively by

$$\Delta X_2(t) = (I_2 + A_{22}M_2)^{-1}[(\Delta A_{21})Y_1(t) + A_{22}\Delta X_2(t + 1)] \quad (39)$$

Similarly, from equation (24) we see that the resulting increment in the initial posthorizon input X_2 is given by

$$\Delta X_2 = (I_2 + A_{22}M^*{}_2)^{-1}(\Delta A_{21})Y \quad (40)$$

The remaining plan increments can be calculated from equations (32) through (34) and (36) through (38). Thus in this case the plan increments depend on the projection of the exogenous enrollments $Y_1(t)$, but not on the projections of the other exogenous variables.

11. *Resource Requirements for a Universal Two-Year College Program*

11.1. INTRODUCTION AND SUMMARY

The coming two decades will probably see a decline in the rate of growth of higher education in the United States. In some fields enrollments will even level off, whereas in others, e.g., the health fields, enrollments may continue to expand significantly. If the percentage of high school graduates who go on to college remains stable, then purely demographic developments will cause undergraduate enrollments to level off or even decline at some point (see Chapter 9). Expansion is likely to occur, however, in undergraduate programs with high academic entrance requirements and in relatively cheaper, perhaps more technically oriented two-year colleges with few entrance requirements other than high school graduation (see Chapter 3 and Miller and Radner, 1975). The latter development, the growth of the junior college system, may well have an important role in increasing equality of educational opportunity, since it not only will make a modest amount of postsecondary education available to almost all high school graduates, but also will provide an additional chance for talented students with poor educational backgrounds to overcome their initial educational handicaps and go on to qualify for entrance to four-year colleges and to universities.

In 1969, over 60 percent of all high school graduates went on to some type of postsecondary education.[1] In this chapter we explore the consequences—in terms of enrollments, teacher requirements, and costs—of bringing the nationwide enroll-

[1]This percentage varied greatly, however, from one state to another. In 1963, the most recent year in which states' residents can be accurately estimated, California ranked highest, with 80 percent of high school graduates enrolled in college, and Maine ranked lowest, with 31 percent. See U.S. Office of Education (1965, p. 89).

ment in the first two years of college up to a level of 90 percent of all high school graduates. For convenience, we shall call this general enrollment target the "universal two-year college program," even though we recognize that it falls short of being a truly universal two-year college plan. The plan should be seen as an exercise that coordinates the different portions of the higher education sector and assesses the resource levels and timing required to accomplish the objective. We use the dynamic input-output model discussed in the previous chapter to forecast the consequences of putting the universal two-year college program into effect under alternative time schedules. It is, of course, debatable whether such a target is optimal or even desirable. We believe, however, that such a target has enough merit to make the exercise interesting.

Briefly, the universal two-year college program's enrollment increase is composed of (1) an increase in the nation's freshman enrollment to 90 percent of the nation's high school graduates, (2) an increase in sophomore enrollment determined by the continuing freshman students, and (3) an increase in upper-division and graduate enrollment sufficient to produce the additional faculty required by the plan's increase in freshman and sophomore enrollment. Actually, three alternative plans are presented. They differ in the length of time necessary to achieve the targeted enrollment rate; we call them the 5-, 10-, and 15-year plans. For each plan, it is assumed that 1972 is the first year in which enrollment is increased. The enrollment calculations show the required manpower necessary for the universal two-year program. These calculations, it must be stressed, are based on a single educational technology, defined as a teacher-student ratio by faculty degree, for each higher education activity; we do not consider questions of allocative efficiency, or of technological change, or of increases in demand for upper-division enrollment arising out of the universal lower-division enrollment experience. An example of technological change is treated in the next chapter.

In addition to the human resources, the monetary costs of the plans are also estimated. These cost estimates do not explicitly take account of expected differences in demand and supply conditions that will arise; rather, they are based on public institution cost-per-student estimates for the 1967 academic year. (Costs estimates will be in 1966–67 dollars.)

In order to get a better feeling for the magnitude of the additional enrollments and resource requirements implied by a given plan, it is useful to have some basis of comparison. One such basis is suggested by the fact that not only have enrollments at the different levels of higher education been rising in absolute numbers, but enrollment *rates* have also been rising. We define (for each level and in each year) the *trend increment* in enrollment to be the difference between (1) the projection of enrollment based upon extrapolation of historic enrollment rate trends and (2) a projection based upon an estimated constant 1972 enrollment rate. For each plan we shall compare the increments in enrollment implied by the plan, to be called the *plan increments,* with the corresponding trend increments. We shall do the same for increments in resource requirements (teacher stocks and dollar costs).

Trends based on the set of institutions that brought forth higher education's "golden age" probably represent in themselves an effort greater than society is willing to carry forward into the last half of the seventies and the decade of the eighties. With the approach to a labor-market equilibrium, priorities change. Diminished additions to public subsidies and an increased awareness of the relationship between the level of public subsidies and the viability of a large portion of the private institutions in the higher education sector are already bringing new financial arrangements that will result in shifting the costs of higher education more onto the future beneficiaries of the experience. The comparison of the plan increments with the trend increments does provide us, though, a measure of the relative effort (relative to the "golden age" trend) society would have to make if it were to attempt to solve the equality of educational opportunity problem with the universal two-year strategy.

The major results of the study can be summarized as follows:

1 When all plans are in full operation, about 1½ million additional students are enrolled in higher education. The plans imply about a 13½ percent expansion in undergraduate education.

2 During the start-up years, the 5-year plan requires roughly 16 times more enrollment than is expected to occur from trend increases in enrollment during the period. The comparable figures for the 10- and 15-year plans are, roughly, seven times and four times, respectively.

When the 15-year plan is at full operation, plan enrollments are still 3½ times the expected trend increments.

3 The timing of requirements for the three plans suggests that, given the demographic characteristics of the United States population, the faster start-up plans are somewhat wasteful in their resource usage.

4 Graduate enrollment required to service the plans is relatively small. In the initial year, the 5- and the 15-year plans require a 3.8 percent and a 1.5 percent initial expansion, respectively, but by full operation only .5 percent graduate expansion is required.

5 The plans cost about $1.5 billion when in full operation. As the enrollment figures suggest, when in full operation the costs of freshman and sophomore enrollment comprise 97 percent of the plans' costs. Using 1967 as a comparative case, this $1½ billion amounts to an 18½ percent expansion in total higher education costs. These figures may be somewhat conservative, though, for they do not include subsidies that might have to be paid to potential enrollees to increase student demand up to the required target enrollment percentage.

6 It seems that there are no major feasibility problems associated with the plans other than that of creating the target enrollment percentages.

Five sections follow: In Section 11.2 the universal two-year program is quantitatively defined, and the plan increments in lower-division enrollments are computed for the years 1972 through 2000. This section also includes discussion of state-by-state measurement of enrollment performance.

In Section 11.3 we briefly define the universal plans in terms of the dynamic input-output model of Chapter 10, and in Section 11.4 we discuss the assumptions employed to estimate the technology and survival coefficients of the model. The faculty-student ratios presented in Chapter 7 play a principal role here.

Enrollment results, comparisons between plan increments and trend increments, and plan feasibility are discussed in Section 11.5. The exercise concludes with cost estimates in Section 11.6.

11.2. UNIVERSAL TWO-YEAR ENROLLMENT DEFICITS

For comparative purposes, and to establish in our own minds what might conceivably be a feasible universal enrollment target, we computed an enrollment performance measure for each state. The enrollment performance measure we used was the ratio of a state's first-time resident higher education enrollment to its high school graduate population. As an aid in estimating the state's resident first-time enrollment, each state's first-time enrollment figure was corrected with the latest (1963) migration rates on interstate higher education attendance. Apparently, these interstate migration rates have not held constant. Both Hawaii and Arizona had performance measures of over 100 percent. Furthermore, Delaware, Arizona, and California were over the 90 percentile range. See Table 89 for enrollment figures

TABLE 89 ***Freshman enrollment by state, 1969 (in thousands)***

	*(1) 1969 first-time enrollment**	*(2) 1969 first-time resident enrollment†*	*(3) 1968–1969 public high school graduates‡*	*(4) 1968–1969 private high school graduates§*
Aggregate United States	1,983.5	1,972.0	2,685.5	310.0
Connecticut	28.4	37.9	35.4	7.9
Maine	6.9	6.2	14.2	3.1
Massachusetts	71.5	60.7	63.4	17.3
New Hampshire	7.2	5.3	9.1	2.6
Rhode Island	13.6	11.2	11.2	2.5
Vermont	6.4	3.0	6.5	1.7
Delaware	7.1	7.6	6.9	1.0
Washington, D.C.	13.3	6.3	6.9	1.9
Maryland	31.1	35.6	45.7	6.5
New Jersey	51.8	86.1	89.6	13.3
New York	156.7	186.2	214.7	42.3
Pennsylvania	90.5	91.2	160.2	72.1
Alabama	23.9	24.9	51.0	1.8
Arkansas	13.8	14.0	26.6	.7
Florida	54.1	58.0	78.3	3.2
Georgia	25.9	25.0	55.3	2.1
Kentucky	22.6	20.1	37.5	5.1
Louisiana	26.7	26.1	49.8	6.3
Mississippi	21.5	20.1	32.8	1.0
North Carolina	49.5	39.7	71.4	1.1
South Carolina	22.5	19.8	39.7	.8
Tennessee	30.3	26.4	52.0	2.7

TABLE 89 ***(continued)***

	(1) 1969 first-time enrollment*	(2) 1969 first-time resident enrollment†	(3) 1968–1969 public high school graduates‡	(4) 1968–1969 private high school graduates§
Virginia	37.0	39.3	59.4	3.9
West Virginia	16.4	14.6	31.2	.8
Illinois	113.3	130.7	124.4	25.2
Indiana	41.5	35.1	72.3	5.8
Michigan	86.0	83.5	119.0	17.7
Ohio	89.8	86.0	140.0	19.3
Wisconsin	50.0	45.9	64.7	11.5
Iowa	29.4	26.2	47.5	5.6
Kansas	27.4	24.8	35.2	2.6
Minnesota	37.0	36.2	62.3	6.6
Missouri	43.7	39.0	54.3	8.2
Nebraska	16.3	14.5	21.4	3.0
North Dakota	8.2	8.5	10.8	1.2
South Dakota	7.8	7.2	12.6	.8
Arizona	28.5	25.4	25.6	1.4
New Mexico	9.1	9.1	18.7	.8
Oklahoma	26.2	24.9	35.8	.8
Texas	94.1	90.8	141.1	5.9
Colorado	26.4	22.7	32.8	2.1
Idaho	9.2	9.9	12.2	.3
Montana	7.4	8.4	12.0	1.1
Utah	16.4	11.0	18.5	.4
Wyoming	5.4	6.0	5.7	.2
Alaska	1.5	2.9	3.4	.2
California	270.3	267.3	266.7	20.3
Hawaii	11.2	14.5	9.8	1.9
Nevada	2.8	3.7	5.4	.3
Oregon	26.9	25.4	33.2	1.7
Washington	48.1	47.2	51.6	2.8

*National Center for Educational Statistics (1969, p. 9).

†Column (1) times export-import coefficient. See Table 90.

‡Barr and Foster (1970, p. 23).

§Simon and Grant (1970).

and Table 90 for interstate migration rates. Table 91 displays the ranked states' performances.

A target figure of 90 percent enrollment was selected as the "universal rate." This was rather arbitrary on our part. It was chosen before our demand calculations were completed, and it now seems a little high to us. But these feelings are somewhat tempered by the fact that five states, according to our best estimates, are already doing better than this universal rate.

We computed three plans. They differ in their start-up intervals, which are 5, 10, and 15 years. For each plan, the annual target enrollment rate was determined as the difference between the 1972 base-year national enrollment performance measure—62.6 percent of high school graduates—and the target figure of 90 percent, divided by the number of start-up years and incrementally added to the previous year's rate. For example, the incremental enrollment for the five-year plan was 5.5 percent per annum. Thus the 1973 five-year plan's enrollment rate was .681.

These plan enrollment rates were then applied to projections of high school graduates, and each plan's annual freshman enrollment increments were determined. We estimated the attrition rate of freshmen to be 36.8 percent (see Miller and Radner, 1975). Sophomore enrollment was computed by multiplying the implied freshmen survival rate of .632 by the plan's previous year's "incremental freshman enrollments." These results are summarized in Table 92 and reported in more detail in Tables 93A–93C.

In addition to the arbitrariness of the target enrollment rate, concentrating on freshman enrollment might be considered arbitrary as well. This consideration led us to compute an alternative universal enrollment deficit, which we shall now describe.[2] However, enrollment deficits calculated with another

[2]For other calculations of state enrollment achievement indices, see Bowker (1965) and Harris (1962). Unfortunately, since their objectives differed from ours, neither of their indices appropriately measures our version of the appropriate two-year college enrollment deficits. For example, Bowker excluded part-time enrollment and did not fully include enrollment in community college technical programs, while over the 1955–1965 decade, according to our calculations based on HEW's *Projections of Educational Statistics to 1975–76,* between one-fifth and one-fourth of two-year college enrollment was part-time. Harris investigated only public institutions. Close to 30 percent of undergraduate degree-credit enrollment, according to HEW's *Projections of Educational Statistics to 1975–76* (p. 18), was under private control.

TABLE 90 ***Interstate migration rate corrections***

State (by region)	*(1) Fall 1963 first-time higher education enrollment state's residents (in thousands)*	*(2) Fall 1963 first-time higher education enrollment in state (in thousands)*	*(3) Export-import characteristic**
Connecticut	16.1	12.1	1.3
Maine	3.4	3.8	.9
Massachusetts	30.8	36.3	.8
New Hampshire	2.5	3.4	.7
Rhode Island	3.4	4.7	.8
Vermont	1.6	3.5	.5
Delaware	2.2	2.0	1.1
Washington, D.C.	3.2	6.8	.5
Maryland	17.0	14.9	1.1
New Jersey	34.5	20.8	1.7
New York	80.2	67.5	1.2
Pennsylvania	47.9	47.5	1.0
Alabama	10.9	10.4	1.0
Arkansas	9.3	9.2	1.0
Florida	28.7	28.8	1.1
Georgia	13.4	13.9	1.0
Kentucky	13.0	14.6	.9
Louisiana	15.7	16.1	1.0
Mississippi	11.3	12.1	.9
North Carolina	17.8	22.2	.8
South Carolina	8.6	9.7	.9
Tennessee	15.3	17.5	.9
Virginia	17.3	16.3	1.1
West Virginia	7.6	8.6	.9
Illinois	64.0	55.5	1.2
Indiana	22.5	26.7	.8
Michigan	40.9	41.2	1.0
Ohio	45.3	47.3	1.0
Wisconsin	20.6	22.5	.9
Iowa	16.2	18.1	.9
Kansas	14.9	16.4	.9

TABLE 90 ***(continued)***

State (by region)	*(1) Fall 1963 first-time higher education enrollment state's residents (in thousands)*	*(2) Fall 1963 first-time higher education enrollment in state (in thousands)*	*(3) Export-import characteristic**
Minnesota	19.9	29.3	1.0
Missouri	22.9	25.7	.9
Nebraska	9.1	10.2	.9
North Dakota	4.4	4.3	1.0
South Dakota	4.5	4.9	.9
Arizona	9.4	10.6	.9
New Mexico	4.6	4.6	1.0
Oklahoma	14.5	15.3	1.0
Texas	52.3	54.2	1.0
Colorado	10.7	12.4	.9
Idaho	5.5	5.1	1.1
Montana	4.8	4.3	1.1
Utah	6.8	10.2	.7
Wyoming	2.4	2.2	1.1
Alaska	.8	.4	1.9
California	152.0	153.6	1.0
Hawaii	4.6	3.5	1.3
Nevada	2.1	1.6	1.3
Oregon	12.1	12.8	.9
Washington	20.2	20.6	1.0

NOTE: All figures are rounded to one decimal place.
*Column (1) divided by col. (2).

TABLE 91 ***1969 freshman enrollment rates and deficits by state, ranked by rate***

State	*Rate*	*Deficit (in thousands)*	*State*	*Rate*	*Deficit (in thousands)*
Hawaii	1.241		*Texas*	.618	41.5
Wyoming	1.002		*Michigan*	.611	39.5
Delaware	.964		*Wisconsin*	.603	21.9
Arizona	.941		*Nebraska*	.594	7.5
California	.931		*Mississippi*	.591	10.4
Connecticut	.874	5.5	*Utah*	.580	5.9
Illinois	.874	3.9	*North Carolina*	.547	25.6
Washington	.867	1.8	*Ohio*	.540	55.8
New Jersey	.836	6.6	*South Dakota*	.534	4.9
Rhode Island	.821	1.1	*Minnesota*	.525	25.8
Idaho	.798	1.3	*Arizona*	.514	10.5
Arkansas	.789	.4	*Iowa*	.493	21.6
Massachusetts	.752	11.9	*South Carolina*	.489	16.6
Oregon	.727	6.0	*Tennessee*	.483	22.8
New York	.725	45.0	*Alabama*	.472	22.6
Washington, D.C.	.715	1.6	*Kentucky*	.472	18.2
North Dakota	.715	2.2	*New Mexico*	.468	8.4
Florida	.712	15.3	*Louisiana*	.465	24.4
Maryland	.681	11.4	*West Virginia*	.456	14.2
Oklahoma	.680	7.7	*New Hampshire*	.454	5.2
Kansas	.656	9.2	*Indiana*	.449	35.2
Nevada	.653	1.4	*Georgia*	.437	26.6
Colorado	.651	8.7	*Pennsylvania*	.393	117.8
Montana	.639	3.4	*Vermont*	.368	4.4
Missouri	.624	17.2	*Maine*	.356	9.4
Virginia	.620	17.1			
ALL STATES	.662				

NOTE: *Rates* computed as 1969 first-time resident enrollment divided by total 1968–1969 high school graduates, col. (2) divided by cols. (3) and (4), Table 89. *Deficits* are .90 less enrollment rate times total 1969 high school graduates, cols. (3) and (4), Table 89.

TABLE 92 ***Plan increment for 5-, 10-, and 15-year plans (in thousands)***

	5-year plan		*10-year plan*		*15-year plan*	
Year	$Y_{13}(t)$	$Y_{14}(t)$	$Y_{13}(t)$	$Y_{14}(t)$	$Y_{13}(t)$	$Y_{14}(t)$
1972						
1973	179.5		88.1		58.7	
1974	365.3	113.4	184.3	55.7	124.0	37.2
1975	563.5	230.9	281.7	116.5	189.0	78.4
1976	762.2	356.1	379.4	178.0	254.1	119.4
1977	963.4	481.7	481.7	239.8	319.3	160.6
1978	986.9	608.9	590.7	304.4	396.2	202.2
1979	999.3	623.7	700.3	373.3	466.8	250.4
1980	987.0	631.6	789.0	442.6	526.0	295.0
1981	977.6	623.8	877.7	498.7	588.7	332.4
1982	955.4	617.8	955.4	554.7	638.1	372.1
1983	914.1	603.8	914.1	603.8	670.6	403.3
1984	880.6	577.7	880.6	577.7	707.1	423.8
1985	859.0	556.5	859.0	556.5	746.2	446.9
1986	858.3	542.9	858.3	542.9	801.9	471.6
1987	862.3	524.4	862.3	542.4	862.3	506.8
1988	863.2	545.0	863.2	545.0	863.2	545.0
1989	882.1	545.5	882.1	545.5	882.1	545.0
1990	905.7	557.5	905.7	557.5	905.7	557.5
1991	929.2	572.4	929.2	572.4	929.2	572.4
1992	953.0	587.3	953.0	587.3	953.0	587.3
1993	976.5	602.3	976.5	602.3	976.5	602.3
1994	1,000.0	617.1	1,000.0	617.0	1,000.0	617.1
1995	1,023.7	632.0	1,023.7	632.0	1,023.7	632.0
1996	1,048.8	647.0	1,048.8	647.0	1,048.8	647.0
1997	1,073.7	662.8	1,073.7	662.8	1,073.7	662.8
1998	1,098.1	678.6	1,098.1	678.6	1,098.1	678.6
1999	1,121.6	694.0	1,121.6	694.0	1,121.6	694.0
2000	1,143.2	708.9	1,143.2	708.9	1,143.2	708.9

NOTE: $Y_{13}(t)$ denotes plan-incremental freshman enrollment for year t. $Y_{14}(t)$ denotes plan-incremental sophomore enrollment for year t.

TABLE 93A ***Universal two-year plan increments: 5-year plan***

	(1) Target enrollment rate*	(2) Increment in rate†	(3) Projected high school graduates (in thousands)‡	(4) $Y_{13}(t)$ Plan increment for freshmen (in thousands)§	(5) $Y_{14}(t)$ Plan increment for sophomores (in thousands)¶
1972	.626		3,179.4		
1973	.681	.055	3,264.2	179.5	
1974	.735	.109	3,351.6	365.3	113.4
1975	.790	.164	3,435.7	563.5	230.9
1976	.845	.219	3,480.4	762.2	356.1
1977	.900	.274	3,515.9	963.4	481.7
1978	.900	.274	3,601.9	986.9	608.9
1979	.900	.274	3,647.2	999.3	623.7
1980	.900	.274	3,602.6	987.1	631.6
1981	.900	.274	3,568.0	977.6	623.8
1982	.900	.274	3,486.9	955.5	617.8
1983	.900	.274	3,336.2	914.1	603.8
1984	.900	.274	3,214.0	880.6	577.7
1985	.900	.274	3,135.2	859.0	556.5
1986	.900	.274	3,132.4	858.3	542.9
1987	.900	.274	3,147.2	862.3	542.4
1988	.900	.274	3,150.2	863.2	545.0
1989	.900	.274	3,219.4	863.2	545.0
1990	.900	.274	3,305.4	905.7	557.5
1991	.900	.274	3,391.2	929.2	572.4
1992	.900	.274	3,478.2	953.0	587.3
1993	.900	.274	3,563.7	976.5	602.3
1994	.900	.274	3,649.5	1,000.0	617.1
1995	.900	.274	3,736.0	1,023.7	632.0
1996	.900	.274	3,827.8	1,048.8	647.0
1997	.900	.274	3,918.5	1,073.7	662.8

TABLE 93A ***(continued)***

	(1) Target enrollment rate*	(2) Increment in rate†	(3) Projected high school graduates (in thousands)‡	(4) $Y_{13}(t)$ Plan increment for freshmen (in thousands)§	(5) $Y_{14}(t)$ Plan increment for sophomores (in thousands)¶
1998	.900	.274	4,007.6	1,098.1	678.6
1999	.900	.274	4,093.4	1,121.6	694.0
2000	.900	.274	4,172.1	1,143.2	708.9

*The difference between .900 and .626 is made up in 5, 10, or 15 years.

†Column (1) minus .626.

‡From Haggstrom's 4-14-71 output. (A set of enrollment projections was prepared for the Carnegie Commission by Dr. Gus W. Haggstrom. A later version of the projections we used appears in Carnegie Commission on Higher Education [1971]. The figures we used were from in-progress work. We shall refer to it as Haggstrom's 4-14-71 output.)

§Column (2) times col. (3).

¶$y_{14}(t) = .632\ Y_{13}(t-1)$.

TABLE 93B ***Universal two-year plan increments: 10-year plan***

Year	(1) Target enrollment rate*	(2) Increment in rate†	(3) Projected high school graduates (in thousands)‡	(4) $Y_{13}(t)$ Plan increment for freshmen (in thousands)§	(5) $Y_{14}(t)$ Plan increment for sophomores (in thousands)¶
1972	.626	.000	3,179.4		
1973	.653	.027	3,264.2	88.1	
1974	.681	.055	3,351.6	184.3	55.7
1975	.708	.082	3,435.7	281.7	116.5
1976	.735	.109	3,480.4	379.4	178.0
1977	.763	.137	3,515.9	481.7	239.8
1978	.790	.164	3,601.9	590.7	304.4
1979	.818	.192	3,647.2	700.3	373.3
1980	.845	.219	3,602.6	789.0	442.6
1981	.872	.246	3,568.0	877.7	498.7
1982	.900	.274	3,486.9	955.4	554.7
1983	.900	.274	3,336.2	914.1	603.8

TABLE 93B ***(continued)***

Year	(1) Target enrollment rate*	(2) Increment in rate†	(3) Projected high school graduates (in thousands)‡	(4) $Y_{13}(t)$ Plan increment for freshmen (in thousands)§	(5) $Y_{14}(t)$ Plan increment for sophomores (in thousands)¶
1984	.900	.274	3,214.0	880.6	577.7
1985	.900	.274	3,135.2	859.0	556.5
1986	.900	.274	3,132.5	858.3	542.9
1987	.900	.274	3,147.2	862.3	542.4
1988	.900	.274	3,150.2	863.2	545.0
1989	.900	.274	3,219.4	882.1	545.5
1990	.900	.274	3,305.4	905.7	557.5
1991	.900	.274	3,391.2	929.2	572.4
1992	.900	.274	3,478.2	953.0	587.3
1993	.900	.274	3,563.7	976.5	602.3
1994	.900	.274	3,649.5	1,000.0	617.1
1995	.900	.274	3,736.0	1,023.7	632.0
1996	.900	.274	3,827.8	1,048.8	647.0
1997	.900	.274	3,918.5	1,073.7	662.8
1998	.900	.274	4,007.6	1,098.1	678.6
1999	.900	.274	4,093.4	1,121.6	694.0
2000	.900	.274	4,172.1	1,143.2	708.9

*The difference between .900 and .626 is made up in 5, 10, or 15 years.

†Column (1) minus .626.

‡From Haggstrom's 4-14-71 output.

§Column (2) times col. (3).

¶$Y_{14}(t) = .632\ Y_{13}(t-1)$.

TABLE 93C ***Universal two-year plan increments: 15-year plan***

Year	(1) Target enrollment rate*	(2) Increment in rate†	(3) Projected high school graduates (in thousands)‡	(4) $Y_{13}(t)$ Plan increment for freshmen (in thousands)§	(5) $Y_{14}(t)$ Plan increment for sophomores (in thousands)¶
1972	.626	.000	3,179.4		
1973	.644	.018	3,264.2	58.8	
1974	.663	.037	3,351.6	124.0	37.2
1975	.681	.055	3,435.7	198.0	78.4
1976	.699	.073	3,480.4	254.1	119.4
1977	.717	.091	3,515.9	319.9	160.6
1978	.736	.110	3,601.9	396.2	202.2
1979	.754	.128	3,647.2	466.8	250.4
1980	.772	.146	3,602.6	526.0	295.0
1981	.791	.165	3,568.0	588.7	332.4
1982	.809	.183	3,486.9	638.1	372.1
1983	.827	.201	3,336.2	670.6	403.3
1984	.846	.220	3,214.0	707.1	423.8
1985	.864	.238	3,135.2	746.2	446.9
1986	.882	.256	3,132.3	801.9	471.6
1987	.900	.274	3,147.2	862.3	506.8
1988	.900	.274	3,150.2	863.2	545.0
1989	.900	.274	3,219.4	882.1	545.5
1990	.900	.274	3,305.4	905.7	557.5
1991	.900	.274	3,391.2	929.2	572.4
1992	.900	.274	3,478.2	953.0	587.3
1993	.900	.274	3,563.7	976.5	602.3
1994	.900	.274	3,649.5	1,000.0	617.1
1995	.900	.274	3,736.0	1,023.8	632.0
1996	.900	.274	3,827.8	1,048.8	647.0
1997	.900	.274	3,918.5	1,073.7	662.8
1998	.900	.274	4,007.6	1,098.1	678.6
1999	.900	.274	4,093.4	1,121.6	694.0
2000	.900	.274	4,172.1	1,143.2	708.9

See notes to Table 93B.

set of assumptions were not sufficiently different from the original deficit calculations to warrant a separate set of plan and cost calculations.

Some states—Utah, for example—enroll a smaller percentage of their high school graduates (or some other measure of eligibility) in the first two years of college, but provide, on the average, a longer higher education experience to those persons who do enroll.

Consider two states with equal populations. Assume that state A has a system of two-year colleges, that state B has a system of four-year colleges, and that no one ever drops out of college in either state. If one-half of the eligible population enrolls in the two-year colleges in state A and one-fourth of the eligible population enrolls in the four-year colleges in state B, then according to our performance measure, state B would be relatively deficient in enrollment by 50 percent. However, both states have the same absolute enrollment. A question remains: Should a state that has a high overall enrollment be required (by our plan) to have increased two-year enrollment?

On the one hand, state A represents the version of the universal two-year college plan previously presented; namely, most people obtain a two-year college education, without appreciable junior and senior enrollment increases. Final two-year status is determined on the basis of students' demand and institutions' evaluation of students' performance during the first two years. Although the number of juniors and seniors is relatively constant, some individuals who formerly would *not* have attended college might continue their education into the final two years, and some individuals who formerly would have continued their education into the final two years might be excluded through student competition. State B (with one-fourth enrollment for four years) does not provide a universal opportunity to achieve a college education. Hence, its first-two-year enrollment should be increased. Our target measure is consistent with this argument.

On the other hand, state B might have been opting for a different output mix from its educational system. If equal opportunity truly characterized eligibility into its higher education system, then one might be reluctant to force the two-year-dominated output mix on that state. Thus a state that had a higher overall enrollment would not be required to increase two-year enrollment.

To investigate the implications of these arguments for our state enrollment index, we constructed another enrollment index, one addressing the previous argument. We took the ratio of each state's 1967 total higher education enrollment to the U.S. Bureau of the Census's series B, 1970, estimate of each state's 18- to 24-year-old cohort, the group most likely to be enrolled. At 38.2 percent, California's enrollment rate was one of the highest. Each state's 1970 enrollment deficit was then computed as the product of the state's 18- to 24-year age-group projection, 1970 population estimate, and the difference between California's target percentage and the state's computed percentage enrollment.

The two indices we computed are compared in column (7) of Table 94. The total enrollment deficit was smaller in only three states. Consequently, we did not think this formulation of the deficit enrollment warranted a separate set of plan calculations.

11.3. THE MODEL

The plan increments in enrollment are based on the dynamic input-output education system model discussed in Chapter 10.

For its present application, the model consists of 24 activities. Most activities refer to a particular school year; e.g., activity 13 refers to the freshman year in college. Some activities refer to a particular type of instruction within some school year; e.g., activity 24 is similar to activity 19, in the sense that both constitute the third year of graduate study, but activity 19 leads to the fourth graduate year toward a Ph.D. degree, while activity 24 terminates with a master of arts degree. A list of these activities and their descriptions appear in Table 95.

The universal two-year college programs specify additional freshman and sophomore enrollments. All other enrollment is induced. Specifying the plan enrollment, the model is used to compute the size and timing of the induced junior through fifth-year Ph.D. enrollments. Subscript 1 in equations (31) through (38) of Chapter 10 denotes activities 1 through 14 in this universal plan, and subscript 2 in those equations denotes activities 15 through 24 in this plan. No plan alters primary and secondary school enrollment; therefore, $\Delta Y_1(t), \ldots, \Delta Y_{12}(t)$ are zero. The values for $\Delta Y_{13}(t)$ *and* $\Delta Y_{14}(t)$ for each plan have

TABLE 94 ***Alternative indices of state higher education enrollment deficits***

State (by region)	*(1) Freshman deficit enrollment (in thousands)**	*(2) 1967 total state enrollment (in thousands)†*	*(3) Resident state enrollment import-export corrected—see Table 90 (in thousands)‡*	*(4) 1970 estimate of 18- to 24-year-old population (in thousands)§*	*(5) (3) ÷ (4); percentage of resident enrollment out of 1970 18- to 24-year-old population*	*(6) Calif. –(5)*	*(7) (6) × (4) (in thousands)*
Connecticut	5.5	95.8	127.9	319	.401	–.019	–6.1**
Maine	9.4	25.5	22.7	124	.183	.199	24.7
Massachusetts	11.9	252.6	214.2	626	.342	.039	24.7
New Hampshire	5.2	25.8	19.1	81	.236	.146	11.8
Rhode Island	1.1	36.9	30.4	122	.250	.132	16.1
Vermont	4.4	16.4	7.8	52	.150	.232	12.1
Delaware	0	15.2	16.3	64	.255	.126	8.1
Maryland	11.4	115.5	132.2	465	.284	.097	45.2
New Jersey	6.6	152.5	253.6	768	.330	.051	39.5
New York	44.5	677.3	804.6	1,981	.406	–.025	–48.6**
Pennsylvania	117.8	347.9	350.7	1,248	.281	.100	125.2
Alabama	22.6	88.6	92.1	436	.211	.170	74.3
Arkansas	10.5	48.5	49.4	232	.213	.169	39.1
Florida	15.3	179.8	192.7	758	.254	.127	96.5
Georgia	26.6	98.5	95.3	604	.158	.224	135.2

Kentucky	18.2	90.2	80.2	398	.201	.180	71.7
Louisiana	24.4	104.2	101.6	459	.221	.160	73.6
Mississippi	10.4	64.7	60.2	307	.196	.185	56.9
North Carolina	25.6	135.0	108.3	673	.161	.221	148.6
South Carolina	16.6	51.8	45.6	378	.121	.261	98.7
Tennessee	22.8	112.6	98.3	487	.202	.180	87.6
Virginia	17.1	117.5	124.9	643	.194	.187	120.5
West Virginia	14.2	52.7	47.0	200	.235	.147	29.4
Illinois	3.9	343.8	396.7	1,199	.331	.051	60.9
Indiana	35.2	163.4	138.1	588	.235	.147	86.3
Michigan	39.5	317.5	308.3	967	.319	.063	60.8
Ohio	55.8	314.0	300.8	1,232	.244	.137	169.4
Wisconsin	21.9	156.6	143.8	479	.300	.082	39.1
Iowa	21.6	99.1	88.4	309	.286	.096	29.5
Kansas	9.2	89.1	80.8	277	.292	.090	24.9
Minnesota	25.8	138.2	135.0	420	.321	.060	25.3**
Missouri	17.2	153.3	136.7	506	.270	.111	56.4
Nebraska	7.5	55.0	48.8	178	.274	.108	19.1
North Dakota	2.2	26.5	27.7	80	.346	.036	2.9
South Dakota	4.9	27.5	25.3	88	.288	.094	8.3
Arizona	0	78.5	70.0	227	.308	.073	16.6
New Mexico	8.4	33.8	34.0	149	.228	.154	22.9
Oklahoma	7.7	100.4	95.4	303	.315	.067	20.3
Texas	41.5	348.5	336.3	1,410	.239	.143	201.8
Colorado	8.7	93.3	80.4	278	.289	.092	25.7
Idaho	1.3	26.4	28.4	86	.330	.051	4.4

TABLE 94 ***(continued)***

State (by region)	(1) Freshman deficit enrollment (in thousands)*	(2) 1967 total state enrollment (in thousands)†	(3) Resident state enrollment import-export corrected—see Table 90 (in thousands)‡	(4) 1970 estimate of 18- to 24-year-old population (in thousands)§	(5) (3) ÷ (4): percentage of resident enrollment out of 1970 18- to 24-year-old population	(6) Calif. −(5)	(7) (6) × (4) (in thousands)
Montana	3.4	23.2	26.1	88	.297	.085	7.5
Utah	5.9	75.8	50.6	141	.359	.023	3.3
Wyoming	0	12.0	13.3	42	.316	.066	2.8
Alaska	.4	5.8	11.2	44	.254	.127	5.6
California	0	974.4	963.7	2,525	.382	.000	0.0
Hawaii	0	27.8	36.0	117	.307	.074	8.7
Nevada	1.4	8.6	11.5	56	.206	.176	9.8
Oregon	6.0	90.3	85.2	231	.369	.013	2.9
Washington	1.8	144.5	141.9	406	.350	.032	13.1

NOTE: A double asterisk indicates an alternative deficit figure smaller than the corresponding deficit used in the plan calculations (col. 1).

*Table 91.

†U.S. Office of Education (1967, Table 9, p. 15).

‡Column (2) × col. (3) of Table 90.

§American Council on Education (1967, p. 9), citing U.S. Bureau of the Census (1966*a*, 1966*b*). *Projected Population* ser. 1-B as of July 1, 1970. Series 1-B assumes continuation of 1955–1960 gross interstate migration rates and very moderate decline in fertility levels. These figures are the most recent 1970 state projections showing age group 18 to 24. Newer total United States projections have been published and are somewhat lower, about 1 percent for 1970 in ser. B.

TABLE 95 ***List of 24 activities in the model of United States education***

	Activity	*Description*
	1	First grade
	2	Second grade
	3	Third grade
	4	Fourth grade
	5	Fifth grade
	6	Sixth grade
Group 1	7	Seventh grade
	8	Eighth grade
	9	Ninth grade
	10	Tenth grade
	11	Eleventh grade
	12	Twelfth grade
	13	Freshman
	14	Sophomore
	15	Junior
	16	Senior
	17	First-year graduate study for Ph.D.
	18	Second-year graduate study for Ph.D.
Group 2	19	Third-year graduate study for Ph.D.
	20	Fourth-year graduate study for Ph.D.
	21	One year of graduate study leading to a primary school credential
	22	One year of graduate study leading to a secondary school credential
	23	Fifth and final year of graduate study for Ph.D.
	24	A third-year terminal M.A. program

been presented in Table 92. We assume that the final demands from the higher education sector, $\Delta F_{13}(t)$ through $\Delta F_{24}(t)$ are not altered by the plans. Thus values for $\Delta F_2(t)$ in equations (31) through (38) of Chapter 10 are predefined as zero.

11.4. THE COEFFICIENTS OF EDUCATIONAL TECHNOLOGY AND FACULTY STOCK SURVIVAL

In the previously discussed equations, the educational technology matrix and the faculty survival matrix, denoted by A and M, required specification. In this section we describe the assumptions employed to specify these matrixes for the plan calculations.

The basic question of the technology matrix is: What faculty-student ratios, by teacher degree, should be used?

Our method in answering this question was to determine a total teacher-student ratio, by level of teacher degree, based on the estimates presented in Chapter 7, and then to disaggregate this total figure by faculty degree according to the following assumptions:

1 We made three teaching divisions in the educational technology: lower division, represented by activities 13 and 14 and describing the two-year college technology; upper division, represented by activities 15 and 16 and describing the four-year college, junior- and senior-year technology; and the graduate division, represented by activities 17 through 24.

2 We decided the question—In which type of institution, public or private, would the expansion occur?—by assuming that the direct and induced enrollment would be allocated according to the present pattern of enrollment by control (1968 data).

3 We assumed that instruction was performed by faculties holding M.A. and Ph.D. degrees. The ratios between these degrees, in the three teaching divisions, again reflect the present pattern of use (1968 data again).

The reader who is not interested in the details of the derivation of these coefficients should skip to Section 11.6.

Lower-division coefficients As derived from Chapter 7, the public and private two-year college faculty-student coefficients are .0446 and .0491, respectively. In 1968, public institution enrollment was 92 percent of the total two-year college enrollment.[3] The control-weighted faculty-student ratio, .0449, was then

[3]See Carnegie Commission on Higher Education (1971).

disaggregated into faculty by degree according to the 1967 two-year college associate professor degree-holding distribution: 85 percent master's degree-holders and 15 percent doctorate degree-holders.

These assumptions resulted in .0382 of a faculty with a master's degree and .0067 of a faculty with a doctor's degree being required for each lower-division student in each plan.

Upper-division coefficients Chapter 7 presented separate faculty-student coefficients for universities, M.A.-granting liberal arts colleges, and four-year liberal arts colleges, by control. These coefficients were weighted according to their 1967 enrollment distribution with one slight modification, which was that only half of the private four-year liberal arts 1968 enrollment—6.7 percent instead of 13.4 percent—occurred in the teacher-intensive private liberal arts colleges. The other half (we assumed) were placed in private colleges that used the public liberal arts technology.

	Coefficient from chap. 7	*Enrollment (in thousands)**	*Percentage of total*
Universities			
Public	.0596	1,750.7	32.7
Private	.0575	625.7	11.7
Comprehensive colleges			
Public	.0525	1,775.1	33.1
Private	.0668	436.4	8.1
Liberal arts			
Public	.0496	53.6	1.0
Private	.0668	716.0	13.4
TOTAL		5,357.5	100.0

*From Carnegie Commission on Higher Education (1971).

These assumptions and distributions resulted in a .0573 total faculty-student coefficient which was distributed between M.A.- and Ph.D.-holding faculty: 46 percent M.A. and 54 percent Ph.D. (see Chapter 9). Result—a .02635 M.A. faculty requirement per student and a .03094 Ph.D. faculty requirement per student.

The graduate coefficients We assumed that all graduate students were taught by Ph.D.-holding faculty. The university faculty–graduate student coefficients from the cross-sectional study of Chapter 7 are .12 and .19 for publicly and privately controlled institutions, respectively. Public and private percentage enrollment was 74 percent and 26 percent, respectively.[4] A weighted university coefficient of .1382 Ph.D.'s per student resulted.

The technology matrix contained the coefficients in Table 96.

Faculty stock survival We assumed that each faculty member works for 35 years and that the distribution of existing faculty was uniform over time. Thus, every year $\frac{1}{35}$th, or 2.86 percent, of the faculty leaves the education sector. The diagonal elements of the M matrix for activities 23 and 24 are .9714. All other elements in M had a zero value.

11.5. RESULTS

Tables 97 through 99 present, in a somewhat aggregated form, the annual enrollment increments for each of the three universal plans.[5]

We notice, first, that the induced increment in upper-division and graduate enrollment is rather minuscule in comparison with the predetermined lower-division enrollment increment. The timing of these enrollments facilitates feasibility; while the lower-division enrollment increment is minimal during the start-up periods, the upper-division and graduate enrollment increments are maximal (although the relative magnitudes of the two groups are so different that little is really gained by this feature).

The three years of negative upper-division increment in the 5-year plan, when it is in full operation, and the single year's negative increment in the 10-year plan suggest that the more rapid start-up plans are somewhat wasteful in terms of physical and human resources, given the projected demographic charac-

[4]Ibid.

[5]More disaggregated results, by activity, appear in Miller and Radner (1975).

teristics of the population. Timing features of this type were brought out in another context in our discussion of the academic demand for Ph.D.'s in Chapter 9.

Notice that at the end of this century, freshman and sophomore enrollment increments continue to rise, while upper-division and graduate enrollment begins to decline. This is due to the planning-horizon problem discussed in Chapter 10. We shall not discuss induced enrollment increments beyond the initial planning horizon of 1988.

The incremental enrollees would enter college in lieu of entering the labor force. The change in induced final demand from activity 12 is consequently negative. Because of the usual high youth unemployment rates, this negative final-demand change should not be interpreted as causing feasibility problems.[6]

Because enrollment rates have historically continued to rise, some of each plan's enrollment increments would be met by these trend increments. Ideally, one would like to predict the future annual enrollments, by level, that spontaneously arise from social, political, and economic conditions within the society and then compare these enrollments with the enrollments required by the plan. The difference between the "planned" and "unplanned" enrollments would be the system's "deficit." The type of comparison that we can actually make in this section is naturally less satisfactory than this ideal comparison, but it is still instructive.

The *trend increment* in enrollment is defined as the increment in enrollment implied by extrapolating historical trends in enrollment *rates* (see Section 11.1). Comprehension of the magnitudes of the *plan increments* will be aided by comparing them with the trend increments. Comparisons are made for lower-division enrollment, for total undergraduate enrollment, and for graduate enrollment.

Table 100 displays the trend increments in freshman and sophomore enrollment. The method of computing these trend increments is similar to the one used to compute the deficit enrollments for each state (Section 11.2). Haggstrom's projected freshman enrollment rates are applied to his projected high school graduates to derive trend-incremental freshmen. The

[6]See disaggregated results in Miller and Radner (1975).

TABLE 96 ***The educational technology matrix***

	1	2	3	4	5	6	7	8	9	10	11	12
1		1.0										
2			1.0									
3				1.0								
4					1.0							
5						1.0						
6							1.0					
7								1.0				
8									1.0			
9										1.0		
10											1.0	
11												1.0
12												
13												
14												
15												
16												
17												
18												
19												
20												
21	.0403	.0403	.0403	.0403	.0403	.0403						
22							.0499	.0499	.0499	.0499	.0499	.0499
23												
24												

13	14	15	16	17	18	19	20	21	22	23	24
1.0											
	1.0										
		1.0									
			1.0								
				1.0				1.0	1.0		
					1.0						
						1.0					1.0
							1.0				
										1.0	
.0067	.0067	.0309	.0309	.1382	.1382	.1382	.1382	.0309	.0309	.1382	.1382
.0382	.0382	.0263	.0263					.0263	.0263		

TABLE 97
Five-year plan's higher education enrollment increments (in thousands)

Year	*Lower-division*	*Upper-division*	*Graduate*
1972		26.7	36.4
1973	179.5	20.2	41.2
1974	478.7	9.0	41.5
1975	794.4	3.3	34.8
1976	1,118.3	1.9	23.3
1977	1,445.1	1.1	10.5
1978	1,595.8	−.3	4.1
1979	1,623.0	−1.4	2.2
1980	1,618.6	−.8	.5
1981	1,601.4	.9	−.9
1982	1,573.2	2.7	−1.2
1983	1,517.9	3.4	.6
1984	1,458.3	4.0	3.2
1985	1,415.5	5.3	5.1
1986	1,401.2	6.0	6.6
1987	1,404.7	6.2	7.9
1988	1,408.2	6.3	9.3
1989	1,427.6	6.3	10.1
1990	1,463.2	6.3	10.3
1991	1,501.6	6.3	10.4
1992	1,540.3	6.2	10.4
1993	1,578.8	6.3	10.4
1994	1,617.1	6.3	10.4
1995	1,655.7	6.2	10.3
1996	1,695.8	4.7	10.2
1997	1,736.5	3.4	10.0
1998	1,776.7	3.4	8.5
1999	1,815.6	3.4	7.0
2000	1,852.1	3.4	5.6

NOTE: In this and succeeding tables, the planning horizon is 1988, whereas the computational horizon is 2000. See Section 10.4.

TABLE 98
Ten-year plan's higher education enrollment increments (in thousands)

Year	*Lower-division*	*Upper-division*	*Graduate*
1972		15.0	21.2
1973	88.1	15.1	24.1
1974	240.0	15.0	24.6
1975	398.2	14.6	24.8
1976	557.4	13.8	24.7
1977	721.5	13.1	24.0
1978	895.1	8.1	22.6
1979	1,073.6	.9	20.8
1980	1,231.6	−.8	15.3
1981	1,376.4	.9	7.8
1982	1,510.1	2.7	1.2
1983	1,517.9	3.4	.6
1984	1,458.3	4.0	3.2
1985	1,415.5	5.3	5.1
1986	1,401.2	6.0	6.6
1987	1,404.7	6.2	7.9
1988	1,408.2	6.3	9.3
1989	1,427.6	6.3	10.1
1990	1,463.2	6.3	10.3
1991	1,501.6	6.3	10.4
1992	1,540.3	6.2	10.4
1993	1,578.8	6.3	10.4
1994	1,617.1	6.3	10.4
1995	1,655.7	6.2	10.3
1996	1,695.8	4.7	10.2
1997	1,736.5	3.4	10.0
1998	1,776.7	3.4	8.5
1999	1,815.6	3.4	7.0
2000	1,852.1	3.4	5.6

TABLE 99 *Fifteen-year plan's higher education enrollment increments (in thousands)*

Year	*Lower-division*	*Upper-division*	*Graduate*
1972		10.2	14.5
1973	58.7	10.6	16.5
1974	161.2	11.1	16.9
1975	267.4	10.8	17.3
1976	373.5	10.3	17.8
1977	479.9	10.0	17.8
1978	598.4	8.5	17.3
1979	717.2	7.1	16.4
1980	821.0	7.2	14.9
1981	921.1	8.3	13.2
1982	1,010.2	9.6	12.2
1983	1,073.9	8.1	12.9
1984	1,130.9	5.3	14.3
1985	1,193.1	5.3	13.6
1986	1,273.5	6.0	11.5
1987	1,369.1	6.2	9.3
1988	1,408.2	6.3	9.3
1989	1,427.1	6.3	10.1
1990	1,463.2	6.3	10.3
1991	1,501.6	6.3	10.4
1992	1,540.3	6.2	10.4
1993	1,578.8	6.3	10.4
1994	1,617.1	6.3	10.4
1995	1,655.7	6.2	10.3
1996	1,695.8	4.7	10.2
1997	1,736.5	3.4	10.0
1998	1,776.7	3.4	8.5
1999	1,815.6	3.4	7.0
2000	1,852.1	3.4	5.6

TABLE 100
Annual trend increments in freshman and sophomore enrollment

Year	*(1)**	*(2)†*	*(3)‡*	*(4)§*	*(5)¶*
1972	.626		3,179.4		
1973	.629	.003	3,264.2	9.8	
1974	.633	.007	3,351.6	23.5	6.2
1975	.636	.010	3,435.7	34.4	14.9
1976	.640	.014	3,480.4	48.7	21.7
1977	.646	.020	3,515.9	70.3	30.8
1978	.652	.026	3,601.9	93.6	44.4
1979	.658	.032	3,647.2	116.7	59.2
1980	.664	.038	3,602.6	136.9	73.8
1981	.670	.044	3,568.0	157.0	86.5
1982	.676	.050	3,486.9	174.3	99.2
1983	.681	.055	3,336.2	183.5	110.2
1984	.686	.060	3,214.0	192.8	116.0
1985	.691	.065	3,135.2	203.8	121.8
1986	.696	.070	3,132.4	219.3	128.8
1987	.700	.074	3,147.2	232.9	138.6
1988	.705	.079	3,150.6	249.9	147.2
1989	.710	.084	3,219.4	270.4	157.9
1990	.714	.088	3,305.4	290.9	170.9
1991	.718	.092	3,391.2	312.2	183.8
1992	.722	.096	3,478.2	333.9	197.2
1993	.726	.100	3,563.7	356.3	211.0
1994	.730	.104	3,649.5	379.5	225.2
1995	.734	.108	3,736.0	403.5	239.8
1996	.737	.111	3,827.8	424.9	255.0
1997	.741	.115	3,918.5	450.6	268.5
1998	.744	.118	4,007.6	472.9	284.8
1999	.747	.121	4,093.4	495.3	298.9
2000	.750	.124	4,172.1	517.3	313.0

*Projected enrollment rate. Projections by Dr. Gus Haggstrom, Carnegie Commission on Higher Education.

†Increment in rate, col. (1) minus .626.

‡Projected high school graduates, in thousands. Projections by Dr. Gus Haggstrom, Carnegie Commission on Higher Education.

§Trend increment for freshmen, in thousands.

¶Trend increment for sophomores, in thousands, .626 × col. $(4)_{t-1}$.

increments in sophomore enrollment are estimated to be 63.2 percent of the corresponding increments in freshman enrollment (see Miller and Radner, 1975).

Tables 101A and 101B display the annual ratios of the 5-, 10-, and 15-year lower-division *plan increments* to the corresponding *trend increments*. During the start-up years, the 5-year lower-division plan increments are roughly 16 times the trend increments, the 10-year lower-division plan increments are roughly seven times the trend increments, and the 15-year plan increments are about four times the trend increments. In 1988, when the 15-year plan has reached full operation, the plan increments are still 3½ times the trend increments, and they continue to remain above the trend increments until the year 2000.

The figures imply that the universal plans are not merely short-run schemes to secure higher enrollment rates—rates that would be reached soon enough anyway. Rather, the concept of universal attendance specified as a 90 percent target figure implies enrollment levels in excess of any anticipated enrollment for at least one more complete generation.

Table 102 displays comparisons between the three plans' incremental enrollments and Haggstrom's total projected undergraduate enrollment.[7] The plans imply a 13.5 percent expansion in undergraduate education over expected enrollment.

The graduate expansion required to produce the teachers for this 13.5 percent undergraduate expansion is roughly ½ of 1 percent, as shown in column (3) of Tables 103A and 103B. The 5-year plan begins with a 3.8 percent expansion, but during full operation it requires less than 1 percent expansion. The 15-year plan begins with a 1.5 percent expansion. Initially, plan increments are double the trend increments for the 5-year plan and four-fifths the trend increments for the 15-year plan. By full operation, plan increments are less than 5 percent of trend increments, as shown in column (5) of Tables 103A and 103B.

It is apparent that the universal two-year college plans considered here would not impose strains on the resources in the higher education sector. Tables 104 and 105 compare the master

[7]A set of enrollment projections was prepared for the Carnegie Commission by Dr. Gus W. Haggstrom. A later version of the projections we used appears in Carnegie Commission on Higher Education (1971). The figures we used were from in-progress work. We shall refer to it as Haggstrom's 4-14-71 output.

TABLE 101A
Comparison of lower-division plan increments to lower-division trend increments (in thousands)

Year	*5-year plan increments*	*Trend increments*	*5-year increment/ trend increment*
1972			
1973	179.5	9.8	18.3
1974	478.7	29.7	16.1
1975	794.4	49.3	16.1
1976	1,118.3	70.4	15.9
1977	1,445.1	101.1	14.3
1978	1,595.8	138.0	11.6
1979	1,623.0	175.9	9.3
1980	1,618.7	210.7	7.7
1981	1,601.4	243.5	6.6
1982	1,573.2	273.5	5.7
1983	1,417.9	293.7	5.2
1984	1,458.3	308.8	4.7
1985	1,415.5	325.6	4.3
1986	1,401.2	348.1	4.0
1987	1,404.7	371.5	3.8
1988	1,408.2	397.1	3.5
1989	1,427.6	428.3	3.3
1990	1,463.2	461.8	3.2
1991	1,501.6	495.8	3.0
1992	1,540.3	531.1	2.9
1993	1,578.8	567.3	2.8
1994	1,617.1	604.7	2.7
1995	1,655.7	643.3	2.6
1996	1,695.8	679.9	2.5
1997	1,736.5	719.1	2.4
1998	1,776.7	757.7	2.3
1999	1,815.6	794.2	2.3
2000	1,852.1	830.3	2.2

TABLE 101B ***Comparison of lower-division plan increments to lower-division trend increments (in thousands)***

Year	*10-year plan increments*	*10-year increments/trend increments*	*15-year plan increments*	*15-year increments/trend increments*
1972				
1973	88.1	9.0	58.8	6.0
1974	240.0	8.1	161.2	5.4
1975	398.2	8.1	267.4	5.4
1976	557.4	7.9	373.5	5.3
1977	721.5	7.1	480.5	4.7
1978	895.1	6.5	598.4	4.3
1979	1,073.6	6.1	717.2	4.1
1980	1,231.6	5.8	821.0	3.9
1981	1,276.4	5.6	921.1	3.8
1982	1,510.1	5.5	1,010.1	3.7
1983	1,517.9	5.2	1,073.9	3.7
1984	1,458.3	4.7	1,130.9	3.7
1985	1,415.5	4.3	1,193.1	3.7
1986	1,401.2	4.0	1,273.5	3.6
1987	1,404.7	3.8	1,369.1	3.7
1988	1,408.2	3.5	1,408.2	3.5
1989	1,437.6	3.3	1,427.6	3.2
1990	1,463.2	3.2	1,463.2	3.2
1991	1,501.6	3.0	1,501.6	3.0
1992	1,540.3	2.9	1,540.3	2.9
1993	1,578.8	2.8	1,578.8	2.8
1994	1,617.1	2.7	1,617.1	2.7
1995	1,655.7	2.6	1,655.7	2.6
1996	1,695.8	2.5	1,695.8	2.5
1997	1,736.5	2.4	1,736.5	2.4
1998	1,776.7	2.3	1,776.7	2.3
1999	1,815.6	2.3	1,815.6	2.3
2000	1,852.1	2.2	1,852.1	2.2

FIGURE 29 ***Plan increments ÷ trend increments in freshman and sophomore enrollment***

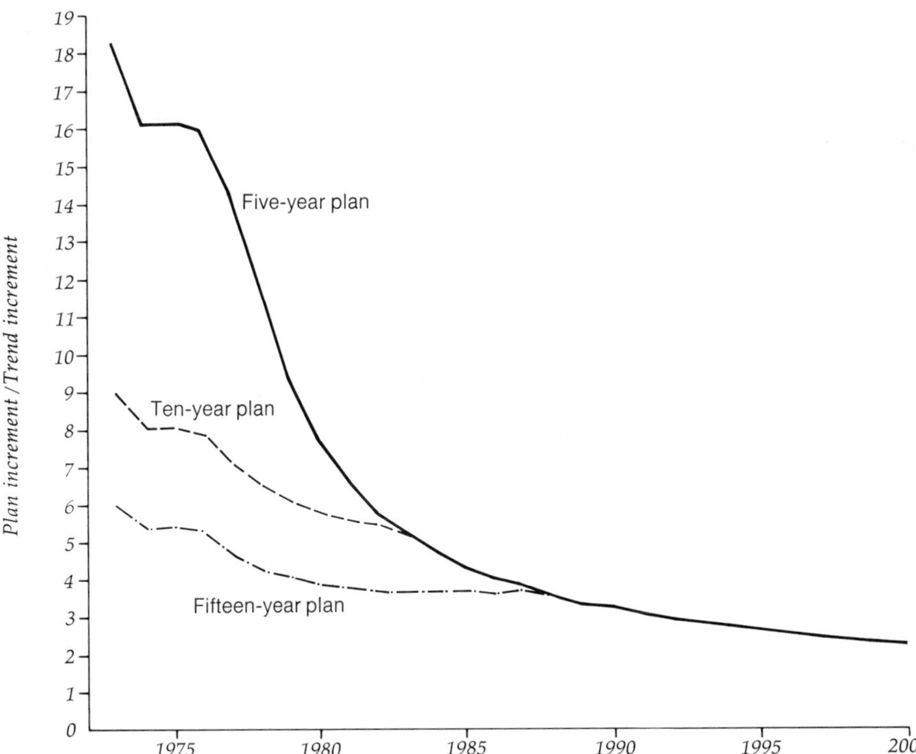

SOURCE: Tables 101A and 101B.

TABLE 102 ***Universal plan summary: undergraduates (enrollments in thousands)***

Year	(1)[a]	(2)[b]	(3)[c]	(4)[d]	(5)[e]	(6)[f]	(7)[g]
1972				8,346.4			
1973	179.5	88.1	58.8	8,817.6	.020	.009	.006
1974	478.7	240.0	161.2	9,261.3	.052	.026	.017
1975	794.4	398.2	267.4	9,655.5	.082	.041	.028
1976	1,118.3	557.4	373.5	9,990.9	.112	.056	.037
1977	1,445.1	721.5	480.5	10,298.7	.140	.070	.047
1978	1,595.8	895.1	598.4	10,605.7	.150	.084	.056
1979	1,623.0	1,073.6	717.2	10,880.9	.149	.099	.066
1980	1,618.7	1,231.6	812.0	11,081.9	.146	.111	.074
1981	1,601.4	1,376.4	921.1	11,222.0	.143	.123	.082
1982	1,573.2	1,590.1	1,010.2	11,229.6	.141	.134	.090
1983	1,517.9	1,517.9	1,073.9	11,065.9	.137	.137	.097
1984	1,458.3	1,458.3	1,130.9	10,828.2	.135	.135	.104
1985	1,415.5	1,515.5	1,193.1	10,543.7	.134	.134	.113
1986	1,401.2	1,401.2	1,273.5	10,317.3	.136	.136	.123
1987	1,404.7	1,404.7	1,369.1	10,225.9	.137	.137	.134
1988	1,408.2	1,408.2	1,408.2	10,237.8	.138	.138	.138
1989	1,427.6	1,427.6	1,427.6	10,374.5	.138	.138	.138
1990	1,463.2	1,463.2	1,463.2	10,586.6	.138	.138	.138
1991	1,501.6	1,501.6	1,501.6	10,859.7	.138	.138	.138
1992	1,540.3	1,540.3	1,540.3	11,205.9	.137	.137	.137
1993	1,578.8	1,578.8	1,578.8	11,566.7	.136	.136	.136
1994	1,617.1	1,617.1	1,617.1	11,927.1	.136	.136	.136
1995	1,655.7	1,655.7	1,655.7	12,287.7	.135	.135	.135
1996	1,695.8	1,695.8	1,695.8	12,652.4	.134	.134	.134
1997	1,736.5	1,736.5	1,736.5	13,021.6	.133	.133	.133
1998	1,776.7	1,776.7	1,776.7	13,393.5	.133	.133	.133
1999	1,815.6	1,815.6	1,815.6	13,764.5	.132	.132	.132
2000	1,852.1	1,852.1	1,852.1	14,122.8	.131	.131	.131

[a]Five-year plan increment in freshman and sophomore enrollment.
[b]Ten-year plan increment in freshman and sophomore enrollment.
[c]Fifteen-year plan increment in freshman and sophomore enrollment.
[d]Projected total undergraduate enrollment.
[e]Column (1) divided by col. (4), ratio (5-year plan).
[f]Column (2) divided by col. (4), ratio (10-year plan).
[g]Column (3) divided by col. (4), ratio (15-year plan).

TABLE 103A
Comparison of 5-year plan graduate increments with predicted graduate enrollment and graduate trend increments (in thousands)

Year	*(1)**	*(2)†*	*(3)‡*	*(4)§*	*(5)¶*
1972	36.4	966.9	.038		
1973	41.2	1,046.0	.039	20.5	2.01
1974	41.5	1,124.6	.037	40.9	1.01
1975	34.8	1,206.4	.029	61.3	0.57
1976	23.3	1,289.6	.013	81.6	0.29
1977	10.5	1,362.0	.008	100.0	0.11
1978	4.1	1,430.8	.003	117.4	0.03
1979	2.2	1,496.0	.001	133.7	0.02
1980	.5	1,555.1		148.6	0
1981	−.9	1,608.1	−.001	161.9	−0.01
1982	−1.2	1,660.6	−.000	174.7	−0.01
1983	.6	1,711.7		186.8	0
1984	3.2	1,753.9	.002	197.1	0.02
1985	5.1	1,786.0	.003	205.6	0.02
1986	6.6	1,805.5	.004	211.8	0.03
1987	7.9	1,807.5	.004	214.9	0.04
1988	9.3	1,794.1	.005	215.5	0.04

*Five-year plan increment in graduate enrollment.

†Haggstrom's middle-value predicted graduate enrollment (Projection B).

‡Column (1) divided by col. (2).

§Graduate trend increments. The trend increment for each year is the difference between Haggstrom's middle projection (B) and his constant rate projection (C). However, these differences are adjusted downward so that the enrollment rates are equal in the start-up year, 1972.

¶Column (1) divided by col. (4).

TABLE 103B Comparison of 15-year plan graduate increments with predicted graduate enrollment and graduate trend increments (in thousands)

Year	*(1)**	*(2)†*	*(3)‡*	*(4)§*	*(5)¶*
1972	14.5	966.9	.015		
1973	16.5	1,046.0	.016	20.5	0.80
1974	16.9	1,124.6	.015	40.9	0.41
1975	17.3	1,206.4	.014	61.3	0.28
1976	17.8	1,289.6	.014	81.6	0.22
1977	17.8	1,362.0	.013	100.0	0.18
1978	17.3	1,430.8	.012	117.4	0.15
1979	16.4	1,496.0	.011	133.7	0.12
1980	14.9	1,555.1	.010	148.6	0.10
1981	13.2	1,608.1	.008	161.9	0.08
1982	12.2	1,660.6	.007	174.7	0.07
1983	12.9	1,711.7	.008	186.8	0.07
1984	14.3	1,753.9	.008	197.1	0.07
1985	13.6	1,786.0	.008	205.6	0.07
1986	11.5	1,805.5	.006	211.8	0.05
1987	9.3	1,807.5	.005	214.9	0.04
1988	9.3	1,794.1	.005	215.5	0.04

*Fifteen-year plan increment in graduate enrollment.
†Haggstrom's middle-value predicted graduate enrollment (Projection B).
‡Column (1) divided by col. (2).
§Graduate trend increments. See note to Table 103A.
¶Column (1) divided by col. (4).

TABLE 104
Comparison of plan increments with cumulated trend increments in M.A. production (in thousands)

Year	*(1)[a]*	*(2)[b]*	*(3)[c]*	*(4)[d]*	*(5)[e]*	*(6)[f]*
1972	6.7	2.3	249.6			
1973	11.3	4.0	270.7	5.7	1.98	0.70
1974	12.3	4.2	292.8	17.2	0.72	0.24
1975	13.3	4.3	314.8	34.4	0.39	0.13
1976	13.6	4.4	337.6	57.2	0.24	0.08
1977	6.8	4.8	360.7	85.5	0.08	0.06
1978	2.2	5.0	380.7	118.8	0.02	0.04
1979	1.1	4.5	339.6	156.9	0.01	0.03
1980	.6	4.5	417.5	199.4	0	0.02
1981	.2	4.1	433.6	245.8	0	0.02
1982	−.9	3.2	448.1	295.9	0	0.01
1983	−1.1	2.9	462.5	349.4	0	0.01
1984	−.5	3.2	476.6	406.2	0	0.01
1985	.6	4.0	488.1	465.8	0	0.01
1986	1.2	4.6	496.6	527.7	0	0.01
1987	1.2	2.5	501.5	591.2	0	0
1988	1.8	1.8	501.3	655.4	0	0

[a] Five-year plan increments in annual M.A. production.

[b] Fifteen-year plan increments in annual M.A. production.

[c] Haggstrom's middle-value predicted annual M.A. production.

[d] Cumulated trend increments in M.A. production. See note to Table 103A for method of calculating annual trend increments.

[e] Ratio of the 5-year plan increment to the cumulated trend increment. Column (1) divided by col. (4).

[f] Ratio of the 15-year plan increment to the cumulated trend increment. Column (2) divided by col. (4).

TABLE 105 Comparison of plan increments with cumulated trend increments in Ph.D. production (in thousands)

Year	(1)[a]	(2)[b]	(3)[c]	(4)[d]	(5)[e]	(6)[f]
1972	1.8	.3	36.1			
1973	1.8	.8	38.9	0.4	4.50	2.00
1974	1.2	.8	42.1	1.6	0.75	0.50
1975	.7	.9	45.7	4.1	0.17	0.22
1976	.6	.8	49.9	8.2	0.07	0.10
1977	.3	.8	54.7	14.4	0.02	0.06
1978	.1	.8	59.5	22.7	0	0.04
1979	−.0	.6	64.5	33.0	0	0.02
1980	−.0	.6	69.5	45.3	0	0.01
1981	.0	.7	73.7	59.0	0	0.01
1982	.1	.6	77.7	74.0	0	0.01
1983	.2	.7	81.3	90.2	0	0.01
1984	.2	.5	84.5	107.4	0	0
1985	.3	.5	87.3	125.5	0	0
1986	.4	.5	90.0	144.6	0	0
1987	.4	.5	92.5	164.4	0	0
1988	.5	.5	94.8	184.9	0	0

[a]Five-year plan increments in Ph.D. production.

[b]Fifteen-year plan increments in Ph.D. production.

[c]Haggstrom's middle-value predicted Ph.D. production.

[d]Cumulated trend increment in Ph.D. production. See note to Table 103A for method of calculating annual trend increments.

[e]Ratio of the 5-year plan increment to the cumulated trend increment in production. Column (1) divided by col. (4).

[f]Ratio of the 15-year plan increment to the cumulated trend increment in production. Column (2) divided by col. (4).

of arts and the Ph.D. degrees required by the plans with the corresponding cumulated trend increments in degree production, for both the 5- and 15-year plans. In three of the four cases the initial ratios exceed unity, but in all four cases the ratios drop quickly to less than 3 percent. We therefore conclude that the manpower feasibility problems associated with the plans would be minimal.

11.6. COSTS

Cost estimates for the universal plans are presented here. The estimates distinguish between the direct costs of the freshman and sophomore enrollees and the indirect costs of the induced upper-division and graduate enrollees required to service the lower division's plan enrollment.

Annual cost estimates are derived from cost-per-student estimates based on O'Neill's figures (O'Neill, 1971) and our plan increments, in 1966–67 dollars.

Table 106 and its accompanying explanation present the methodology and assumptions associated with our cost-per-student estimates. Graduate student costs are estimated here at $3,681, upper-division student costs at $1,475, and lower-division student costs at $982.

In terms of the actual feasibility of the plans, these cost figures must be interpreted as conservative because they do not include any direct student subsidies. Such subsidies may be required to increase the demand for higher education up to the plans' required annual enrollments. The cost estimates do include an estimate of capital costs.

The universal 5-, 10-, and 15-year plans' costs are presented in Tables 107, 108, and 109, respectively. Costs naturally vary according to the rate of start-up. The universal plans cost about $1.5 billion when in full operation. The 5-year plan starts, and annually increases, at roughly $200 million a year, and the 15-year plan costs roughly one-third of that figure.

The total cost of higher education in 1966 was $8.1 billion (O'Neill, 1971). Thus the long-run costs for the universal plans amount to about 18.5 percent of 1966 total higher education costs.

TABLE 106 ***Calculation of costs per student, public institutions, 1966–67 (in current dollars)***

Type of student	*(1) Total credit hours (in thousands)*[a]	*(2) FTE students (in thousands)*[b]	*(3) Cost factor*[c]	*(4) Adjusted FTE students (in thousands)*[d]	*(5) Percentage of adjusted FTE students*[e]	*(6) Annual costs for instruction (in millions of dollars)*[f]	*(7) Annual instructional costs per FTE student*[g]
Graduate	7,124	254.4	3.75	954.0	18.55	919.9	3,616
Upper-division	46,916	1,675.6	1.50	2,513.4	48.87	2,423.3	1,446
Lower-division	46,916	1,675.6	1.00	1,675.6	32.58	1,615.6	964
TOTAL	100,956	3,606.0		5,143.0	100.00	4,958.8	1,375

[a]O'Neill (1971, Table A-10, p. 71). Upper-division = lower-division by assumption.

[b]Calculated by dividing col. (1) by 28, as suggested in O'Neill (1971).

[c]See O'Neill (1971, p. 14). Factors are based on estimates of relative costs of graduate, upper-division, and lower-division education.

[d]Column (2) times col. (3). FTE students are weighted by relative costs.

[e]Each of the first three lines of col. (4) is divided by 5,143.0.

[f]Column (5) times 4,958.8. See O'Neill (1971, p. 92). Total instructional costs are divided among the groups according to the percentages.

[g]Column (6) divided by col. (2).

TABLE 107 ***Costs of 5-year universal plan (in millions of 1966–67 dollars)***

Year	(1) Direct costs	(2) Indirect costs	(3) Total costs	(4) (2)/(3)
1972		170	170	1.0000
1973	173	178	351	.3513
1974	461	163	624	.2611
1975	765	130	896	.1458
1976	1,078	87	1,165	.0747
1977	1,393	39	1,432	.0277
1978	1,538	14	1,552	.0093
1979	1,564	6	1,570	.0037
1980	1,560	0	1,560	.0003
1981	1,543	−2	1,541	−.0012
1982	1,516	0	1,516	−.0003
1983	1,463	6	1,470	.0047
1984	1,405	17	1,423	.0121
1985	1,364	26	1,390	.0188
1986	1,350	32	1,383	.0234
1987	1,354	37	1,391	.0269
1988	1,357	42	1,400	.0305
1989	1,376	45	1,421	.0322
1990	1,410	46	1,457	.0319
1991	1,447	46	1,494	.0312
1992	1,484	46	1,531	.0305
1993	1,521	46	1,568	.0297
1994	1,558	46	1,605	.0290
1995	1,596	46	1,642	.0281
1996	1,634	43	1,678	.0260
1997	1,673	40	1,714	.0239
1998	1,712	35	1,748	.0203
1999	1,750	30	1,780	.0169
2000	1,785	25	1,810	.0138
TOTAL			40,295	

NOTE: Costs are for public institutions only.

TABLE 108 ***Costs of 10-year universal plan*** **(in millions of 1966–67 dollars)**

Year	(1) *Direct costs*	(2) *Indirect costs*	(3) *Total costs*	(4) (2)/(3)
1972		98	98	1.0000
1973	84	108	193	.5620
1974	231	110	342	.3239
1975	383	110	494	.2236
1976	537	109	646	.1690
1977	695	105	801	.1319
1978	862	93	956	.0978
1979	1,034	76	1,111	.0689
1980	1,187	53	1,241	.0435
1981	1,326	29	1,356	.0217
1982	1,455	8	1,464	.0057
1983	1,463	6	1,470	.0097
1984	1,405	17	1,423	.0121
1985	1,364	26	1,390	.0188
1986	1,350	32	1,382	.0235
1987	1,354	37	1,391	.0269
1988	1,357	42	1,400	.0305
1989	1,376	45	1,421	.0322
1990	1,410	46	1,457	.0319
1991	1,447	46	1,494	.0312
1992	1,484	46	1,531	.0305
1993	1,521	46	1,568	.0297
1994	1,558	46	1,605	.0290
1995	1,596	46	1,642	.0281
1996	1,634	43	1,678	.0260
1997	1,673	40	1,714	.0239
1998	1,712	35	1,748	.0203
1999	1,750	30	1,780	.0169
2000	1,785	25	1,810	.0138
TOTAL			36,618	

NOTE: Costs are for public institutions only.

TABLE 109 ***Costs of 15-year universal plan (in millions of 1966–67 dollars)***

Year	(1) Direct costs	(2) Indirect costs	(3) Total costs	(4) (2)/(3)
1972		67	67	1.0000
1973	56	75	131	.5697
1974	155	76	232	.3312
1975	257	78	335	.2328
1976	360	79	439	.1805
1977	463	78	541	.1453
1978	576	74	651	.1149
1979	691	69	760	.0914
1980	791	64	855	.0752
1981	887	59	947	.0630
1982	973	57	1,031	.0562
1983	1,035	58	1,093	.0533
1984	1,090	59	1,149	.0518
1985	1,150	56	1,207	.0471
1986	1,227	50	1,277	.0393
1987	1,319	42	1,362	.0311
1988	1,357	42	1,400	.0305
1989	1,376	45	1,421	.0322
1990	1,410	46	1,457	.0319
1991	1,447	46	1,494	.0312
1992	1,484	46	1,531	.0305
1993	1,521	46	1,568	.0297
1994	1,558	46	1,605	.0290
1995	1,596	46	1,642	.0281
1996	1,634	43	1,678	.0260
1997	1,673	40	1,714	.0239
1998	1,712	35	1,748	.0203
1999	1,750	30	1,780	.0169
2000	1,785	25	1,810	.0138
TOTAL			32,940	

NOTE: Costs are for public institutions only.

FIGURE 30 ***Universal two-year college costs***

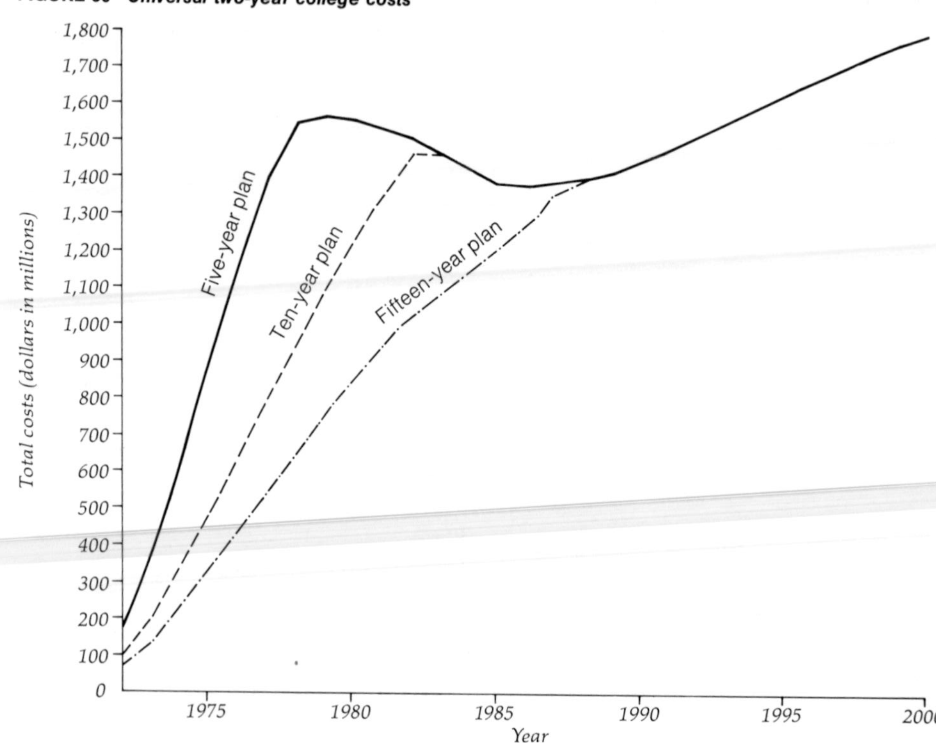

SOURCE: Tables 107, 108, and 109.

FIGURE 31 Universal two-year college program

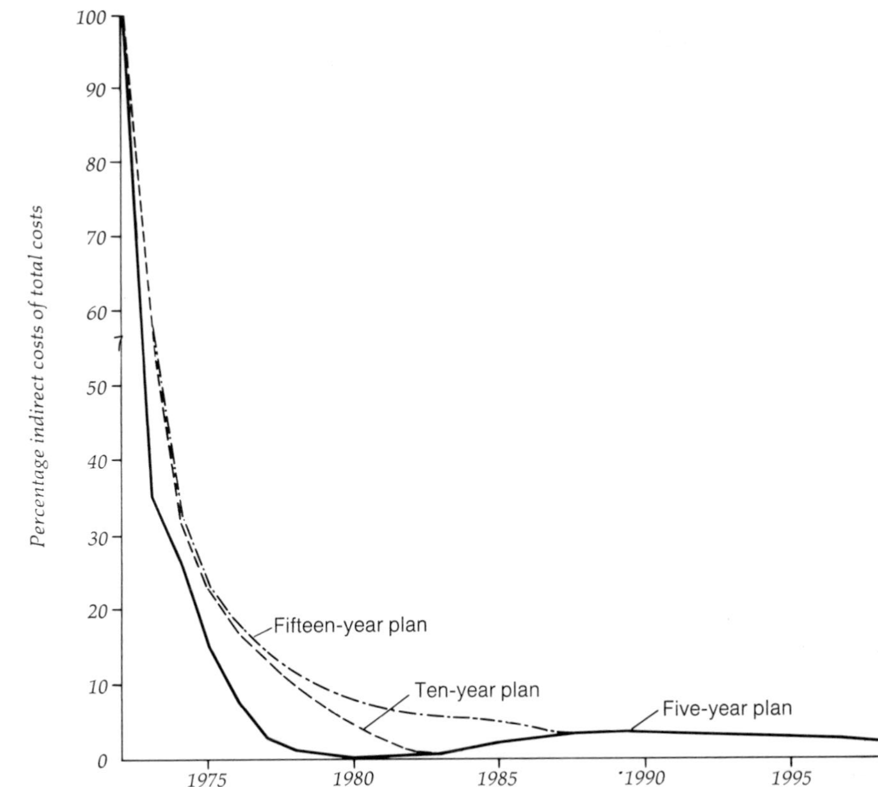

SOURCE: Tables 107, 108, and 109.

12. Resource Requirements for a Compensatory Primary and Secondary School Program

12.1. INTRODUCTION AND SUMMARY

The low achievement of large numbers of students in primary and secondary schools is a matter of increasing concern in our society. Low achievement is highly correlated with certain "disadvantages" in the student's background, especially poverty and racial discrimination. It also bars students from going into higher education and into high-paying jobs. Thus low achievement in primary and secondary schools appears to be a key element in the vicious circle of poverty and disadvantage.[1]

One class of methods that has been proposed for eliminating this element is "compensatory education." Generally speaking, compensatory education involves allocating more than average resources to the education of students from disadvantaged backgrounds. These additional resources may take the form of specialized programs, an increase in the general quality of teachers, an increased number of counselors, improved facilities, etc.[2] A particularly simple form of compensatory education is an increase in the teacher-student ratio.

A plan of compensatory education in the primary and secondary schools can affect higher education in at least two ways. First, it can increase the output of high school graduates who are qualified to enter institutions of higher education. Second,

[1]We do not claim that the removal of inequality in academic achievement would in itself result in the removal of inequality of income; see, for example, Jencks (1972).

[2]The literature on this topic can be separated into studies of the productivity of resources used in education and studies of the financing of education. The objectives of the first group are to understand how compensatory education might work, what characteristics resources should have in order to improve student learning, etc. Some examples are Bowles (1970); Bowles and Levin (1968*a*, 1968*b*,); Coleman et al. (1966, 1968); Guthrie (1970); Hanushek (1970, 1971); Levin (1970); Michelson (1970); Mood (1970).

it can increase the demand for teachers, some or all of which will be met by increasing the output of institutions of higher education.

In the present chapter we estimate the resource requirements of compensatory education plans in which the student-teacher ratio for disadvantaged students in United States primary and secondary education would be reduced from its present level to a target level of 6 to 1. This target level has been chosen to illustrate the quantitative impacts on higher education of a *dramatic* change in the student-teacher ratio for disadvantaged students in primary and secondary education. Little is known about the relative efficacy of different student-teacher ratios, although it would appear that small changes cannot be expected to produce significant results in achievement. Nevertheless, it seems to us plausible that such a low ratio, coupled with appropriate teaching techniques, could produce substantial gains in achievement among students.

Functioning compensatory programs would have levels of complexity that exceed those represented in our exercise. For example, personnel would require differential training levels. Within each level, a multitude of differentiated skills might be required, and each might be produced by a separate higher education program. It is likely that the dynamic input-output model we used could be extended to cover these complexities.

For lack of a better estimate, we have used the number of nonwhite students only as a crude estimate of the number of students in need of compensatory education. We would have preferred to base this estimate on some direct measure of educational disadvantage, since we realize that many white students fall into this category and many nonwhite students do not.

The resource requirements that we calculate are both in terms of manpower (i.e., increased stocks of teachers in primary and secondary schools, increased output of such teachers in primary and secondary schools, increased output of such teachers from institutions of higher education, and increased enrollment of students in higher education to be trained as teachers) and in terms of dollar costs. These requirements have a dynamic aspect because of the variation in enrollment and because of the lead time required to train teachers. A further dynamic element is introduced if we take account of the fact that the time path of resource requirements depends on the speed with which the target teacher-student ratio is achieved. We consider three different start-up times: 5, 10, and 15 years.

The resource-requirement computations are based on the dynamic input-output model of the educational system presented in Chapter 10 and on the cost-per-student estimates presented in Chapter 11. In the explication of our exercise we emphasize the increased numbers of faculty induced by the plan. We compare the distributions of the increased graduate enrollment and the increased faculty by fields, education, and other. For completeness, rough cost estimates for each program are included.

As defined in Chapter 11, we shall use the terms *plan increment* and *trend increment* to describe our results. The plan increments are those increases in quantities (enrollments, teacher stocks, etc.) which are required by the plan, in comparison with the quantities that would have been implied by an extrapolation of historical time series at *constant* rates. The trend increments are the corresponding changes in quantities that would be implied by extrapolation of historical trends in *changes in those rates.* (See Chapter 11, page 365, for precise definitions of these terms.)

Summary of empirical data The objective of the compensatory plans is to increase the teacher-student ratios for disadvantaged children in primary and secondary schools from the 1969 levels of .0403 and .0499, respectively, to a target level of 1 to 6, or .16667 (the same target level for both primary and secondary schools). There are three plans; they differ only in the time necessary to reach the target teacher-student ratio. This time interval will be called the "start-up time." We consider alternative start-up times of 5, 10, and 15 years. Each plan begins in 1972 with a total enrollment of 7.4 million disadvantaged children, which increases to 10.0 million by 1985.

Summary of results By 1987, when all the plans would have reached full-scale operation, an increment of approximately 1 million primary and secondary school teachers would be needed. This is equal to half of the 1969 stock of practicing elementary and secondary school teachers. Although this need not place a great strain on the system in the long run, all the plans would appear to face bottlenecks in teacher training if all the additional teachers were new college and university graduates. However, two sources for the relief of such bottlenecks suggest themselves. First, there is a reserve of persons qualified to teach at the primary and secondary levels. In order to tap this reserve, some inducements to return to the classroom would have to be provided, such as higher pay, alternative work schedules (including part-time appointments), and short courses for teacher retraining. Second, the decline in the academic demand for Ph.D.'s that was projected in Chapter 9 could free resources for teacher training. This shift in resources would require that many undergraduate and graduate students shift their goals from college and university teaching to primary and secondary school teaching and also that many students at the doctoral level shift their goals from research-oriented academic careers to careers in teacher training. The various quantitative dimensions of the requirements and bottlenecks associated with the different start-up times are described in detail in Sections 12.4 and 12.5.

On the cost side, by 1987 the annual cost increments for all plans would be about $12 billion, not counting capital costs for primary and secondary schools. This is probably a low estimate, since we have used moderate estimates of teacher salaries and have not accounted for any increase in costs per teacher that might be needed to tap the present reserve. Of this $12 billion, only about $1 billion represents costs induced in the higher education sector. (Figures are in 1966–67 dollars.)

Although the different start-up times of the plans do not affect the long-run annual costs, they do affect the initial costs. Longer start-up times result in smoother time series of higher education faculty and student requirements, which are more efficient from the point of view of resource utilization. Thus the initial induced higher education cost of the 5-year plan is $1.6 billion, whereas the corresponding initial cost of the 15-year plan is only $600 million. Details of all the cost estimates are presented in Section 12.6.

Postscript The research for this chapter was essentially completed in 1971. During the final stages of that work, new information and new developments appeared—and have appeared since then—that bear on our estimates and projections. On the one hand, enrollment projections for primary and secondary education are being revised downward in the light of recent demographic trends. Furthermore, demographic factors and fiscal problems have contributed to a poor market for teachers that has been developing during the last few years. This development has led many undergraduates to shift out of education majors, leaving excess capacity in schools of education. Therefore, we could probably train many more teachers currently without an increase in overall enrollment in higher education or an increase in faculty in schools of education. A sharp increase in the demand for teachers would draw students back into education majors and draw into teaching recent education graduates who have accepted nonteaching jobs. All these factors would make the compensatory education plans even more easily feasible than we have estimated.

On the other hand, some of these factors work in the opposite direction. Fiscal problems in the schools may have resulted in increased student-faculty ratios, so that an even greater reduction in student-faculty ratios might be needed to achieve the target ratios of the compensatory plans. The recent shift away from education majors means that the total stock of teachers may be less than we estimated.

The net effect of these recent developments is thus difficult to estimate, but it probably is in the direction of making the plans easier to implement. In any case, it is clear that the next decades present a special opportunity to carry out a significant program of compensatory education at the primary and secondary levels.

12.2. THE MODEL

Our analysis is based on the dynamic input-output model of the educational system presented in Chapter 10. As in Chapter 11, the model consists of 24 activities. Most activities refer to a particular school year; e.g., activity 2 is the second grade. Some activities, however, refer to a particular type of instruction within some school year; e.g., activity 21 is graduate study to produce primary school teachers. These activities are again listed and described in Table 110; however, the activities are grouped differently here from the way they are in Chapter 11.

For our present problem, we assume that enrollments are specified exogenously for primary and secondary education (group 1), while final demand is specified exogenously for higher education (group 2). Thus, in equations (31) to (40) of

TABLE 110 ***List of 24 activities in the model of United States education activity***

	Activity	*Description*
	1	First grade
	2	Second grade
	3	Third grade
	4	Fourth grade
	5	Fifth grade
Group 1	*6*	Sixth grade
	7	Seventh grade
	8	Eighth grade
	9	Ninth grade
	10	Tenth grade
	11	Eleventh grade
	12	Twelfth grade
	13	Freshman
	14	Sophomore
	15	Junior
	16	Senior
	17	First-year graduate study for Ph.D.
Group 2	*18*	Second-year graduate study for Ph.D.
	19	Third-year graduate study for Ph.D.
	20	Fourth-year graduate study for Ph.D.
	21	One year of graduate study leading to a primary school credential
	22	One year of graduate study leading to a secondary school credential
	23	Fifth and final year of graduate study for Ph.D.
	24	One-year graduate M.A. program leading to teaching in higher education

Chapter 10, *subscript 1 refers to activities 1 through 12, whereas subscript 2 refers to activities 13 through 24.* The exogenously specified enrollments and final demands are assumed to be unaffected by any of the compensatory plans.[3]

The derivation of the principal teacher-student coefficients

[3]This last assumption is particularly questionable, since a successful compensatory plan would presumably result in an increase in high school graduates qualified for higher education and therefore in an increased demand for places in higher education.

for these compensatory plans is discussed in Section 11.4. Two additional comments are necessary.

First, in these compensatory plans the teacher-student coefficients in primary and secondary schools increase over time. Their change is discussed in the following section.

Second, activities 21 and 22, the one-year post-B.A. program leading to the primary school teaching credential and the secondary school credential, respectively, are taught with the technology used in the upper-division undergraduate program.

The Group 1 technology matrix for the program is displayed in Table 111. To the division of activities into two groups

TABLE 111 ***The final education technology matrix for compensatory plans, group 1*** ***(see p. 389 for group 2)***

	1	*2*	3	*4*	5	*6*	*7*	*8*	*9*	*10*	*11*	*12*
1		1.0										
2			1.0									
3				1.0								
4					1.0							
5						1.0						
6							1.0					
7								1.0				
8									1.0			
9										1.0		
10											1.0	
11												1.0
12												
13												
14												
15												
16												
17												
18												
19												
20	.17	.17	.17	.17	.17	.17						
21							.17	.17	.17	.17	.17	.17
22												
23												
24												

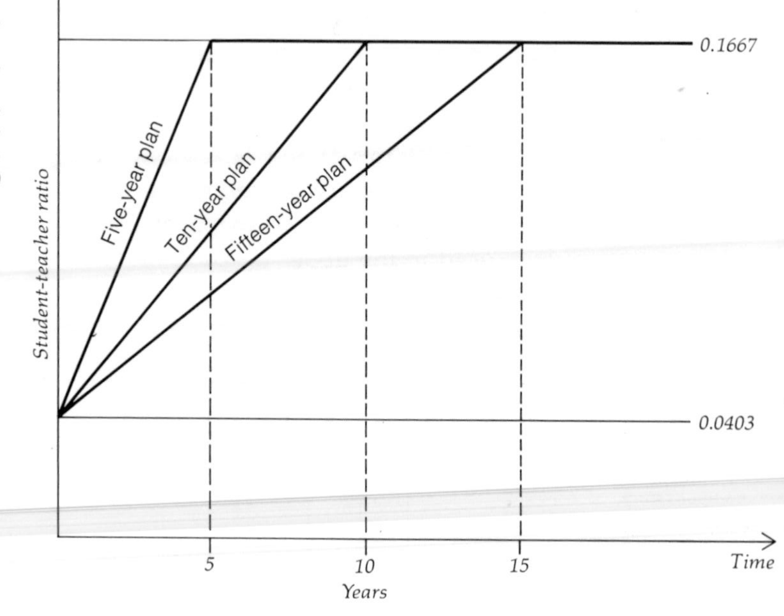

FIGURE 32A ***Illustration of the change required in teacher-student ratios by the three compensatory plans—primary school ($a_{21,1}$ through $a_{21,6}$)***

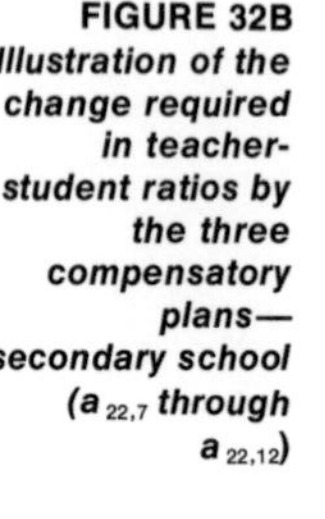

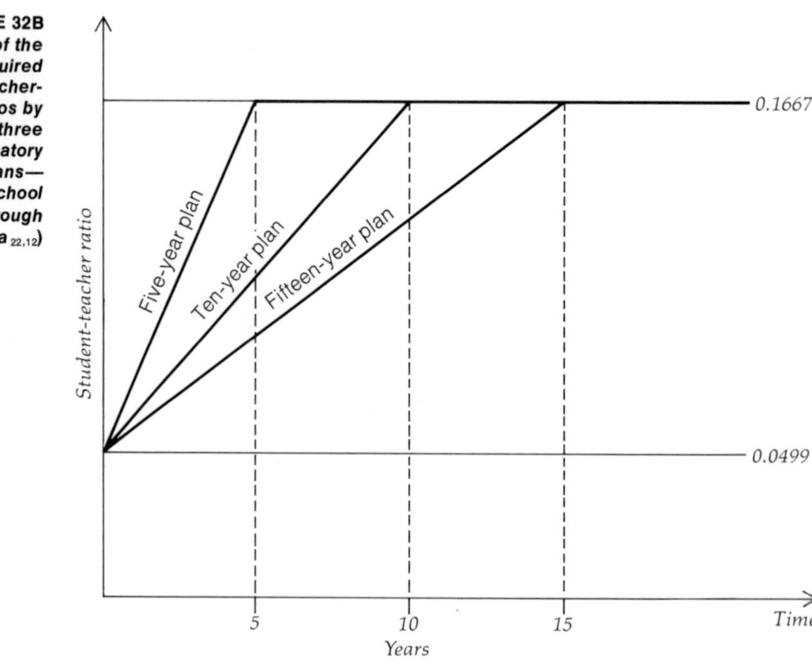

FIGURE 32B ***Illustration of the change required in teacher-student ratios by the three compensatory plans—secondary school ($a_{22,7}$ through $a_{22,12}$)***

corresponds a partition of the education technology matrix, denoted by A, into four blocks. Increasing the primary and secondary school teaching requirements changes the coefficients in A_{21}, the lower left block.

12.3. DATA

Figures 32A and 32B illustrate the change over time, for each plan, in the primary and secondary school compensatory technology. Figure 32A represents primary school activities (elements $a_{21,1}, a_{21,2}, \ldots, a_{21,6}$ of A_{21}), for which the 1969 teacher-student ratio is .0403; Figure 32B represents secondary school activities (elements $a_{22,7}, a_{22,8}, \ldots, a_{22,12}$, of A_{21}), for which the 1969 teacher-student ratio was .0499 (National Center for Educational Statistics, 1969*b*, Tables 3 and 5). For each plan, the objective is a teacher-student ratio of 1 to 6 (.16667) for disadvantaged students in both primary and secondary schools. This target is to be met linearly over a period of 5, 10, or 15 years.

The elements of $\Delta A_{21}(t)$ are defined as

$$\Delta a_{ij}(t) = a_{ij}(t) - a_{ij}(1969).$$

As we noted in Section 12.1, we have used projections of the number of nonwhite students as proxies for estimates of the number of disadvantaged students. There are, of course, many disadvantaged white students, and, on the other hand, many nonwhite students would not be considered disadvantaged. We assume that all disadvantaged students are enrolled in public schools. Since these data are broken down by age rather than by grade in school, we assume that persons aged 6 through 11 are enrolled in grades one through six (primary school activities) and that persons aged 12 through 17 are enrolled in grades seven through twelve (secondary school activities).

The projected population of nonwhite persons by age—values of $Y_1(t)$—was obtained from the Bureau of the Census.[4] We used the series B projections, which are considered by the Bureau of the Census to be moderately high. The fertility rates used in these projections assume only a modest drop in fertility. In light of the recent precipitous drop in fertility rates, it now seems that the series D projections would have been a better choice. The table below compares these two projections

[4]U.S. Bureau of the Census (unpublished data); projections by age and race.

TABLE 112 ***Projections of nonwhite enrollment in primary and secondary school, 1972 to 2000 (in thousands)***

Year	$\sum_{i=1}^{6} Y_{1i}(t)$	$\sum_{i=7}^{12} Y_{1i}(t)$
1972	3,876	3,554
1973	3,847	3,649
1974	3,851	3,731
1975	3,890	3,796
1976	3,954	3,212
1977	4,080	3,894
1978	4,263	3,882
1979	4,451	3,852
1980	4,638	3,857
1981	4,823	3,895
1982	5,004	3,959
1983	5,182	4,084
1984	5,358	4,267
1985	5,530	4,454
1986	5,698	4,641
1987	5,859	4,825
1988	6,013	5,006
1989	6,156	5,183
1990	6,289	5,358
1991	6,412	5,530
1992	6,527	5,697
1993	6,635	5,858
1994	6,749	6,010
1995	6,849	6,155
1996	6,960	6,286
1997	7,079	6,409
1998	7,208	6,524
1999	7,348	6,632
2000	7,501	6,738

for the nonwhite population of primary and secondary school students at five-year intervals, 1972 to 1987.

Nonwhite, aged 6 to 17 (in thousands)

Year	*Series B*	*Series D*	*Ratio B/D*
1972	7,429.99	7,429.99	1.00
1977	7,973.46	7,345.77	1.08
1982	8,963.59	7,145.63	1.25
1987	10,684.31	7,896.20	1.35

The population-projection differences would produce significant changes in our results. We see from the text table that the gap between the two projections grows continuously. We shall argue in this chapter that the principal problems associated with the plans occur in the short run and are aggravated by shorter start-up times. During the start-up period, however, the two projections are most alike. Thus, although the series D projections would require fewer resources, this probably would not drastically reduce feasibility problems. In the long run, the series D projections imply about 20 percent fewer students in primary and secondary schools. Thus the long-run costs with the series D projection should be approximately 20 percent less than the costs we have calculated.[5]

12.4. RESULTS

The manpower requirements for the three compensatory plans are presented in this section. We also explore the effects of the plans on the higher education sector. The question of program feasibility will be raised in the subsequent section.

The plan increments in enrollment in higher education for the three compensatory education programs appear, in a somewhat aggregated form, in Tables 113A–113C.[6] When the plans are fully operative, they require an annual increment in higher education enrollment of about 675,000 persons. This increment appears to be allocated rather uniformly over the undergraduate years; approximately 275,000 in the lower division and approxi-

[5]For a more complete description of the assumptions and methodologies employed in the census projections, see U.S. Bureau of the Census (1967).

[6]Disaggregated results appear in Miller and Radner (1975).

TABLE 113A
Annual plan increments in higher education enrollment—5-year plan (in thousands)

Year	*Total*	*Lower-division*	*Upper-division*	*Graduate*
1972	1,143.18	401.87	526.25	215.07
1973	1,019.02	200.66	579.42	238.94
1974	875.50	205.45	401.87	268.17
1975	713.34	211.07	200.66	301.60
1976	528.67	222.10	205.45	101.12
1977	549.48	232.35	211.07	106.06
1978	574.49	245.99	222.10	106.40
1979	608.37	264.22	232.35	111.81
1980	640.04	277.00	245.99	117.05
1981	668.88	283.88	264.22	121.33
1982	695.38	288.51	277.00	129.86
1983	715.05	292.83	283.34	138.88
1984	727.04	296.25	288.51	142.28
1985	737.16	299.31	292.83	145.02
1986	745.78	302.20	296.25	147.33
1987	753.41	304.85	299.31	149.25
1988	760.50	307.20	302.20	150.71
1989	766.72	309.63	304.85	150.71
1990	772.86	311.76	307.60	153.50
1991	778.24	313.84	309.63	154.77
1992	784.96	317.13	311.76	156.07
1993	793.27	322.66	313.84	156.77
1994	784.96	328.54	317.13	157.55
1995	815.16	335.06	322.66	157.43
1996	798.03	310.14	328.54	159.35
1997	778.84	281.72	335.06	162.05
1998	757.52	281.72	310.14	165.65
1999	733.26	281.72	281.72	169.82
2000	705.53	281.72	281.72	142.09

FIGURE 33A ***Annual plan increments in higher education enrollment—5-year plan***

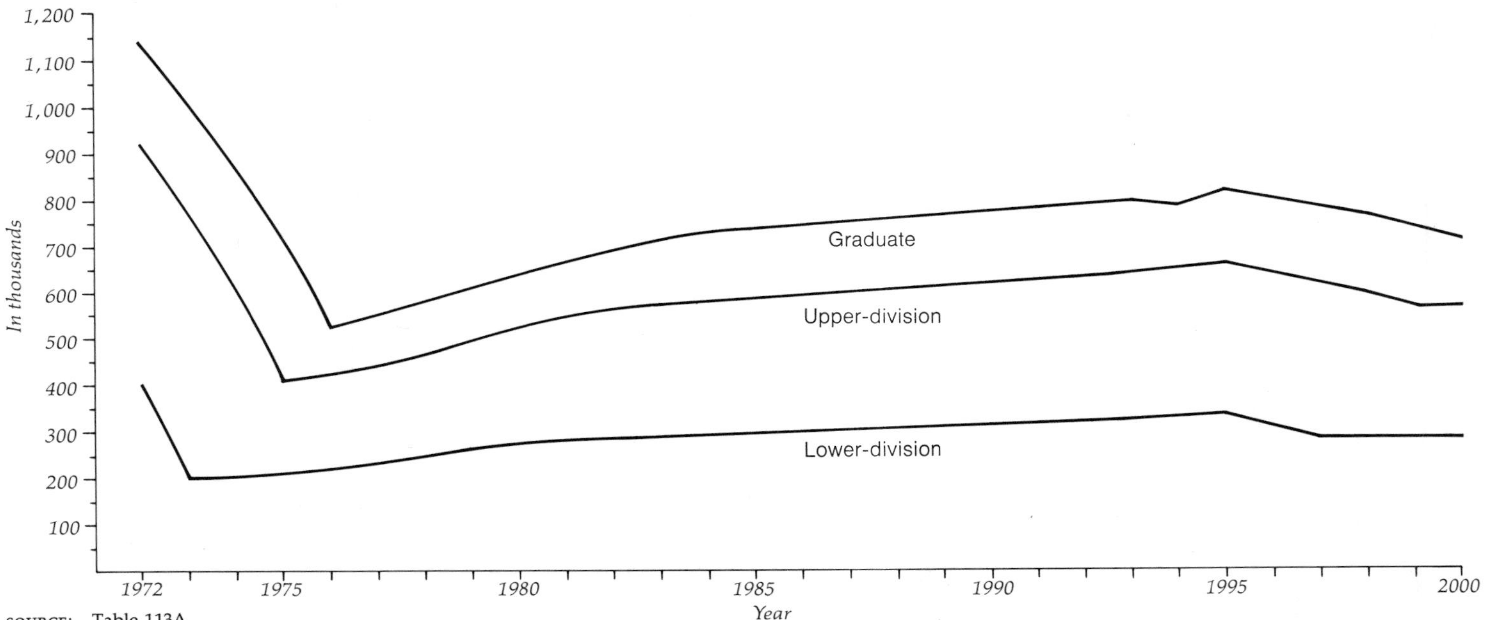

SOURCE: Table 113A.

TABLE 113B ***Annual plan increments in higher education enrollment—10-year plan (in thousands)***

Year	*Total*	*Lower-division*	*Upper-division*	*Graduate*
1972	643.39	288.62	240.37	114.39
1973	700.52	315.52	265.97	119.02
1974	767.14	347.12	288.62	131.39
1975	836.21	378.68	315.52	142.01
1976	911.15	415.20	347.12	148.83
1977	877.93	335.65	378.68	163.60
1978	838.44	245.99	415.20	177.25
1979	796.54	264.22	335.65	196.67
1980	740.83	277.00	245.99	217.83
1981	668.68	283.34	264.22	121.33
1982	695.38	288.51	277.00	129.86
1983	715.05	292.83	283.34	138.88
1984	727.04	296.25	288.51	142.28
1985	737.16	299.31	292.83	145.02
1986	745.78	302.20	296.25	147.33
1987	753.41	304.85	299.31	149.25
1988	760.50	307.60	302.20	150.71
1989	766.72	309.63	304.85	152.24
1990	772.86	311.76	307.60	153.50
1991	778.24	313.84	301.63	154.77
1992	784.96	317.13	311.76	156.07
1993	793.27	322.66	313.84	156.77
1994	803.21	328.54	317.13	157.43
1995	815.16	335.06	322.66	157.43
1996	798.03	310.14	328.54	159.35
1997	778.84	281.72	335.06	162.05
1998	757.52	281.72	310.14	165.65
1999	733.26	281.72	281.72	169.82
2000	705.53	281.72	281.72	142.09

FIGURE 33B ***Annual plan increments in higher education enrollment—10-year plan***

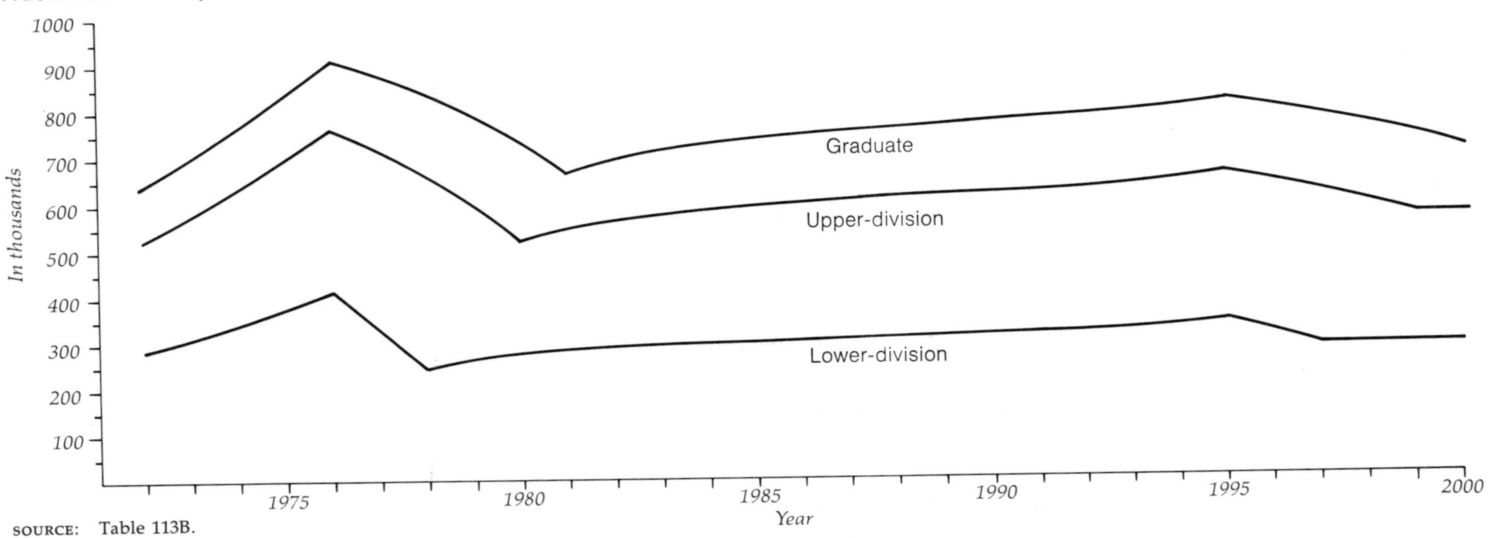

SOURCE: Table 113B.

TABLE 113C ***Annual plan increments in higher education enrollment—15-year plan (in thousands)***

Year	*Total*	*Lower-division*	*Upper-division*	*Graduate*
1972	428.29	193.88	160.20	74.21
1973	470.81	212.91	176.42	81.47
1974	515.14	232.08	193.88	89.18
1975	561.56	250.33	212.91	98.12
1976	611.87	272.85	232.08	106.94
1977	663.02	295.15	250.53	117.34
1978	722.27	323.45	272.85	125.97
1979	792.63	361.79	295.15	135.69
1980	866.18	396.76	323.45	145.96
1981	941.95	426.95	361.79	153.11
1982	934.10	366.38	396.76	168.95
1983	907.60	292.83	526.95	187.82
1984	866.99	296.25	366.38	204.35
1985	813.14	299.31	292.83	221.00
1986	745.78	302.20	296.25	147.33
1987	753.41	304.85	299.31	149.25
1988	760.50	307.60	302.20	150.71
1989	766.72	309.63	304.85	152.24
1990	772.86	311.76	307.60	153.50
1991	778.24	313.84	309.63	154.77
1992	784.96	317.13	311.76	156.07
1993	793.27	322.66	313.84	156.77
1994	803.21	328.54	317.13	157.55
1995	815.16	335.06	322.66	157.43
1996	798.03	310.14	328.54	159.35
1997	778.84	281.72	335.06	162.05
1998	757.52	281.72	310.14	165.65
1999	733.26	281.72	281.72	169.82
2000	705.53	281.72	281.72	142.09

FIGURE 33C ***Annual plan increments in higher education enrollment—15-year plan***

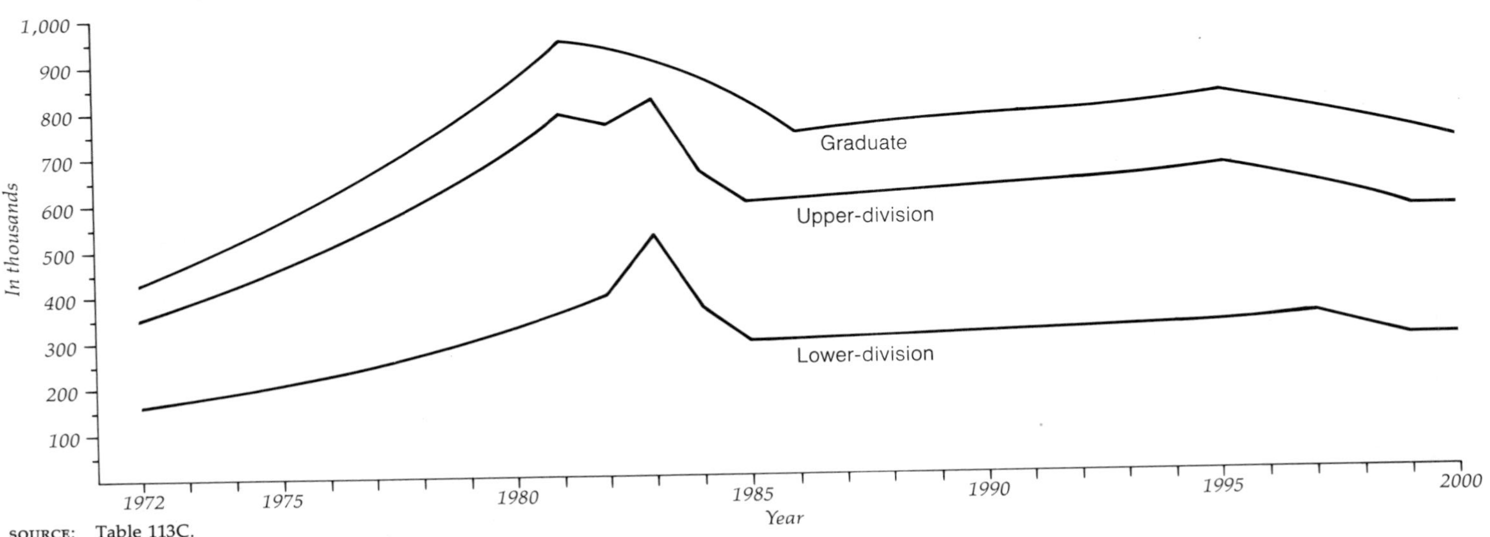

SOURCE: Table 113C.

TABLE 114
Higher education enrollment trend increments (in thousands)

Year	*Undergraduate trend increments*	*Graduate trend increments*
1973	19.6	20.5
1974	59.4	40.9
1975	98.6	61.3
1976	140.8	81.6
1977	202.2	100.0
1978	276.0	117.4
1979	351.9	133.7
1980	421.2	148.6
1981	487.0	161.9
1982	547.0	174.7
1983	587.4	186.8
1984	617.6	197.1
1985	651.2	205.6
1986	696.2	211.8
1987	743.0	214.9
1988	794.2	215.5
1989	856.6	214.2
1990	923.6	213.0
1991	991.6	212.5
1992	1,062.2	212.8
1993	1,134.6	214.6
1994	1,209.4	218.2
1995	1,286.6	223.5
1996	1,359.8	239.1
1997	1,438.2	237.6
1998	1,515.4	245.7
1999	1,588.3	254.4
2000	1,660.6	263.4

SOURCE NOTE: The undergraduate trend increments are Haggstrom's freshman plus sophomore trend increments doubled. The graduate trend increment for each year is the difference between $G(t)$ of Haggstrom's middle projection (B) and $G(t)$ of his constant rate projection (C). However, these differences are adjusted downward so that the enrollment rates are equal in the start-up year, 1972; therefore the trend increments start with 1973.

mately 275,000 in the upper division. An additional 125,000 students are enrolled in graduate school. The overwhelming majority of these graduate students are pursuing primary or secondary teacher training; a relatively small proportion are pursuing a graduate education that would qualify them to teach in institutions of higher education.

Would this increased enrollment precipitate changes in historic higher education trends? How large an impact would a plan's adoption have on the higher education system?

Exploring the answers to these questions will require the definition of two terms: *trend increment* in enrollment and *plan increment* in enrollment. Trend increment in enrollment, at a given level in a given calendar year, is the difference between (1) the projection of enrollment, in that level in that year, based upon extrapolation of the historic trends in enrollment rates and (2) the corresponding projection based upon the assumption that enrollment rates will remain constant at their 1972 levels. For each plan we shall compare the increments in enrollment implied by the plan—the plan increments—with the corresponding trend increments.[7]

Haggstrom's projections are used to calculate the trend increments in enrollments. Table 114 lists the undergraduate trend increments and a mean value of the graduate trend increments.

The ratios of the plan increments in undergraduate enrollment to the trend increments in undergraduate enrollment for the 5-year compensatory plan and for the 15-year compensatory plan are shown in Table 115. Although each plan immediately requires more students than is expected from trend increments, the ratios show that within a decade, trend increments are actually greater than plan increments.

The ratios for plan increments in graduate enrollment to trend increments in graduate enrollment appear in Table 116. In the first five years, the ratios of plan to trend increments for the 5-year plan are, on the average, greater than 5. After that, plan increments in graduate enrollment are lower than trend increments in graduate enrollment. Plan increments for the 15-year plan are close to the trend increments from 1976 to 1985, and are lower thereafter.

The internal transformations within higher education caused

[7]See Sec. 10.5.

TABLE 115
Ratio of plan increments in undergraduate enrollment to trend increments in undergraduate enrollment

Year	*5-year plan*	*15-year plan*
1972		
1973	44.9	19.864
1974	10.224	7.171
1975	4.176	4.700
1976	3.037	3.587
1977	2.193	2.699
1978	1.696	2.161
1979	1.412	1.867
1980	1.241	1.709
1981	1.124	1.620
1982	1.034	1.395
1983	.981	1.225
1984	.947	1.073
1985	.909	.909
1986	.860	.860
1987	.813	.813
1988	.768	.768
1989	.717	.717
1990	.671	.671
1991	.629	.629
1992	.592	.592
1993	.561	.561
1994	.534	.534
1995	.511	.511
1996	.470	.470
1997	.429	.429
1998	.391	.391
1999	.355	.355
2000	.339	.339

FIGURE 34 ***Ratio of plan increments in undergraduate enrollment to trend increments in undergraduate enrollment***

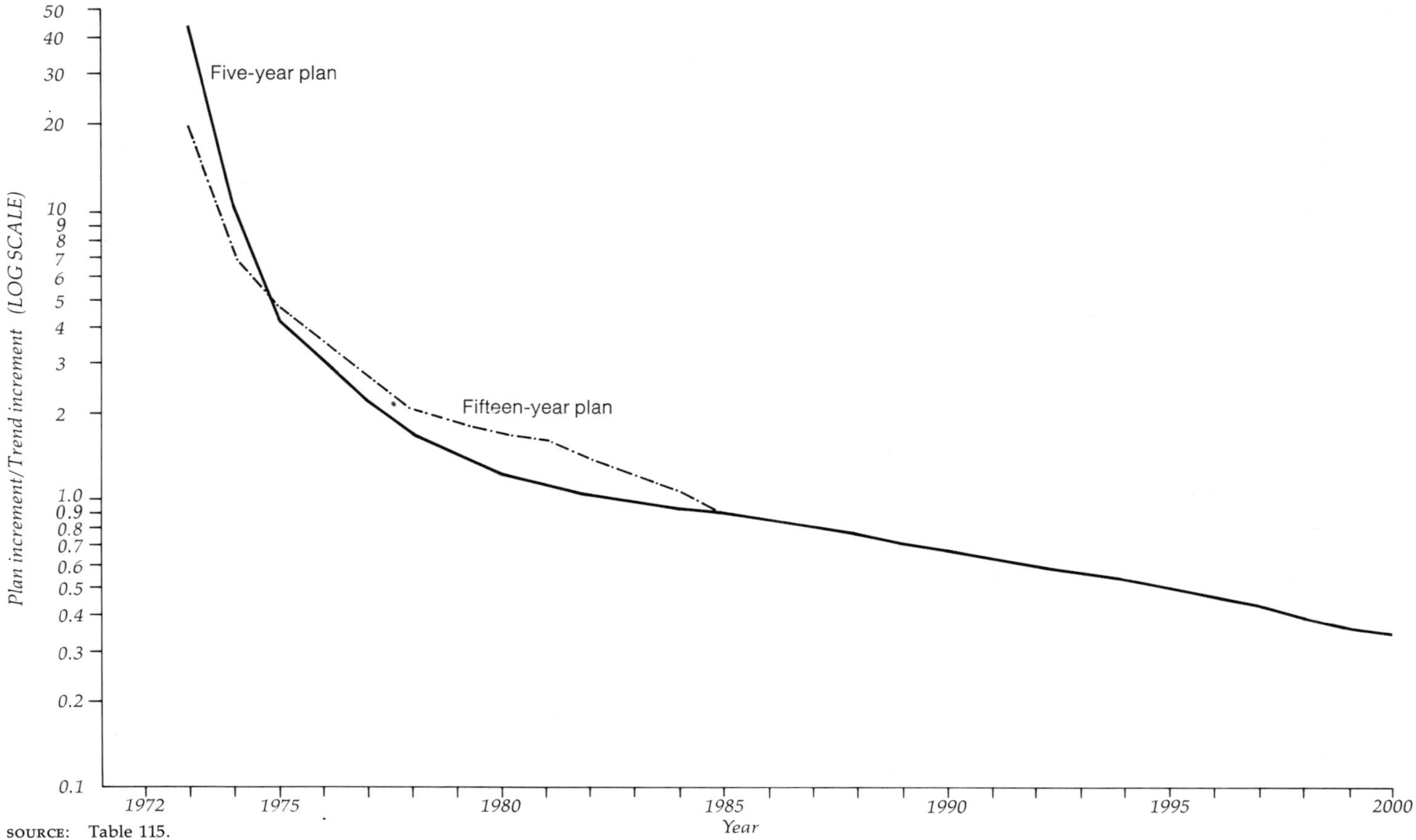

SOURCE: Table 115.

TABLE 116
Ratio of plan increments in graduate enrollment to trend increments in graduate enrollment

Year	*5-year plan*	*15-year plan*
1973	11.66	3.97
1974	6.56	2.18
1975	4.92	1.60
1976	1.24	1.31
1977	1.06	1.17
1978	0.91	1.07
1979	0.84	1.01
1980	0.79	0.98
1981	0.75	0.95
1982	0.74	0.97
1983	0.74	1.01
1984	0.72	1.04
1985	0.71	1.07
1986	0.70	0.70
1987	0.69	0.69
1988	0.70	0.70
1989	0.70	0.71
1990	0.72	0.72
1991	0.73	0.73
1992	0.73	0.73
1993	0.73	0.73
1994	0.72	0.72
1995	0.70	0.70
1996	0.67	0.67
1997	0.68	0.68
1998	0.67	0.67
1999	0.67	0.67
2000	0.54	0.54

FIGURE 35 ***Ratio of plan increments to trend increments in graduate enrollment***

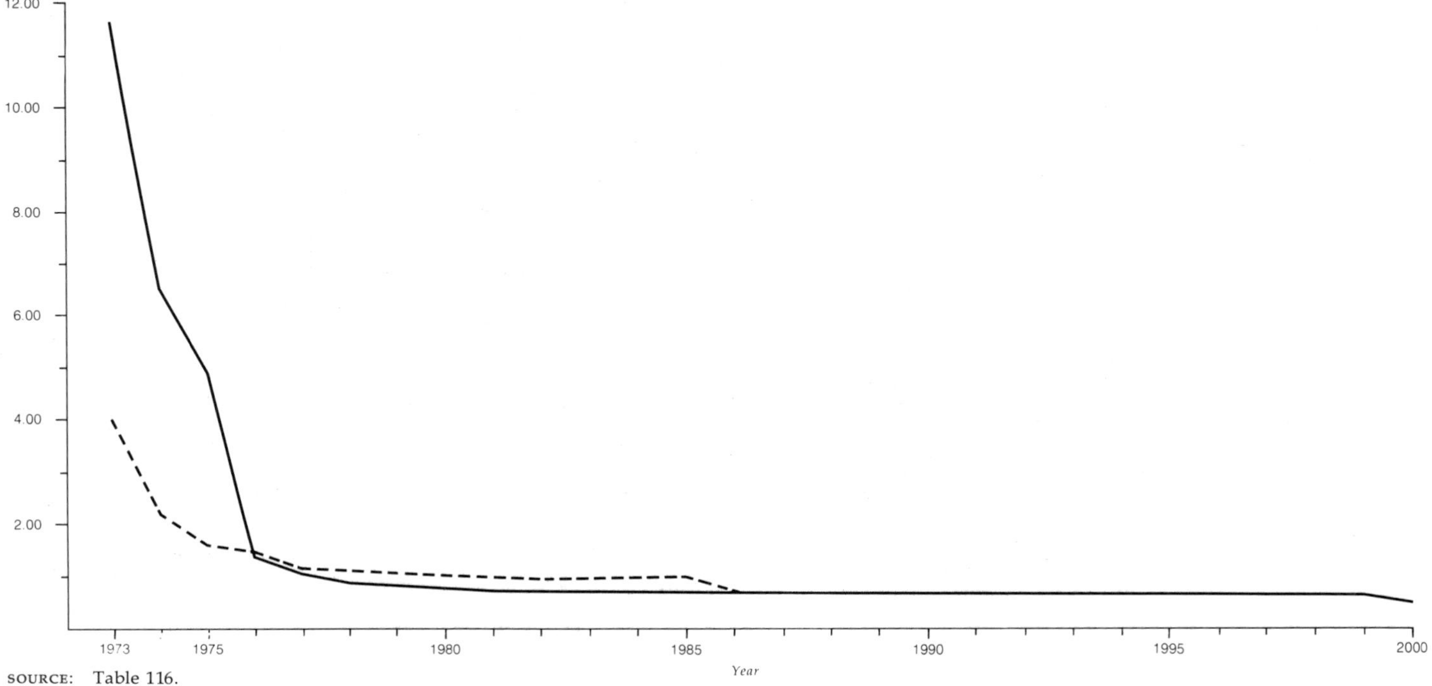

SOURCE: Table 116.

by the adoption of one of these plans are highlighted by a comparison of shifts in incremental enrollments among activities. In our model of the higher education system, teaching credentials are awarded after one-year post-B.A. programs. Consequently, the internal reallocation of enrollment would be revealed in our model as a shift in the proportion of total graduate students who are in schools of education. The ratios of plan increments in school of education enrollment to the corresponding plan increments in total graduate enrollment appear in Table 117. We see that almost all plan increments in graduate enrollment are in schools of education.[8]

One can therefore think of the ratio of the plan increments in total graduate enrollment to the trend increments in graduate enrollment as approximating the ratio of plan increments in school of education enrollment to trend increments in total graduate enrollment.

The implementation of a compensatory plan obviously results in a certain shock to the system. In order to discuss the size of the shock, one must keep in mind that the short-run effects of a plan are distinct from its long-run effects.

The size of the required initial stock naturally varies according to the start-up time of the plan. When we separate the plan increments in students into school of education students and other graduate students, we see that the 5-year compensatory plan requires some diminishment in other graduate school enrollment as well as an increase in school of education enrollment.

Only the 15-year plan requires a less radical increase in school of education enrollment. In its initial year, however, even the 15-year plan requires virtually all resources allocated to expansion in graduate enrollment.

When the plans reach full operation, which will be described as the "long run," the plan increment in school of education enrollment will be approximately 50 percent of total graduate enrollment. In 1970, 254,500 graduate students (31 percent of the total, 816,207) were in schools of education (Simon & Grant, 1971, p. 73).

[8]More than 100 percent of the planned increment in enrollment goes into schools of education in the first four years of the 5-year compensatory plan. This rather curious result is due to the fact that the plan actually causes the increments in enrollment to diminish slightly in other parts of graduate school.

TABLE 117
Ratio of plan increments in school of education enrollment to plan increments in total graduate enrollment

Year	*5-year plan*	*10-year plan*	*15-year plan*
1972	1.036	.914	.885
1973	1.052	.913	.888
1974	1.033	.939	.891
1975	1.016	.961	.898
1976	.940	1.008	.905
1977	.939	1.012	.910
1978	.935	1.009	.912
1979	.941	1.001	.933
1980	.947	.995	.954
1981	.953	.953	.995
1982	.960	.960	1.005
1983	.966	.966	1.007
1984	.968	.968	1.002
1985	.969	.969	.997
1986	.970	.970	.970
1987	.970	.970	.970
1988	.971	.971	.971
1989	.972	.972	.972
1990	.973	.973	.973
1991	.973	.973	.973
1992	.973	.973	.973
1993	.977	.977	.977
1994	.981	.981	.981
1995	.993	.993	.993
1996	.995	.995	.995
1997	.994	.994	.994
1998	.992	.992	.992
1999	.989	.989	.989
2000	.977	.977	.977

FIGURE 36 ***Ratio of plan increments in school of education enrollment to plan increments in total graudate enrollment***

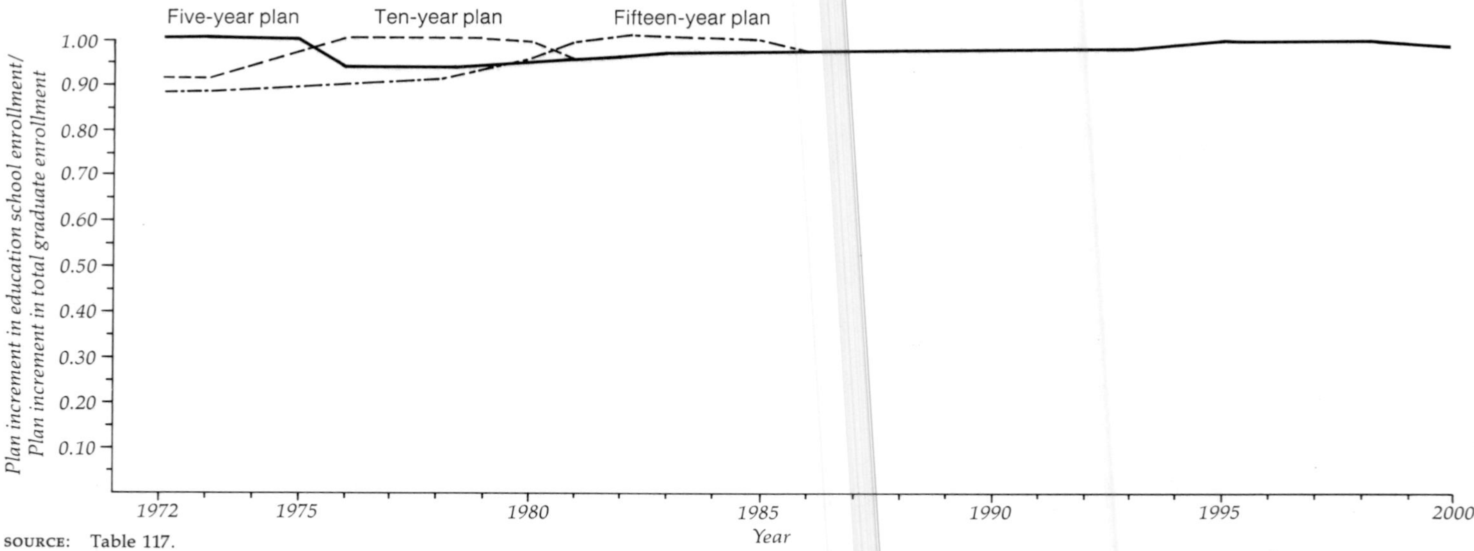

SOURCE: Table 117.

The plans require that, in the long run, 50 percent of all graduate students be enrolled in schools of education. This implies a 67 percent expansion of enrollment in graduate schools of education. Graduate training in education is qualitatively more like upper-division instruction than graduate school instruction. In fact, we assumed that school of education technology is the same as upper-division technology. One should therefore think of this expansion of graduate schools of education as similar to an expansion in upper-division instruction, rather than as a radical shift in graduate instructional emphasis.

Having briefly explored the effects of the plans on student enrollment, let us turn to the plans' effects on higher education faculty. The total increments in faculty required by each plan appear in Table 118. A most interesting situation appears in this table, which is illustrated by the corresponding figure. For all three plans there is some period, during the start-up phase, when more additional faculty are required than will be required when the plan reaches full operation. In the initial four years, the requirements of the 5-year plan drop from an increment of 59,000 faculty down to 38,000. In full operation (1978) the plan actually requires only 30,000 additional faculty. This figure rises slowly thereafter. It is not until 1988 that 40,000 additional faculty are required. This condition is present in an attenuated form in the 15-year plan as well. The 15-year plan begins requiring almost 23,000 additional faculty members. Requirements rise annually for over a decade; in 1982 almost 49,000 additional faculty are required. Requirements then diminish until the plan is in full operation. In 1986, a little over 39,000 additional faculty are required.

To avoid the condition whereby large numbers of faculty would first be hired and then, in a relatively short period of time, fired, one would probably favor compensatory plans with longer start-up times. Further discussion of feasibility appears in the next section.

In Table 119 the plan increments in higher education faculty appear by degree. The 5-year plan begins requiring about 25,000 Ph.D.'s and 35,000 M.A.'s. By the time the plan is in full operation, these requirements are roughly halved. The 15-year plan begins requiring an additional 10,000 Ph.D.'s and 13,000 M.A.'s. As the plan progresses, these figures slowly rise to a

TABLE 118
Plan increments in stocks of higher education teachers (in thousands)

Year	*5-year plan*	*10-year plan*	*15-year plan*
1972	59.4	34.1	22.8
1973	54.8	37.0	25.0
1974	46.8	40.3	27.4
1975	37.8	43.6	29.8
1976	28.0	46.9	32.5
1977	29.0	45.9	35.2
1978	30.3	44.8	38.2
1979	32.0	42.3	41.6
1980	33.7	30.1	45.2
1981	35.2	35.2	48.7
1982	36.7	36.6	48.7
1983	37.7	37.7	48.2
1984	38.3	38.3	45.9
1985	38.5	38.8	42.9
1986	39.3	39.3	39.3
1987	39.7	39.7	39.7
1988	40.7	40.1	40.1
1989	40.4	40.4	40.4
1990	40.7	40.7	40.7
1991	41.0	41.0	41.0
1992	41.3	41.3	41.3
1993	41.7	41.7	41.7
1994	42.1	42.1	42.1
1995	42.6	42.6	42.6
1996	41.9	41.9	41.9
1997	41.2	41.2	41.2
1998	40.0	40.0	40.0
1999	38.6	38.6	38.6
2000	37.2	37.2	37.2

FIGURE 37 ***Plan increments in stocks of higher education teachers (in thousands)***

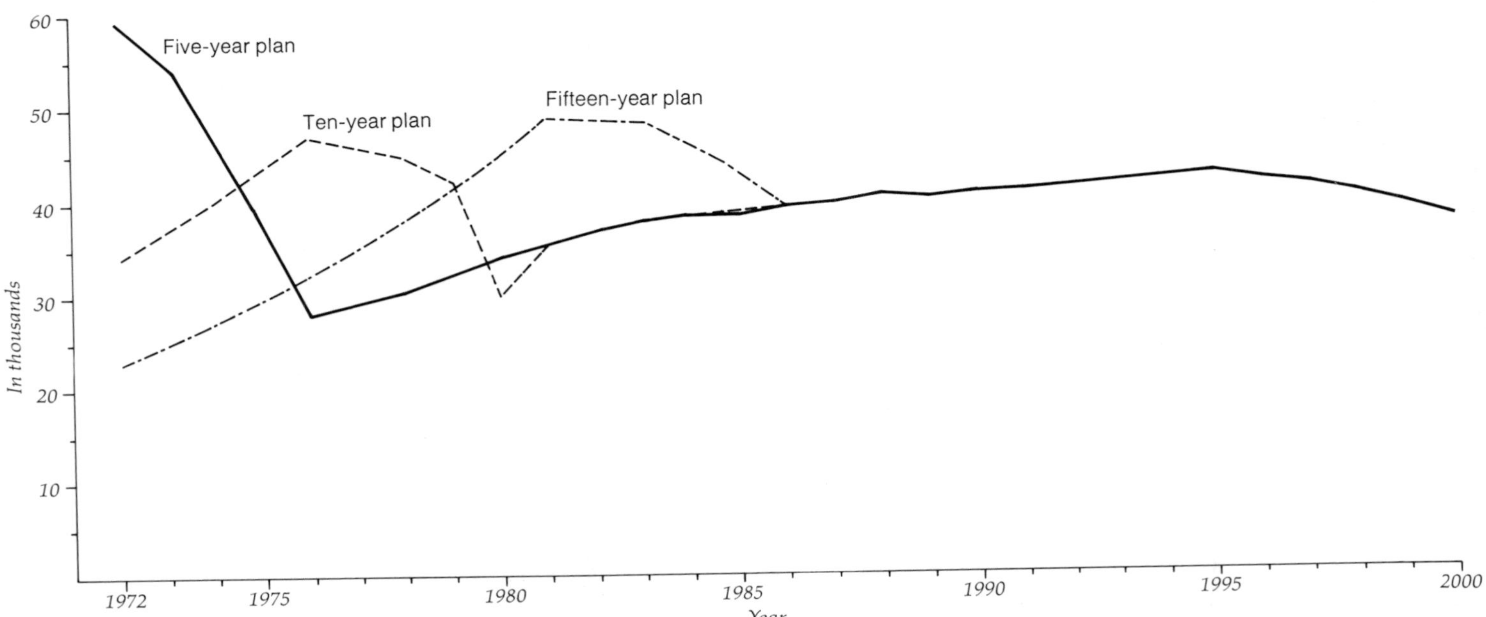

SOURCE: Table 118.

TABLE 119 ***Compensatory plan increments in faculty stock, by degree (in thousands)***

	5-year plan faculty stock increments		*10-year plan faculty stock increments*		*15-year plan faculty stock increments*	
Year	*M.A.*	*Ph.D.*	*M.A.*	*Ph.D.*	*M.A.*	*Ph.D.*
1972	35.2	24.2	20.1	14.0	13.3	9.5
1973	29.5	25.3	22.0	15.1	14.7	10.4
1974	25.7	21.1	24.1	16.2	16.1	11.3
1975	21.4	16.4	26.2	17.3	7.5	12.4
1976	16.4	11.7	29.0	18.0	19.1	13.4
1977	17.0	12.1	27.1	18.8	20.7	14.5
1978	17.9	12.5	25.0	19.8	22.6	15.7
1979	19.0	13.1	24.1	18.1	24.9	16.7
1980	20.0	13.7	22.8	16.3	27.3	17.9
1981	20.8	14.4	20.8	14.4	29.8	18.9
1982	21.6	15.1	21.6	15.1	28.9	19.9
1983	22.2	15.5	22.2	15.5	27.4	20.8
1984	22.5	15.8	22.5	15.8	26.3	19.6
1985	22.8	16.0	22.8	16.0	25.0	18.0
1986	23.1	16.2	23.1	16.2	23.1	16.2
1987	23.3	16.4	23.3	16.4	23.3	16.4
1988	23.5	16.5	23.5	16.5	23.5	16.5
1989	23.7	16.7	23.7	16.7	23.7	16.7
1990	23.9	16.8	23.9	16.8	23.9	16.8
1991	24.1	17.0	24.1	17.0	24.1	17.0
1992	24.3	17.0	24.3	17.0	24.3	17.0
1993	24.6	17.1	24.6	17.1	24.6	17.1
1994	25.0	17.2	25.0	17.2	25.0	17.2
1995	25.4	17.2	25.4	17.2	25.4	17.2
1996	24.7	17.2	24.7	17.2	24.7	17.2
1997	23.8	17.3	23.8	17.3	23.8	17.3
1998	23.2	16.7	23.2	16.7	23.2	16.7
1999	22.6	16.0	22.6	16.0	22.6	16.0
2000	21.8	15.3	21.8	15.3	21.8	15.3

maximum of a little over 20,000 Ph.D.'s and almost 30,000 M.A.'s; then they drop off slowly again.

In Table 120 we list the ratios of the plan increments in faculty stocks to the cumulated trend increments in degree output (M.A. and Ph.D.), for the 5- and 15-year plans. We see that an initial feasibility problem exists with the 5-year plan. The 5-year plan requires Ph.D. faculty stock increments in 1972, 1973, and 1974 that are 63, 13, and 4 times the respective cumulated trend increments in degree production. However, by 1979 the plan increments in both M.A. and Ph.D. faculty stocks are less than half the corresponding cumulated trend increments in degree production. Initial increments for the 15-year plan are also larger than the corresponding cumulated trend increments in degree production, but are considerably less than those for the 5-year plan. After 1979 the 15-year plan faculty stock increments are less than half the corresponding cumulated trend increments in degree production, thus providing a smoother transition.

The increments in the stocks of primary and secondary school teachers required by the three plans are listed in Table 121. The 5-year plan requires about 1 million teachers in five years, and the 10-year plan and the 15-year plan require a little under one-half million and between one-quarter and one-third million in that time, respectively. In 1980, the 5-year plan requires a little over 1 million, the 10-year plan a little over 900,000, and the 15-year plan a little under 600,000 teachers.

To convey some feeling for the size of these requirements relative to the existing stock of teachers, Table 122 shows the ratio of plan increments in stock to the 1969 stock of practicing public education primary and secondary school teachers.

It is here, in Table 122, that the magnitude of the plans under consideration becomes most clear. When the 5-year plan is in full operation in 1977, it requires an increment in teaching staff almost equal in size to half the 1969 existing public elementary and secondary school teaching staff. At that time (1977), the increments for the 10- and 15-year plans are, roughly, one-quarter and one-sixth the size of the 1969 stock of practicing teachers, respectively.

12.5. FEASIBILITY

Having explored the magnitudes of students and faculty personnel required by the plans, we turn now to the question of feasibility. In manpower terms, the question is: Will enough teachers be available? We shall examine this question in terms

TABLE 120
Ratios of plan increments in faculty stocks to cumulated trend increments in degree output, 5- and 15-year plans, M.A. and Ph.D. degrees

	5-year plan		15-year plan	
Year	*M.A.*	*Ph.D.*	*M.A.*	*Ph.D*
1973	5.18	63.25	2.58	26.00
1974	1.49	13.19	.94	7.06
1975	.62	4.00	.22	3.02
1976	.29	1.43	.33	1.63
1977	.20	.84	.24	1.01
1978	.15	.55	.19	.69
1979	.12	.40	.16	.51
1980	.10	.30	.14	.40
1981	.08	.24	.12	.32
1982	.07	.20	.10	.27
1983	.06	.17	.08	.23
1984	.06	.15	.06	.18
1985	.05	.13	.05	.14
1986	.04	.11	.04	.11
1987	.04	.10	.04	.10
1988	.04	.09	.04	.09
1989	.03	.08	.03	.08
1990	.03	.07	.03	.07
1991	.03	.07	.03	.07
1992	.03	.06	.03	.06
1993	.03	.06	.03	.06
1994	.02	.05	.02	.05
1995	.02	.05	.02	.05
1996	.02	.05	.02	.05
1997	.02	.05	.02	.05
1998	.02	.04	.02	.04
1999	.02	.04	.02	.04
2000	.01	.03	.01	.03

NOTE: Plan increments taken from Table 119. Trend increments calculated by same method as for graduate trend increments; see Note to Table 114.

TABLE 121 ***increments in primary and secondary school teachers required by the 5-, 10-, and 15-year compensatory plans (scaled in thousands)***

Year	*5-year plan*	*10-year plan*	*15-year plan*
1972			
1973	228.1	104.5	65.7
1974	461.3	204.9	132.8
1975	701.3	311.8	201.9
1976	951.5	423.3	273.9
1977	970.5	539.5	348.8
1978	992.4	661.9	427.6
1979	1,012.5	787.7	508.3
1980	1,036.7	921.6	594.2
1981	1,064.6	1,064.6	685.9
1982	1,095.0	1,095.0	783.4
1983	1,132.1	1,132.1	890.4
1984	1,175.6	1,175.6	1,008.4
1985	1,210.3	1,219.3	1,132.5
1986	1,262.2	1,262.2	1,262.2
1987	1,304.2	1,304.2	1,304.2
1988	1,344.7	1,344.7	1,344.7
1989	1,383.5	1,383.5	1,383.5
1990	1,420.7	1,420.7	1,420.7
1991	1,456.4	1,456.4	1,456.4
1992	1,490.5	1,490.5	1,490.5
1993	1,523.0	1,523.0	1,523.0
1994	1,554.3	1,554.3	1,554.3
1995	1,584.6	1,584.6	1,584.6
1996	1,614.0	1,614.0	1,614.0
1997	1,643.4	1,643.4	1,643.4
1998	1,673.0	1,673.0	1,673.0
1999	1,703.4	1,703.4	1,703.4
2000	1,735.1	1,735.1	1,735.1

TABLE 122 ***Ratios of plan increments in elementary and secondary school teachers to the 1969 public school stock****

Year	*5-year plan*	*10-year plan*	*15-year plan*
1972			
1973	.118	.052	.033
1974	.201	.124	.066
1975	.356	.105	.101
1976	.475	.212	.131
1977	.485	.270	.174

*The 1969 stock of elementary and secondary teachers was 2,013,836 (National Center for Educational Statistics, 1969*b*, Table 3, p. 10).

of the three "manpower" types necessary for the production of teachers: (1) higher education faculty, (2) graduate students, and (3) persons who are qualified to teach in primary and secondary schools. We find that the start-up problems of these compensatory programs are far more acute than those associated with the universal two-year college program.

Stock of higher education faculty For the year 1974, the plan increments in faculty are 46,800 for the 5-year plan, 40, 300 for the 10-year plan, and 27,400 for the 15-year plan (see Table 118). The cumulated production trend increment is 24,000 (see Table 120). Thus the respective plan increments are 188 percent, 162 percent, and 110 percent of the corresponding trend increments.

These figures imply that the plans may well *not* be feasible. It is impossible to produce higher education faculty instantaneously, and it hardly appears possible that this many additional faculty could be recruited from among people who are qualified for higher education teaching but who are not currently teaching. The only other way to meet this short-run feasibility problem is by increasing the student-faculty ratios in higher education. This, however, raises the question of whether primary and secondary school teachers produced with increased student-faculty ratios would compare in quality with teachers produced under higher ratios. The original objective of compensatory education might be defeated by the very method of creating more teachers.[9]

[9]These comments illustrate the importance of research on the determinants of quality in higher education.

Graduate students The compensatory education plans require an increase in enrollment of graduate students, both to produce increased numbers of primary and secondary school teachers and to produce additional higher education faculty (see Table 117 for percentages of each). In Table 116 the plan increments in number of graduate students are compared with the corresponding expected trend increments.

For the 5-year plan, the plan increment in graduate enrollment for 1974 is more than six times the trend increment; for the 15-year plan, the plan increment is more than two times the trend increment.

However, the problem is not simply one of numbers of graduate students. On the one hand, enough teachers could be produced if a larger proportion of graduate students could be induced to become primary and secondary school teachers. On the other hand, even if the plan increment were met in total, there might still be too few teachers if other professional fields attracted these additional students away from teaching. The question of feasibility depends, then, not so much on total numbers of graduate students as on the numbers that prepare for primary and secondary teaching. The implication is that the plans are not feasible without some actively pursued concomitant policy, such as traineeships and higher teacher salaries, to induce graduate students to become primary and secondary school teachers.

Stock of primary and secondary teachers In addition to the potential numbers of graduate students who might be induced to teach, the existing stock of potential teachers includes a large reservoir of qualified primary and secondary school teachers (mostly women) who are not currently teaching.

Table 123 indicates that in 1960, the number of these potentially recruitable teachers was approximately 35 percent of the number of active teachers. Recall that the compensatory plans require increases in stocks of teachers on the order of 50 percent (see Tables 121 and 122). If that 1960 inactive-active ratio is anywhere in the ball park, we note, with some relief, that that reserve teaching labor force could go a long way toward meeting any plan's requirements.

As with recruiting graduate students, social policy will play a determining role in inducing these qualified teachers to return to teaching. Alternative work schedules, such as half-time or

TABLE 123 ***Comparison of labor reserve with labor force, by level of teaching, age, and sex: 1960 (in thousands)***

	Male			*Female*		
Level of teaching and age	*Persons in labor force*	*Persons in labor reserves*	*Labor reserve as percentage of labor force*	*Persons in labor force*	*Persons in labor reserves*	*Labor reserve as percentage of labor force*
25 to 34 years old						
Public elementary	60,785	1,170	1.9	169,061	142,641	84.4
Public secondary	104,426	2,239	2.1	47,906	35,812	74.8
35 to 44 years old						
Public elementary	53,988	528	1.6	171,463	52,449	30.6
Public secondary	68,645	832	1.2	51,247	15,235	29.8
45 to 54 years old						
Public elementary	20,810	369	1.8	243,310	33,230	13.3
Public secondary	50,035	593	1.2	67,563	7,859	11.6
55 to 64 years old						
Public elementary	10,427	730	7.0	144,218	27,575	28.2
Public secondary	27,383	1,378	5.0	42,168	7,951	21.0
TOTAL	376,499	7,839	2.1	942,966	322,770	34.2

NOTE: Teachers in the labor reserve are persons "who had taught at any time in the 10 years preceding the 1960 census."

SOURCE: Folger and Nam (1967, pp. 104–105).

quarter-time teaching positions, might prove effective, given the preponderance of females in the reserve.

The successful recruitment of teachers who are presently unemployed and not in the market for a teaching position would have the beneficial effect of reducing both plans' graduate student requirements. This in turn would decrease faculty requirements, alleviating, to a certain degree, the need to increase student-teacher ratios in higher education.

We have thus far defined the feasibility question in terms of available manpower resources. We have not considered the organizational arrangements necessary to enable teachers to be either produced or used. Higher education institutions are notorious for their inability to make changes in their teaching methods and their governing structures very rapidly. This comment seems pertinent, given the plans' long-run requirement of a 50 percent increase in graduate enrollment in education and the subsequent changes in institutional faculty and administrating structure that would be likely to accompany these figures.

This discussion brings out the importance of research into the recruiting of qualified teachers who are not teaching.

12.6. MONETARY COSTS

The compensatory programs explored in this exercise require huge numbers of personnel. The exercise amounts to establishing a public primary and secondary school educational system half again the size of the present system. In this section we report the costs of establishing and operating this "new" system in 1966–67 dollars.

As in the previous exercise (the universal two-year college plan discussed in Chapter 11), we have separated the total costs into direct and indirect components. The direct component includes the salaries of the compensatory primary and secondary school teachers required by the plans. It does not include any primary or secondary school capital costs that would be associated with the plans.

Table 124 displays the numbers of primary and secondary school teachers for the three plans and the direct costs of the plans. The latter have been calculated on the basis of $8,500 as the annual salary of a compensatory teacher.

When the plans are in full operation in 1987, the direct costs are roughly $11 billion per annum. The 5-year plan begins requiring almost $2 billion and annual increases of $2 billion. In the initial years, the 15-year plan's costs are roughly one-third of the 5-year plan's costs.

The induced higher education enrollments determine the indirect costs. Costs-per-student estimates are discussed in Table 106 in Chapter 11; they are estimated at $964 for lower-division students, $1,446 for upper-division students, and $3,616 for graduate students. We have assumed that the graduate education programs are taught with upper-division faculty-student coefficients and have estimated their costs accordingly.

Table 125 displays the induced, or indirect, costs of the plans. They are roughly $1 billion when in full operation. Owing to the rather wasteful timing features of the faster start-up plans, the 5-year plan begins requiring $1.6 billion. The most efficient plan in terms of resource timing, the 15-year plan, requires $600 million in higher education costs at its beginning.

Table 126 displays the total costs of the three plans. The $12-

TABLE 124 ***Teacher requirements (in thousands) and direct costs for the 5-, 10-, and 15-year compensatory plans (in millions of 1966–67 dollars)***

Year	*5-year plan*		*10-year plan*		*15-year plan*	
	*Primary and secondary teacher stock**	*Direct cost*	*Primary and secondary teacher stock**	*Direct cost*	*Primary and secondary teacher stock**	*Direct cost*
1972						
1973	228	1,938	104	888	65	558
1974	461	3,920	204	1,741	132	1,128
1975	701	5,961	311	2,650	201	1,715
1976	951	8,087	423	3,598	273	2,327
1977	970	8,248	539	4,585	348	2,964
1978	992	8,435	661	5,626	427	3,634
1979	1,012	8,606	787	6,695	508	4,320
1980	1,036	8,811	921	7,833	594	5,050
1981	1,064	9,048	1,064	9,048	685	5,830
1982	1,094	9,307	1,094	9,307	783	6,658
1983	1,132	9,622	1,132	9,622	890	7,568
1984	1,175	9,992	1,175	9,992	1,008	9,571
1985	1,219	10,363	1,219	10,363	1,132	9,626
1986	1,262	10,363	1,219	10,363	1,132	9,626

1987	1,304	11,085	1,304	11,085	1,304	11,085
1988	1,344	11,429	1,344	11,429	1,344	11,429
1989	1,383	11,759	1,383	11,759	1,383	11,759
1990	1,420	12,076	1,420	12,076	1,420	12,076
1991	1,456	12,379	1,456	12,369	1,456	12,379
1992	1,490	12,668	1,490	12,668	1,490	12,668
1993	1,523	12,945	1,523	12,945	1,523	12,945
1994	1,554	13,211	1,554	13,211	1,554	13,211
1995	1,584	13,467	1,584	13,467	1,584	13,467
1996	1,614	13,719	1,614	13,719	1,614	13,719
1997	1,643	13,968	1,643	13,968	1,643	13,968
1998	1,673	14,220	1,673	14,220	1,673	14,220
1999	1,703	14,479	1,703	14,470	1,703	14,479
2000	1,753	14,748	1,735	14,748	1,735	14,748

*Primary and secondary teacher stock = sum of increment to stock for activities 21 and 22. Direct cost = $8,500 × primary and secondary teacher stock.

TABLE 125
Indirect costs: induced higher education costs for compensatory primary and secondary programs (in millions of 1966–67 dollars)*

Year	*5-year plan*	*10-year plan*	*15-year plan*
1972	1,596	888	591
1973	1,531	961	650
1974	1,348	1,048	711
1975	1,141	1,137	776
1976	739	1,223	845
1977	768	1,223	916
1978	799	1,219	995
1979	842	1,166	1,083
1980	885	1,097	1,176
1981	926	926	1,268
1982	967	967	1,292
1983	1,000	1,000	1,305
1984	1,018	1,018	1,258
1985	1,033	1,033	1,192
1986	1,045	1,045	1,045
1987	1,056	1,056	1,056
1988	1,066	1,066	1,066
1989	1,075	1,075	1,075
1990	1,084	1,084	1,084
1991	1,092	1,092	1,092
1992	1,101	1,101	1,101
1993	1,110	1,110	1,110
1994	1,121	1,121	1,121
1995	1,132	1,132	1,132
1996	1,121	1,121	1,121
1997	1,109	1,109	1,109
1998	1,081	1,081	1,081
1999	1,050	1,050	1,050
2000	992	992	992

*The indirect costs for any year are the sum of the costs per student times the number of students enrolled. Costs are differentiated by three levels: lower-division, upper-division, and graduate. See Table 106 in Chap. 11.

TABLE 126
Total costs of compensatory plans (in millions of 1966–67 dollars)*

Year	*5-year plan*	*10-year plan*	*15-year plan*
1972	1,596	888	591
1973	3,470	1,850	1,208
1974	5,269	2,789	1,839
1975	7,102	3,788	2,492
1976	8,827	4,821	3,173
1977	9,017	5,809	3,881
1978	9,234	6,846	4,630
1979	9,449	7,862	5,403
1980	9,697	8,930	6,227
1981	9,975	9,975	7,098
1982	10,275	10,275	7,951
1983	10,622	10,622	8,874
1984	11,011	11,011	9,829
1985	11,396	11,396	10,818
1986	11,774	11,774	11,774
1987	12,142	12,142	12,142
1988	12,496	12,496	12,496
1989	12,835	12,835	12,835
1990	13,160	13,160	13,160
1991	13,471	13,471	13,471
1992	13,770	13,770	13,770
1993	14,055	14,055	14,055
1994	14,332	14,332	14,332
1995	14,600	14,600	14,600
1996	14,840	14,840	14,840
1997	15,077	15,077	15,077
1998	15,302	15,302	15,302
1999	15,529	15,529	15,429
2000	15,740	15,740	15,740

*The annual total cost is the sum of the annual direct cost, Table 124, and the annual indirect cost, Table 125.

billion long-run annual cost in 1987 must be interpreted as a low estimate; primary and secondary capital costs are not included. Further, teachers' salaries have been priced moderately at $8,500 per annum and thus do not reflect the probable increase that would be required to recruit teachers back into the labor force.

References

Adkins, D. L.: "The American Educated Labor Force: An Empirical Look at Theories of Its Formation and Composition," in M. S. Gordon (ed.), *Higher Education and the Labor Force,* McGraw-Hill Book Company, New York, 1973.

Adkins, D. L.: *The Great American Degree Machine,* The Carnegie Commission on Higher Education, Berkeley, Calif., 1975.

American Bar Foundation: *The 1961 Lawyer Statistical Report,* Chicago, 1961, 1964.

American Council on Education: *American Universities and Colleges,* Washington, 1952, 1956, 1960, 1964, 1968.

American Council on Education: *Cartter Report: An Assessment of Quality in Graduate Education,* Washington, 1966.

American Council on Education: *A Fact Book on Higher Education,* Washington, 1967.

Astin, A. W.: "Undergraduate Achievement and Institutional 'Excellence,'" *Science,* vol. 161, no. 3842, 1968.

Balderston, F. E., and R. Radner: "Academic Demand for New Ph.D.'s, 1970–1990: Its Sensitivity to Alternative Policies," Ford Foundation Program for Research in University Administration, paper P-26, University of California, Berkeley, 1971.

Barr, R. H., and B. J. Foster: *Statistics of Public Elementary and Secondary Day Schools, Fall 1969,* U.S. Office of Education, 1970.

Bowker, A. H.: "Quality and Quantity in Higher Education," *Journal of the American Statistical Association,* vol. 60, no. 309, March 1965.

Bowles, S.: "Towards an Education Production Function," *Education, Income, and Human Capital,* National Bureau of Economic Research, New York, 1970.

Bowles, S., and H. M. Levin: "The Determination of Scholastic Achievement: An Appraisal of Some Recent Evidence," *The Journal of Human Resources,* vol. 3, no. 1, pp. 3–24, Winter 1968*a*.

Bowles, S., and H. M. Levin: "More on Multicollinearity and the Effectiveness of Schools," *The Journal of Human Resources,* vol. 3, no. 3, pp. 393–400, Summer 1968*b*.

Campbell, R., and B. N. Siegel: "Demand for Higher Education in the United States," *American Economic Review,* vol. 57, June 1967.

Carnegie Commission on Higher Education: *The Open Door Colleges: Policies for the Community Colleges,* a report and recommendations, McGraw-Hill Book Company, New York, 1970.

Carnegie Commission on Higher Education: *New Students and New Places: Policies for the Future Growth and Development of American Higher Education,* a report and recommendations, McGraw-Hill Book Company, New York, 1971.

Carnegie Commission on Higher Education: *The More Effective Use of Resources: An Imperative for Higher Education,* a report and recommendations, McGraw-Hill Book Company, New York, 1972.

Carnegie Commission on Higher Education: *Higher Education: Who Pays? Who Benefits? Who Should Pay?* a report and recommendations, McGraw-Hill Book Company, New York, 1973.

Cartter, A. W.: "Scientific Manpower for 1970–1985," *Science,* vol. 172, no. 3979, pp. 132–140, 1971.

Coleman, J. S., et al.: *Equality of Educational Opportunity,* U.S. Office of Education, 1966.

Coleman, J. S., et al.: "Equality of Educational Opportunity: Reply to Bowles and Levin," *The Journal of Human Resources,* vol. 3, no. 2, pp. 237–246, Spring 1968.

College Entrance Examination Board: *SCOPE (School to College: Opportunities for Post Secondary Education),* Center for Research and Development in Higher Education, University of California, Berkeley, published in New York, December 1966.

College Entrance Examination Board, Educational Testing Service: *College Board Score Reports: A Guide for Counselors and Admissions Officers,* Princeton, N.J., 1971.

Corazzini, A. J., D. J. Dugan, and H. G. Grabowski: "Determinants and Distributional Aspects of Enrollment in U.S. Higher Education," *The Journal of Human Resources,* vol. 7, no. 1, 1972.

Creager, J. A., and C. L. Sell: "The Institutional Domain of Higher Education: A Characteristics File for Research," *ACE Research*

Reports, vol. 4, no. 6, American Council on Education, Washington, 1969.

Denison, E.: "Measuring the Contribution of Education and the Residual to Economic Growth," in *The Residual Factor and Economic Growth*, Organization for Economic Co-operation and Development, Paris, pp. 13–55, 1964.

Feldman, P., and S. A. Hoenack: "Private Demand for Higher Education in the United States," *The Economics and Financing of Higher Education in the United States*, a compendium of papers submitted to the Joint Economic Committee of the Congress of the United States, part IV, "The Structural Outlook for Institutions of Higher Learning," Washington, 1969.

Flanagan, J. C., et al.: *The American High School Student*, technical report to the U.S. Office of Education, Cooperative Research Project no. 635, Project TALENT Office, University of Pittsburgh, Pittsburgh, Pa., 1964.

Flanagan, J. C., and W. W. Cooley: *One Year Follow-up Studies*, technical report to the U.S. Office of Education, Cooperative Research Project no. 2333, Project TALENT Office, University of Pittsburgh, Pittsburgh, Pa., 1966.

Folger, J. K., and C. B. Nam: *Education of the American Population*, Government Printing Office, Washington, 1967.

Froomkin, J.: "Approaches to Forecasting Demand for College Graduates and Ph.D.'s," (unpublished). Cited in D. Wolfle and C. V. Kidd, "The Future Market for Ph.D.'s," *Science*, vol. 173, no. 3999, pp. 784–793, August 1971.

Galper, H., and R. M. Dunn, Jr.: "A Short-Run Demand Function for Higher Education in the United States," *Journal of Political Economy*, vol. 77, no. 5, 1969.

Ghali, M., W. Miklius, and R. Wada: "The Demand for Higher Education Facing an Individual Institution." (Mimeographed.)

Guthrie, J. W.: "A Survey of School Effectiveness Studies," *Do Teachers Make a Difference? A Report on Recent Research on Pupil Achievement*, U.S. Office of Education, 1970.

Haggstrom, G. W.: *The Growth of Higher Education in the United States*, unpublished manuscript, Carnegie Commission on Higher Education, Berkeley, Calif., 1971*a*.

Haggstrom, G. W.: "The Growth of Graduate Education in the Post-Sputnik Era," unpublished, revised degree projections received from the author, 1971*b*.

Hanushek, E.: "The Production of Education, Teacher Quality, and Efficiency," *Do Teachers Make a Difference? A Report on Recent Research on Pupil Achievement,* U.S. Office of Education, 1970.

Hanushek, E.: "Teacher Characteristics and Gains in Student Achievement: Estimation Using Micro Data," *American Economic Review: Papers and Proceedings,* vol. 61, no. 2, pp. 280–288, May 1971.

Harmon, L. R., and H. Soldz: *Doctorate Production in United States Universities, 1920–1962, with Baccalaureate Origins of Doctorates in Sciences, Arts, and Professions,* National Academy of Sciences, National Research Council, Washington, 1963.

Harris, S. E.: *Higher Education: Resources and Finance,* McGraw-Hill Book Company, New York, 1962.

Hoenack, S. A.: "Private Demand for Higher Education in California," unpublished doctoral dissertation, University of California, Berkeley, 1967.

Hoenack, S. A.: "The Efficient Allocation of Subsidies to College Students," *American Economic Review,* vol. 61, no. 3, part 1, pp. 302–311, June 1971.

Hood, W. C., and T. C. Koopmans, (eds.): *Studies in Econometric Method,* Cowles Commission Monograph 14, John Wiley & Sons, Inc., New York, 1953.

Jacobson, P. H.: "Cohort Survival for Generations since 1840," *Milbank Memorial Fund Quarterly,* vol. 42, part 1, pp. 36–53, July 1964.

Jencks, C.: *Inequality: A Reassessment of the Family and Schooling in America,* Basic Books, Inc., Publishers, New York, 1972.

Jencks, C., and D. Riesman: *The Academic Revolution,* Doubleday & Company, Inc., Garden City, N.Y., 1968.

Jewett, J. E.: *College Admissions Planning: Use of a Student Segmentation Model,* Ford Foundation Program for Research in University Administration, November 1971.

Johnson, H. G.: "The Keynesian Revolution and the Monetarist Counter-Revolution," Richard T. Ely Lecture, *American Economic Review, Papers and Proceedings,* vol. 61, no. 2, pp. 1–14, May 1971.

Kohn, M., C. F. Manski, and D. Mundel: *A Study of College Choice,* paper presented at the North American Regional Meeting of the Econometric Society, Toronto, December 1972.

Kuhn, T. S.: *The Structure of Scientific Revolutions,* 2d ed., The University of Chicago Press, Chicago, 1970.

Levin, H. M.: "A New Model of School Effectiveness," *Do Teachers*

Make a Difference? A Report on Recent Research on Pupil Achievement, U.S. Office of Education, 1970.

Luce, R. D., and P. Suppes: "Preference, Utility, and Subjective Probability," in R. Luce, R. Bush, and E. Galanter (eds.), *Handbook of Mathematical Psychology,* John Wiley & Sons, Inc., New York, vol. 3, 1965.

McFadden, D.: *Conditional Logit Analysis of Qualitative Choice Behavior,* Institute of Urban and Regional Development, University of California, Berkeley, May 1973.

McFadden, D.: *The Measurement of Urban Travel Demand,* Institute of Urban and Regional Development, University of California, Berkeley, February 1974.

Marschak, Jacob: "Economic Measurement for Policy and Prediction," in W. C. Hood and T. C. Koopmans (ed.), *Studies in Econometric Method,* Cowles Commission Monograph 14, John Wiley & Sons, Inc., New York, 1953.

Massachusetts Metropolitan Area Planning Council: *Higher Education in the Boston Metropolitan Area,* Commonwealth of Massachusetts Board of Higher Education, Boston, 1969.

Massé, P.: *Le Plan, ou l'Anti-hasard,* Gallimard, Paris, 1965.

Medsker, L. L., and D. Tillery: *Breaking the Access Barriers: A Profile of Two-Year Colleges,* McGraw-Hill Book Company, New York, 1971.

Michelson, S.: "The Association of Teacher Resources with Children's Characteristics," *Do Teachers Make a Difference? A Report on Recent Research on Pupil Achievement,* U.S. Office of Education, 1970.

Miller, L. S., and R. Radner: *Demand and Supply in Higher Education in the United States: A Technical Supplement,* Carnegie Commission on Higher Education, Berkeley, Calif., 1975.

Mood, A. M.: "Do Teachers Make a Difference?" *Do Teachers Make a Difference? A Report on Recent Research on Pupil Achievement,* U.S. Office of Education, 1970.

Mooney, J.: "Attrition among Ph.D. Candidates: An Analysis of a Cohort of Recent Woodrow Wilson Fellows," *The Journal of Human Resources,* vol. 3, 1968.

Morgan, J. N., et al.: *Income and Wealth in the United States,* McGraw-Hill Book Company, New York, 1962.

National Center for Educational Statistics: *Advanced Statistics on Opening Fall Enrollment: Basic Information, 1969,* Washington, 1969*a*.

National Center for Educational Statistics: *Statistics of Public Schools,* Washington, 1969*b*.

National Center for Educational Statistics: *A Taxonomy of Instructional Programs in Higher Education,* Washington, 1970.

National Commission on the Financing of Postsecondary Education: *Financing Postsecondary Education in the United States,* Washington, 1973.

O'Neill, J.: *Resource Use in Higher Education,* Carnegie Commission On Higher Education, Berkeley, Calif., 1971.

Pugliaresi, L.: "Inquiries into a New Degree: The Candidate in Philosophy," Ford Foundation Program for Research in University Administration, paper P-13, University of California, Berkeley, 1970.

Schwartz, M. A.: *The United States College-Educated Population: 1960,* report no. 102, National Opinion Research Center, University of Chicago, October 1965.

Simon, K. A., and W. V. Grant: *Digest of Educational Statistics,* National Center for Educational Statistics, Washington, 1971.

Solow, R.: "Technical Change and the Aggregate Production Function," *Review of Economics and Statistics,* vol. 39, no. 3, pp. 312–320, August 1957.

Taubman, P., and T. Wales: *Mental Ability and Higher Educational Attainment in the 20th Century,* a technical report prepared for the Carnegie Commission on Higher Education, Berkeley, Calif., 1972.

U.S. Bureau of the Census: *Statistical Abstract of the United States, 1930 through 1972,* 1930–1972.

U.S. Bureau of the Census: *Historical Statistics of the United States: Colonial Times to 1957,* 1960.

U.S. Bureau of the Census: *Current Population Reports,* ser. P-25, no. 326, Feb. 7, 1966*a*.

U.S. Bureau of the Census: *Current Population Reports,* ser. P-25, no. 354, Dec. 8, 1966*b*.

U.S. Bureau of the Census: "Projections of the Population of the United States, by Age, Sex and Color to 1990, with Extensions of Population by Age and Sex to 2015," *Current Population Reports,* ser. P-25, no. 381, 1967.

U.S. Bureau of the Census: "Demographic Projections for the United States," *Current Population Reports,* ser. P-25, no. 476, February 1972.

U.S. Bureau of the Census: *Census of Population 1970, Characteristics of the Population: Number of Inhabitants,* vol. 1, part A, sec. 1, pp. 1–43, 1970.

U.S. Office of Education: *Annual Report of the United States Commissioner of Education,* 1879–1917.

U.S. Office of Education: *Biennial Survey of Education in the United States,* 1918–1946.

U.S. Office of Education: *Earned Degrees Conferred, Annual Report,* 1948–1969.

U.S. Office of Education: *Residence and Migration of College Students, Fall 1963, State and Regional Data,* 1965.

U.S. Office of Education: *Higher Education General Information Survey,* National Center for Educational Statistics, Washington, D.C., 1966.

U.S. Office of Education: *Opening Fall Enrollment in Higher Education,* 1967.

U.S. Office of Education: *Advanced Statistics on Opening Fall Enrollment: Basic Information, 1969,* 1969.

U.S. Office of Education: *Statistics of Public Schools,* 1969.

U.S. Public Health Service: "Physicians, Dentists, and Professional Nurses," *Health Manpower Source Book,* no. 9, 1959.

Wolfle, D.: *America's Resources of Specialized Talent,* Harper & Row, Publishers, Incorporated, New York, 1954.

Wolfle, D., and C. V. Kidd: "The Future Market for Ph.D.'s," *Science,* vol. 173, no. 3999, pp. 784–793, August 1971.

Index

PART I: AUTHOR INDEX

PART II: SUBJECT INDEX